A Long Road
from China

A Long Road
from China

Z. Charlie Li

To order additional copies of this book, contact:
Xlibris
1-888-795-4274
www.Xlibris.com
Orders@Xlibris.com
774891

CONTENTS

PREFACE

One of the major reasons that I resigned from my laboratory director position in 2015 was to give myself time to complete this autobiography. After two years of effort, this book has finally met with our readers.

This autobiography describes all the ups and downs of my dreams and the arduous course of my life. If compared with other autobiographies, this book contains several distinct characteristics. My experience covers several decades that were filled with major political movements in China, including Great Leap Forward, three years' famine period, the Cultural Revolution, reform and opening of China, in addition to studying in the US and becoming a US citizen as well as a successful entrepreneur.

During this ever-changing era, as one of many peasants' children with aspirations, I diligently pursued my dreams. When I met challenges and frustrations, I held my head up with perseverance, never gave up, and continued to explore, overcome obstacles, and work with the tenacity of determination toward my goals. This indomitable pursuit of my dream spirit enables me to achieve one goal after another.

My entrepreneurial experience was different from others because I started my venture with no business knowledge and experience, no patented and advanced technology, and with very limited capital. I accomplished my goal of becoming a successful entrepreneur because of my passion about my business and my persistence in my pursuit.

My dreams included my family life and public service. My view of love and family is with unique aspects. I set my own standards of love. I always maintain my tradition of hardworking and conservative living standards, but for public welfare, I have been generous. And I have established and sponsored a number of public welfare projects. Thus, my life pursuit naturally includes my contribution to build a better and a more harmonious society.

ACKNOWLEDGMENT

I want to dedicate this book to my lovely wife, Lisong Zhang, for her endless support and contributions to the pursuit of my dreams and to our family. Especially during my graduate school and entrepreneurship, she stood by me and coped with all kinds of challenges and bore the responsibility of caring for and educating our children. After I realized my dreams, she shared with me the happiness of success. I am grateful for her tolerance, magnanimous understanding, encouragement, and supportive role of my devotion to public service and philanthropy.

This book is also dedicated to my father, Hengnan Li, and my mother, Yuekui Qin. They have worked hard all their lives to raise six of us. When the family was in extreme difficulty, they urged us to stay the course and obtain an education. My achievements today are due to my parents' support and encouragement.

I want to thank my brothers and sisters (Zhenming, Zhenshen, Zhenhai, Liming, and Huiming) and my sisters-in-law and brothers-in-law (Mingnan Pu, Meiqiong Chen, Xuemei Qin, Liwei Lu, and Haihong Wang) for their help and the sincere care of my parents.

Finally, I would like to thank all my teachers for their education and knowledge—my master's adviser, Dr. Richard Bruce, and PhD adviser and mentor, the late Dr. Jerry W. McClure, for their guidance and support. My special thanks goes to Mrs. Frances McClure for editing this autobiography.

Zhenchang "Charlie" Li

September 2018
Champaign, Illinois

1

RICE TEMPLE AND DUQIAO MOUNTAIN

Hometown and My Family (1954)

I was born in 1954 in Rong County, Guangxi Zhuang Autonomous Region, China. The county comprises thirty-four square kilometers and has a population of about eight hundred thousand. The Xiu River, about two hundred to three hundred meters wide, runs from west to east through the city and continues on into Guangdong province, eventually entering the South China Sea. The older portion of the city is located on the north side of the river. The recent rapid development of the county's economy has led to the expansion of the city toward the south side of the river. Many new businesses are located in the commercial park several kilometers south from the river. In the northwest of the county lie the Darong Mountains, running from northeast to southwest, at about thirty-five kilometers in distance. To the southwest is Paradise Mountains, which are part of the Yunkai Mountain Range that runs from northwest to southeast, also about thirty-five kilometers long. The region's climate is subtropical, with abundant precipitation and lush forest.

My family lives in the village of Qiaobei, which is on the north side of a mountain at Rong County named Duqiao Mountain. This mountain consists of eight major peaks spread over about thirty kilometers of the mountain ridge. Many deep valleys, caves, and upright rocky walls bring out many ridges and valleys, which display the jagged, hilly features.

In addition to being beautiful, Duqiao Mountain also hosts a Taoist temple. From the beginning of the Ming Dynasty up to the last century, the mountain has had the twentieth cave of the thirty-six Taoist caves, which affords a long cultural and religious history. In the middle of Qingshou Rock Hill lies Qingshou monastery, a temple hosting five hundred arhats (Sanskrit, meaning "one who is worthy") or Pali arahants. In Buddhism, it is a perfected person who has gained insight into the true nature of existence and has achieved nirvana (spiritual enlightenment). These sculptures were well arranged in rows in five natural caves, each housing a hundred arhats. The monastery has four ceremonial Buddhist activities for daily prayers, chanting, and burning incense as a way of paying respect to the ancestors.

1-1: Duqiao Mountain of my hometown village

1-2. *Fo* is a word for Buddha carved on the wall of Duqiao Mountain

In addition to the main rock caves, Duqiao Mountain has about three hundred other caves. In some of these caves, there were fortifications of the Tang Dynasty, fighting among different tribes or rebellions against government forces. There were mud, or stone, houses in the Lotus Rocks, built in the late Ming and early Qing Dynasty, including seventy-two units of the houses and bodhisattva (a person who is able to reach nirvana but delays doing so out of compassion, in order to save suffering beings). Some caves are situated high up on the cliffs. They can only be reached by climbing a rope. Because some of caves are difficult to reach, bandits used them in resistance to the liberation forces of the new China in 1950–1951.

A particularly legendary cave, called the Rice Temple, is the subject of a beautiful legend. A long time ago, a visitor came to see this mountain. He was attracted to the strange rocks, caves, and the overall beauty of the mountain. One evening, immersed in the beautiful landscape, he did not want to go home. He climbed partway down the mountain and found an entrance to a cave. He entered and walked toward the inside of the cave, where he began to glimpse wonderful scenes. A large hall in the middle could accommodate up to a hundred people. There were carved stone chairs, tables, bowls, and other items for daily use. With all daily necessities available, he did not want to leave. At dinnertime of that evening, he was fascinated when he saw a small hole, which was called a rice grotto, in this natural cave that was presumably used by humans in both modern times and in antiquity. The legendary story continues to say that this visitor could collect rice from this small hole every day, and the amount of rice that could be collected was just enough for him to consume daily. If he had a visitor, the hole would provide more rice but also just enough to feed the guest, and it never gave out too much or too little. However, later on, because some greedy people wanted more rice, they chiseled some stone away to enlarge the hole, hoping for more rice to be flowing out of the hole. Unexpectedly, this action completely changed the fortune. To penalize these greedy people, the hole never provided rice again. This magic legend of the Rice Temple has been passed down for many generations, adding to the mysterious atmosphere associated with Duqiao Mountain.

In addition to the many beautiful scenes in Dugiao Mountains, the city of Rong County is also a well-known historical city. This city was established over 1,700 years ago. During the period of Tang Dynasty to the Ming Dynasty, it housed one or more government offices/agencies of the state, the district, and the county levels. It always played an important role as a political, cultural, economic, and military center. In a more modern time, several famous figures in the Republic of China such as Huang Shaoxong, Huang Xuchu, Xia Wei, Wu Tingfong, Yang Yuangong were all born in the county. In addition to being a unique political center, since Song Dynasty, Rong County has been the home to advanced technology in ceramic making, which is still an important part of exports in our local economy today.

Since my earliest infancy, I have fallen in love with the Duqiao Mountain. As the years went by, I grew to love her more and more. She represents the home of my ancestors, now some nineteen generations in all. The mountain provided us with resources and offered us a place to work, live, and play.

My great-great-grandfather Li Wei had three sons. Li Aireng, the eldest; Li Aiqi, the middle; and Li Aixiang, the youngest. In a sense, I had two grandfathers. The first, my biological grandfather, was Li Aixiang, who was born in 1896 and died in 1961. My biological grandmother was Yang Shi, who was born in 1898 and died in 1978. Her name was a universal name—Shi. In ancient China, most women had no name but instead used Shi as their name, with only their family name to distinguish them as individuals. My biological great-grandparents gave birth to three sons—Li Songnan, Li Hengnan, and Rongnan—and a daughter, Li Zhihua. My stepgrandfather, Li Aireng, was born in 1889, but the date of his death was not known. My stepgrandmother, Liu Shi, who was born in 1900 and died in 1975. My great-uncle Li Aiqi and my great-aunt had four sons—Li Gueinan, Li Dongnan, Li Binnan, and Li Xinnan—and two daughters—Li Ruiqiu and Li Ruikuei. Thus, my grandparents and granduncles had seven bothers and uncles and three sisters and aunts.

Because Li Aireng and Liu Shi had no heirs, they adopted Li Hengnan and Li Binnan and thus became my stepgrandparents. My father, Hengnan, and my uncle, Binnan, became their heirs. My stepgrandfather joined the army when he was young. He was promoted to company commander in about 1920. Subsequently, he was appointed the head of Mei County in Guangdong province. However, due to his illiteracy, he was removed from his position only a few months later. My stepgrandfather's first wife was named Zou Shi (1989–1944); his second wife, my stepgrandmother, was from Hunan Province, where they met and married during the time of the civil war. She came home riding on a donkey that was pulled and accompanied by my stepgrandfather. Aside from my father, my uncle, Binnan, also lived with my family until 1950s. I did not see my stepgrandfather, but my stepgrandmother helped my parents raise us.

In the olden days in China, the relationship between brothers and sisters was a close one. Adoptions between brothers were very common; if one brother was in difficulty, other brothers and sisters would help. Closely related families stuck together. That was why it was easy for my stepgrandfather to adopt my father and my uncle. This ancient tradition is slowly fading away in modern China.

My father was born in August 18, 1924. He was in school for only about a year. He can read and understand some simple letters and newspapers. When he was six years old, he was sent to help others raising cattle for three years. He did not receive any compensation for his work, other than food. After returning home, he joined the family in farming. Before the birth of the new China, the People's Republic of China, our family rented about five mu (one acre is equivalent to about six mu) of paddy field. Because a deposit was required, many poor families could not afford to rent. My grandparents had a relatively good relationship with a landlord, so they were able to rent the field for many years. From each of the two harvests of rice, my grandparents sent to their landlord, in accordance with their rental contract, a certain amount of rice. The amount of rice required by a landlord differed between renters, depending on the relationship between the landlords and the renters. For my family and most other families, it was usually about half of what was harvested.

Because the planting of rice and other crops is highly seasonal, the whole family must work their hardest in the planting season. It is absolutely crucial that farmers are focused and get the crops planted in a timely manner. Otherwise, the yield could be substantially reduced. However, during the slack period between two planting and harvest seasons, my father used to follow my grandfather to do a second job in hopes of making a few extra yuan for his family. My biological grandfather knew how to brew rice wine and how to make bricks and tiles. He brought my father along to work with him, even when he was still a child, and taught him the necessary skills until my father was able to do them by himself. My father was grateful for Grandfather's help because he learned many skills from him that many others never had a chance to learn.

However, even these two craft skills were insufficient to make a living, either because there was not enough demand or because there was too much competition in these areas. My father, therefore, had to learn a third skill of building houses. His mentor lived in a small village called Four-Mei Village about two miles away from our home. My father was his apprentice for many years. In the countryside, housebuilders were not required to undergo any systematic technical training and had no need for a certificate for building houses. A recognized master always acted as the contractor to take on projects. This master, as the head of a house-building project, then determined the number of technical persons needed. In general, a builder's team included a few technical staff and a number of assistants and laborers. My father became a technical member after a number of years of working for the team. Until he was over forty years old, he was allowed to train one or two of his own students and could occasionally act as the head of a house project.

Before 1980, all houses in countryside were built with mud bricks measuring 4 by 8 by 12 inches and were mostly with two floors. The ground-level floor was seven to eight feet in height, which is the main living space; and the second floor, usually four to six feet high, was for storage. The roof was covered with tiles. The critical skill required for construction was the ability to lay the mud bricks in a straight line and to make the corners perpendicular to the other walls. The most common tools for my father were a meter ruler, a muddy razor, a wooden plate board measuring about 0.2 by 6 by 10 inches, a ruler, and a pendulum hanging on a fine and durable string. I recall that my father made 0.5–0.6 yuan a day in the 1970s and about 1.0 yuan in the 1980s. Of course, his two meals a day were free, which were offered by the owner of the house during the house construction.

In old China, many girls—from newborn babies to ten to fifteen years old—from poor families were "sold" or "given" to a "foster family" and raised, called child brides. Such a foster family usually had a young son or sometimes a grown-up man who would be formally married to the fostered girl when she reached the age of about fourteen to fifteen. Some fostered families sometimes would not wait until the girls reached this age to complete the marriage. Child brides were common at the time due to the fact that many families in countryside were very poor. In addition, there was no family planning and no way to avoid pregnancy, which led to the uncontrolled birth of babies. As a result, when a baby girl was born, the options could be either to let her die or to sell or give her to someone who could afford to raise her. In a sense, becoming a child bride could save the girl's life. On the other hand, for a family who could afford to take on a girl for a few years, it was beneficial to the family because an arranged marriage would be certain, and the young girl could help with the family farming. Even though the child bride arrangement appeared to be a win-win system at the time, it is against the laws of marriage in the new China and in many countries around the world.

My mother, Yuekuei Qin, was born into a poor family that lived about three miles away from our home. She did not know her own name in writing. Fortunately, as a farmer and a housewife, literacy was not important. So long as you were physically strong and willing to work hard, you could be a good daughter-in-law. My mother is both a good daughter-in-law and a good mother.

My parents are the hardest-working couple in the world. Despite the conditions they endured at the time, they were able to raise us, a total of six brothers and sisters. In addition to me, the second of the six, were my elder sister, Li Zhenming; two younger brothers, Li Zhensen and Li Zhenhai; and two younger sisters, Li Liming and Li Huiming, born in 1951, 1957, 1963, 1968, and 1972 respectively. Although ours was not the family with the most children in the countryside at the time, it was considered a large one in the village. Not only were my parents able to feed such a large family but they also raised us and made sure we had the best education in the area. My stepgrandmother, working alongside my parents, also played an important role in raising us. In addition to the work and duties assigned and required by the production team, my family divided the various responsibilities through something like this: my father was mainly responsible for making money and dealing with matters outside the house; my mother handled everything related to the home, including farming, gardening, and housework; while my grandmother took care of the children and the cooking. We all felt deep affection, gratitude, and respect for our grandmother.

During the period of the establishment of the new China, the People's Republic of China, the central government policy was to divide the peasants and landlords into several categories: landlords, rich farmers, medium-rich farmers, submiddle farmers, poor farmers, and extremely poor farmers, covering from the richest to poorest farmers in the countryside. The government's allocation policies allowed the poorest to receive the most and the richest to receive either far less or even nothing at all. My family was placed in the submiddle farmer category during this nationwide agrarian reform because my father rented a few mu (less than an acre) of paddy fields and owned a cow. Therefore, the allocation to our family was below the average. Since submiddle and middle farmers are close to the groups of poor farmers and poorest farmers, we were still considered a part of the revolutionary class and were respected in our society.

In my childhood, our family lived in a space of about three hundred square feet, which was similar to the size of one floor in a modern condo. The whole house consisted of three units of a similar size, accommodating three grandfathers and granduncles' families. It is a two-story house, built with mud-brick walls and a mud-tile roof. The ceiling of the second floor was about five to six feet in height and was used mainly for storing rice grains and other food items in jars. There were plenty of mice up there, and my father tried many means to fight them off, from poisoning, mouse-catching traps, and a mice-catching cat, etc. The first floor had a bedroom and a living room, with a small eight-by-eight-feet kitchen attached to the side of the main unit. The living room was further divided into two portions, one about six feet by ten feet and the other was fourteen by ten feet. The smaller portion was occupied by a bed for my grandmother, and the larger portion was used as a dining area and playroom for the children. There were two dining tables, a square four-by-four-foot table at four-foot height and a shorter three-by-three-foot table for the children. As a comment practice, our family members did not always eat meals at the same times, which could actually ease the crowded situation a bit. When the tables were not in use, they were pushed back against the wall to make room for us to play. Grandmother and the children spent most of their time in this room.

The bedroom was in the rear of the house unit. There was an open patio, a portion of the house without roofing, connecting the front living room and the rear bedroom. It was our bathroom and clothes- and handwashing area, with a drainage and a water reservoir. Two full-size beds, placed end to end, filled the twelve-by-ten-feet space of the rear bedroom, while the other side of the bedroom contained a wardrobe, a rice jar, and a urine bucket. As the house was so small, all the family, prior to 1970, slept in three beds with two to three people in each. In general, the youngest one or two children slept with our mother and the older boys with our father or grandmother. This arrangement continued up to the Chinese Cultural Revolution when our new house was built.

By 1964, the housing shortage became a very serious problem. As my two younger brothers and I grew up, three people sleeping in one four-foot-wide bed became more and more of a problem. Two of us slept at one end of the bed and one at the other end. Making thing worse was the fact that my parents were still young enough to have more children. To deal with this housing crisis, my father applied to the production team, a production unit organized by the formation of people's commune, in about 1955–1956, for a piece of hillside with areas of about forty by twenty feet for us to build a new house. Because the empty lots and spaces around the small village had all been allocated to various poor and poorest families, our family had no land allocation that could be used for the site of a house. My father got an approval for the hill site, which was so steep it was not fit for building our house. To level this site, my father worked very hard continuously for several years. He used a hoe to loosen the soil whenever he had time during the day. When it rained, he wore a raincoat and shoveled the soil into a stream of water that had been prechanneled to our site from the hilly mountain by my father. This water carried the loosened soil away. Therefore, whenever there was a heavy rain, my father and my mother would be working on the site. I also helped with the work many times when I was seven to nine years old. Without the help of water, my father would not have been able to get the lot leveled, especially since there was no place to pile the soil he had dug out. At that time, many families did the same in order to save manpower. However, this practice caused a great deal of silt to wash down into the river, not only damaging the farmland but also contaminating the environment and the drinking water. My father continued this work several times a week for four or five years and was eventually able to level off an area of about forty by fifteen feet with an outer soil wall of about twenty feet in height, barely enough for a house and a limited easement.

While digging out the lot, my parents also planned out the building project, collecting necessary materials and drafting a floor plan. The main building materials were mud bricks made by my father. The wood for supporting the second floor, windows, doorframes, and rafters was all collected and prepared by my parents. Because the mountains and forests belonged to the production team, my father had to apply and pay a fee for a permit from the captain of the production team. After the approval by the captain, the application was submitted to the village government called production brigade to obtain approval from the village administrator before he could cut down any trees. Since the trees were located far away on the other side of the Duqiao Mountain, my father carried them back one by one, often making these trips once or twice a day. As a result, the preparation of lumber often took months or even years. If we needed help, we could ask neighbors. This type of "neighbors help one another" system was in common practice for decades or even generations in our village. A house with one living room and two bedrooms required about a hundred pieces of lumber at about fifteen feet long and with a diameter of four to six inches. Preparation for building our house took us about five years.

In the countryside in China, except during the time of the Cultural Revolution, every family would pick a specific time on a specific day to start building a house. This so-called good day or auspicious day was chosen by a Mr. Feng Shui (similar to a geomancer or fortune teller or witch) who was believed by some for being capable of picking a good fortune time for commencing building a house. This Mr. Feng Shui claimed to have learned techniques and skills, either by passing down from his ancestors or learning from another master. It is specific to the minute and hour of the day as the most favorable movement. It was believed that one has to lay down the first piece of brick, stone, or concrete at the correct moment in order to receive the good fortune in the future. After the house was built, one also chose another good day on which to move in. A ceremony and big feast often took place on the moving-in day. Many neighbors, friends, and relatives would be invited to the celebratory gathering. Fireworks, live music, and performances may also accompany the festivities, depending on the economic situation of the family. Apart from the marriage ceremony, this event is still the major tradition in our countryside. My father followed the same tradition when constructing our house. Because my father was himself a builder, he did most of the work on our house himself. To ensure its quality and to show respect to his mentor, he asked his master to help with the construction. Because there are rains from time to time in our subtropical regions, it is important, once started, to complete building as fast as possible. My father, therefore, asked neighbors and others to help him. Most house construction takes place in the fall and winter because there is less rain.

Our house took a couple of months to complete, with one living room and two bedrooms covering a total area of about 450 square feet. Because the new house was only about 300 yards away from the old one, we all ate in the old house; and my father, brothers, sisters, and grandmother slept in the new house. This arrangement continued for about ten years until we could put an addition on the side of the new house. By then, the oldest house was deteriorated to a point that continuing living there was not safe anymore. After the kitchen was put up, our whole family was moved out of the oldest unit. By then, our living conditions had finally improved.

My hometown has plenty of mountains, forests, and vegetation, as well as clean water and fresh air; and my parents were both very diligent and hardworking persons. Nonetheless, a comfortable life remained impossible. The legendary Rice Temple no longer helped us with rice, and my childhood was filled with unrealistic dreams.

2

GREAT LEAP FORWARD AND THREE-YEAR DISASTER

My Childhood Was a Nightmare (1954–1961)

In today's society, our children have more food than they can eat. They often throw away food because they don't like that particular food or because they've taken more than they can eat. Whenever our three children throw food away, we always tell them, "Please don't waste food, as wasting food is a crime." Their response might be a glance, an innocent expression, or worst of all, a protest: "If you don't want to waste it, then you can eat it" or "We have so much food, so we are not wasting it but helping farmers." Our children's minds work differently from ours. They have no idea that there was a time when our generation had no food to eat. I often whisper to my wife that we inherited our parent's genes of working hard and treasuring every bit of food, so why did our kids not inherit such genes from us? When we can't persuade our children, we often eat their leftover meals. Although this is inappropriate from the health and hygiene standpoint, my memory of past days without food makes me still keep on doing it.

I was born in the early years of China liberation, when a major country-wide movement organized by the Communist Party had just begun. The cornerstone of the party's effort was to enact land division policies and carry about land reform. This was an unprecedented reform in that the government took over all the lands from landlords and whoever the owner the land was and then redistributed to all population according to classifications designated by the government. This redistribution policy made the poorest farmers get the most land and the richest landlords get less. This reform led to an explosive growth in agricultural production and an improvement in the peasants' living standards in the early 1950s. But those good days for farmers did not last long because

11

another movement called the people's commune movement began in 1955, which turned the original family-unit production model into a production-team model or people's commune production model. There were two basic levels in is production model: production brigade and production team. The former was at the grassroots level of government that reported to the people's commune. The production teams were the basic farming and production unit consisting of from a few dozen people to more than a hundred of farm population. Our production brigade had about thirty production teams. Each team was not only a production unit but also a self-distribution unit. This movement was considered as the first step toward the final goal of Communist Party that all people would share the abundant resources and produced foods either equally or according to their needs; everyone would work as hard as they could and not ask for more pay than others. With this model, the government could motivate a large portion of the population to work together on any large construction project that could not be done otherwise by an individual or a small group of people since there were no machines available and every bit of work was done manually.

However, this team-production and distribution model did not reach its intended purpose of collective production and equal distribution because (1) we greatly overestimated the morale and willingness of the peasants to participate and (2) we hyped the masses' level of enlightenment while underestimating the complex feudal ideology of the people. As a result, the equality policy severely dampened the enthusiasm of the masses, resulting in a decline in food production, which led in turn to uncertainty about people's living standards.

Making things worse were the Socialist Education Movement and the Great Leap Forward Movement (GLFM) in 1957–1958. I was then only a few years old, just starting to begin to remember things. Like many other children, my wish at the time was to have food to eat, clothes to wear, water to drink, and a happy childhood. Unfortunately, my dream was unrealistic. In a sense, my childhood was a nightmare caused by these two nationwide mass movements followed by a three-year period of difficulty. I did not know what GLFM was. In the beginning, I was just curious as to why, at the midday and evening mealtimes, adults and children all went to the same location. I followed my parents to the same place. I soon realized that everyone went to the collective canteen (the big cafeteria) to eat. This was apparently the egalitarian people's commune, equality, and an iron rice bowl that would not break and would always have rice in it.

The idea of eating together and of eating as much as one wanted was fascinating to me, but it was equally interesting to see that after meals, most people went to work together. Some worked in the paddy fields, while others went up the mountain, cutting trees and carrying wood back for cooking and burning. Still others were building a reservoir in an adjacent village. However, none of these observations was as puzzling to me as when I saw people surrounding a burning carbon furnace and pushing bellows. "What are they doing with this?" I asked my father. He explained to me that these people were trying to make steel.

Indeed, the steel movement was an integral part of the GLFM, in which Chairman Mao's Central Committee called for all members, including peasants, of people's communes and rural cooperatives to join in this steel movement and in all prodemocracy activities, striving for the big industrial leap forward. The central government had set a national goal of steel production at tens of millions of tons and a half ton of grain per capita. The aim of the country was to equal the living standards of developed countries. As a small boy, I did not know the exact meaning of steel production at ten million tons and had no idea of what the world's advanced standard of living was. I saw that my parents put together our old iron pot, sickle, and tin debris as well as anything that might contain iron in it into a container, which they carried to a location where there was a carbon-burning furnace. Neighbors and villagers all did the same. All these materials were used for making steel. My elder sister and other schoolchildren hunted everywhere for pieces of scrap iron that they handed in at their respective schools. Because the GLFM provided food to everyone in the people's commune, individual family no longer needed to cook, which made most families "contribute" their iron bowls and iron pots, whether new or patched, to the steel-making site. The furnace for my village was in a central location in a small village nearby, where people worked in the furnace day and night, trying to make steel. The national steel-making movement probably lasted about half a year. A lot of trees on the mountain were cut down, much manpower was expended, many natural resources were used up, and agricultural production was greatly affected; but still, due to insufficient firepower from the burning of carbon and the low level of steel-making technology involved, steel production proved to be a complete failure.

The agricultural production movement was the other major part of GLFM, complementary to the industrial steel movement. It was said that agricultural production must achieve its intended level. However, in order to achieve high yield of a ton of rice per mu (about 0.15 of an acre) in two planting seasons annually, people moved the preharvest rice from one field to join the next field of rice just before they were harvested. This treating practice was to make sure the highest yield possible because when calculating the rice yield, farmers only accounted for the area from one field instead of two fields. They showed this display field to visitors and journalists, who eventually reported the high-yield production of rice. Everyone knew that this was a cheat because moving rice plants together was unnatural, and when the wind blew, the rice plants that had been moved could not stand up. Even as a five-year-old, I knew it was impossible to achieve the high yield described in the propaganda under the conditions and crop cultivation technology of the time. The actual yield of the natural rice field was about half or even one-third of the amount claimed. This practice was a complete bolshie, which unfortunately became a laughing tale of an agricultural satellite production for years.

Why did people deceive themselves about this satellite production of rice? To understand this phenomenon, we must consider the attitudes and practices of the socialists at the time. The central government set a goal, and the cadres at various levels of government followed. They knew they had to obey the order since if a cadre could not comply, he or she would be criticized or even lose their job. Because everyone knew such a high yield was impossible, all they could do was to tell lies and thus be able to pass the government inspection and keep their job.

The steel production in industry and the satellite production in agriculture during the GLFM was supposed to lead to more steel for construction needs and more food for us to eat. It was supposed to keep our meals free of cost and enable us to take whatever we wanted to eat. It was also believed that socialism and communism were just around the corner. I certainly enjoyed this life because I could eat as much as I wanted. I could play with other kids, and I did not need to do any housework. I thought that communism might be just what was happening around me, that perhaps my dreams had just come true!

Unfortunately, this state of affairs did not last. It was a pity to have to let such a good dream go away so soon. Only a few months later, the central government, the cadres, and the people woke up and realized that the current central policy was a mistake. Local governments knew from firsthand information that a severe shortage of food was approaching. They could not afford to continue the "eat together and take what you want" practice. As a result, they started implementing the first change. Our one big pot was divided into three smaller pots, the one big village into three subgroups according to people's last names, and then a proportion of food was distributed to each group according to the number of person in it. The resources designated to each group were to be managed by the group leaders. It was thought that such division would save food and create a planned and better life. Immediately after this division, some people remained doubtful about the new practice and felt that this change would not save the smaller pots. In contrast to these pessimistic people, there were some strong believers of the GLFM. For instance, one cadre exclaimed dramatically that "unless you could see the Duqiao Mountains fall, the big cafeteria practice would be here to stay."

Now, food was allocated to each person, a change from "take what you want to an allocation to you accordingly" style but still in the format of eating and working together. In a sense, it was this very equality for everyone that had led to the laziness and decreased productivity. It did not take more than a couple of months for many cadres to realize that the new arrangement would not improve conditions but instead make them worse and worse. Less and less food was available. Compounding the wrong policies of central government were a series of natural disasters. Dry weather caused many paddy fields to dry up, and a significant portion of the paddy fields could not be planted with rice. Moreover, even if rice was planted, the lack of water caused the crop to die, and the production of rice was severely reduced. The fall in production was most severe in Guangxi and Guangdong provinces. As a result, the food was soon gone. There was no incentive for people to work harder and produce more. Soon enough, there was little foods left in canteens. As a result, all canteens, big or small, were eventually closed down after less than a year in existence. Three years of disaster (sometimes also called three years of difficult times) began. My childhood life took a dramatic turn for the worse in 1959.

The result of this change was that the "iron bowl canteens" practice had all gone, and small portion of rice left over from "eating and working together" practice was divided and allocated to each family according to the number of children and adults in each family. Obviously, the allocated food was too limited to solve the hunger, which led to a nationwide problem of hunger and famine. To alleviate the problem, the central government put out a new policy allowing the people's commune to designate a portion of the land and fields for peasants to farm by themselves. Such a policy was in striking contrast to the GLFM because now individual family could plant what they wanted and harvest and consume what they produced. Although the main portion of land and field were owned by the people's commune, this small portion of land at about 5–10 percent of the total tilled acreage played an important role in helping peasants survive and get over the crisis.

Exacerbating the effects of the misguided central policy of the GLFM were natural disasters and the need to repay Soviet debts. Starting in 1960, the relationship between the Soviet Union and the People's Republic of China went from unstable to worse. The Soviet government tore up the contract signed by the two governments in the early 1950s. The Soviets withdrew all their experts from China and demanded China repay all money borrowed from them during the liberation of China and the Korean War. The total debt was said to be about 600 billion yuan, and 250 billion yuan still remained to be paid off at the time. This demand of immediate payment forced China to spread its resources, making the disaster even worse. It was believed that the three difficult years from1959 to 1961 were due to a combination of a wrong central government policy, natural disasters, and the repayment of debt imposed by the Soviet Union.

Our family received a small portion of allocated rice when the big and small canteens dissolved. The ration of allocations was apparently based on the number of people per family and the number of adult laborers. We had two adult laborers (our parents) and five nonlaborers (my brothers and sisters) in our family. How to survive on such a small amount of food became a major concern for my parents, who were worrying about food every day.

In the following next two years, a lot happened to me, our family, and to the people living nearby. Although I cannot remember many of them, a few striking experiences linger in my memory. Those listed here represent what occurred at the time and reflect the reality of the society as a whole. Because we had only a small rice allocation, my parents did everything they could to make it last longer. First, they first divided the rice into smaller portions for each meal.

This change forced us to change from dried cooked rice to rice porridge (or rice soup). In doing so, we could make a large pot of porridge with about half a pound of rice in the morning for lunch. In the evening, we might increase the amount of rice to about a pound or so, which meant that each family members could have two large bowls of porridge at each meal. I sometimes "enjoyed" the porridge, although it was without meat or other nutritious items but with only a small bit of salt with a few drops of oil. However, eating porridge like this made us get hungry again very quickly. We frequently felt hungry by midnight and had little energy during the day. Second, in order to fill our stomachs or make us just feel fuller, my parents started to collect wild vegetables and fruits from the mountains. For example, we collected mushrooms and wild yams to cook and eat. We collected the inner layers of bark from pine trees and mixed them with rice powder to make a kind of fried pancake. We harvested stems and leaves of sweet potato, chopped them into small pieces and mixed them with rice before cooking. This helped our hunger pangs. Unfortunately, when everyone in the village did the same as my parents did, the edible wild vegetables and fruits were rapidly exhausted. Our crisis continued because farm production is highly seasonal, and it takes time to produce a yield of crops.

My parents, therefore, had to come up with other solutions to alleviate our hunger, one of which was eating chaff. As we all know, the chaff of rice grain, or the chaff bran, has no nutritional value but only fiber. If used in small quantities in food recipes today, rice chaff bran may provide some health benefits as fiber. However, when we were severely malnourished and hungry, eating this husk bran caused serious problems such as suffering from constipation and causing extreme stomach pain. Due to the lack of medicine for treating constipation, eating husk bran and other innutritious stuff led to many deaths in our county.

Another marginal food was a pancake made primarily with pumpkin, pumpkin stems and leaves, and with a small portion of rice flour. This was again mostly fiber and contained only limited amount of nutrients. It filled our stomachs but with little health value. Many people again experienced intestinal cramps and suffered constipation.

As the three years of natural disasters continued, more and more people suffered from edema all across the nation. My father and my aunt both suffered from edema. People with such disease could not walk or do fieldwork because of their swollen legs and hands. They had to be sent to a clinic (more like public house where all such patients were placed) for treatment. While my father suffered swollen leg and hands, my mother was thin and bedridden. Although both of them stayed in the clinic for different symptoms, their diseases were apparently due to severe malnutrition, energy deficiency, and a heavy workload over a long period of time. Our parents formed the backbone of our daily life and in our family. Without them at home, we all were very sad and anxious. If the famine continued, they could die, and we would not know what might then happen to us.

When I was six years old and had witnessed the effects of famine on my family, I started to feel sympathy for my parents' bitterness. One habit I developed, according to what I was told many years later by my grandmother, was that I often ate a half meal (or would half fill my stomach) and then pretended to be full so that we could save a little more food for my parents. Also, even if I was hungry, I would not cry as some other children might. My grandmother later told me many times about how wonderful and passionate I was because I tried to help my parents during these difficult times.

Since 1962, the private plot had become part of the collective economic policy, which permits individual families to use a small area of land (a field) on a long-term basis and to plant what they want in their spare time. It is intended to supplement the yields of the production ream of the people's commune and to improve the living standards of the peasants. Peasants had the right to plant in the plots but not own them since ownership remained with the government. This policy was enacted from 1955 to 1957 but was abandoned during the GLFM.

The three years of disaster period was a hard lesson to learn for our government and for each of us. A successful policy should be able to motivate farmers to work harder and to produce more to meet the needs of the society. That was why many people considered that allowing farmers to plant their private lots was a good policy. In addition, our local government also allowed farmers to plant crops such as yams and sweet potatoes on the hilly mountain sides, where there was usually no limit placed on cultivating virgin land. This policy motivated all the hungry farmers not only to plant in their private plots but also to dig out large areas in the hills to plant sweet potato and yams. Before long, we could harvest plenty of vegetables and other crops, and our food situation improved dramatically. I was so glad that my family survived the GLFM and three-year difficult period. As a boy of eight years old, my nightmare childhood was finally over, and now I could go to school and hope for a better life.

3

A THREE GOOD STUDENT

Primary School (1961–1965)

When I woke up from the bad dream of three years of disaster, I realized that good things were happening for me and for the people in our village.

Our central government had adopted a new policy to help peasants overcome the difficult time by allowing small portions of land and paddy fields, also called private lots, to be planted on and crops to be harvested by farmers. The problem of our food shortage was gradually resolved, so like other children, I did not have to eat wild vegetables, sweet potato, and sparse rice porridge in my main meals any longer I could eat thick rice porridge, or cooked rice leftover from the previous night the next morning, porridge for lunch, and cooked fried rice for dinner.

This eating pattern was also a common routine for most families in our village prior to the GLFM, which was disrupted during 1958–1961. Our rice was mostly from the distribution/appropriation by the production team, a basic collectivization unit of the people's commune. But our vegetables were from our own private plots. The variety and availability of vegetables for us depended greatly on the seasons and sometimes the weather prevalent in our area.

The most common vegetables included, but were not limited to, water spinach, cabbage, lettuce, Napa or Chinese cabbage, and eggplant. Meat remained to be a luxury item for our family because we could only afford two to four pounds of pork a few times a year. In general, a couple pounds of pork was purchased for the traditional Chinese holidays such as Spring Festival and Midautumn Festival. For a family of eight, each of us often had only a few pieces of pork.

Furthermore, because we had a shortage of vegetable oils for cooking, whenever we purchased pork, we did not select lean pork but picked the fatty pieces. We cut out the fatty portion and fried the fat out, collecting it for daily cooking. My parents often said to us that fatty meat was tastier and made us feel fuller in our stomachs. Apparently, they did not know fatty meat could provide more energy than lean meat. If we ever had the opportunity to eat all the meat we wanted, it would be the time when we raised a big pig then killed it for selling at the free market.

Most of the time, my parents and grandmother let the children eat first before they would reach their chopsticks into the bowl of meat. Fortunately, my brothers and sisters all had already developed an attitude of sympathy toward our parents and grandmother, so we consciously ate only a few pieces of meat and always left some for them.

Our cooking oil was manufactured from peanuts, milled and squeezed into oil by our production team. It was then distributed to each family in the village.

Occasionally, we used our private plot to plant some peanuts for oil. Our family was normally allocated thirty to forty pounds of peanut oil per year, depending on the harvest yield for that year. If the quantity of peanuts from private plots were minimal, the amount of oil per person was about two to five pounds per year. It was a common practice that each family would use fats from pork for cooking for at least six months annually. Another way of getting oil was from the free market. My father could make a purchase after he sold his firewood.

As a child, I really liked to eat the small pieces of pork rinds left from the rendered fat. I knew at the time that it was delicious but did not realize until later that trans fat produced during the high temperatures and repeated frying is the reason for such a good taste, but it was not good for our health.

I went to the first-grade primary school at seven years old. In the 1950s, there were no preschools and kindergarten in our village. This was common in most of the country villages in China. Because my family for generations was not literate, there were no books or other kinds of literature in our home. I never had an opportunity to read a storybook or have a story told by my parents. My parents worked hard day in and day out throughout the year to raise us and provide for us. I stayed with my grandmother and played with my siblings and other kids or occasionally helped my family before my school age. In comparing myself to the kids from most cities, my educational background and my knowledge were definitely not good at all.

The primary school I attended for the first two years was named Stone Foot Elementary School. The school got its name from the name of the Stone Foot Village, which was so named because it was situated on the base or foot of the rocky stone of South Mountain. The school was centrally located in our village of about 150 families. The school had two grades, first and second. There was one class for each grade with about twenty to thirty children. There was one teacher for each class who taught language and math. Other courses taught included physical education and music, primarily singing.

This elementary school was less than half mile away from my home. It was about a ten-minute walk, passing through a paddy field area and up a short hill.

On my first day of school, my elder sister accompanied me and registered me for the school. I recall that I was very happy on that day, possibly because I had been looking forward to school for quite a while because I wanted to learn as much as my elder sister.

For the next two years, I walked to school in the morning and came home for lunch at noon. After lunch, we often had nap time. We finished all our work at school and hardly ever had any homework in the afternoon. From the first day on, I appeared a step ahead of most other pupils in the class. I completed assignments faster, memorized everything better, recited text faster, read the story/text loudly, and never shied away from standing up in front of the class. As result, I soon became a leader and was elected as the captain of the class. I knew that I might not be that good, but because it was in my village, perhaps it was just like an old saying that said, "When there are no tigers in the mountain, the monkey is the king!" Because of my ability, it seemed that most of my teachers always gave me a thumbs-up which, in turn, encouraged me do more with greater confidence. The more praises and encouragement I received, the more confidence I had, the faster progress I made, and the more goals I had achieved. As a result, I was selected by the class and students as a three good student, an honorable recognition for achievement in morals, physical fitness and intellect.

Beginning in the third grade, I entered the Qiaobei Central Elementary School. This school was located in the center of four villages under the jurisdiction of our township. All students who had completed the first two years of elementary school in their home villages would be qualified to attend this school. It was from third to sixth grades. Our big village, consisting four smaller villages, had a population of about three thousand people. The total students from the four villages were placed in one or two classes for each grade. During these four years, I had some very nice teachers who taught us Chinese language, math, and geometry. These teachers were highly regarded in the township because they had high school diplomas. In our countryside, many other teachers might have had only a middle school diploma. Definitely, no one had a bachelor's degree. This was very different from the West where most teachers must graduate from college with teaching certificates in order to qualify for teaching. From the standpoint of education, without highly educated teachers, it was impossible to train first-class students. However, this did not seem to bother peasants because most farmers did not know what to expect from teachers for their children in the first place. They considered that farming did not require much intelligence or knowledge because they had been good farmers for generations, even without going to school at all.

The teaching method we had was like a duck-filling approach, in which children were generally filled with textbooks and formulas. Teachers usually did not make any effort to promote or foster a student's curiosity. Students were not encouraged to ask questions, especially questions that were not related the textbook. Anyone able to recite the text or formula would be considered a good student. For this reason, most teachers were not challenged, and their qualification was hardly ever evaluated by the school district or by the public. For this reason, because I was good at reciting text and stories, table arithmetic 99, and other formulas, I was naturally considered a top-tier student. I often got good grades when tests were given, which was more or less based on recital ability instead of on the comprehension or problem-solving skills.

My language proficiency was comparable to other children in the school, but apparently, it was not as good as the children who attended the schools in the city. Throughout my primary school, I did not read any book outside the textbooks that were used in our class. My composition was as bad as it could be because I could not write any story even if it were as short as a few sentences of a simple story.

Not until my fourth grade did I make any significant progress in writing. I was fortunate to have a teacher named Mr. Li teaching our Chinese language class. I learned some skills and knowledge of composition and essay writing in his class. My writing actually got better and better as years progressed. Later, my essays were often read to the class as examples. I received honors and awards many times from fourth to sixth grade.

Chinese Young Pioneers was founded by the Communist Party at the beginning of the new China. It is a children's organization created and sanctioned by the Communist Youth League leadership. Beginning in my third grade, I joined this organization through recommendations of my teachers. I had been longing to join because I respected and admired my elder sister who wore a red scarf around her neck to school every day. She wore an armband with one red stripe and later two red stripes. The red scarf is worn by all members of Young Pioneers, but the stripes represent the official position of the student within the youth organization. A squad captain leading a small group of five to seven members wore one red stripe. The captain of a squadron that is composed of at least two squads wore two stripes. And the captain of at least three squadrons wore three stripes. For each of our Young Pioneer members, the opportunity to join this organization was not freely open to everyone. Its members were selected by the teachers and the school. Being a member of the organization was a particularly happy and glorious thing for any student. I am proud to be one of them.

As all other members of the Youth Pioneer organization, I was required to attend school meetings where all students from different grades participated. At the meeting, the school principal introduced us on the stage in front of the other students and the teachers. We stood under the flag of the Young Pioneers to swear, "I am a Chinese Young Pioneers member. I swear by the flag that I will do things in accordance with the Chinese Communist Party's guidance—studying well, doing good work and a good job—to be prepared and ready to contribute to the cause of communism." I started as the Young Pioneer member and gradually progressed to squad captain and then squadron captain. If it were not for the Cultural Revolution, I might have progressed to be a captain of the Young Pioneers.

Throughout the years of my elementary school, I not only studied hard and made sure that I was a top-tier student in my grade but also actively and enthusiastically participated in various activities. I was educated a lot about the communist ideology and often taught to be trained and nurtured to be successful in communism.

My elementary school progressed smoothly. I was a step ahead and had more comprehensive learning than most other rural children of the same age. Specifically, I was able not only to recite and memorize better but also to answer questions faster and sometimes to extrapolate and draw conclusion more rapidly. My self-confidence was higher than most students in my class. My exams always went well, and my grades were always good. I was awarded and honored as a three good student and an excellent Young Pioneers, as well as becoming the squad and then a squadron leader each year. I was very lucky to be born with my intellectual capability. Numerous awards I received with certificates were posted on the wall of our living room and were comparable to those of my elder sister. I was one of the best students in our village. I was very proud of myself because I not only earned it for myself but also for my parents as well.

4

A POOR CHILD FAST TO BE A BOSS

Middle School and Moneymaking Dreams (1964–1967)

The Agricultural Cooperation Movement in 1956 was a collectivization movement that led to the food production model for the countryside with the production brigade as the lowest level of government. This was the equivalent of a township government. Next were production teams, which were the basic units of agriculture production and distribution under the production brigade. This production model reclaimed all lands and fields previously assigned to an individual family during the land reform of 1950–1951. The land was owned by the government, and it was designated to be used by the production teams. Each production team was about ten to fifty families, mostly with one to a few surnames from the same ancestor or who had several of the same ancestors.

Our production team was called Datang production team with about twenty families with three surnames Li, Qin, and Chen and a total population of approximately seventy people. The production team produced mainly rice, sweet potatoes, peanuts for oil, and other food items.

In the planned economy of China, the central government assigned an annual GDP as well as the amount of rice or other main staple food items to be produced by all production teams across the nation. The government purchased rice from farmers, paying only a symbolically low price. The obligation placed on each production team depended on area of land assigned, the size in mus (each mu = about 0.165 acre), depending on land fertility and water resources.

This obligation was called *gong-guo-liang*, which was like a tax on the farmers who were paying in rice for the right to use government lands. Rice collected by the people's commune was stored in grain reservoirs that were spread across the country. Regardless of the amount of rice produced by our production team, the amount of the rice we were obligated to give to the government did not change. Consequently, in a dry year, after fulfilling the government obligation, each team member or each family would receive a considerably less rice than in a good harvest season.

Obviously, a change in the weather in any given year led to the fluctuation and instability of the farmers' incomes which, in turn, affected their lives. This was in sharp contrast to those called country persons who worked in government manufacturing companies or the educational system where the appropriation obligation was fixed.

If it were a disastrous farming year, the difference would become even more striking. The farmers' obligation might be as high as 50 percent of the total rice crop produced by the production team When this occurred, there was a food shortage for the farmers. If there was a disaster in any given year that led to hunger, then the government could return a portion of the taxed rice to farmers to ease the food shortage.

The organization structure of our Datang production team was composed of the production team head, a political head, a treasurer, an accountant, a recorder, and the storage keeper, all of whom managed our team with seventy to eighty people. Half of the adults planted sixty to seventy mu (about ten acres) of rice in paddy field, with the other half planting another thirty mu (fifty acres) of dry field on the hillsides of the mountainous areas for other crops such as sweet potatoes and peanuts. Our team was assigned more mountainous acreage than total arable acreage. These mountainous fields were an important part of our income for our team because we could harvest lumber and rosin to sell for cash.

The production and distribution models were geared toward socialism. All teams members worked together to produce rice and our other produce. After the fulfillment of the gong-gou-liang, the rice and other products were distributed to each person or family in the team. The distribution, or allocation, consisted of two parts: the average amount per capita accounted for 70–80 percent of total produce, especially rice, and the earned portion (about 20–30 percent), which was based on work points earned and accumulated for each family.

This allocation system took into consideration the basic living requirement of food for each person and, at the same time, determined the take-home amount for the best-working farmers and the lazy farmers.

At the first glance, it appeared to be a fair system from the standpoint of socialism since a family with more laborers who worked harder earned more work points and received higher allocations. However, looking at this system more carefully, we find a number of unfair outcomes because it created a situation that made most people not work as hard for the team, leading to low productivity.

Han lao bao shou, another term for iron rice bowl, was used to describe the people who worked for the government and nationalized manufacturing and enterprises that always received the same appropriation (salary, foods, oil, and meat, etc.) regardless of whether it was a good or bad production year.

These people, the country persons, included the cadre, clerks, and staff in the government; manufacturing and enterprise workers; and schoolteachers. In other words, all people except farmers were unfairly considered country persons.

Production in any given year was greatly influenced by many uncontrolled factors such as flooding, drought, crop disease, or insects that could cause a severe reduction of rice and other crops. This unstable income and the hard life of peasants was used as a key differentiation between the country persons and farmers. This was also the main reason that all peasants longed to be a country person.

In describing the country person, there were several other terms that were used, including *han lao bao shou, iron rice bowl,* or *imperial food eater,* all implying those who received fixed salaries had their food, including meat and oil, and all of life's necessities that were in short supply for the farmers.

I witnessed this unfair distribution system and decided that I wanted to be a country person when I grew up. My dream and my life goals were established at a very early age.

From my first days in primary school, I felt that as a good child, I had to be a good student in school and a good helper at home. At that time, many families often considered schooling useless. Children, too, thought that getting good grades in school was not as important as earning work points at home, and gaining book knowledge was not as appealing or as important as learning how to do farming and housework to make money and to grow up with the skills of raising a family. I am fortunate to have a father who was different from most others because he encouraged us to go to schools and to get an education, and we did.

I often thought that listening to my parents and my grandma would be an important indication of a good child. This included no fighting among brothers and sisters and making no trouble at home. Helping my parents was equally important as well. Our family lacked laborers, and my parents were the only full-time laborers, with six kids and a grandma as none-adult laborers. My parents had to work very hard to raise us. To be able to help them out, my elder sister and I joined in the labor force, doing the kinds of farmwork that would be considered by today's society, especially in the developed countries, as unlawful child labor practice. Although it is still happening in China today, it occurs on a much more limited basis and less frequently.

When I was about eight years old, I followed my mother and my elder sister to the field to work. The normal farmwork included removing weeds, loosening soil between crops, planting rice seedlings, and harvesting the rice and other crops.

When we worked in my Datang team, we earned work points, which were used for calculation of our annual allocation of rice and for earning some cash. Earning as many work points as possible would increase our take-home rice and cash at the end of the year. Starting from seven to eight years old, all children in most families would join the labor team. These child laborers were sometimes considered by those families who were without children to be unfair because children earned a share of the total distribution that would have been divided among all adult laborers. Since the number of families with children significantly outnumbered those without children, this practice continued for decades in China without much change.

In general, children's work points were determined through the Ping-Gong meeting where all peasants were present, and they appraised or judged the points for each child earned each workday. Because children were physically weaker with a lower productivity rate compared to strong adult laborers, children often started with about two to three work points each day and gradually earned five to eight points, depending on the age, physical strength, and work skills.

This was still much lower than the best laborers, who usually earned ten points a day. Although my sister and I earned a few points a day at the beginning, with all my sisters and brothers working, our earned work points added up and could be the equivalent of half or even a full-time strong laborer during the summer months when school was in recess. Children were the major contributors in our Datang team, and we were proud to be contributors to the family.

At the beginning of my farmwork participation, I mostly did light labor such as hand removing weeds or using a light hoe for digging out weeds and loosening soil between the crop rows. Because our dry field was mostly clay soil, it was important to loosen the surface soil for better aeration and for better retention of the soil water to prevent moisture evaporation, both necessary for the crops to grow.

Our team planted mostly peanuts and sweet potatoes on nonirrigated farmland in the spring season. These crops require fertilizing a couple of times during the growing season, removing weeds, and loosening the soil once or twice as well. If weather was dry, watering the crops manually might be required. Just like all children, I liked harvesting peanuts at the end of summer then picking the peanut kernels from the roots because we could sometimes secretly eat a few as snacks. Although a few adults might sneak a few peanuts to eat, kids were more closely watched. Most people felt that a snack was not worth it because we all needed every peanut for oil production.

The farming season for that area is based on the twenty-four solar terms, starting in February in a Western calendar: spring begins, the rains, insects awaken, vernal equinox, clear and bright, grain rain, summer begins, grain buds, grain in ear, summer solstice, slight heat, great heat, autumn begins, stopping the heat, white dews, autumn equinox, cold dews, hoar-frost falls, winter begins, light snow, heavy snow, winter solstice, slight cold, great cold. There are fifteen days for each solar term and six terms in each quarter.

In the south of China, the main crop is rice, and it is planted twice a year, although there are three planting seasons a year in the southern part of China in the Hainan province. In practice, farmers know that the first term of spring begins is usually around February 6. When spring begins, farmers should begin preparing the field and seedbeds for sowing rice. The process is for farmers to first soak the seeds in water for one to two days then remove them from the water and leave them in a basket for a few days at room temperature to allow seed germination. At the same time, the seedbeds are prepared in either a small area of a paddy field or in a terraced area with water or irrigation available. After seeds are sowed and germinated and the seedlings grow to about four to six inches high, which usually takes about twenty-five to fifty days depending on the weather, the seedlings are ready to be transplanted to paddy fields.

The paddy fields are prepared by plowing soil under a layer of water with a cow pulling the plow. This procedure turns over the surface soil, weeds, and the debris. The field is then leveled off with another procedure by pulling a tooth harrow, also pulled by a cow, over the previously plowed field. The plowing and harrowing procedures could be repeated if the cow- and manpower are available. Our team did it just once due to the lack of such cow-power. I helped take care of the cow from the time I was eight years old and did it in the summer during my school recess for a few years. I could not operate the plow and harrow until I was twelve to thirteen years old because these tools are heavy and need to be lifted at end turns in the paddy field. That is why not many women or girls could plow the paddy fields. This kind of work is said to be a man's job in farming, a necessary skill that I had to learn and master in order to be a man. This type of farming operation now has been largely replaced by farming machines.

As an old saying goes, "Spring is the start of an important season not to miss because if we do, the yield of crop production will be greatly affected." Farmers take this very seriously and do all that they can to sow and transplant the rice to the paddy field as soon as they can and as weather permits. This is a practice that all successful farmers must keep in mind. Transplanting rice seedlings often occurs in March and April. If everything is well planned and prepared for, the transplanting of the paddy fields could be completed within ten to twenty-five days. The planting season should be over by the solar term grain rain, which is before the end of April.

I started doing transplanting of rice when I was about eight years old. This is considered a more difficult farm job because it requires some skill in order to do a good job. In order to do this kind of farmwork, I held a block of rice seedlings of about 0.5 by 4 by 10 inches in one hand and, with the other hand, separated five to ten seedlings from the seeding block; then I took the seedling, with its roots and soil, and inserted it into the leveled paddy field. The seedlings inserted had to be such that the distance between adjacent two rows was eight to ten inches and between each bundle of seedlings, about three to five inches. The goal was to make sure that it formed straight rows, at an even distance between bundles, with about the same number of seedlings in each bundle at about the same depth of about one to two inches into soil surface.

Just like other children, I had to learn from my elder sister and my mother for a while before I could do it independently. At first, the seedlings I inserted were either too diffuse and fell horizontally into the field. At other time, I might pick out too many or too few of the seedlings. Still another time, I inserted the seedlings too deep into soil. We were all required to improve to meet the standard before we were allowed to transplant independently.

During the rice seedling transplant, I stood in the paddy field, bending my back, facing the paddy field and my back facing the sun. Keeping this position for hours, even without doing anything, would had been a challenge for most people. It was necessary for me to coordinate my hands and my feet, busily taking the seedlings from the block that I held in my hand and then inserting them into soil while moving my feet backward through the field. I got so tired in the beginning that I wanted to stand up and rest for a while. However, because I was only one member of a team working in the field doing the transplanting, I had to complete my portion of field as fast as the others to keep the rows of seedling straight from one person to the next. If I were too slow, it would slow down the speed of others. Therefore, I had to keep working. To ease the pressure on me, I worked beside my mother or my elder sister because whenever I slowed or was in trouble, they could help me out.

When the seedling transplanting day was over, I felt so terribly tired that I went to bed as soon as I finished my dinner. By the morning, when I was awakened by my mother or my grandmother, I still felt tired and wanted to just sit on the doorstep for another five to ten minutes, doing nothing. Occasionally my father would yell at me, "Why you are so tired, I never looked this tired when I was your age!" I knew that I could become stronger and that I should not let my father down, so I stood up, brushed my teeth, had some breakfast, and then joined the other people in the paddy field for another day. It was fortunate that in those days, it would not last for more than a week, either because during rainy days, paddy fields could not be planted or for some other reason, we could not work. I could rest and physically recover.

For the next thirty to fifty days after the rice seedlings had been transplanted, our main responsibilities were to take care of the crops. We fertilized the rice crop, usually about fifteen to twenty days after transplanting when the seedlings had become firmly anchored in the soil and new roots had grown. Along with the fertilizer application that was done by several experienced adults capable of spreading fertilizer evenly by hand, the rest of us, mostly ladies and children, followed, removing weeds by hand and loosening the surface soil with one foot moving the top surface soil with thin layer of water around and around to make sure that all surface soil between rows of rice crops was well mixed to produce a cloudy and thick muddy layer. To balance ourselves to prevent stepping on rice seedlings or falling, each person usually held a cane in one hand and pulled weeds with the other hand. Weeds were collected and were disposed or pushed with our feet deep into the soil of the paddy field.

This farmwork may seem to be an easy job, but this was only because we balanced ourselves with one foot deeply anchored into the soil and with a cane in our hand. Our legs were sometimes cut by the rice leaves and some muggy paddy fields could be as deep as two feet, thus making it difficultly for us to move. There were leeches in most paddy field, and some people teased the children, saying that the leeches particularly liked the legs of young children because it is easier to attach themselves to the younger skins of their legs. Although I hardly believed it, I was certainly afraid of leeches, especially when I had scratches on my leg that attracted leeches. I sometimes cried at the beginning of my fieldwork when I had leeches biting and I could not remove them no matter how hard I tried. The leeches would sting, and they attached themselves firmly. After a number of tries, I finally found that applying some my own saliva to the leeches then rubbing back and forth was an effective way to remove leeches from my leg. I slowly got used to it.

The rice growth season is normally 80–150 days, depending on the species we were planting. We often started the harvest the first season crop around slight heat and great heat (around July). The busiest season for farmers are the months of July and August in our region because it was a time of harvesting the first crops and the planting the second crops in this season. We needed to set aside most of our other activities these two months so we could harvest the rice as soon as it ripened and plow the paddy field to bury the rice straw immediately.

When we completed the rice harvesting, which usually took us about two to three weeks, the paddy field was leveled off with the harrow, so it was ready for the next seedling transplanting. It was not uncommon for the harvesting and the transplanting to overlap each other during that season. In order to have seedlings ready or the second season, in the spring, we often planted about 5 percent of the paddy field with a rice species that needed a shorter growing season. This selected rice was usually ready for harvesting in June, making the field available to be a seedbed for nurturing seedlings for second crop season. Since I participated in all these proceedings at an early age, I knew how to do this kind of farmwork.

Harvesting rice was another major farm responsibility that I did when I was a child. At that time, harvesting rice crops was done manually.

Ripened rice was cut down to about four inches above the ground or the water line. It was then laid in bundles in the rows of the paddy field, which was wet during the first harvest season, but the soil was dry during the second harvest season. This kind of work was done mostly by women and children. Then a second group of farmers, mostly men, pulled a large five-by-four-three-foot or a six-by-four-by-three-foot rectangular wooden bucket into the paddy field that sat in one place. The men picked up bundles. Standing at a corner of the bucket and holding the grain heads firmly with both hands, they struck the head of the rice hard against the side wall of the bucket to loosen the grains so that they fell into the bucket. The force exerted by a man and the maturity of the grains determined how many strikes would be needed to make sure all the rice grains dropped off into the bucket. The rice was collected at intervals in bamboo-woven buckets then carried home to be dried under the sun on an open concrete surface area. The straw that was removed from the grain was then either returned to the paddy field as organic fertilizer or collected as feed for the cow or utilized for other purposes. Just as any other farmwork, I had to learn before I could cut the rice straw and then later how to hold the grain to strike it against the bucket to release the grain correctly.

I learned a painful lesson doing the harvesting work. Cutting rice straw was done with a sharp-toothed, rainbow-shaped knife. One hand holds the knife, and the other hand holds the rice straw. Both hands must be well coordinated in order to do this job quickly. In the beginning, I could not do it easily, and I cut my fingers several times before I could master the technique. Today, I can still see the scar on the little finger of my left hand as a memory of this farm job.

As in every production team in our production brigade (township), the recorder of our Datang team registered, on an hourly basis, the daily attendance of each person. There was no easy communication between the team captain and laborers, no big brass bell to call together the farmers, and each day's work and scheduling was mostly unknown to one another. The team captain decided the kinds of work and the starting time each day.

Every morning, the captain whistled and shouted loudly the kind of work and the assignments, as well as the work schedule. In order for every member to hear, the captain went from one end of the village to the other and whistled, followed by shouting. He alternated this sequence several times as he walked back and forth. Sometimes there were several jobs, and sometimes the men were assigned a job that was different from the women's job. The children generally followed the women's work. After lunch breaks, the captain repeated the morning's routine unless the responsibilities were clearly assigned in the field before the lunch break.

The captain divided the work into two section each day, morning and afternoon. When a person worked two sections, it was recorded as one day or eight hours of work for that day. If only one section, a half day, was worked, that would be recorded as four hours. By the end of month, a summary would be given by the recording clerk for the total work hours of each person. This was divided by eight to determine the number of days worked by each person.

A meeting was held either every two months or, most likely, every six months to determine the points for each working day for each person. The highest number of points for a workday of eight hours was ten points for best laborer. Then for next level would be nine points then eight points or seven points or less. For a child, depending on the age, physical capability, and skills, the points could start at two or three points and gradually move up the ladder to close to eight points for a high school student. When each person's work points per day had been determined, the total work points would then be calculated.

Sometimes, the determination of a person's work points that were earned was unfair. There were multiple reasons for this. First, the appraisal was held only once every two or even six months by the time of appraisal meeting. How could anyone remember who was the best worker and who had made the most contribution to the team on a particular day or week several months ago? Secondly, very few people would speak up at the appraisal meeting because they were either accustomed to being silent or did not dare to say anything against anybody. They were afraid to speak against anyone who might retaliate against them if they spoke up.

There were numerous examples that showed that these meetings often led to a so-called one-person appraisal or scoring. As an example, someone might speak bad words before the meeting, saying that if anyone said anything against him during the appraisal, it would result in that person receiving low work points, and he would take action against the person who spoke out against him. Under these circumstances, the general outcome was silence when that person's name was called. After the scoring, the meeting mediator repeated calling for the number of points a few times, then one person closely related to him would yell out "Ten points." Since no one would dare openly object or oppose the score, that person received the full score of ten work points per day, even though his performance might deserve only eight or nine points. This appraisal system to determine work points greatly affected the attitude and the moral spirit of all the other laborers.

The total work points accumulated at the end of the year were used to determine the allocation and distribution of rice and farm produce to each family. The allocation was determined by two factors: the number of members of a family and the total number of work points that were allocated to that family. Because the per capita allocation was based on the total population of our Datang team in a given year, the allocation of the portion of earned work points was a major factor in determining whether a family received a larger ration of rice than average. The same was true for other produce, such as sweet potatoes and peanut oil.

All allocated rice and farm produce was priced according to the national pricing policy. The total farm income, plus certain business sideline income, was used by our accountant to calculate the total annual income of our team. Then our accountant calculated the compensation total, or salary, for each ten work points (or one day equivalent) by dividing the total revenue income, minus the total expenses for fertilizer, pesticides, etc. divided by the total accumulated work points that had been converted to day equivalents. Through this exercise, the accountant then calculated the income of each family according to the total work points earned and the total amount of rice and farm produce allocated to each family. If the end calculation showed a positive amount, this was the take-home cash income for the year; if it were a negative number, this indicated that the family was required to pay that amount in order to receive all rice and produce allocated to the family.

My Datang team was considered a relatively poor team in our township. It was not because we had fewer resources or that we had less manpower. It was because our team did not have a good captain and management team. Because our leadership was not as good, our members were not united and were less willing to work harder. Consequently, our total income was always less than the neighbor teams. Our team income was substantially lower, with a compensation rate in the range of 0.1–0.4 yuan (RMB) per working day. This rate was about half the income of most of the other production teams. Since each team had a fixed amount of allocation of rice by the government per capita, or per mu, the income from this portion should be similar among all production teams. The difference in total income would depend on the sideline business income generated by each production team. This income could come from raising and selling pigs, medicinal crops, and bricks/tiles, etc. Unfortunately, we had fewer sideline businesses compared to other teams. As a result, some young men in our team could not find a girl to get married to because many girls would not want to marry someone from such a poor team.

Due to several children and a retired grandma in our family, no matter how hard my parents worked or how much fieldwork we did to compensate our parents, our year-end income was always negative. In some years, we paid 50–100 yuan, while other years, we paid up to 120–150 yuan in order to receive all the allocation of rice for our family. Once we knew what we needed to pay to the Datang team, my father set up a prioritized budget plan. The first priority was to pay the team all we owed so that we could bring home all the rice that was allocated to us. This was important because our family depended on this for our yearlong food. Next was the expense of going to school. My father placed this priority in the budget right after food because he wanted his children to be educated and to learn. Tuition then was not very expensive, only a few yuan per semester. Although the cost of education was not much compared to buying back rice, it was critical that we had the notebooks, pens, inks, etc. in order to study and to learn. We were fortunate to have a father who set aside money as one of his top priorities because he was very concerned of our education.

After food and school, our third priority was clothing. We, like all children, always looked forward to a new set of clothes each year, but our family's economic situation often made it impractical. We have an old saying that goes, "The new three years and the older three years, sew-sew and patch-patch for another three years." Younger brothers and sisters had to wear clothes from elder brothers and sisters year after year. It was a common practice throughout my childhood that my father tried hard to sew a new set of clothing for us each year. In the 1950s, my mother and my grandma were able to wear gunny, a linen-like fabric; and part of the cloth was used for our clothing. In the late 1950s and 1960s, we purchased fabric from stores. Then we hired a tailor to help make a set of clothes for each of us. As for shoes, we all liked a brand called Liberation shoe. Generally, we had a pair of new shoes every other year. Again, younger brothers and sisters would wear those from the elder ones. Often the shoes were patched multiple times until they were completely unwearable. More often than not, it was a common routine that we did not wear shoes to school and to work in the field. My father made at least two pairs of rice-straw sandals a year for himself and my mother, and he made me and my elder sister each a pair too. These straw sandals were worn whenever we went to the mountain, collecting firewood and twitch grass. In this way, we saved money to purchase regular shoes.

To come up with the cash needed, my father had adopted a number of approaches. First, our family lived through very mean and lean conditions to save money—eating less meat and purchasing only what was necessary for our daily life, such as salt, soy sauce, and oils. We did not buy any expensive items that were not absolutely required for our living. Of course, in a planned economy such as China's at the time, there were really not much to buy in the marketplace.

Our second approach was to earn some extra money. In addition to farming as his primary job, my father had a second job as a house construction technician. This was a part-time job, mostly in the period between fall and winter when the regular planting seasons were mostly over. His compensation in the 1960s was about 1.0 yuan per day. He would keep 0.2 yuan for our family and the other 0.8 yuan submitted to the Datang team to receive work points equivalent to one day of participating in farming. This arrangement was required by the rules set up by the team management, and if not obeyed, my father would not be legally allowed to do this work. If he broke the rules, he would be stopped and probably would be called to the "study" by the officials of production brigade. The income received by Datang team from the likes of my father was added to the total income for distribution at the end of the year. As a result, my father made only 20 cents a day in his second job plus the compensation of Datang team, usually at a rate of between 0.2 to 0.5 yuan per day, which was added to our family income from the Datang team. My father seemed happy to receive 20 cents extra cash a day by working as a construction technician compared to farming.

Our third approach was to do as much sideline business as possible. Unfortunately, the policy from the central government that was enforced was that no capitalist activity was allowed. As a result, our options for sideline earnings in our countryside were limited to just mainly raising poultry, planting medicine crops, selling firewood, and selling twitch grass.

Family farming is the most common sideline business in our village. Since the people's commune had allocated to each household a small private lot of field, we could use the lot to grow vegetable for self-consumption. In addition, we could plan more for raising pigs, a common practice in most countryside across the nation. In general, my family raised at least two pigs at any given time, one as mother pig (sow) and the other as pig slaughtered for pork. To raise a piglet from 40 pounds to a 250–400-pound pork pig, the size considered for slaughtering, it usually took us about fifteen to eighteen months. This was somewhat slower than other families that could raise a pig at the similar size in only twelve to fifteen months. The time needed to raise a pig was several times longer than that of current, modern pig farms. This was because it was 100 percent organic and no hormones were used.

In a planned socialist economy, our pig was also a part of a "planned" market in which we were required to sell one qualified pig to the government in order to obtain an allowable certificate to slaughter the next pig we raised. After my family sold one pig to the government weighing about two hundred pounds, we received a certificate from the production brigade government. The government purchased all meat pigs for allocation to country persons who worked for the government, schools, stores, factories, public enterprises, etc. All these people received meat coupons monthly and were guaranteed to have meat every month, another benefit of "iron rice bowl" holders.

My family would spend the next year and a half raising a second pig, most likely to about 250–300 pounds. When we felt the pig was ready for slaughter, we went to the government with the certificate and applied for an approval to slaughter our pig. As a child of eight to twelve years old, I liked the slaughtering event a lot because, on the one hand, I would have the opportunity to eat a good meal with plenty of meat with viscera, or internal organs, and on the other, the slaughtering itself was an interesting process.

For example, kids, just like adults, often got up very early in the morning, usually at about 3:00 to 4:00 a.m. Because there was no power-shock or quick-kill method for killing a pig, my father hired a butcher, or slaughter master, and called on several adult neighbors to help. No matter how hard they tried, occasionally a pig could still get away. If this happened, it was not uncommon to see ten to twenty minutes of struggle between the pig and the people. The pig was killed by inserting a sharp knife into the throat of the pig then releasing it to collect the blood. The killed pig was placed in hot water so the hair could be scraped off with a knife. The belly was split open, and the internal organs were removed and collected. Part of the pork would be sold to the neighbors, but most it would be sold in the free market. We usually kept five to fifteen pounds for the family, unless we could not sell it in the market. If this happened, we might do a second day of sale or we kept it and salt dried it in the sun. We usually made about 100–150 yuan for the pig after expenses and after all our work for eighteen to twenty-four months. It was an important part of our family income.

With the mother pig, our family usually raised two litters of piglets each year. Each litter consisted of three to fifteen piglets, with an average of about ten. Raising sale piglets was different from raising pork pigs because the focus was different. When we raised pork pigs, we spent more on nutritious feed in the last three months before they were slaughtered for the market. For the sale of piglets, we provided nutrition for the nursing mother pig during the first thirty days after the piglets were born, then our attention shifted to feeding the piglets well for the next thirty to fifty days. When piglets grew to about thirty to sixty pounds, which usually took us about seventy to a hundred days, they were considered ready for the market.

In contrast to pork pigs, there was no need to get a certificate from the production brigade in order to sell our piglets. All my father had to do was to visit the free market a few times, one or two days just before he planned to take the piglets to the market. These visits to the market were mainly to assess the market conditions. On the day he took the piglet to market, my father informed neighbors and friends to come over to receive the piglet they had orally reserved. It was a general practice that the customers who had reserved a piglet would be invited to have a breakfast with us. All piglets were well-fed before weighing, and then each one was placed in a bamboo basket. After the reserved ones were taken away, my father and one or two other adult helpers would carry these piglets on their shoulders and walk ten kilometers to the county free market to sell them. If my father could not sell them all on the first day, he would carry the unsold piglets back home and wait seven to ten days before going back to the free market. Because of the pressure and the frightening effect on the piglets, the piglets needed time to recover to normal before the next trip to the market. If we were lucky, we could sell all the piglets on the first day, or more commonly, we sold them on a second or even a third trip to the market. For each litter of piglets, we often made about 100–150 yuan after all our expenses for feed. About two months after giving birth to the piglets, the mother pig would be separated from the piglets to recover in order to be ready for next fertilization either by a male pig or by artificial insemination.

Feed for the pork pigs, the mother pig, and the piglets was mostly from our private lot. Also, they were often fed rice from the rice we received from the distribution by the Datang team. If we did not have enough rice for the pigs, since we had to take care of our family need first, we might go to the market to buy more feed. During the winter months when all crops grow slowly, my sister and I often went to paddy field or the dry field to harvest wild weeds and vegetables used as feed for the pigs.

A by-product of our preparation of the rice was rice bran that was fed to the pigs. At that time, we shared a rice processing room with several close-related families. There was a large impact L-Dou, a chest-like fan, and a small stone mill. We placed the rice into a semicircular tube, using foot power to raise the L-Dou to about a meter in height and then let it fall down to impact the grain. The head pressure was heavy enough to make the husks separate from the grains. After about twenty to thirty minutes, all rice and husks were separated. If we wanted to get a bit more rice bran, we might repeat the process for a longer time. Next, we transferred all of it to a manual chest fan to separate the chaff, rice bran, and rice completely.

The stone mill there was used to grind the rice into powder to make rice noodles or rice cakes. I started helping my family when I was about seven years old to learn these critical survival skills. Now the rice preparation process was replaced in the late 1960s by a mechanical mill driven by a diesel engine machine.

In additional to raising pork pigs and piglets, we also raised chicken and ducks. Our method of raising chickens was not as good as it was for raising pigs since it often took more than a year to raise a chick to an adult weighing four pounds. We could raise only a few chickens each year, so most of them were consumed by our family. In order to make money from poultry, we began raising ducks. From May to June of each year, my father purchased twenty to forty ducklings from the free market. It took only sixty to eighty days for them to become adult ducks for the market. Because the growth season of ducks coincided with my school recess, my main job in these two months was to care for the ducks. To speed up their growth, I spent considerable time digging earthworms to feed them during raining days and catching frogs at night by hearing them croak or feeling them with my hand in the paddy field. I collected insects when I could find them in order to increase the duckling's nutrition. Usually starting in June, when harvesting of the rice crop began, I took the flock of ducks to the rice paddy when the harvesting of rice had just been completed. There would be other flocks of ducks taken by other children or retired adults who had taken their ducks as well. To prevent a mix-up of the different flocks, I often marked my ducks with a marker, or I cut off some feathers in the same spot on each duck.

Just as any other duck-raising person, I tried to let our ducks follow the harvesting by the farmers. I knew that the rice lost in the field and the insects that dropped off the cut rice straws would be eaten up by the first flocks of ducks in the field, so there was competition among us. This followed the famous saying "The early bird catches the worm." If my ducks could not get enough food, I had to feed them when we returned home in the evening, so I had every incentive to find the feeding field with rich food for my ducks. By August to September, our ducks weighed three to four pounds and were ready for the market. We often ate a few, but most of them were sold in the free market. Each duck could be sold for about two to four yuan, and with thirty ducks, we could generate sixty to a hundred yuan per year.

Planting medicinal herbs on private lots was a common practice for many farmers in our village. The most common herbs were *Ophiopogon japonicus*, *Aconitum polyschistum*, and *Rehmannia glutinosa*. I helped in removing weeds, watering the plants, and drying the roots after the herbs were harvested. These medicinal herbs were planted according to the state-planned program. The income from herbs was limited and possibly provided the family twenty to forty yuan annually. It was a supplemental income for the family, and I was happy that I could help.

The slogan "Living in mountain, depending on mountain provided" was used by farmers in our village. This slogan describes the fact that there are rich resources in mountains and the people who live in the mountain or in a close by area should find ways to use the mountain resource for their lives. Selling firewood collected from Duqiao Mountain was a good example of using the mountain resources. When I was six or seven years old, I went to the hills and collected branches and ferns for fires used for cooking. When I was eight to ten years old, I went to the mountain to cut firewood and carry it back home for our own use or to sell in the free market. Most of the time, I went with my father, mother, and my friends; but sometimes, I did it just by myself. I often left for the mountain right after my school was over at about 3:00 p.m. It took one hour to get to my destination where I worked for a couple of hours, and I then carried the firewood on my shoulder back to my home. Because the weight of the wood I carried was usually equivalent to my own weight, it usually took me about an hour to an hour and a half to get home. When I got home, it was 7:00 to 8:00 p.m. in the evening.

Cutting firewood was a hard, laborious job. I once had a terrible experience. One day, I went to the mountain by myself. While I was gathering the wood, I held a branch of the pine in my left hand and, with my right hand, held the big knife to cut the branch. As I made the cut, the knife slipped, hitting my left hand, cutting the flexor area. A piece of skin and muscle was cut off, and I lost a lot of blood. Fortunately, it did not cut an artery or a main vein, but a deep scar remains today.

When our firewood was dried, my father, and sometimes I, would carry it on our shoulders to the free market that was about ten kilometers from our home. My father was able to carry 140 to 160 pounds, while I could carry 70 to 90 pounds. The price for firewood was about one to two yuan per 50 kilograms. We usually sold firewood ten to twenty times a year for our family income.

Another of our sideline business was cutting and harvesting thatch, the twitch grass, as a major sideline income source for my family. The brick-and-tile factories in our areas often used this grass to cover the clay bricks and clay tiles they made to prevent rain damage. Thatch grass is a wild perennial grass that grows in the mountainous areas and is sparsely distributed. One could find small patches here and there on the mountainside. By May or June, the grass is likely to grow to 1–1.5 meters in height and is suitable for harvesting. There were a few dozen families in our village, including my family, who participated in this sideline business.

Because the Duqiao Mountain was so large and no one knew where the grass was located, we all hoped for luck as we searched for it. We began in the areas or spots where we harvested the previous year. Sometimes we were lucky to find a few clusters of thatch, while other times we spent hours trying to find it. Our past experiences provided only a starting point, but there was no guarantee we would find it. Most times, we could find only a few plants growing here and there. The day before we went out to search for the grass, my father, my mother, and sometimes I and my elder sister too went to bed earlier than usual because we often got up at about 4:00 a.m.

After our breakfast, we went to the mountain with a couple of ropes, a carrying pole, a saw-tooth knife, and a pot of porridge. When we found the thatch, we would cut it and lay it down on the bare surface, or on a canopy of fern, and let it dry under the sun. If we were unlucky and could not find a patch of thatch, we had to settle on picking and cutting thatch from dense ferns, one by one, or a few at a time.

Because it was in summer of a subtropical region and the weather was very hot, we usually sweated a lot. We might take a break from time to time to drink mountain stream water or eat the porridge we brought with us. But more often than not, we worked continuously without taking any break until noon. We ate our lunch of porridge or occasionally with some dried rice, then we took a short break under a tree. After a short rest, we worked until 5:00–6:00 p.m. or even until 7:00 p.m., if we did not get enough thatch.

We tied all the thatch into two bundles and carried one on each end of the pole on our shoulders all the way back home. The two bundles could weigh anywhere from 100 to 150 pounds for my father and 40 to 80 pounds for me if we were lucky to find the thatch and then how well the sun dried it. Usually, we got home between 7:00 and 9:00 p.m. Sometimes, my father or my mother went to the mountain alone for the thatch. I remember there were a few times when my father or mother did not get home by nine to ten o'clock at night. Then, our family would be very worried about their safety. When this happened, my elder sister and I would take a flashlight to look for our parents. Sometimes they were late because they had too-heavy bundles or perhaps they were too tired. Still there might be times when they were sick or hurt or had wasp stings that caused a swollen face. But fortunately, there was never an accident for any of us. As we think of all this now, it was, indeed, a very scary time in our lives.

After we got home, we dried the thatch, arranging it according to length into bundles, and then stored the bundles in our living room. This kind of labor-intensive fifteen-hour workday could obviously be done only a few times a month or ten to twenty times a year. To market our thatch, my father first went door to door, or brick factory to brick factory, to ask our former customers if they wanted to buy. These customers had sometimes asked my father for thatch whenever they needed it. Often a verbal agreement was all that was needed to make the deal. A long-term relationship established between my father and the factories was crucial. After we received an order, we would dry the thatch in the sun the next day. We removed the shortest thatch and rebundle it to make it look nice and neat and about the same length.

My father and my mother, and sometimes my elder sister and I, each carried two bundles of thatch and walked more than ten to twenty kilometers to deliver the thatch to the buyers. Because it was a competitive market for selling thatch, the price was about four to eight yuan per fifty kilograms in 1960s. My bundles weighed about twenty-five to thirty kilograms and was worth two to four yuan. This had taken me two to three days of hard work.

Although cutting and selling thatch had been an important source of our cash income, we looked beyond the thatch to find other ways to make a yuan or two. One way was to cut the stems of *Thysanolaena maxima* and sell it to paper mills. *Thysanolaena maxima* is a bamboo-like plant with slender thumb-size stem consisting of 1.25-millimeter fibers suitable for papermaking. It grows on hillside, especially on the edge of rocks and cliff. The government apportioned a certain number of stems to each production brigade for a specified period of each year for a penny (RMB) per pound.

After my school ended at about 3:00 p.m., my sister and I, and sometimes with some classmates, went to Duqiao Mountain to cut the stems. We returned home with a bundle of stems of forty to eight pounds by eight o'clock in the evening. The next morning, I carried the bundle on my shoulder to the buyer's station to sell before I went to school. I made about 0.5 yuan. Often, I did this a dozen times or so each year and made 5–10 yuan for the year.

The leaf of *Thysanolaena maxima* can be used for wrapping sticky rice called *zongzi*, a traditional cuisine for the Chinese New Year celebration in the Southern China. Every year before the Spring Festival, I followed my parents to the mountain, collected leaves, and sold them to the public in a farmers' market. My family was able to make ten to twenty yuan each year by doing this. Even fifty years later, my father still enjoys doing this sideline business!

From a child to an early teenager, I had experienced and acquired all the necessary skills in farming, in sideline businesses such as raising poultry, and in the moneymaking practices needed to be a successful farmer. I quickly became a competent farmer during my childhood. What I learned then made me a more endurable, more hardworking, and more persistent person when I grew up.

5

LONG LIVE CHAIRMAN MAO

The Cultural Revolution (1965–1971)

During the most memorable period of my childhood, I experienced rapid changes in China, including the Socialist Education Movement (SE) and the Cultural Revolution. Each of these big social movements was accompanied by many smaller ones, one after another, and produced serious consequences similar to the past.

The older generation of cadres and intellectuals had been subjected to relentless blows and letdowns. The country was in a turmoil and distress. Students could not go to school, and if they were in school from time to time, they would not study. Instead, they participated in the Cultural Revolution, joined Red Guards, or went to the north with destination of Beijing to join the rally with Chairman Mao. They traveled across the nation, lighting the torch of the Cultural Revolution. And they created villains of royal and separatist factions and engaged in class warfare.

Many people throughout the nation sang red songs, danced with loyalty to communists, and recited the Mao's quotes. We shouted out slogans like "Break four olds and build four news," "Long live Chairman Mao," "Long live the Communist Party," and "Carry out proletarian struggle to the end."

The consequence of all these actions was that the Chinese civilization of thousands of years was destroyed and the country's economy was almost ruined. Young people in the cities were sent to countryside for laboring, and the village children returned home to do farming. The Chinese educational system and scientific research were brought to the brink of collapse. The Cultural Revolution took away ten years of the lives of our youths and caused our economy to retreat for at least ten years.

When I was eleven to twelve years old, a teacher from the small village of my mother came to Datang team and lived with my family. Another teacher came with him and stayed with another family. Both of them were sent to our team by the Committee of Organization Department of Rong County to engage in campaigns of social education propaganda. SE was considered premovement of the Cultural Revolution. At that time, Chairman Mao had observed a certain "unhealthy development" in the country, and to curtail its further progress, he put forward a "class warfare" concept that was considered a part of SE.

At the end of 1963, the entire country initiated the pilot program of rectifying the society by carrying out small *Siqing*, which was designated as Four Cleanups of clearing up accounts, warehouses, property, and work points. The purpose was to make sure that cadres in each production team and production brigade, or township, were not making false claims to cash, farming produces, fixed assets, or work points, all of which were the goals of SE.

This movement was further developed as Five-Against Movement in certain areas as the Campaign of Anticorruption, Antispeculation, Antiextravagance, Antidecentralism, and Antibureaucracy, while in other areas, the Four Cleanups evolved to Big Four Cleanups movements as Clearing Politics, Economy, Organization, and Ideology. Although these movements, from small to bigger cleanups, were considered as step forward campaign by cadres from countryside to the higher levels of county provincial governments, most people did not understand what this really meant to them. The centerpiece of the SE goal was the universal campaign of the class struggle, or conflict, in which people with different interests would go against one another, either openly or secretly. The situation became especially severe when the people with power, such as cadres in various governments, went against the five kinds of people comprised of landlords, rich people, rebels, bad guys, and right-wing extremists, as well as those who did not agree with the central policies of the Communist Party. The main job of the propaganda team was to check all cadres in our Datang team. The process of Four Cleanups was first to hold a meeting to ask each cadre to undergo self-criticism and to confess if they had problems. Next, other peasants spoke out to reveal or to criticize any problems that might exist in the cadre.

Because my family was that of an average farm family, just like most other families, we went to the self-criticism and confession. They checked the work of the recording clerk for any wrongdoing by recording more points than were really earned. They checked the cashier's records for missed accounting or misappropriation of the team's funds. They reviewed the records of the accounting officer for any mishandled records and possible corruption. The team captain was searched for embezzling public funds, and the warehouse keeper's records were searched for any missing public produce or taking any produce taken home illegally. If the team found a problem, the cadre involved was ordered to correct and return any unlawful items immediately.

Our Datang team cadre members were found with very few problems, but it was different in other production teams, where some major corruption and items unlawful taken home were uncovered. This Four Cleanups Movement had, indeed, cleaned up some remarkable problems in certain organizations and helped solve some critical issues that had existed in the countryside for years, although the means of completing this task was unnecessarily enlarged and extended into the class criticism movement.

When the Four Cleanups and Five-Against movements took place in 1963, I was still in elementary school. These movements affected me only slightly. But by the time the SE moved to the front stage in 1965, I had just graduated from primary school. According the curriculum of school education of the country, I would enter my next school, middle school, and then high school. At that time, we had primary school, middle school, high school as a six-three-three system, representing six years, three years, and three years of education, respectively. However, as soon as the Cultural Revolution began in 1966, this system was broken and modified to a five-two-two system.

The propaganda of this change was because the strategic direction of the nation needed students to graduate earlier, to participate in the workforce earlier, and contribute to the social fabric of the nation earlier. This changed not only the educational system in the country but also the name of our middle school, from the people's commune to production brigade, and the high school's name from the county to the people's commune or township. This change marked the beginning of an era of civilian-run high schools and middle schools.

The change in education system led to several important issues. One was the lack of classrooms, and the other was the need for additional facilities. Before the change, the campus and the facilities in our primary school were barely enough for grade 1 to grade 6. Now the school needed to add the middle school classes and a lot more students. Without additional construction, it was difficult to accommodate the needs of the school. This led to the combination of fifth grade and sixth grade into one class as the first-year class of the middle school. Additionally, each class was increased in size to obtain more space for extra classes that otherwise wouldn't be available. Even though some of teachers from high school were reassigned to middle schools, there was a shortage of teachers, and there were certain teachers from former middle schools that were transferred to civilian-run middle schools.

To partially overcome the severe teacher shortage, the central government established a general policy for civilian-run schools that would require each production brigade to raise money for salaries and food produce such as rice from each production team to be used for hiring the teachers. These civilian-sponsored teachers were supposedly selected by the heads of all production teams; however, the cadres in the production brigades usually had the power to determine and finalize selection of the teacher candidates before submitting the names for approval by the office of the people's commune. The compensation included a cash salary and rice, plus oil and certain allocation coupons, all collected from production teams of the production brigade according to the allocation methods established by the government of the county. Although a portion of teacher's salaries was budgeted and financed by the government, the new teachers hired were mostly classified as civilian-supported teachers.

In addition to the civilian-funded teachers, there were other projects funded by the same manner, such as the barefoot doctors, the cadres of the production brigade, and the operators of joint projects such as water reservoir or power production station. There were three to five barefoot doctors in our production brigade with population of about three thousand. These doctors did not have academic training, but some might have a nursing school diploma. Others might have only had some limited experience gained from parents or grandparents. Some barefoot doctors claimed that their medicinal experience and knowledge were the treasures of their ancestors, passed down from generation to generation. This is completely different from current Western medicine where qualified doctors must graduate from medical schools and pass residency requirements. Although the barefoot medical practice has changed considerably over the past two decades in China, there are still clinics scattering around the county that many patients visit.

In addition to the civilian-supported teachers and barefoot doctors, all cadres in our Qiaobei Production Brigade were funded by the same program. Farmers felt that all these sponsored programs had taken a big bite out of their pie. Adding to the problem was that the payout for these programs had nothing to do with how good a job the sponsored teacher or barefoot doctor performed. In addition, the sponsors usually had very little authority to determine who would be hired as our teachers and as our barefoot doctors or even the cadres of our production brigade. Instead, these people were selected by the government or by a specific officer through some backdoor practice. This caused a strong negative effect on the farmers, and it damaged the relationship between the sponsored person and the farmers in the countryside.

As an example, the farmer-supported teacher received a compensation of about twenty-five yuan per month, along with about 250–300 kilograms of rice per year. This relatively stable compensation was also slightly above the average income of farmers, so many people wanted this kind of job. Although there were certain criteria to be met (these candidates would be graduates from middle school or high school), the candidates most commonly selected were based not on their qualifications but on the relationship between the candidates and the cadres of the production brigade.

However, once the candidate was hired as a teacher, he or she often considered the job unsatisfactory because the job was not permanent and the compensation was not equal to those directly compensated by the government. To narrow the gap of compensation between these two types of teachers, the farmer-supported teachers were allowed to take part in farming in a production team, thus receiving additional income. This initially appeared to be good for the production team because more manpower for farm production would lead to a higher farm production. However, many farmers disagreed with and sometime argued against these practices and arrangements because the farmers felt that teachers and the barefoot doctors had already received a good compensation and should not compete with the farmers for a distribution of the proceeds of the production team. When these disagreements between farmers and teachers became more intense, these teachers preferred spending time on their private plots, raising poultry and taking care of their own sideline business. They went to the school at the same time as the students and went home when the school day was over. They could work many hours a day at home and give very little effort in their preparation and teaching at the schools. Indeed, I was one of the young men who wanted to be a teacher when I grew up. Interestingly, I became a substitute farmer-supported teacher for about a month when I returned from my high school.

Because the educational system had changed, my sixth-grade class was forced to combine with the fifth-grade, creating one grade. As a result, the level of learning and education for these two groups of students was quite different. This large class made the teaching more difficult. Since fewer students wanted to learn during the Cultural Revolution, plus the fact that the training of how to teach and how much should be taught to students was not required by the school official, these changes did not lead to additional major issues. Students in the sixth grade, like me, spent more time in school than they should but did not learn as much as they were supposed to learn during the year of 1965.

My elder sister studied at the Rong City Middle School at the beginning of Cultural Revolution in 1966. Her school was soon disrupted and became half-time schooling and half-time participating in the Cultural Revolution. She joined the Red Guards early and participated in the cultural movements such as posting *dazibao* (big character poster) and carried out the class struggle against the *dangquanpai* (capitalist faction, capitalist roader), who were usually the head with the power of the county sheriffs, school principals, and various government agencies. The struggle, based mostly on argument and literate meaning, later evolved into attacks on human rights and physical abuse. Almost everyone who held power was targeted as capitalist or socialist road blocker during this time. This class struggle developed into one that included certain teachers, government officials, and other social clerks. The middle school my sister attended was closest to the county government, and the Red Guards there were most active in a class struggle against capitalist roaders.

In 1966, my sister took part in the march to the north with a destination of Beijing, the capital of People's Republic of China. She was one of a large group of Red Guards from our county, walking fifty kilometers to the city of Yulin. There, she and her team boarded a train loaded with Red Guards that carried them to the next city north. These Red Guards participated in the class criticism and the activities that were occurring all over China. They shared their experiences and learned from one another about the Cultural Revolution. After a short stay in each city along the way, these Red Guards then boarded another train heading further north. If they could not catch a train, they might walk for a day or two to the next city near any railroad station adjacent to the city. My sister spent half of her time marching and half of her time riding on trains. It took my sister and her group several weeks before they reached Beijing in October of 1966.

I admired my sister very much because she was able to travel to Beijing, where Chairman Mao lived. There was a mammoth rally where my sister saw Chairman Mao from a long distance, and I thought to myself, *If I were three years older, I could be one of them there too.*

Toward to the end of my elementary school, I set my goal to attend college. However, because of the Cultural Revolution, my middle school years were nearly completely wasted. There was a widespread rumor circulating throughout the country that there was no use to study. This caused many children in our village to not go to school and to not learn at home as well. Many children would rather help their parents to earn work points than be educated. Our school had no curriculum or specific requirements for its students. Normal school activity was considerably reduced. I was fortunate because my parents thought of the school differently from most other families. They wanted us continuing going to school and insisted that learning was a lifetime benefit and believed that we should keep going to school.

The teaching in our school closely followed the political movement in our nation. It was obviously tied to the Cultural Revolution, and one of a few focuses in our language class was to study the headlines of the *People's Daily*, an official newspaper for the Communist Party. Our teacher often started the class by reading a few selected topics related to the Cultural Revolution that was then followed by discussion. Some of questions we discussed were on how to keep up with the national political movement, how to raise awareness of class struggle, and how to maintain consistency with the policy of the central committee of the Communist Party. In addition, we were also required to do self-criticism and to criticize others, as well as setting our goal to become a communist successor.

Another important part of language class was to study the Chairman Mao quotations, study the Old Threes: "Serving the People," "Yugongyishan (Yugong Moved a Mountain)," and "Memorable Bethune." Apparently, I was good at reciting Mao's quotes and memorizing the stories of the Old Threes. I read them out loud in school and recited them at home. I was touched and sometimes even moved by these Old Threes, especially by the spirit of Yugongyishan. This story was about a person named Yugong who set out to move a mountain that was sitting in front of his house. He was brave and determined and willing to work very hard and persistently. He claimed that he would dig this mountain until his death, then his sons and daughter would pick up what he left off and continue digging to move the mountain. In doing so, his heirs would keep digging from one generation to the next. He strongly believed that the mountain would not grow any taller and that the continuous digging and moving earth bit by bit would eventually one day move the mountain. In the legend, Yugong's determination and action moved the god who then carried the mountain away. I read this story many times and particularly admired the vigorous spirit of Yugong. This story helped me to comprehend the old famous sayings that said, "Nothing in the world couldn't be done, as long as the one's conscientious" and "An iron bar can be ground into a needle." Although I did not learn much school knowledge as I was supposed to and I lost several years of my golden time in my middle school, I did learn something useful that has actually benefited me when I experienced difficulty and challenges in my life during the next few decades.

In the early 1950s when my hometown was liberated by Communist Party, the landlords, rich peasants, the counterrevolutionists, the bad guys, and the right-wing extremists were all classified as Five Kinds of Black Bad Persons or Black Five Kinds or Five Classes. At the bottom of our society, these Five Kinds formed our class enemies, and they were the antithesis of the people's proletariat, the target of mass peasants in class struggle. They were subjected to disciplinary action at all times. Although at the time, I did not know much about why these Five Kinds were placed into the five classes, I was told repeatedly that they were not our friends and that we had to stand up against them and that we should not stand alongside them or even their children. Their children were segregated from most students in our school and from other children at home as well.

My wife was born into a rich peasant's family right before the liberation. Her grandfather and grandmother worked very hard and saved money for decades and finally had enough money to purchase a few mu of paddy field for themselves. Because their family lacked someone to do the labor, they hired a couple of long-term workers. During the land reform in 1951, because they owned some land, they were, unfortunately, classified as rich peasants. This classification affected her life from the time she was a young child. She was treated unequally in elementary school, middle school, and high school. She was segregated in her production team and was often assigned the difficult tasks but did not earn the work points she deserved. She wore the stigma of rich peasant until 1978 when she passed the entrance exam and went to college.

By contrast, I was luckier. My family was classified as tenancy, which was considered not the poorest peasants, but with whom the revolutionists would still unite with as friends for the revolution and class struggle. This tenancy group was considered the most effective assistants of the revolutionary team. I was educated with revolutionary thought and ideology starting from my childhood, and I witnessed the so-called revolution and class warfare.

Despite the different forms of class struggles, the most common forms of class warfare were basically the same. In every interrogation conference, the target was always the Black Five Kinds. The production brigade appeared to schedule the conference with a preprepared list to take into consideration the interrogation of one or more of the Black Five Kinds. If a landlord, a rich peasant, or a bad guy knew how to impress the cadres in the production brigade, he or she might be less likely to be interrogated. Otherwise, that person would be the target of interrogation. In addition to constantly worrying about being interrogated, the members of Black Five Kinds were often assigned to do the most difficult and most labor-demanding jobs. To humiliate these Five Classes even further, they had to do the dirtiest or heaviest work, but they earned the lowest work points per day. Whenever a production goal was not reached or delayed, the head of a production team would ask farmers at any meeting to uncover the cause, which was often led to the Black Five Kinds members. They then proceeded with class warfare against the Five Kinds. In short, we used all the class struggles as reasons to vigorously pursue the class warfare in order to achieve both the revolution and productivity victoriously. This was widely used in our county during the Cultural Revolution.

Another aspect of Socialist Education sweeping across the nation was called Shing Education, in which all citizens were educated with a movie named *The White Haired Girl*. The main character of the movie was a girl born in a very poor peasant's family whose father could not provide food for her family. As a result, her life was miserable. Her father had to "give her away" to a big landlord as payment for his debt. The girl would not accept such an arrangement and fought it vigorously. Eventually, she escaped from the landlord and lived in a mountain cave for years where her hair turned from black to white. She was finally liberated when the Liberation Army came into town. Afterward, she was able to live as a normal person with a happy life.

This fiction, or at least partially fictional story, moved a lot of people with sympathy for her bitter life and then her good life under the leadership of the Communist Party. The central government propagated this story to educate us and to make sure that we all would love our Chairman Mao, the Communist Party, and our People's Republic of China. Without them, we could be just like this little white-haired girl without any hope of having good life. I watched this movie many times, and each time I was deeply moved and occasionally sobbed, just as some others in the audience.

This movie was often associated with the Shing Conference and eating Shing dishes. The Shing Conference could be held in the square of our middle school where more than a thousand of farmers and children could attend. It could also be held by each production team where twenty to forty peasants were present. Shing foods were often the inferior foods, such as wild grass, rice kernel shelf powders, and squash vines, etc. The worse the foods tasted, the more effective it was in bringing out the people's memory of their poor life in the past and the better way they were living as a result of the Shing Conference. Generally, an older peasant, usually someone with the most difficult life in the past, would be the main speaker at the conference. The other people then followed by recalling their past bitter life. Finally, we ate Shing foods while the speaker was crying. This moved many people including me to crying and sobbing along with the speaker. This was the high point of the Shing Conference.

The Shing Conference was accompanied with class struggle and class warfare during which one or two landlords, or Black Five Kinds, would be the targets. During these meetings, the leaders of the conference would often motivate the attendees to shouting out together, "The evil of landlords!" "Fighting with landlords to the end!" "If there's no Communist Party and no Chairman Mao, we would have no good life!" These repeated educational slogans were effective in brainwashing the younger generation. We slowly developed a hatred for the landlords and Black Five Kinds and accepted the communist ideology to realize our communism.

The *People's Daily* printed in the early days of the Cultural Revolution an editorial, "Swept All the Monsters." This article marked the beginning of the so-called Destroy Old Fours and Set New Fours movements across the nation. Old Fours, which were claimed to be inheritors of thousands of years of feudalism, with "old ideas, old culture, old customs, and old habits." As opposed to the Old Fours were the New Fours or "new ideas, new cultures, new customs, and new style." We in our countryside joined the national force to break down "blind faith, emancipate one's mind, and to destroy and sweep all of bad publicity, superstition of witches, geographic fortune tellers, and clerics." Part of the movement included destroying all the old books, arts, handcrafts, and antiques. Because my family had been farmers for many generations, we did not have any books related to the Old Fours except an old print of *Pedigree of Li's Clan*. My father took the risk of preserving this print, while many others had to give it up. All books collected by the Production Brigade were burned to ash.

Nowadays, at every traditional Chinese holiday such as Midautumn Festival and Chinese Spring Festival, we pay our respects to ancestors and bring food to an ancestral temple with a statue inside, which we share with our common ancestors spiritually or through imagination. All settings inside the temple, such as incense pots and memorial tablets, were thrown out and destroyed during the movement of the Destroy Old Fours in early the Cultural Revolution.

Another old custom was when the people got sick, or if someone unfortunately passed away, the witches would be invited to the temple to do some superstitious activity that was claimed to drive away ghosts or bad spirits so that the sick person could soon get better. This credulous belief in and reverence for supernatural beings was deeply rooted in the mind of many people. Therefore, there were some positive aspect of the Destroy Old Four movement. The front-runners of this movement were the Red Guards. I was still a boy and could not understand a lot of what was behind it. It was like a revelation for me when the Red Guards destroyed the Old Fours and set up the New Fours.

Socialist Education Movement at its late stage was coupled with the Cultural Revolution. Although I could not remember much of Cultural Revolution, there are a lot of records and archives one can access today. According to the records chronicling the events of our Rong County, the Cultural Revolution closely followed the entire country, specifically the development of Guangxi Zhuang Autonomous Region of Guangxi Province.

Records indicate that at the beginning at any normal meeting, people with disagreement would be verbally abused and criticized. However, this was later evolved to resorting to violence.

In 1967, two factions were formed, the United Camp and the Rebellion 4.22 Camp. Generally, the former was in support of the Chairman of Guangxi Province, Mr. Wei, and the latter was in support of another Provincial Officer. The two factions were organized all over the province and appeared to be artificially created, possibly promoted by the central government in Beijing for a specific purpose. Indeed, the two factions were created in every province across the nation.

In general, the factions acted against the leader of province, Mr. Wei in Guangxi, who was regarded as antiorganization and also called the rebellion faction. The supporting faction of the principal leader, Mr. Wei, was referred to as loyalists. After the formation of two factions or camps, the army and many other organizations, from the provincial level to the grassroots units, were considered as loyalists. Red Guards from most schools were loyalists at the beginning, but a great portion of them later joined the rebellion camp.

At times, there was no way to tell who was in which camp because everyone could take a stand at will. Cadres fought one another, students argued with one another, and the Guangxi military changed its stand at will because both factions claimed that they represented the worker class and the political direction of Chairman Mao and Communist Party. Each carried out their own agenda and propaganda. It later involved fighting one another. This led to a social disturbance and turmoil in Guangxi. Toward the later stage of Culture Revolution, the Loyalist Camp evolved into the United Camp, which was supported by the army. The Rebellion Camp, which consisted of many different people with complex backgrounds, often created more turmoil and vandalism and was often considered as an unfavorable or unjust camp by the peasants.

The fighting of two camps in our county occurred mainly at the Licun Commune. On September 7, 1967, the 4.22 Camp, or Rebellion Camp, took over the United Camp with twenty-six guns. On September 13, the United Camp and 4.22 Camp opened fire at each other, killing six persons of the United Camp. This fighting occurred again on September 26, and another six persons from the United Camp were killed. On the same night, the United Camp raided the 4.22 Camp and killed six persons there. On December 25 to 27, 1967, the United Camp sent four hundred fighters to fight the 4.22 Camp headquarters, killing twelve and injuring twenty-one persons. After the raid, some people from the 4.22 Camp escaped to Guangdong Province.

In additional to the fighting in Licun, there was scattered fighting around the county, which did not result in any loss of life. However, as the Cultural Revolution entered the winter of 1967 and the spring of 1968, Guangxi set off the Red-Storm movement aimed at the Black Five Kinds. The propaganda was that the Black Five Kinds and their children were planning to resist and wanted to kill cadres and peasants.

In order to motivate the mass of farmers in this campaign, the County Revolution Committee developed slogans saying, "If you don't kill them, they will kill you," "Long live Communist Party," Long Live Chairman Mao," "Carry class struggling to the end," "Long live proletarian struggle," etc. As a result, each production brigade established a form of the highest peasants' court to carry out class warfare against the Black Five Kinds. This unlawful and unjust Red-Storm led to the killing of hundreds, or possibly thousands, of Black Five Kinds and their children in our county.

In our Qiaobei Production Brigade (Qiaobei Township), class struggle and conferences were held either at Qiaobei Central School or the headquarters of the village. I remember that at one class struggle conference, the targeted landlords wore a "high-hat" and a cloth or a patch labeled with their names and the "criminal facts." They were forced to kneel in front of about two thousand peasants and children. Their "criminals facts" that had occurred prior to the liberation or the planned resistance were read out loud by a cadre of the production brigade, then someone motivated the crowd with slogans like "Knock down Black Five Kinds, then give another step. Make them never get up again," "Long live the dictatorship of the proletariat," etc.

This was followed by a number of these Five Kinds being taken to the base of a mountain where they were killed. This massacre did not just happen in our county but also across our province and other parts of nation. Some people used this Red-Storm movement for their own personal interests to retaliate against or to kill innocent people who might had said or done something to the retaliators or to the retaliator's family in the past. The mass killings included a significant numbers of rebellion members from the 4.22 Camp.

In the spring and summer of 1968, along with the Red-Storm movement, there was the establishment of the Country Revolutionary Committee. This was called the second phase of the organized movement. In this phase, many Black Five Kinds were killed in a planned, organized, and orderly manner. I remember that in our brigade, a landlord surnamed Han was charged with participation in the Anti-Communist National Salvation Corps and the presumed attempt to overthrow socialism. Of course, he denied the allegations. He was hit on the head with a three-inch-thick wood stick, and he bled to death. This made other Five Kinds extremely anxious and panicked. Some committed suicide, using poisonous pesticides or by hanging themselves. These kinds of deaths of thousands of people occurred across our province because of the propaganda campaign that was against the Anti-Communist National Salvation Corps that was supposedly organized by "Black Five Kinds."

Also, in 1968, a third phase of the movement began, as soon as the central government put out the Seven-Three Proclamation. The Revolutionary Committee, the Guangxi Army, and the Rebellion Group of the United Camp used this proclamation as a secret, double-edged sword, spread rapidly through newspapers, TV, and other media to label some factions of the 4.22 Camp as the enemy, who were then attacked and killed., The worst of it was that some of the people had already surrendered, but they were still killed.

After the Cultural Revolution, to clean up the Three Kinds of People who had been defined as fighters, vandals, and robbers, the direction of our National Central Committee was that supporters and followers of Lin Biao and Gang of Four were categorized as rebels and the supporters of Deng Xiaoping and veteran cadres were loyalists. Although the Three Kinds of People existed in both camps, only those named loyalists and conservatives were given a politically favorable position. Those who were rebels were less likely given any consideration for a governmental post. However, in Guangxi, none of these three kinds of people, regardless of their supporters and followers, were not given any recognition in politics.

Although the formation of two political camps was a result of the specific historical condition, the outcome of Culture Revolution was to destroy our society in order to reach the political goals of Chairman Mao and the many others, such as the Gang of Four. It developed to the seizure and the large-scale destruction of social fabric, or holocaust of the nation, to become a cult for Chairman Mao. It set the economy back ten years, and it caused the death of millions nationwide. In our county alone, at least two thousand people died unnaturally. Fortunately, there was little impact on my family as a whole, although my sisters, my brothers, and I were affected emotionally because our golden period of learning and acquiring knowledge was wasted. From this viewpoint, our loss was irreparable.

My family treated Chairman Mao as a cult god. My father admired Chairman Mao with a lot of respect. He repeatedly said to us that "Chairman Mao was our life saver. Without him, we would not have a good life nowadays, and as long as we have Chairman Mao, our life will get better and better, our future will be bright." Not only did my father say these things but he also put it into action. He encouraged us to read Mao's quotations, listen to Mao's speeches, and to nurture ourselves to become a socialist successors. He directed us to hang the Chairman Mao's picture on the center wall of our living room, which is still there today. I carried *Little Red Book* with me, and I read and recited Mao's quotes all the time. I knew that I had no talent in music, but during the Cultural Revolution, I sang out "Red Song" loudly and with passion, and I learned the loyalty dance from my elder sister. Such a fanatic mass movement was widespread, well-known, and well participated by millions all over the country.

6

MY COLLEGE DREAM

High School (1971–1973)

The Cultural Revolution had resulted in near destruction of the Chinese economy and the death of millions of innocent people throughout the country. Similarly, our educational system had also been completely undermined. Students would not go to school, and teachers would not teach. It was catastrophic for all children and the entire nation. Our golden age of learning was being lost. This became a lifelong regret for my generation.

Within a few years of the Cultural Revolution, the central government began to impose a seven-year compulsory education policy. This policy required that rural children were to be given the opportunity to go to school for seven years, from first grade to middle school (equivalent to junior high school). Previously, it was six years of elementary school and three years of middle school. At first glance, this appeared to be good for all children, especially those in the countryside. However, because of the influence of the Cultural Revolution, most peasants felt that it was useless to go to school and that to get good grades was not as important as getting more work points on the farm. This nearly universal stand caused many children not to complete seven years of education. Most likely, more than half of children in our village would not finish as many as five years of schooling.

Prior to the Cultural Revolution, all middle and high schools were located in the city of Rong County or in several designated locations scattered within the county for easy accessibility by students. However, when the change was implemented, all middle schools were delegated to local level under the production brigade at the village level. Our middle school was located at the Qiaobei Central School, where a portion of the original elementary school was divided to make room for middle school. Some middle schools, including our school, were later named the Agricultural Middle School because we were located in the farming area and the students were from peasant families of the village. This school was further developed to include Agriculture High School a few years later. Regardless of name change, it remained the same with not much schooling, teaching, or learning. In the end, we did not learn much during the two years of middle school.

During 1966–1970, the admission to college through entrance examination went the way of the Cultural Revolution and was suspended across the nation. In 1967, within less than two years of the Cultural Revolution, a directive from the Central Committee from Beijing ordered all schools, including universities, primary, middle, and high schools to commence classes immediately. Although many schools did not open until 1968, or later, all universities remained closed because they were so badly devastated with the persecution of cadres and teachers during the previous years.

In 1968, Chairman Mao gave a new directive with several emphasis: (1) the college education period should be shortened from four years to three years; (2) admission qualification should be based on class background and pure ideology; (3) students should have manufacturing work experience or farming experience; (4) students should be recommended by his/her production unit and, after several years of study, students should return to the production unit to serve; and (5) the university should invite the experts from manufacturing or farming with experience to teach the students.

To implement and enforce these directives, worker-peasant Mao-Zedong propagation teams were organized and entered the universities. Beginning in 1970, some universities reopened admission and resumed classes, while others did not until 1971 and 1972. The five-year suspension or closed college education was finally over. However, now the admission procedures and requirements were completely different from before the Cultural Revolution. One thing directly affecting me was that no entrance examination was given for admission and all students had to be recommended from the production level. This policy did not allow the most intellectually qualified students admission, but it meant that those with "good class backgrounds" and those with a "good relationship" with cadres were able to access the "back door" and were admitted.

With the gradually reopening of college education, the students at schools of all levels returned to the classroom. In our countryside, the people's commune (township) held entrance exams for high school admission. I passed the exam and entered a high school named Chengxian High School in 1971. This high school was renamed from Rongxian High School because all county-level high schools were transferred to the People Communes as a result of education reform. Because Chengxian was the closest people's commune to Rongxian County High School and was within the Rongxian City. It was a natural beneficiary of this county high school.

Many teachers there were from a key high school in Guangxi, making it the best known high school in the county. There were a number of excellent teachers, like chemistry teacher Wang, math teacher Lou, and physics teacher

Lou, all of whom had twenty to thirty years of teaching experience in their respective fields. They were recognized in the county and in Yulin City region as knowledgeable, skillful, and most respected teachers.

Our 1973 grade or class consisted of two classes named numbers 731 and 732. There were sixty students in each class. We were from all nineteen production brigades under the Chengxian People's Commune. There were ten students from our brigade from a population of about three thousand. Based on the acceptance of only ten students in the total of junior high graduates of at least fifty, our admission was selective and competitive. Anyone admitted to this high school was considered to be in the top tier of students in their respective junior high classes. The students who were not admitted to this high school attended the Agriculture High School in our production brigade.

Just like most students entering this class, I had a big dream that after graduation from high school, I would be able to pass the entrance exam to enter college. We studied hard and acquired a lot of knowledge in math, chemistry, and physics in the two-year period.

There was an urgency at the time because most students were aware that the college entrance examination would most likely to be resumed. Our school and most of the teachers believed that Deng Xiaoping could regain his position in the central government. I could feel and sense the competitive atmosphere in our classroom. Our class adviser, who was also the instructor for the political course, always provided a summary report that described our grade profile. This included the top 5 to the top 10 highest student scorers for each exam and then compared that to the highest student scorer of the next class, 732. If our average score and the number of top ten scorers were not as good as the other class next door, he often asked us to analyze it and find the reason for it. Although his practice did not made students feel better, he did indeed created a competitive atmosphere to encourage our students to learn more.

All students entered the 1973 class had little understanding of Mandarin because all primary schools and middle schools in the county were taught the local dialect. This dialect originated from Cantonese, but due to the long history of development, our dialect was somewhat different from its mother Cantonese. In addition, it is completely different from official language Mandarin (Putonghua). In high school, we had a language teacher who taught in Mandarin, but because he had very strong accent, his pronunciation was difficult to understand. Despite his broad knowledge and strong foundation of classical Chinese, we could not understand half of what he taught in the first semester. Most of the students showed little enthusiasm toward his lectures. Because I never had opportunity to learn classical Chinese until then, it was hard for me in his class too. I felt that I was not learning as much as I should. It was in his class that I started speaking Mandarin that was accompanied with both my own dialect and the accent from the language teacher. As a result, my spoken Mandarin is somewhat hard to understand by Mandarin-speaking people from the north of China today.

Compared to primary school and middle school, I felt a little more pressure in high school. Apparently, the students were more talented than the students in middle school. Most students in the class had a clear goal of getting a high score on the college entrance examination and that they were going to college. There were three girls in our no. 1973 class who were also known as Three Rongs. They had the same first name, Rong. Their grades, measured through exams and quizzes, were consistently in the top 5 percentile of the class. My grades were also right there with them. I was generally considered as a top-tier student among the boy's group.

At that time, the political landscape was rapidly changing. There were many signs, from the central government in Beijing to grassroots levels of village government, and from news media to publication outlets, that had led us to believe that the entrance examination for college admission would soon be resumed. In our high school, there was pressure on our teachers to teach as much as they could. In our classroom, all the students were very enthusiastic about learning. The combined efforts between the teachers and the students resulted in the best 1973 class in learning and acquiring knowledge in the 1970s. Indeed, this statement was not exaggerated because about 30 percent of our classmates were admitted to college in the first year of college entrance examination, which resumed in 1977. It was recognized that the examination for my class was the most competitive one in the history of China because the college admittance rate for that year was only about 2 percent.

In additional to studying as our main responsibility in high school, we participated in learning from peasants, workers, and from the army. These educations were part of a curriculum for all high schools across the nation. Learning farming was an easy part because all of us in our school came from countryside. We already knew most the farming procedures and understood how to grow crops. On the other hand, learning from workers was very different because we had no such experience. Our lessons were given in a manufacturing facility owned by the high school where workers manufactured various parts for agricultural machines and equipment, such as tractors and rice harvesters. We had lessons a few times in a couple of semesters. During these classes, we usually watched the operation of the workers and occasionally received some hands-on experience. Several workers there had graduated from our own high school in 1971 and 1972. I respected them very much and thought to myself that if I could be a worker like them, it would make me the happiest young man in the world.

Mandatory learning from army was another lesson for all students. We were trained using the general disciplines of the army, but since the training was given by a retired veteran or a head of People's Militia unit, our training was mostly focused on general routines such as formation, left and right turns, and march-walk, etc. We learned the position for shooting but did not have the chance to fire a gun. Therefore, such lessons were not serious and were merely set to meet the requirements of our curriculum.

Farming and gardening was the main part of our labor class. One propaganda prevailing at the time was that attending farming practice was a necessary strategy for antirevisionism and would prevent revisionism. It was considered that it would be excellent in training ourselves to become a communist successor. Therefore, in accordance with the direction of the upper governments, our high school officials required that all students participate in farm and garden work in the designated fields or lots.

In general, we learned the complete farming cycles for each crop from seedling to harvest. We worked twice a week in the afternoon, each for about forty-five minutes to an hour. All students were divided into small groups that took turns watering and fertilizing the vegetables the first thing in the morning in any dry day. We harvested the vegetables according to a schedule arranged by the students' cafeteria. Because we fertilized vegetables with human excrement and urine, as well as livestock waste, based on organic food standards today, what we produced might be considered as organic vegetables. However, these vegetables were actually severely contaminated by microorganisms because sometimes we harvested them just a couple of days after fertilizing. Fortunately, such contamination was not a problem because we washed the vegetables with channel water that ran through the campus from a distance water reservoir to farmland before sending them to the cafeteria. They were washed again with tap water before being chopped up and then cooked at the boiling temperature before being served to the students. This so-called self-planting and self-supply practice was the main way to supply ourselves with fresh vegetables for our meals. It helped us to solve the shortage of vegetables and to save money to reduce our dependence on support from our parents.

In addition to supplying fresh vegetables to our own cafeteria, we sent inferior and surplus vegetables to a pig farm owned and operated by our high school. Students were assigned in small groups to join the livestock team each day to help with raising pigs and cows. There were twenty to thirty pigs in stock at any given time of the semester. At midterm or at the end of the semester, some of the large pigs were slaughtered and supplied to the cafeteria to improve our nutrition.

There was one large cafeteria in our high school shared by about five hundred students from the six classes of 1972 classes and two classes of 1973. All classes took turn helping the cafeteria workers prepare vegetables for cooking. Each class was also divided into small groups of usually between five to ten students who helped cafeteria workers with putting cooked vegetables into cups containing about 1.5 pounds of cooked rice.

When class was over at noon and in the evening at 5:00 p.m., each student brought his/her own bowl to the cafeteria to pick up food. All food was dished up and placed on designated tables for each class. We picked up a container of it and each put the food and vegetables into our own bowl. We then washed the public container and returned it to the cafeteria for the next use.

Because most students were beginning to grow more, many, especially male students, required more calories and more than one cup of food. A few times during a semester, I ate two cups in a meal, one that was finished before I was halfway back to my dormitory.

Although allowed, it was unfortunate that most students did not have the financial resources to eat more than one cup of food on a frequent basis. To ease the hunger, many students went home on the weekends to improve nutrition. When they came back to school on Sunday, they brought with them a full container of food with meat and eggs as Monday treats for the people in our dormitory.

I was seventeen years old when I entered the high school. I was relatively skinny and short, with only about forty kilograms in weight and 155 centimeters in height, and based on my current weight and height, seventy-five kilograms and 175 centimeters, I shouldn't have been that short at that age. It has been often said to me that my retarded growth was a result of the Great Leap Forward and the three years' disaster periods, when I did not get enough food to eat during this critical stage of my physical development. I knew that it was not the main cause, and it had to do with the way of my personal development. Needless to say, if I were not the smallest one in our class, I was definitely not a handsome and attractive boy at the time. This shortcoming did not stop me from being a notable student in the class, because I was full of self-esteem and confidence. I brought with me the leadership skills I had learned in my primary and middle schools. I was brave and talented enough to start doing things from the beginning of the first semester that would resonate well with students and teachers, and I was slowly recognized as one of the student leaders. As an example, I was courageous enough to lead the morning callisthenic exercises for the class. In the military training class, I was a leader for the training and, at times, for formation and march-forward, etc. In general, in a class of all new students, like our No. 731 class, it was not easy for a student to stand up in front of the class to play a leadership role. But I did it, and I was able to do it well.

Because the Cultural Revolution had destroyed the moral relationship between teachers and students, our school were desperately in need of improving this relationship. I realized this, and early on, I put it into practice to comply with all school rules and regulations. I developed a good relationship with the class adviser and all the other teachers. In doing so, I received more help from the teachers, and I enjoyed my strong relationship with them, which continued into the following decades. My achievement at high school was well recognized, and I became a member of the Communist Youth League, which was a prestigious honor at the time.

Two years of my high school life quickly passed by. Although I was a successful graduate with high honors, I was hugely disappointed that there was no college entrance examination taking place. We studied hard, and we learned a lot in math, physics, and chemistry. But because of the interference of the Gang of Four (Jiang Qing, Wang Hongwen, Zhang Chunqiao, and

Yao Wenyuan), and the Zhang Tiesheng's 73-White-Paper Hero, who was an example of handing over blank answer sheets in exams but who was considered a "good college student." Our higher education system and our education policy and directive that had been formulated in the past few years remained unchanged. Deng Xiaoping's comeback failed, and we had no hope of going to college.

My dream of becoming a college student had become an illusion, and it put my life into a terrible spin. The uncertain situation that was filled with lots of twists and turns haunted me for the next few years.

7

IMPERIAL FOOD DREAM

Return Home (1973–1974)

The Mountains and Countryside (M and C) Movement began in 1955 and was promoted until the late 1950s. This was further promoted nationwide during the Cultural Revolution in 1960s. This M and C Movement was booming in 1969 after Chairman Mao issued the statements, "Rural area is a vast world, where there can be great" and "Young people to the countryside to accept the education of poor and lower middle peasants was very necessary."

The purpose of this movement was to eliminate the Three Differences (worker-peasant difference, urban-rural difference, and physical-mental difference). To carry out Chairman Mao's order, the Chinese government organized a large number of urban intellectual youth, mostly between ages fifteen to eighteen, to leave the city and to settle and to work in rural areas.

In the early years, some young people did indeed become rooted where they were sent and made contributions toward building the poor countryside. However, many of them brought along with them the ideal and comfortable life they had enjoyed in the city. They did not realize the challenges they faced. This led to serious consequences for the M and C Movement in the years that followed.

There are two operating modes for M and C: the Big Farm and the Rusticated Team.[1] The former included production corps and military farms, etc. In this model, young people were sent to the state's remote areas with vast lands and cultivated farms. They were placed under various production brigades, and they participated in mass agricultural production and/or mass industrial production.

---

[1] Educated or rusticated youth (*zhiqing*) from the cities were sent down to work in the rural areas.

Prior to1968, M and C mainly begun with this model. Later it was a queue model in which one to two people were placed in a selected family in countryside where they were to accept education from the peasants. This education included living with the families and working in a farming production team. They worked and participated in distribution and apportionment of agricultural production. This was the main model in the M and C Movement after 1968.

Due to the disruption of high education because of the Cultural Revolution, large numbers of junior high and high school students remained in the cities. This was often referred to as *laosanjie*, in which all students from middle schools and high schools in 1967, 1968, and 1969 (a total of six classes) remained in the city. These young people only had to do the political activities of Cultural Revolution.

Along with the establishment of Cultural Revolution Committee in 1968, the central government realized the major issues—that these youths who remained in the cities without jobs added to the unrest in our society. In order to resolve this serious problem, Chairman Mao and the Communist Party decided to organize a large-scale mass movement of sending them to rural areas. According to statistics, the total number of youths sent to the countryside during the Cultural Revolution was more than sixteen million, about one-tenth of urban population.

There were two middle school young people sent to our Datang production team. They were placed with a peasant family, a household classified as a poor family at the time of liberation of new China. The host became the "helper" of these two young girls in our production team.

Just as all other students in the rusticated team, the two girls in our team were to live with the family in order to learn how to live in the village, how to blend themselves into the farming life, and how to farm for food.

Because they had no knowledge of, or experience, in farming and countryside life, they had to begin with the basics. They had to be taught how to hold a shovel and hoe, how to use sticks on their shoulders to carry two buckets or bundles of things, and they learned how to plant rice seedlings in the paddy field. Basically, they were required to learn everything involved in farming and independent living.

It was hard for them in the first few weeks. Their hands were blistered, and their shoulders were red and bruised. They could not do the work of farmers most of the time, especially the heavier farmwork.

Some of the rusticated girls in different teams cried and escaped back to their parents in the city. However, because their personal government account had been transferred to the countryside, they had no choice but continue in their assigned farmwork.

To ease the pain of the rusticated girls and boys, the county and the people's commune governments required that the cadres of each production team assign lighter work to them to do in the beginning of their farm life. Also, if they returned to their parents in the cities for a short stay, the production team should not put too much pressure on them. Because they were young, it was understandable that they wanted to be with their parents and wanted to have some good food from time to time. Usually after a few days, they came back to the village and continued their reeducation process.

The rusticated girls in our team got help from the peasant families but also from young single men who wanted to become friends with them. After one to two years of work with our farmer at the village, the girls had gradually learned how to do all the farmwork.

It was claimed by some that the achievements of these youths supported the evidence of Chairman Mao's quote that "accepting poor and lower-middle peasant's re-education is necessary." It was considered to be the concrete embodiment of guarding against revisionism!

"Going to the countryside to the country where they are needed" was a loud slogan issued from the top of the Communist Party. It was because of this slogan that many youths in the cities were motivated and went to the villages. However, this M and C Movement began to slow down, and it was hardly mentioned in less than two years. The reason was twofold: first, these rusticated youths worked along with farmers during the day and joined political study or meetings at night. They earned only a few yuan a month in addition to a few hundred pounds of rice per year, which was barely enough for one person's consumption. These youths felt that by working on the farm, they saw no future and began to express their frustration, posting many questions to the government. Second, farmers had been complaining that these girls and boys came to the countryside to rob the people of jobs and food. This dissatisfaction became a somewhat-epidemic phenomenon across the county. Because of resistance from both the M and C youths and the countryside people across the nation, the central government had to recall most of youths back to the city after about three years. By 1974, most of them had returned to the city.

When I graduated from high school in 1973, the M and C Movement had slowed down, and youths returned to the city. Because I was from the countryside, it was much easier for the government to ask people like me to return home. My returning home had little to do with the M and C Movement.

The higher education system, especially the college education, had adopted the recommended enrollment system in which the admittance of students started with the selection of the mass of peasants, workers, and cadres at the basic production level, such as farm production teams and manufacturing units. In this enrollment system, all high school or middle school graduates must have at least two years of experience working in farming or manufacturing. The major problem of this recommended enrollment policy was that the process was very subjective because there was no national standard to be followed. In addition, a "recommended candidate" did not have to be the best qualified intellectually but had to have the best relationship with those people who had power at various levels of the governments, including the production brigade, people's commune, and the county. This recommendation process created a surge of backdoor entries of many cadres across the country. In the end, the most highly qualified high school graduates might not have had the opportunity to go to college.

I was extremely disappointed that there was no college entrance examination in those years. The exams were the most effective way to select the most talented high school graduates for college. I had studied so hard and achieved so much in the two years of my high school, and based on the ranking of my overall grades, I should have had an excellent chance of becoming a college student if the entrance exams had been given. Now I returned home without knowing what my future might hold. I stood on the same starting line as other young people who might or might not even be comparable to my qualification but who had an advantage over me because they had a backdoor relationship. I was completely at a loss and could not do anything to help my situation. I knew that no one could help me under the current society and the education system. Instead of sitting around and waiting for changes to occur for the better, I adjusted my goal and decided to make the best out of it. I still believed that as long as I worked hard and kept up with my work, I should be able to come out of this depressing period as a winner. I was a strong believer that "no matter where it was placed, gold would always have a chance to shine."

Although my parents both were illiterate peasants, they always knew what was best for us. They encouraged us to find our way out the countryside, to leave farming behind, and to become a worker or a cadre when we grew up. They wanted us to become a person joining those millions as an imperial food eater or imperial food person who received monthly salaries and allocations of food from the government. These people were proud of their upper status in our society because they had a stable income and food allocations regardless of bad weather and disasters that had greatly affected the peasants' income and life. Therefore, to become an imperial food eater was a dream of all young people. I took this seriously and made up my mind that when I grew up, I would do everything I could to become one of those people.

Based on the situation I was in after I returned from high school, I had three ways that could lead me to this imperial food dream. I could be recruited as a worker, promoted to a cadre position, or be recommended for college. I knew that none of these routes were available for me. I had to prepare myself in the coming years to meet the requirements of at least one of them. In order to achieve my goal, I set out with a plan. First of all, I made sure that I was one of best young farmers in my Datang production team. In achieving this, I leveraged my high school diploma by helping our team in political studies and helping peasants in their night school to eliminate illiteracy; I also worked diligently and showed the team leaders that I was a good farmer in the field. As a result, my effort was recognized and praised by most peasants within a few months after I returned to the village.

I had one disadvantage in the beginning working on the farm. I was a skinny young man when I returned from high school. As a main laborer who should have good health and be physically strong, I lacked the physical strength and could not carry the heavy weights that many peasants could do. Fortunately, I quickly developed body strength, and within about a year, I grew to be a man with body size of above 70 percentile of all the men in our team. This allowed me to shoulder-carry 130–140 pounds comfortably.

I realized that being a good farmer was not good enough to be considered a leading youth and that I should to be recognized not only by our production team but also by the cadres of my Qiaobei Production Brigade, which was equivalent to a township government. I thought to myself that I could become our team's leader or captain. However, my elder sister and my parents did not agree with me with this plan because they felt strongly that our team was difficult to lead and to manage.

There were about eighty peasants and their children in the team, consisting of people with three surnames—Li, Chen and Qin. We were naturally divided into three subgroups according last names. It was hard to unite these subgroups into a team. Even within each subgroup, there were always more disagreements than agreements. Some people always created more trouble than solutions while others often argued intensively with one another without a final decision being made. Most people did not even care how well the production team did. Because of these historical challenges, few peasants wanted to be the team leader. My sister was concerned that if I became captain of the team but could not lead it to achieve better results, it might damage my reputation and hurt my credibility. This in turn could affect my pursuit of my imperial foods dream.

I agreed with my sister's analysis and did not pursue the captain position, but instead I did a good job as a farmer. But I still had to find a way to attend certain meetings organized and held in the Qiaobei Production Brigade and the people's commune. It was only with the opportunity of attending these meetings that I could have chance to meet the cadres of the brigade and the propaganda team from people's commune and county government. Fortunately, there were several approaches that I could use to make myself known to the public. One was to join the Communist Youth League Committee. The others were to join the Amateur Propaganda Team and the Militia Brigade.

I brought with me the prestigious membership of the Communist Youth League, granted when I was at high school, which was my political asset. This membership, often considered as a stepping stone to Communist Party membership, was imperative to my imperial foods dream. Young men and women with this membership often had the advantage of being the first ones recommended as candidates for workers, cadres, or colleges. As soon as I returned to my village, I joined the branch of Communist Youth League of Qiaobei Production Brigade and played an important role in developing our Communist Youth League.

The secretary of the branch of the production brigade was a veteran and a member of the Communist Party. He was a good leader with the objective of growing and expanding the membership of the branch of the Communist Youth

League. We had only a few of members, and his first task was to complete the organization structure, including appointing a leader of four sub-branches, or groups, one in each village of about sixty to one thousand people. I was selected as the group leader of our village. The other three groups were also designated with a leader each. Altogether, we formed the five key member leadership committee. We worked together to develop memberships, achieving from the original ten members to about two hundred members within two years. The Communist Youth members played an important role in the evolution and growth of our brigade.

In addition to the youth league, I joined the Amateur Arts Propaganda Team. This team was actually under the Communist Youth League branch, and all five key members of the youth league were the activists in the amateur team. There were twenty to thirty0 young people with the main actors and actresses of a handful of youths, which included me. In the beginning, the performance skill was not especially good for most of us, but we all worked hard to improve. We gathered for rehearsal in the headquarters of the Qiaobei Production Brigade twice a week from 7:30 p.m. until 10:00 p.m. It was a twenty-five to forty minutes' walk for most of us to go home. Our attendance remained high even if it were raining in the summer or cold in the winter. Our rehearsal programs closely followed the political development of the country. We selected certain episodes from the then-popular shows and movies. We self-directed our chorography. In order to be consistent in with the country's politics in our performances, we had to include the revolutionary model operas that were promoted according to the guidance of Chairman Mao's proletariat literature course. We rehearsed episodes of two operas, *Taking Tiger Mountain by Strategy* and *White-Haired Girl*. After we had practiced for several months, we went to each village to perform in front of the peasants. And we performed in competition shows in the Chengxian People's Commune, where we were selected for second place out of nineteen propaganda teams.

During the first half of 1974, the main political movement in China was Criticizing Lin and Confucius. The Gang of Four of Jiang Qing and her associates had purposely used this political movement to purge Zhou Enlai's associate, Deng Xiaoping, and other elder leaders and revolutionists, alluding that this was the right verdict.

As a young man, I actively participated in these political studies and criticism meetings. Although I had a limited understanding of the reason behind such movements, I followed the mainstream of masses, speaking and discussing them at various meetings. My active participation led me to become a known youth in the brigade. I knew that recognition and trust by the county propaganda team and by the cadres of the brigade was crucial for my route to become an imperial food person.

During 1973–1975, our slogans was, "Agriculture learned from Dazhai and industry learned from Daqing, and all people nationwide learned from the Liberation Army." These Three Learns were the directives of Chairman Mao and were vigorously promoted in every part of China. Accompanying these movements was another political movement to train and cultivate young cadres in party organizations and to build teams of cadres at all levels of government with a combination of elderly, middle-aged, and young members. This same policy was carried out in our county and production brigade. To start this process, qualified candidates of youths were first identified by the propaganda team and the government of the brigade. Once identified, candidates were given further training. These candidates were to one day be qualified as cadre members in our county. In our village, a scheduled adjustment of the government was planned for 1975. The selection of the new government body would require the combination of the three ages of cadres. My efforts and my outstanding performance coincided with this political development, and I was naturally considered as a strong candidate for the young cadres.

To become a cadre,[2] one important criterion was that the candidate should be a Communist Party member. It was common at the time that majority of young people wanted to join the party, not only for promotion from farmer to cadre but also for future recruitment to be workers and teachers, so my next goal was to become a Communist Party member. Because I had been a Communist Youth League member for a couple of years and because of my experience in the amateur propaganda team, I was identified as one of a few party member candidates in our brigade. To be a qualified candidate, we had to understand the purpose of joining the Communist Party to serve the people wholeheartedly and impartially, to willingly sacrifice ourselves in order to liberate all mankind, and to fight to realize communism for all. For most people, these were high-sound and grand and truth statements that did not have real meaning personally.

To put into words the thoughts and action of individuals like me and for most other people, the objective in joining the party was at least, in part and in the short run, to achieve our dream of being promoted and recruited to be a worker, a cadre, or a teacher.

Once I was selected as a candidate, a propaganda team member and a designated party member served as my mentors. They explained to me the by-laws of the Communist Party and pointed out what I needed to improve. After I submitted my application, I was seriously "cultivated" in order to qualify for party membership. During this cultivation period, I actively participated in such movements as class struggle / class warfare, propagation of liberation battles, and criticism of Lin and the Gang of Four. My performance was appraised by the masses and the propaganda team. Then my mentors brought my candidacy status to the branch party members' meeting for evaluation. If there were any issues thought to be inconsistent with the criteria of party membership, I was required to improve it within a specified time frame. At last, my candidacy was

---

[2]   A *cadre* was a public official holding a responsible or managerial position, usually full time, in party and government.

presented to the whole Communist Party in our Qiaobei branch, and it was passed by a raised hand vote. After final approval by the party committee of the people's commune, I was sworn in under the party flag to officially complete my joining the Communist Party. This whole process was normally a long one, usually taking several years; but due to the movement's new cadre policy that required a speedy way to promote the youths to various governmental posts at several levels, my party membership process was simplified and shortened to about a year.

Family planning or planned parenthood shouldn't have anything to do with the imperial foods dream because parenthood and imperial foods were completely different things. For me, however, there was some relationship between them. My goal of becoming an imperial foods person required me to play a leading role among young people in the Qiaobei Production Brigade. Family planning in China in 1970s and1980s was used to encourage each couple to bear only one child, which was later referred to as the one-child policy. Starting in 1974, our county government sent to each brigade a family planning propaganda team of two or three members who were from county governments, state-owned enterprises, or agencies, as well teachers and selected temporary workers and youths. This team was expanded to four to six members by adding a youth from the production brigade. The reason behind this move was that family planning was difficult to do, and it was a task of persuasion that required a continuous and persistent effort.

With a critical number of propaganda team members present, it helped when the team encountered unwillingness and challenges from resisting families. I was one of added members to the team in our brigade. As an unmarried young man, I was reluctant, but I had no choice about joining the team since I wanted to play a leading role in every new movement and keep my leading status quota as a youth.

The members of the planning parenthood team first studied the documents from upper government to understand the policy, then we learned basic knowledge and slogans about family planning from the propaganda team members. The most frequently used examples were the following: "Family planning is a national policy and strategy," "It is a long-range plan of socialism," "The fewer pregnancies, the healthier births," "The fewer births are good for both our country and for our own family," "Late marriage and late childbearing are the basis of eugenics," "New social equality between men and women; giving birth to boys or to girls is the same," "Sons preference to girls is the black sheep of feudal ideas," "We must to clean them up," etc.

At the beginning, I had no idea how complex and challenging this was. I soon realized that this was one of toughest jobs around at the time. The reality was that there was only a small percentage of families that did not really want to have any more children. In the past, they didn't know what to do to prevent it. Now, not only were there techniques to help them but there was some compensation or subsidies to them for their willingness to control births. For these families, it was an easy job to get them to respond and complete the birth control procedures.

The next group that the family planning committee encountered was those of the Communist Party members, families with one or two party members and families with at least one member as an imperial foods person. Although most of the childbearing women in this relatively small group were reluctant to consider the birth control procedure because of the status of personal, family, and political backgrounds, most of them eventually agreed to the birth control. In this small group of targeted birth control individuals, a relatively high percentage of them were educated and, in some cases, were themselves cadres. They could argue and debate with our team elegantly on the subject of birth control, but in the end, only about half of the women in this group accepted the birth control procedures.

The most challenging and difficult group accounted for the majority of childbearing women. In this group, no one was willing to accept family planning. This was a complex group with a variety of reasons for not responding to the birth control policy. Some of them were filled with the family feudal concept and ideology that the more children, the better; and they felt that a big family was the status symbol for prosperity, blessings, and happiness. Others preferred boys to girls because they considered that only boys were capable of keeping the family history going and the family tree growing. Still others were just opposed to the propaganda team without any solid reason. Because of the legacy of thousands of years and because of the serious lack of social welfare in China, every family wanted to have a son or sons who could take care of them when they got sick and old or died.

To deal with this group of women, our propaganda team first held meetings in the production team to educate them on the importance of family planning and birth control. We then went to each specific family to help solve the specific problem these women might have. Most likely, we made an additional effort to educate and persuade the husband and wife together to accept the family planning policy. If it were still not effective, the family planning propaganda team worked with cadres of our production brigade and the county work propaganda team. The general approach was to "educate" them at their home and not allow them to work. It was obvious that every peasant had to work in order to receive work points and allocations of rice, and by sitting at home with our team, they wasted time with nothing to gain. Some women surrendered to the team after a couple of days of this kind of action. For the most resistant groups, the women and their husbands who did not accept the policy were called to the office of brigade and were educated by a one-on-one basis. This could include a long education and meeting, criticism at mass meetings, and/ or using other means that would make them feel uncomfortable and sometimes somewhat desperate. This highly pressurized approach could get some of the unwilling women to accept the birth control method.

Although there were a lot of tactics used, we did not use any physical abuse or monetary fines during the time I was involved. When the one-child policy was really enforced within the next several years, there were plenty of examples of physical abuse, along with financial fines, including, but not limited to, removing personal assets from the household such as pigs and cows in addition to cash, removing the career post of workers and cadres, and reducing the salary of the civil servants and the cadres. Forcible measures plus financial fines and the propaganda promotion played a role in carrying out the one-child policy in China.

One example was an elder farmer in our village, who with his wife had six girls at the time the family planning policy began. He was a well-regarded figure with leadership skills of organizing and carrying out all work for his production team. When the propaganda team approached his family, he strongly objected to the policy. He dragged his feet on accepting the policy and later sent his wife away during another pregnancy. It was not until after his boy was born that the birth control measure applied to his wife. Many people in the village considered that he had set a bad example for the brigade. As a result, many families did not accept birth control until they had a boy.

As any of the other political movements in China, the family planning movement slowed down within a year. To me, my part-time job was very short because my next assignment was coming. This time, I was designated as a leader of a militia company of about sixty young men and women to participate in the construction of the Xiaodong Reservoir. By then, I had been farming for about two years after I returned from my high school. I did many different kinds of work, participated in various activities, and joined the Communist Party, regardless of whether I did it voluntarily or reluctantly. I certainly did it for one simple dream: to jump out of countryside and to become an imperial foods eater.

8

"THE PARTY WANTS YOU TO BE A SECRETARY"

A Cadre's Life (1974–1977)

The Agriculture Learning from Dazhai campaign created a huge wave across the nation. Organized by Chairman Mao in 1963–1964, the campaign encouraged peasants to accept an advanced model of agriculture. This model was established according to the practice of farmers in the village of Dazhai production brigade, which had built a new people's commune for all their farmers to live in a gorgeous collective housing community. It was claimed that Dazhai had entered a new socialistic collectivism society. This movement reached its peak about the same time as I returned from high school to work as farmer in 1973–1975.

This movement lasted for fourteen years and ended in 1978. It touched the heart of every cadre and farmer in countryside across the nation who aspired to build their own Dazhai communes, but only to find out about the wasteful resources. Eventually, all failed.

Our slogans during this period were "Agriculture learning from Dazhai" and "We want to learn from Dazhai, to build our county as a Dazhai County, our township as a Dazhai township, and our production brigade as a Dazhai brigade." Surprisingly for me then, I had an idol to worship: a young lady who, in her twenties, was a young party secretary of the Dazhai Brigade. She was promoted nationwide as the advanced model or symbol of a communist successor. I respected her so much that I made up my mind to learn from her, hoping that one day in the future I would also be a model for others to learn from. Although there were many things to learn from the Dazhai movement, one that stood out to me was how to motivate masses of cadres and peasants to reclaim more paddy fields and dry land in order to produce more rice and produce. To do this, our county government would gather the mass of the power of the farmers to make terraced fields from hills and mountains and block the rivers with dams to increase the land for farming.

The influence of the Learning from Dazhai movement led to the construction plan of a water reservoir named Xiaodong Reservoir in our county. The reservoir is located in the Northwest Mountains of Stone Township of the county. With its high altitude of 1,500–2,000 meters above sea level, once completed, it could provide irrigation to vast farmlands, including both the existing farmland and the reclaimed fields from hilly mountains that were at lower altitudes than the reservoir. In 1974, the plan of reservoir's construction was completed, and the relocation of the residents proceeded smoothly. In China at that time, there were no earth-moving machines or other machines that could be used for this kind of project. All the work had to be completed manually with lots of manpower. Consequently, the county government adopted a human sea tactic to organize a large source of manpower from the county population to work together on the project.

A militia group, organized at the county level, was led by militia commander. This militia group was composed of thirteen militia battalions, one from each people's commune. The leader of our battalion was an officer of Chengxian Commune.

The project was divided into various phases. In the early phase, our Qiaobei Production Brigade had a team of about sixty militia members, organized as a company. I was designated as the commander, and a young lady was a deputy commander. There was a total of nineteen companies, one from each production brigade in our battalion. Our company was divided into two militia categories, one of which composed of two militia classes. We left for our destination, Xiaodong, in September 1974.

Xiaodong was about fifty to sixty kilometers away from the City of Rongxian. We rode in the back of open trucks for about two hours before reaching the base of Xiaodong Mountain. There were no roads accessible by truck or bus from there. We jumped off the truck, gathered our luggage containing a few clothes and a quilt, and carried it walking for more than an hour uphill to reach our destination of Chongjin Village. This was a small village with a couple dozen families, located on a hillside with an altitude higher than that of the water reservoir. Our company was placed in small groups in the houses of several families in this village.

The first phase of our work was to prepare the groundwork and site conditions suitable for a large-scale militia teams to arrive later. Our first job was to build sheds for ourselves and for those who would come later. After building the sheds for temporary living, our next priority was to construct roads and bridges. This was important since when the larger number of workers came, we would need roads to transport people and their supplies. It took us only about a couple of weeks to complete the shed construction, and then we immediately started with road construction.

Our company was assigned a small section of the road, possibly less than a hundred meters in length. We used shovel and hoes to loosen soil and to rake it in order to loosen the soil. When we met large rocks, we made holes using iron rods and hammers manually in order to set explosives. This was all very hard work and was extremely labor-intensive. The palms of our hands were bruised within a couple days of work. Our palms were thickening with another layer of callouses developed within a week's time because no gloves were available for us to wear. Fortunately, most of our members were young, in our twenties and thirties, and such hard work did not result in anyone falling behind. It took about a month or so for us to complete our section of the road construction.

The phase 1 of our assigned task was completed before the Chinese New Year of 1975. The county government was planning for an organized large scale of massive work to construct the reservoir after the Spring Festival. The county office this time called for about half of the adult farmers across the county to work in groups, with each group working for a period of one to two weeks at a time. The approach and the execution of it was to make sure that there were thousands of people working at any given time, day in and day out, twenty-four hours a day and thirty days a month. All these participants took turns every ten days to two weeks by bicycling or walking to and from the reservoir site. This kind of strategy of large-scale manpower movement back and forth was a high waste of manpower. In addition, it was very difficult to organize and manage all these people. In the end, the construction project was completed by smaller militia groups, or commandos, organized from all nineteen of the people's communes on a semipermanent basis. These young men and women were given jobs as workers in factories owned by our county and the people's communes in return as compensation for their work and their contributions to the construction of the Xiaodong Reservoir.

My tenure in leading our company in the initial phase of the construction project was relatively short and only for about two months. However, this short experience helped me develop my leadership skills considerably. I was proud of my capability to lead our militia company composed of young farmers from diverse backgrounds and coming from thirty production teams. We were able to come together and work in a military lifestyle in a harmonized manner. Our daily routine included getting up collectively in the morning, eating the same food, working together on the same project with our maximum capabilities, then studying or meeting together in the evening. I was very pleased to have the deputy commander working along with me. She was a couple years older than me and was just like a big sister. She often helped me by not only fully supporting my work as commander but also with my daily life. The two months of working as a commander was a memorable experience for me.

At about the same time that I led the militia team in the reservoir construction, there was another rapidly developing political movement around the country. This appeared to be a country-strategic move to establish young people as communist successors at the various levels of government from production brigade and people's commune to county, province, and even to the central government. Plenty of propaganda was spreading around the nation that focused on cultivating and training young people as leaders and successors. The strategic directive was set to ensure that various cabinets would be composed of older, middle-aged, and young members. Programs were established to identify the potential young candidates who were provided the opportunity to show his or her qualifications. Once selected as final candidates, these young persons were given advanced training and were finally promoted to posts at the identified levels of government. Because the members of leadership team were not democratically elected, as long as a recommendation was made by an existing leader at a higher official hierarchy, the promotion was usually valid.

Our work achievements during the two months in the construction of the Xiaodong Reservoir was recognized by the militia group and the battalions' headquarters. After we had completed the first phase of construction, both the deputy commander and I, along with several others, were recognized as excellent leaders in the reservoir project. We were selected as promising youth candidates for future governmental posts of the people's communes and the county. This unexpected opportunity made me extremely happy because this was something that I had been looking for over the past a few years. Right after the new year of 1975, we in a group of five were selected and sent to Licun People's Commune for a trial cadre training. Although it was said to be potential and trial in nature, all of us had a clear understanding that this was only procedural and that unless we did badly during this practice, we would be future cadres. I was excited because I felt that my dream of becoming an imperial food eater could soon be a reality.

We arrived at Licun People's Commune in January. I was assigned to Taiping Production Team of the Taiping Village Production Brigade. I was placed in the Li family. This family, with the mother Li and two brothers, was a red family because it was considered poor class as designated at the time of land reform in the early 1950s. The older son of the family was in service in the military, and the younger son was in elementary school. The mother Li was a respected cadre and farmer in the production team. I liked this family very much because Mother Li cared for me a lot and made me feel at home. I sometimes felt that she was just like a mother for me. I gave a portion of my salary supposedly for daily living to Mother Li according to the requirements of the county government. She cooked delicious meals every day, and I ate every meal with her and her younger son. More importantly, she told me all about what was going on in this production team, which helped my job tremendously.

Our training was focused on three major areas: to eat and live with farmers in order to develop our ability to establish a tie with them, to study and to organize various activities with cadre and the farmers to train our leadership skills, and to farm with the peasants to make sure that we were good at doing agriculture work. Because I was from a farmer's family, working on the farm was not a problem for me. I adapted to the workdays and the farming practice easily. We worked during the day and studied politics, such as learning from the Dazhai spirit and assessment of work points, in the evening.

Our project of agricultural learning from Dazhai was to block the side flow of the river and to rebuild the river-retaining wall in order to enlarge a paddy field. In addition, we combined small paddy fields to make a larger one. The project was done manually over a period of a few weeks. Again, it was the mass strategy of human power on one specific project. In addition to the project, other farmwork included the caring of the winter crops such as wheat and tobacco. At the beginning of the spring, our attention was shifted back to preparation of the rice seedbed and the paddy field for spring crops. I participated in all aspects of the farming work throughout the season.

Because we had good management members in the team, we were able to complete all farm tasks on time according to the requirement of the administration of the production brigade. This obviously made my training a lot easier.

Time really flew by quickly, and our trial cadre training went smoothly. In May of that year, some of us got calls to return to the county office where they were immediately promoted to the permanent cadre posts. Unfortunately, I was not one of them. By about July and August, while I was still in this cadre trial period, a couple of others were called and promoted. My cadre trial was completed by August, but after a short meeting at the county office, I was told to return home and wait for a decision.

Although I felt reasonably confident that I had performed well during the seven-month cadre trial, I was very uneasy with the waiting. As days went by, I became increasingly anxious and sometimes nervous, especially when all the other four young people had been called with a cadre position. I knew that my chance of becoming a cadre was diminishing, and I could not understand why. I was depressed and started to believe that the outcome must be related to my lack of a relationship with government officials.

While I was in my depressive mood, I was called to the office of party secretary office of the Chengxian People's Commune. I nervously entered his office, and even before I was asked to sit down, he said to me, "If you don't get to be a cadre, you should realize that you are a Communist Party member, and the Party wants you to stay in your production brigade as a future party secretary of the branch."

This, just like a judgment, was a big blow to me and made me feel terrible and miserable. It was not because I was neither incapable of nor incompetent to hold a cadre position, but instead I was helpless with the party's arrangement. Now my dream of becoming an imperial food eater remained elusive, and I had no choice but to accept the reality. So despite my unhappiness about the outcome, I decided to do what was called for. By then, I realized that I was indeed a victim of the combination of elder-middle-youth government in our countryside.

A production brigade was the most grassroots rural administrative organization. The cadres of production brigades did not belong to the national allocation and welfare system and, therefore, their wages and food rations were based on an agreement between all production teams and the brigade, taking into consideration the general guidelines from the governments of the people's commune and the county. Therefore, the compensation for all cadres in each production brigade was funded or sponsored by production teams of the brigades. In general, the grain appropriation was slightly above average of all the production teams, usually in the range of three hundred to four hundred kilograms of rice annually per cadre. The cadre's salary, also from the production teams, was within the range of twenty-four to thirty yuan (RMB). They bought rice at a set price, defined by the county government. Because of the funding nature of the cadre positions, the jobs of cadres were not secure. They could be replaced from time to time as long as the upper government saw someone unfit for a cadre's job. The farmers of the commune elected new officers under the direction of the party secretary of the people's commune or the propagation team from the county.

There was little motivation among these cadres to do a good job in their positions because it was a temporary employment coupled with the nonincentive distribution system. The amount of allocations for all cadres was fixed at a preset level, which provided no incentive to cadres to work harder and do a better job. Because the portion of grain allocation was less than that of a good production team, to compensate for this, the cadres were allowed to participate in laboring and earning work points in their selected production team, usually their home team.

However, this policy was challenged by the farmers who had lower incomes than the cadres. Additionally, the home team also felt it was unjust because the cadre took a share of their distribution. Still others criticized the fact that the cadres were given double earnings and took home twice what they were entitled to since they already had a full allocation for their jobs. In order to ease the critical voices of the farmers, many cadres elected to stay out of the laboring. In doing so, they eased the concern on the one hand but lost credibility as a good laboring cadre.

One might reasonably assume that by taking money and rice from the farmers, all cadres should serve the peasants to the best of their ability. However, this was in fact not the case. Most cadres did not feel responsible for their jobs. Some of them stayed at the office rather than visiting the farmers and the production team to resolve real farm problems. Others loved the bureaucracy and did not listen to the opinions of the peasants. Still, others used their power to gain advantages, such as recruiting workers and cadres for their family and friends or against those farmers who expressed different opinions. All these unethical practices by certain cadres created a tense relationship between the farmers and the cadres.

There was a general perception by most farmers that a greater portion of the cadres had not done a good job for them. However, one had to agree that the cadre's job in the production brigade was a difficult one, and many talented young people did not want this kind of job.

Due to the political and operational practices from various governments, most cadres acted as a conduit to pass information from the upper to the lower levels of governments, a passive kind of communication that bored most young people.

There were numerous meetings focusing on so many different issues such as politics, learning from Dazhai, welfare, and the many agriculture production and related practices. As a result, the cadres could have meetings almost every day. Our peasants often said that our cadres were almost full-time meeting goers. The production team captain and the political captain often spent an average of half of their time attending meetings. The peasants often called cadres meeting cadres.

It was strange and ridiculous for cadres of the people's commune and the production brigade to tell the farmers when, what, and how to do farmwork when the peasants knew exactly what they should plant in spring and summer and what to harvest in the fall. They had been farmers for generations, and our ancestors did not hold meetings to tell farmers about what to do, so why now? It was through executive orders. Some of the orders from the upper government did not make much sense, and they could make the cadres' job difficult to do. Consequently, the peasants did not want to learn farming technology and did not play an active role in decisions of farming and production because they knew that government officials would tell them when and what to do. All they needed to do was to follow directions and the orders from the government.

The passive obedience of the cadres was a common phenomenon across the country. Because of the influence of traditional Chinese ideology, the eating-drinking-playing phenomenon was then widespread in the countryside. Some cadres in our brigade ate meals and drank alcohol here and there. Some would have half of their meals in peasants' homes, or they were invited for meals in nearby restaurants. Some cadres on a field trip for investigation or observation of crop growth frequently walked into a peasant's house where a lunch or dinner could be served. This kind of free meals became a common occurrence.

Some peasants were not happy about it because they did not prepare for the unexpected "visitor" like this, while others might be pleased and welcoming because they wanted to have a good relationship with the cadres. These peasants might serve good meals and a drink in the hope for future promotions and recruitment opportunities. It was not uncommon to see cadres coming out from a peasant home semidrunken or to find a cadre who was drunk and lying down on the side of a road.

There were instances in which a cadre drank too much alcohol at a local restaurant right before a meeting and could be seen and smelled by the attendees at the meeting. This unwelcomed behavior left a bad impression of the cadres. Everyone knew this was a bad habit and an unfair advantage taken by the cadre, but there was no easy way to change it. It was widespread across many parts of the nation and had become an accepted epidemic by most of the cadres and a greater portion of peasants.

There was a famous old saying in traditional Chinese that said, "Take one's short hand; eat one's mouth soft," which means that if you take things from other people, your hand would be tied and can't do what is supposed to be the right thing to do. If you eat another person's food and drink another's alcohol, you would not dare to speak up on what is right or wrong, and mostly, you would think against your will and not in the best interests of the society. This had led to the prevalence of relationship or backdoor practice in China.

Well before I accepted the assignment of the party as a branch party secretary of my brigade, I fully realized these existing problems. That was why I was very unwilling and reluctant to be named to this post. Because there was very little democracy, all cadres were named to various posts according to the upper leaders' decision. For my promotion process, I was first called by a member of the propaganda team, along with a cadre in our brigade, to a meeting room. They repeated what was told to me by the party secretary of our people's commune that "the Party wants you to be our branch party secretary, and as a party member, you must set the country's and people's interest above your personal interest. You must obey the arrangement by the party and serve the people wholeheartedly."

This elegant language, or better yet, slogans, were frequently cited or quoted by all officers at various level of governments. It was the real communist ideology that if every communist could do it accordingly, the society would be beautiful, and all people would be happy with their lives. Unfortunately, this did not always resonate well because the human nature was often selfishness. When an ideology was set against the natural laws of development, it was hard to see how it worked all the time.

For me, however, I had no choice but to accept the situation as I was listening to them and accepting their education. The propaganda team member wanted to ease my concern of being tied to the production brigade for the rest of my life by indicating to me that if I did a good job, the upper government would see it and I would have chances to be promoted to be a national cadre. I knew that this was one of many strategies to get me to agree to their plan. Of course, if I didn't accept this arrangement, I would loss my status in my Qiaobei Production Brigade and the Chengxian People's Commune. My future career would be in jeopardy.

When everything appeared to be ready, the leader of the propaganda team brought my name as the only party secretary candidate to the branch party committee for discussion. Since this was under the political movement of the country to establish governments combining the youth-, middle-, and elder-aged cadres, fewer would express opposition against this kind of arrangement.

Then, my candidacy was brought up to a special meeting of a branch communist party where I was voted into my position by the raising of hands. After approval by Chengxian People's Commune Party Committee, I was formally introduced as the branch party secretary of Qiaobei Production Brigade in the fall of 1975.

Our branch party committee consisted of five members, one from each village and the fifth person from the largest village. This arrangement was in practice for many years in order to give representation of cadres in each village. One committee member was elected as the captain of the government. Because the Communist Party was the controlling body of the branches of the government, the captain also had to be a member of Communist Party Committee in our branch. From the standpoint of responsibility and authority at this lowest level of government, the branch party secretary was the most powerful person in charge in the production brigade. There was little democratic process in governing, and there were fewer things that would need all members to agree on. This process was widespread across our county. As a result, from the first day I began my post, I was a key figure in charge of our brigade. If things did not go as well as planned, or as expected by the upper leaders, I would be the one responsible for it.

There was plenty of work laid out ahead of me in the first few months. I wanted to get the new party committee on the same page and hoped they would agree with me on my plan and agenda. In order to do so, I had to receive the support of the immediate past party secretary. He was now the vice party secretary, who was also called the secondhand person. He was presumed to be my mentor to train and to help me become a competent secretary. I knew that he had some dissatisfaction when I was named to the post he held in the past, and I anticipated some reluctance on his part. But with my honest approach in showing my respect to him, things actually turned out better than I had anticipated. Our good relationship was soon established. I took the same approach and attitude toward the other cadres of the committee and soon established a good relationship with them as well.

With a relatively united branch party committee in place, my attention turned to carrying out our routine works around the brigade. It was unfortunate that most of responsibility fell on one person, me. Whether it was the vice secretary or the captain of the production brigade, all the committee members were usually only listeners and left their responsibility to me. This had little to do with my leadership style, but at the time in China, the cadres at every production brigade and in the people's commune were the same. It became a universal issue that the party secretary was one to be responsible.

Since my job started from day 1, I had plenty of meetings to attend whether they were held in the people's commune or at the country government. In general, for every meeting I attended, I would hold the same type of meeting and pass the meeting content to the cadres of our production teams. Roughly one third of the meetings were related to political studies, one third on agriculture production and practices, and the last third on various issues such as family planning, planned parenthood, and the one-child policy and practice. My time spent on various meeting exceeded 60–70 percent of my time. This was the same case with other cadres because whenever there was a meeting for the cadres of a production team, all cadres from the brigade would be required to attend. My other 30–40 percent of time could be spent on visiting different production teams and dealing with specific problems that rose within the villages.

It did not take long for me to realize that this job was a much more difficult than I had originally anticipated. There were many different issues that were hard to deal with, such as if I criticized a cadre too strongly for the slowness or delay of crop planning, the cadre was not happy to be criticized. On the other hand, if I did not push to get the jobs done on time, the upper government and the people's commune party secretary would criticize me for my inability to complete the task. Indeed, every cadre in the production team level knew what to do in their farming work. They knew exactly when to sow the rice, when to transplant the seedlings to the paddy field, and when to fertilize and harvest their crops. However, the cadres from our county government to my Qiaobei Production Brigade did not give the farmers their freedom to do their jobs because we felt that if we gave them too such freedom, we might loss control and might not be able to accomplish the planned acreage of the main rice crop.

As a result, farmers would always take on tasks that were given passively so we often had to force a schedule on the cadres of the production teams. This, in turn, led to an unrealistic practice of giving administrative orders that not only wasted resources but also damaged the relationship between the production team and the production brigade. Just as no one would disagree or oppose orders or suggestions of the upper secretary and governments, the cadres from production teams would not oppose what I asked them to do either. There was a common saying that "we must keep our ideology and our acts consistent and on the same page with upper communist party, especially with Central Communist Party."

Although I felt bored after a few months on the job, I had to keep going and do my best for the job. There were more than three thousand people in our brigade, divided into thirty production teams. Two production teams were located in the remote mountain areas, so to reach these two teams, I needed to walk almost two hours each way including uphill and downhill. For this reason, our cadres rarely visited them. When I became the party secretary, I established my plan to visit every production team at least once or twice annually, including these two remote teams. My goal on my visits was to understand more about the peasants' life, their concerns, their farming, and their sideline businesses. Also, I visited the paddy fields of each production team once a month to understand the growth of rice and other crops. I used this practice as my commitment to be a better leader who would be able to keep the best interest of the farmers in mind. Furthermore, I continued physically working with the farmers once a week. In addition, I tried to avoid being called an eating cadre to distinguish myself from other past cadres. In brief, I did all what I could to ensure the farmers I served would remember me as a good young cadre.

Forty years later, when I visited a peasant in our village, she praised me as one of those cadres who was frequently seen in the paddy fields of the Qiaobei Production Brigade and who helped farmers solve specific problems. This made me feel that my past hard work had been recognized by the peasants. I always tried to be a better listener and problem solver than the other cadres.

However, the most challenging work for me was how to bring our own production team up the speed with the other twenty-nine production teams in our brigade. Our team was recognized as a slower team that had difficulty completing the tasks that were laid out and announced by our committee. Since it was my home production team, it should not always drag on the progress of the production brigade, or I would have trouble putting my agenda through with other production teams. Accordingly, I had to spend a lot of time working on improving my home production team. Through some hard work and timely help, within about twelve months or so, our production team gradually got better and finally reached the middle of the pack in the brigade.

After a year of service as the party secretary, I felt a little more comfortable with the job as everything seemed to be going smoothly, and my authority had gradually been established. The Chengxian People's Commune and Rongxian County government considered that I had completed transition from a naive cadre to a more reliable cadre. However, just about this time, I became bored and started to feel that this job, in the long run, was not for me.

During the two years of my post, I tried to follow the developments of the political movements of the nation. One of these movements was Learning from Dazhai. The most widely spread slogans in our county and our brigade were that "politics is the commanding, class struggling is the key, promoting production, learning from Dazhai, to surpassing Dazhai, and to reach the victory of both revolution and production." However, as everybody knew, Learning from Dazhai was only a skin-deep experiment.

A good example of Learning from Dazhai was the construction of the Xiaodong Reservoir. During my tenure as the branch party secretary, our county government set up another project named Oil Tea Garden of Ten Thousand Mus (about 1,500 acreages). This project was to be located near the public roads in order to show off its glory and grand majesty when it was completed. This was a big and important project that had created some madness around our people's commune and Rongxian County.

The plan for the Tea Garden project was to dig out terraces on the many hilly mountains to be connected one to another. The terraces surrounding each mountain was to be built by using a large number of peasants. The county government divided the project into multiple stages in several regions of the county. Our people's commune was given a certain acreage by the county that was to be divided and assigned to each production brigade. Our production brigade was given about 1,000 mu (about 150 acres), and we followed the same used by the county and people's commune governments and divided our acreage for all production teams. After we measured and set the terraces marks, we issued an order that all production teams should start the project and complete the assigned acreage within a few weeks. Several hundred farmers went to the mountains and worked on the project at any given time. We cut down the trees, cleared the brush and vegetation, dug out the yellow-brownish soil, and then the terraces were finally built. Immediately after that, oil tea seeds were planted, and the terraces were managed by a team from our brigade.

Unfortunately, in the end, there were few oil tea trees growing on these terraces. It was another failure of Learning from Dazhai projects. Forty years later, when I visited my hometown, I felt badly about it because I was a leader in our brigade that lead and participated in this wasteful project.

9

GLORYING AND ILLUMINATING ANCESTORS

President of Student Union (1978–1982)

My dream of becoming an imperial food eater was getting away from me when I was appointed a branch party secretary. Two years on the job appeared to be long enough for me to realize that the road to reach my dream was long, bumpy, and boring. Throughout, I was anxiously hoping that a miracle could occur to change my situation and I would have a better fortune. To everyone's surprise, like a spring thunder waking up the sleeping earth in the country, the central government announced the resumption of the college entrance examination in October of 1977. This strategic change in the education policy was significant in the history of China because it helped to rebuild the country into a modern and glorious nation.

It was known that the ten years of the Cultural Revolution in China had led to the destruction of the educational system, a severe shortage of technical talents, and large technical gaps for a generation. China was fortunate to have creditable and reputable leaders like Deng Xiaoping in power after the Cultural Revolution. For me, the announcement of entrance examination was like throwing me a straw that could save a hungry sheep. My immediate feeling was that now I would not need to wait for a recommendation and a backdoor channel in order to attend college. All I needed to do was to pass the entrance examination in order to realize my college dream.

However, because I had been away from school for more than five years, I felt that most of what I had learned from high school had already been forgotten. My daily work as a party secretary did not help because the job did not require any math or science. Consequently, I was concerned about how to regain my knowledge before the entrance exam. If I failed to pass this exam, it would be more difficult for me to develop my career path from the cadre route because I might not be given the same treatment by the party secretary of people's commune and the other upper officials.

However, this concern was soon overtaken by my dreams and my aspirations. I was bored during the previous two years. I did not like the routine of the secretary with meetings almost daily. I followed the instructions of the upper government without much independence, and I did not know where I was headed without a career goal. In brief, I didn't like where I was, and I had to find a way to leave my post. The college examination that I had been waiting for so many years presented the best chance for me to become an imperial food eater. I soon made up my mind to participate in the exam, and in the process, I found a number of challenges that I had to overcome.

The immediate challenges were to find time to study and to prepare for the exam that was less than two months away. As a branch party secretary, I had my hands full every day from morning to evening. I knew I would not have time to study if I kept doing this full-time job, so as I analyzed the situation, I concluded that I could not resign from my post to study full time. I also realized that it would be better for me to not annoy the propaganda team or the party secretary of the people's commune because to do so, if I failed to pass the entrance exam, would undermine my future career. I knew I had to deal with this in a diplomatic manner.

I first consulted my vice secretary of the branch party in hopes for his support, then I shared plan with the other cadres in our team, asking them to agree for me to have two months of time off. To my surprise, they actually all understood and supported my request. I then applied to the party secretary of the people's commune, who also approved my request because of the promotion of education by multiple media and the political movement of the nation.

After I got this much-needed time off, I hurried back to the high school from which I had graduated to speak to the director, the political teacher of my class, and to the math, physics, and chemistry teachers. They all were very supportive of my request to take part as a student in their classes to study for the exam. Just as one of a couple hundred of students, I was back in the school with all my effort to prepare for the college entrance examination.

As soon as I arrived at the school, I felt lost. I was hungry to learn, and I wanted to jump-start my acquisition of knowledge, both new and past learned. Since I left the high school, I was no longer familiar with any of my textbooks, so I had to start all over again. I brought with me with the anxiety and a little nervousness for the first week or so, but then I started feeling better by the fourth and fifth weeks. However, the date of the exam was quickly approaching.

Even though I was good at my studies when I was at high school and my studying during the last few weeks helped me regain most knowledge of what I had learned in the past, I did not do very well on the tests. I had entered the testing with a heavy mind, knowing that I had to pass this exam. This mind-set may have placed more pressure on myself than it should have and could have been a factor affecting my examination. Luckily, the test scores were evaluated based on all students taking the exams. Because most students might have not been well-prepared in such a short time either, many of them did not get the scores they expected. I was confident that I would be able to meet the minimal point requirements to meet the criteria for the four-year college admission.

This was the first entry class after the Cultural Revolution. Every applicant was required to file a school application indicating the major applied for. This application had to be completed before the test days. For most students, including me, it was not easy to complete the application. Many of us were afraid of not being admitted if we selected a college that required higher scores than we could achieve. On the other hand, if we selected a school merely based on making sure to be accepted but was not the school or the major that we liked, we might also regret entering the name of that school on the application if our scores met or exceeded the admission requirements for a better college. However, if one selected a good college as preference but did not achieve a score to meet the admission score criteria, this could lead to no admission and the loss of a college opportunity.

The admission process was that best schools, especially the nationally ranked universities and colleges, were given first priority to select a student. If one was not picked by this first group of schools, the applicant's name was then given to the second-tier colleges, then in turn to a third tier, and finally to a two-year college. Because there was no computer selection process used, each examinee's score sheet and application could be placed in the unaccepted pile of applications and could be easily lost or not being seen until much later in the rounds of selection. That was why some students who had high scores got only admission to the third-tier colleges or even a two-year college.

In order to play it safe, I decided to apply for Guangxi Agriculture College as my first selection and the Guangxi University as my second. Both schools were in my home province, and by doing so, my application would not leave the province. This would reduce the possibility of it being misplaced or lost. The fact that I had been a farmer and a branch party secretary of my production brigade were the major reasons behind the selection of these universities. This should make me a better fit in an agriculture college and as an agronomy major compared to other universities. My ultimate goal was to leave the countryside to become an imperial food eater, so it did not matter that much to me as to what school I could attend. I was willing to sacrifice an ideal college in exchange for a better chance of admission. Fortunately, today this type of college exam and admission policy has been changed so that all students know their scores and admission score requirement for each college before their applications are completed.

In addition to completing the college application, each student was required to pass a political review process. The purpose of this review was to "ensure students were qualified politically to enter a college." This was obviously influenced by the ideology of the Cultural Revolution as in one of the three-parts quote by Chairman Mao that "as a communist successor, one must be completely fits all three criteria of Moral, Knowledgeable and Physical standards." I felt that as a member of the Communist Party and a branch party secretary, my political review should be an easy one with all green lights along the way.

However, in regard to meeting the physical standards, I was somewhat concerned. It was a national policy that every applicant who met the entrance scores had to take part in a physical checkup. The admission policy appeared to require that each accepted student had to be healthy. Even as a normal person without any signs of unfitness for college study, if the checkup showed any unhealthy physical profile, that person could still be declined. In Western countries, this would be considered a discrimination and would be against the laws on equality. My concern was that during the physical checkup to join the People's Army, I had a heart murmur, and this could make me fall within the unfit parameter for college admission according to the health standards. Therefore, I asked a teacher who knew the president of the hospital where the physical checkup was to be conducted to keep an eye on my physical examination records. It was later considered by some that my opportunity to attend college was because of the recommendation and the help that I received from certain people, or else I would not have had the opportunity to go to college. I, of course, disagreed because the opportunity I earned was through my own personal effort.

My exam and college application were completed, and there was nothing else I could do but to continue my duty as the branch party secretary as I waited. Although my busy schedule and duties kept me fully occupied, just as every other applicant, I could not stop thinking of the admission letters from the colleges. When each day passed, I felt it longer than the previous day. Fortunately, I had only to wait for a couple of weeks before the admission letter came. The whole process from the exams to receiving the college admission letters was only for a few weeks. Because all tests were scored by teachers manually due to precomputer age, it was considered as an unusual race against the time for the government. I thanked God for receiving such a fast miracle.

The news that I was admitted to the Guangxi Agriculture College was quickly spread to all my production brigade and to the people's commune. With a population of about three thousand people in our brigade and several dozen young men and women taking part in the entrance exam, only two of us were admitted to a four-year college. It was a truly veritable one-out-of-a-hundred selection. Historically, our brigade had had very few who could be qualified as scholars, and it was rare to have students who had gone through the college exam process in the previous two decades. Most of our teachers' highest diplomas were from high school, and very few had the two-year college associate degree. At the time we were in middle and high schools, the widespread thinking was that going to school was not as good as going up to mountain, and getting high grades at school was not as important as earning work points on the farm. Therefore, one could proudly claim that whoever made it to college was rare and had an astonishing accomplishment in our village.

My accomplishment meant even more to our family because the family had been farmers for many generations. Our ancestors, and even my parents, were illiterate. My father hardly finished one year of elementary school. My mother was a child bride, and as such, she did not have any chance to go to school. She could not even recognize her own name, nor could she do any simple addition or subtraction. She was completely illiterate. Tracking back five generations, none of our ancestors had been a scholar or had any scholarly related profession. Therefore, my admission to the college was considered as a glorious and illuminating accomplishment honoring our ancestors.

To celebrate my admission to the college, I consulted with my parents, and we decided to celebrate this occasion out of the limelight by impressing the public with lights on the faces of the family. This was especially for my father and mother because they finally had a son who would be going to college, something that every family dreamed about. My parents really wanted to spend some of their hard-saved money. They encouraged us to have a celebration because they felt that they would never again be looked down by some people in the village. Now, they could look up and live as proudly as everyone else in the area.

However, in my village, the relationship between the neighbors had always been uneasy. Some people did not like to see others having a life better than theirs. They were jealous when someone had a happy occasion such as sending their children to college, so when the opportunity arose, they would try to use their power to suppress others. This was the characteristic of small peasant thoughts and ideology.

My family had directly suffered from this type of jealousy and practice. As an example, one year, our production team fell behind in completing the farm production target; and we were criticized by the production brigade, who demanded the reason and an explanation for failing. The political captain of our production team told the brigade that my father was the cause because he did not participate in labor work in the production team and this affected others, resulting in the slow farming output. He was what might be called a scapegoat to the brigade by the cadre of the brigade, and he was required to join in a "study" section for "education." He was one of only a handful of peasants in the class. In this kind of education class, everyone had to admit the wrongdoing and promise that they would not do it again in order be released from the class. My father was nervous and surprised to be a bad example for a completely unwarranted allegation. My father's absence from the farming work was because he did sideline work for some cash in order to buy back the team allotment of the rationed rice for our family.

It was a common practice at the time. When a production plan could not be completed on time or if a production goal could not be reached, the cadres in the production brigade and the production team would always start with a class struggling meeting. The first scapegoat was mostly a Black Five Kinds person. Since our production team did not have Five Class people in it, it was natural for the cadres to move down the chain to get someone as a scapegoat. My father happened to be this person. The political captain of our production team told my father that no matter how well I did, I should prepare to stay in the countryside for several years before I could have any chance of being recruited as a worker or to be promoted to a cadre position, unless my father begged him for help. It was under such a suppressed environment that I could become a college student. This was undoubtedly a mockery and showed contempt for these people.

Inviting friends and relatives to our organized banquet for celebrating with us was a long tradition in our village, and it was exactly what we planned to do this time. My admission date to the college was right after Chinese New Year in 1978. Lunar Chinese New Year was the biggest celebration in China, so we decided to use this holiday to hold our banquet. I invited all my teachers and friends to this party, as well as our relatives and neighbors. The total guests were more than a hundred sitting at twelve to fifteen tables, with eight at each table.

For this occasion, we provided plenty of food to eat with lots of rice wine and cigarettes for the gentlemen who loved liquor and smoking. I took this opportunity to express my appreciation to the cadres of the production brigade who had supported me during my tenure as the party secretary and for giving me the time off to study for the entrance exam. I also thanked the friends of my youth for supporting me when I was the vice secretary of Communist Youth in our village and the captain of the militia team for the construction of Xiaodong Reservoir. Of course, I would not forget my teachers who educated me from a child to a college student. I proposed toasts to all guests during this gathering. And last, but not the least, I thanked my parents, the neighbors, especially uncles and aunts, brothers and sisters, and nieces and nephews for being our neighbors and for being with my family during both good and bad times.

It was common across the country that the celebration for this 1977 class for college was widely held by many students. It appeared that most of the students had been dreaming for the college opportunity since their high school years. Just like me, they had been disappointed when there was no entrance exam given at the time of graduation from high school. Returning home as farmers or for the Up the Mountain to the Countryside movement added to the tragedy of our misfortune. It was not until now that we had gotten this recognition of being a college student. As a result, most of us seemed to have a common thought in mind to release our suppressed pressure and our trapped emotions with great fanfare by showing our exuberance and celebrating the return to our happy life.

When the exciting and emotional party was over, everything returned to normal. My mind began to settle down to prepare for college. Indeed, I did not have much to prepare for because a small suitcase was more than enough for my clothing and daily necessities. My parents and my family did not give me any more suggestions on how or what to do in the college because they totally believed in my ability and my independence. One concern my parents had was how much money they would need to prepare for me over the next four years of college. Because I have five other sisters and brothers at home, my parents hoped that they would not need to come up with much money, if anything at all, to support me since they expected that I would receive scholarship support from the government.

I got my bag packed in the morning, and then, wearing my sweater with a tunic jacket and my liberation shoes, I walked to the county bus station. From there I boarded the bus to the city of Yulin and then transferred to a train. This was my first time to ride on a train and my first time to go to the capital Nanning City of Guangxi Zhuang Autonomous Region (a Zhuang minority province). I sat on the train with my heart beating in time with the rumbling sound of the train. I could not keep myself calm whether I closed my eyes or not. My brain was filled with the memory of the past decade, especially what had happened to me and to other young people. If the Cultural Revolution had not ended, if Deng Xiaoping was still in jail and if the Gang of Four came to power and if . . ., how would I and other youths have our college dream come true? I was one of those lucky young people, and more importantly, I was now able to leave the countryside and could become an imperial food eater after my graduation in four years. The more I thought about all these life challenges, the happier I felt.

It took five to six hours to arrive at the Nanning City in the evening. We were picked up at the Zhangganling Railroad Station by the classes '75 and '76 from our college. It was February 16, 1978, a special date that turned the page of my life to a new one. Now I was twenty-four years old.

My class, called class '77, was different from any other classes in the history of college because all students were not only admitted to college at a somewhat strange time but it was also the smallest group of new students admitted. We were among only about 290,000 new students admitted in the nation. This was very unusual class because normally, a college exam is given in the summer and entry to college is in the fall. Our class was tested in the fall and entered the college in the winter. The class '78 was only six months away from our class '77.

As soon as I entered the campus of Guangxi Agricultural College, I was strongly attracted to it right away. This college was separated in 1952 from Guangxi University as an independent college. By 1997, the college was again merged into Guangxi University to form a comprehensive university. The university, which is located in the western suburbs of Nanning City, was established in 1928 by Shaohong Wang, who was the governor of Guangxi government and first president was a famous educator, scientist, and democratic revolutionary leader, Dr. Ma Junwu. The Agriculture College was founded a few years later in 1932. The university and the college are considered as one of the older universities in the country. To describe my experience with the university, I will focus mainly on the Guangxi Agriculture College that I attended.

Nanning has a subtropical climate with plenty of rainfall, high temperatures, and high humidity, all of which are good for growing perennial plants. There were about 170 hectares of college campus. In addition to the class buildings, the office building, dormitories, and both inside and outside sport facilities, there are multiple farms, horticultural gardens, animal farms, and fishponds. A high ratio of green areas covered with trees and crops up to the areas of building structures makes the campus a beautiful park for people who like to walk, enjoy the beauty, and smell the aroma of the flowers. From the entrance of the college gate to the teachers' residence is a wide shaded avenue of dense mango and eucalyptus trees. Two large ponds are located in the center of campus with two pavilions erected in the center of the ponds, making it an ideal place for friends gathering and dating. The school library is located next to one pond, and when it is sunset, the shadows reflected on the clear water adds to the beauty of the campus. There are several paths for students to walk around the ponds in the morning and in the evening to speak or read English in, to have conversation with friends, or just to take a walk after a day of a heavy workload or to relieve pressure and tiredness. In brief, the beauty of our college was recognized as the top 10 campuses in the country.

The college has a large experimental farm station to grow various crops such as rice, sugarcane, and corn, as well as a horticulture garden with numerous fruit trees and flowers where students can learn and practice. It has a large veterinary farm to raise pigs, cows, and other livestock to provide not only an experiment station for students but also meat for the campus cafeteria to improve the nutrition for both students and teachers.

Unfortunately, many attractive scenes that were seen forty years ago have gradually disappeared because of the rapid expansion of Nanning City and the construction that has taken most of farms and horticulture gardens. Fortunately, the main part of the campus is still beautiful.

Although this is an old university campus, academically, it is a common and an average university in China. During the World War II, a number of famous professors and educators moved to the south and to our college to teach. However, after the liberation of China in 1949–1950, these professors returned to the north because it is a frontier province and in an ethnic minority region, plus Guangxi's economy was not as good as other provinces. Guangxi Agricultural College, although a good university, when to compared other top-tiered universities in the nation, was not highly ranked. When I entered the college, we had only an undergraduate student curriculum and no graduate programs. By 1981–1982, we had only a few graduate students, but it was not until the middle of 1980s that the college had a few professors qualified for supervising doctoral students. Fortunately, there have been significant changes since 1990s.

There were five separate departments in our colleges: agronomy, horticulture, plant protection, animal husbandry and veterinary science, and agricultural machinery. The department of agronomy was the largest department with five classes, which were divided with two in agronomy, two in sugarcane, and one in meteorology. There was a total of 150 students admitted in class '77; each class had thirty students. Among these thirty students in my class, there were twenty-four males and six females. Two weeks later, two more students were added to each class because the government expanded the class to include some experienced technical people. Our class added classmates Mr. Wei and Mr. Huang, both of whom were agriculture technicians, one from County Farm Bureau and the other from a people's commune agricultural station. Due to their rich experience and because they were older in age than we were, we quickly called them big brothers. There were three other students with similar backgrounds as I in our class, who had been cadres and Communist Party members of our respective production brigades before admission to the college. Four of us, plus one girl, were later organized as the activity group for the Communist Party group in the class.

Most of the students admitted to our college were from Guangxi regions. Because of the diverse nationalities in our province and the uneven economic development in most mountain areas, students in our class were from different backgrounds and nationalities. Some students were high school graduates from between 1966 and 1968, the so-called three old classes, while others were from high schools who had graduated from 1971 to 1977. Some were manufacturing workers, clerks, cadres, and the staff of enterprises and institutions; while others were from the cadres of people's commune and production brigades. Some of us were more than thirty years old while others were only seventeen. Further analysis of the student population indicated that the reason for most students to select this agriculture college was the desire to be accepted to a college in the first place. Most of us had considerable experience in agriculture, which was considered as an important factor for the admission selection process. In general, students from countryside were older in age than those from cities who had little farming experience.

There was considerable pride in our class '77. This was in sharp contrast to the class '76, which was the last class of students admitted to the college by recommendation instead of by entrance examination. Because the class '76 were composed of students with mostly red backgrounds and were recommended by various levels of government and organizations, these students lacked the self-esteem of the later classes. They should not have felt this way because most students from class '77 did not give them the cold shoulder and were not discriminatory. We knew that it was not their fault that they were in the class '76. It was the product of the Cultural Revolution. A considerable portion of students in that class had good backgrounds, and if they had taken part in the entrance exam as we had, some would have passed and would have been admitted just as we were. It was unfortunate that the society gave them a "looked down on" feeling and they were treated differently from class '77 and the later classes. This was reflected with the job assignments after graduation from the college with fewer graduates getting good jobs in the cities and universities.

Most of them were sent back to the county or people's commune they had come from.

When we got to the college, all curriculum established during the past several years of the Cultural Revolution were thrown out, and those from prior to the Cultural Revolution were readopted. One obvious change was to focus more on teaching instead of on field practice as it had been for the class '76. To graduate, our class was required to complete about 120 credits. Accordingly, we were assigned four main courses in each semester or the equivalent of 16 credit hours. No students could choose what class to take, but instead, all courses were mandatory. In general, two courses were given, each for two hours, in a classroom teaching conducted in the morning of each day. The basic courses required, such as botany and general chemistry, were taught in a large class format with all 120–160 students attending. For the more select, focused courses, the class size was limited to the specific major. For example, sixty-four students majoring in agronomy would be in the same class, while those majoring in meteorology would be limited to thirty-two students of that major. Only a few specific courses might be arranged in the small class-size setting.

There were two groups of required courses to be taken: general requirements and major-specific requirements. The former was mathematics, chemistry, physics, and political science; and the latter depended on the specific major. For an agronomy major, the required courses were organic chemistry, inorganic chemistry, botany, plant physiology, biochemistry, soil science, and statistics. Our major specialty courses were crop cultivation and crop breeding. Because class '77 was the first year of the resumption of college education after the Cultural Revolution, certain curricula were not developed in time for use in the first year; therefore, we were not given the courses of calculus and general physics, which were later required for the class '78 and beyond.

The afternoon was often reserved for laboratory and field experimental sections. These sections were an important part of our curriculum. Due to the influence of the Cultural Revolution and Chairman Mao's ideology, political science was required and taught for two semesters. Our political slogan was to "train all-around qualified college students." In addition, labor courses and physical education classes were required as part of our curriculum.

Field trials or field practice was an important part of our education in agronomy. The goal of our college education was to train qualified technical experts in agriculture. Most of us, after graduation, would be assigned positions in various levels of government, guiding and leading the revolution of agricultural science and agriculture production. Therefore, we were required to fully master the techniques in crop breeding and crop cultivation. Because most of us came from countryside, we had some general understanding of the process and practice of crop cultivation, although we might lack in comprehensive understanding of how and why crops were cultivated the way they were. In contrast, our knowledge in crop breeding was very different. For generations, farmers had never bred crops but always set aside of a portion of the grain, such as millet, from the previous harvest season to be used as seeds for the next year. They did not have any concept of deterioration of inbreed seeds. As each cultivation season proceeds for the same crop, the inbreed seeds would have a significantly negative impact on the crop yield.

Before 1978, there was an early hybrid rice cultivated in Guangxi, although most of us had no idea of hybrid rice breeding, especially the genetic and biological mechanism behind the hybrid rice. For example, we didn't understand why a hybrid rice seed requires three lines of rice crops to produce sterile male, a maintainer of male sterility, and a male sterile restorer. We did not know anything about the genetic mechanism of hybrid rice seeds or why only the first generation of hybrid rice F_1 gave the highest yield while the second generation F_2 and F_3 gave abnormal growth and low yield. These issues related to crop breeding were particularly interesting because it also had significant implication on the biological evolution, including the reason why the government would not allow the population to inbreed, which would give birth to an inferior offspring.

There was no undergraduate supervisor for our class '77 except for a head teacher or political worker. This full-time teacher was responsible for taking care of issues among all students in our class. Although no thesis was required, the department had a program to provide additional learning opportunities to those students with high grades. In our class, six students were selected to participate in a research project organized by a crop professor. Several other students were with another teacher on crop breeding using gamma x-ray. The reason why these specific projects were not open to all students was because it was not required by our curriculum, plus there were not enough teachers or resources for this kind of extra work for all students. Since it was in the first year of formal college after the Cultural Revolution, it was understandable that the school needed time to develop a systemic and appropriate program for undergraduate education. Such an approach at a small scale was easy to conduct, manage, and control.

Radiation breeding was thought to have great potential in crop breeding as a new technology. This technique was markedly different from the technique of three-line hybrid rice breeding. Its principal mechanism is that when seeds are subjected to high-energy isotope cobalt 60, which gives out gamma x-ray, the genetic materials, or DNA, of seeds would mutate, which could lead to new species. Through selection in the field trials, one could select a good crop if the change of genetic material had led to beneficial characteristics and traits. I was selected along with about a dozen other students from our class '77 to participate in this project. Our experiments were conducted in a basement laboratory on the farm. We had limited radiation protection equipment at the time. Some thirty years later, when we gathered for a campus reunion, we learned that two students of this small group of participants had passed away from cancers. This became an unpleasant memory for years among us.

Similar to three lines of rice breeding, tissue culture was another exciting technology that most of us wanted to learn. We were very curious about it. It had just been applied to sugarcane production. In this technique, we selected a complete nutrient profile in a sterilized medium suitable for crop development then transferred a small piece of tissue (i.e., leaf) to the medium and cultured it under a specific set of conditions. After a period of a few weeks, this tissue would be developed into a callus, which in turn developed into small seedlings. In general practice, sugarcane is not propagated through seeds but through its organs, called asexual propagation. Farmers use a good portion of sugarcane stems for planting. This not only reduces the yield of sugarcane used in sugar manufacturing but also requires intensive labor for planting. By using seedling from tissue culture technology, we could reduce the cost of both labor and propagation compared to the traditional practice in sugarcane planting. In addition, this technology is easier to be adopted by autonomous operation. Our tissue culture class included training in medium preparation, disinfection and aseptic operations, and transferring callus cells, field seedling cultivation, and transplant technology.

Our daily routine during the four years of college was that we had lecture classes in the morning and laboratory sections and field practice in the afternoon. Activity and exercise in the late afternoon and free period was mostly used for study in the evening from 7:30 to 10:30 p.m. In the morning, after the breakfast, we often had twenty to thirty minutes to study English, either by reading out loud on the sidewalk of the ponds or by reciting words on the way to classroom. We often studied with best friends in small groups, mostly in the classrooms, sometimes in the library, and occasionally in the dormitory. Due to the limitation of quiet areas for study, just as many other students in our class, either my study partner or I often went to a preselected classroom to "occupy" a couple of chairs with our book bags setting on them. This behavior would not have happened if there had been a sufficient quiet environment for all students.

The classes '77 and '78 shared many similarities. We both were admitted to the college through entrance examination, we were mostly from countryside with relatively poor families, and most of us depended on the scholarship from the university. Although the school funding was allocated by the education department of Guangxi government, most of students would not be able to receive full assistantship to cover all the cost of living expenses even though assistantships were said to be had on an as-needed basis. If we compared it to today's students, ours was much more challenging and more difficult.

Our dormitory was limited in availability. Our living conditions were hard for any young person of the present time to imagine and understand. Our dormitory room was about 12 by 14 feet, enough for two double-stacked single beds (about 3 by 6 feet) on each side, with an upper and a lower bed or a total of eight beds as the maximum number. Because we had twenty-six male students in our class '77-1, we were assigned to four rooms, each occupied by six or seven students. Only one or two bed spaces that were not occupied would be used for storing suitcases and hanging clothes. Our shoes were stored on the floor directly under our beds. Our study desks at about 3 by 1.5 feet was placed in front of our bed. The single stool was pulled out for sitting on for study and pushed back under the desk when not in use. When someone climbed to the upper bed, the students had to step on their desks as a first step. The rooms were used mainly for sleeping, including a lunchtime nap. It was the place where we ate our meals or had interaction with other students. It was also used as a study place if students elected not to go to the classrooms or to the library. During a raining day, we often stayed in the dormitory when we didn't have classes. There were no washers and dryers in the dormitory. Our clothing was hand-washed and hung out of the window to dry in the sun. If it were a raining day, clothing would be hung inside the room, usually in the unoccupied bed areas. Because of the crowded space with wet cloths hanging, our apartment was usually wet and smelly, especially when it was a humid day outside.

In addition to the poor housing conditions, our daily meals were also not great, although one could have said it was better than many parents in the countryside had to eat. Our farmer parents usually ate a dried staple rice meal and two porridge meals daily and only occasionally with meat. But we at the college had two dried rice meals with some meat and one morning breakfast with steam buns and steam bread or rice noodles. The college had one big cafeteria for all students. Students ate the same meal with no choice on the type of meals we wanted, nor could we have any preference for certain foods. By the third year, the school relaxed the rules somewhat to allow some students who could afford it to get more food and allowed for more selections of certain type of the food they wanted. Some students brought their own electric wire heater to the apartment for cooking some simple food to improve nutrition. Some students who came from nearby cities often went home during the weekend to improve their living standards. Those with relatively good financial conditions might eat out one or twice a week. I never tried to compare myself with these students because all these luxury items appeared to be quite remote to me.

I had six brothers and sisters, plus a grandma, at home with only my father and mother as laborers, which qualified me as having a difficult family financially. I originally expected to receive a higher scholarship compensation from the university. In fact, my expectation was set a little too high and unrealistic because most of my classmates came from the countryside with a similar living background as mine. They were all expecting to receive maximum scholarships as I did. However, the school did not have all the resources to meet such demands. Since I was a student leader and should be in sympathy with these students, I elected to keep my good composure during the assignment of student scholarships in the class. At the end, I accepted approximately 80–90 percent of my expectation. This scholarship covered my meals. My expenses for daily necessities was mostly supported by my parents.

My busy study schedule and the challenge of our living condition did not interfere with my enthusiasm and my commitment to serve as a student leader, the president of the student union of Guangxi Agriculture College. I was proud of representing our college to attend the Nineteenth National Student Congress of Federation from May 3 to May 9 of 1979. There were 450 representatives attending this congress meeting, representing about one million students in colleges and universities nationwide. Communist Party and state leaders Hua, Deng, and other leaders met with all student delegates and took pictures with us. The central task of the conference was to hold high the great banner of Mao Zedong's thought, to carry out and execute tasks according to the party's general guidelines, and to comprehensively implement the party's educational policy. At the meeting, a key organizer and past president, on behalf of the National Student Federation of the eighteenth session of the Bureau of the Commission, gave a report with title of "Continuing the Inheritance of May Fourth Tradition, Dedicated to the Four Modernizations, Nurture Ourselves to Become Qualified College Students in Moral, Intellectual, and Physical Development." The general assembly adopted the statutes of the all-China Students' Federation and elected the board of the National Federation of the Nineteenth Committee. He continued on his election as president of the National Student Federation.

There were twenty-three delegates, five females and sixteen males, plus two leaders from our Guangxi Province. We represented more than ten major universities across the province by attending the conference. There was only one representative from our college. Before going to Beijing, we gathered in the provincial facility, held a short meeting, and were provided with instruction and points of interest. We arrived in Beijing by train about two days in advance of the conference. After the meeting, our delegation had arranged for sightseeing of Beijing, including the Great Wall, Forbidden City, Tiananmen Square, Chairman Mao Memorial Hall, Summer Palace, Temple of Heaven Park, and some famous shopping centers such as Wangfujing and Xidan. Upon our request, the head of our delegation booked our tickets, and we returned home by plane.

It was a dream come true for me that I got this opportunity to attend the conference and visit Beijing and the beautiful sceneries. I was excited when I was on the plane going back. Who would have thought that, as a farmer's child growing up in the Cultural Revolution, I would have such opportunities to meet and have pictures taken with the then Communist Party leaders and government leaders. I suddenly felt that I was one of luckiest young men in my college and our county. I obviously could not hide my satisfaction and my happiness. I knew that this good outcome was not just simply by luck, but it was because of many years of persistent effort, starting from my middle and high school to returning home as a farmer and as a party branch secretary and now as the president of the student union of our college. I said to myself that all my efforts in the past was well worthwhile. I made up my mind that I should continue to serve the students to the best of my ability in the next couple of years.

After we returned to our college from the conference, I felt that my position was more important than ever. I had a greater responsibility to lead our student organization. My first job was to convey the spirit and the content of the meeting of the Nineteenth Confederation to our students. We used various means, such as meeting and posters, to promote the tasks of the meeting. We called on all students in the college to study harder and to devote our effort to make contributions to the realization of the four modernizations. At the same time, I also assisted the Guangxi Student Confederation to organize the Fourth Federation Congress in November of the same year.

The conference was held in Nanning on November 5–17 of 1979. The main task of this assembly was "to insist standard principals of practice as a test for the true . . . and to become well-rounded modern, qualified students and the contributors to new long march of four modernizations." As one of the members of the preparatory committee, I led our college delegates in participating in the general assembly. I was elected as one of officers of fourth session of the confederation. Our Guangxi Agricultural College was selected as one of a handful of key members as the university's executive directors.

From both the National Conference of the Federation and the Guangxi Conference of Federation, we could see the policy changing in the central governments. From now on, all students' organizations and activities would be similar to those practices prior to the Cultural Revolution. In continuing the effort, National Federation organized a summer camp in Guilin for students across the country in August 1980. I had the privilege to lead a group of representatives from our college who were participating in this camp. In the summer of 1981, Guangxi's Fourth Student Federation organized a camp for students from various universities of Guangxi Province. This camp was organized by our key executive university members, including me, with a similar format of the National Federation camp. The camp was held at Lu Mountain of Jiangxi Province. The Communist Youth and our student union coled a delegate of about a dozen or so representatives from our college, mostly student leaders from the college and the departmental student organizations, to attend this camp—from Nanning by train to Wuhan and then by ship through Jiu River to Lu Mountain. The whole camp lasted about a week. Every participant appeared to be very happy with this camping opportunity.

In our college, all student activities were organized by the student union and the Communist Youth Offices. The latter was particularly important because it was staffed with multiple full-time teachers in both the college level and the departmental level. In contrast, all officials in the student union were voluntary, so it made a lot of sense for both bodies to coordinate and to organize activities and to even collaborate with the offices of physical education. For example, we helped with a campus-wide basketball tournament, volleyball and ping-pong tournaments, and track and field competitions, etc. In general, we organized one or two performances that included ballroom dancing and singing. Overall, the participation rate in these types of social gatherings by students was not high. One reason might be due to the close mindedness and the less-liberated thinking from many students who grew up and were educated during the Cultural Revolution. I was in the same camp because I had hardly tried learning dancing or singing in my four years of college.

Compared to the arts and recreation activities, most students were more interested in physical exercise. We had morning broadcasts of gymnastics right after we got up every day, then the next ten to twenty minutes was freestyle exercise before breakfast. In the late afternoon, between 5:00 and 6:30 p.m., students ran and played various sports. Although I was an average student in a number of sports, I participated in running and basketball, and I represented our department in track and field competition for the 1,500-meter run, as well as joining the departmental basketball tournament. I even broke my front lower right tooth during a competition of a basketball game. This broken tooth could not be repaired or fixed at the Nanning City Hospital and the implant of a new tooth also failed. I did not have it repaired with a bridge by an American dentist until twenty years later.

The end of four years of college life was quickly approaching. Now every one of us faced a major decision to get a satisfactory job after graduation. In China, all college graduates were under the country-planned economy and planned employment, meaning that all graduates were guaranteed a job, but the job might or might not be what one liked.

Generally speaking, students from the cities would like to have a job in their home cities, and students with good grades who ranked in the top 5 percentile wanted a job in the university or a specialty two-to-three-year college, within the provincial government, or in research institutes. Student leaders and Communist Party members, or youth members, sought a cadre position in various government positions at the provincial, city, or county levels. Because the backdoor relationship and practice was still prevalent, some students with parents with power and good relationships with the school could gain some advantage over those who did not. All of us hoped for the best job possible, but unfortunately, we had only limited good ones for a portion of the sixty-four graduates majoring in agronomy.

My grades had been ranked in the top 10 percent for my four years in our class, I had been a student cadre as the president of the student union, and I was considered to be a moral example as a pacesetter in the New Long March of Guangxi Province. Because of my achievements, I was in an excellent position for a good employment prospect. Our department of agronomy planned that I would become a political worker, taking care of student matters in the department because I had been involved in politics, educating or leading others for many years, including the past four years of college. Although this was considered a good job by many graduates, it was not my preferred choice.

I had become bored with this kind of work, from being the branch party secretary in our production brigade to my work as a political leader in college. I wanted a chance to be more professional and more technically challenged. Accordingly, I expressed my interest in teaching, in both the college and in the two-year technical school. I had made up my mind that this time around, I did not want to accept an arrangement like the branch party secretary as I had in the past because I was a communist.

My strong qualifications finally convinced the department to assign me a job as an assistant teacher, the equivalent of an assistantship in Western universities, in the botany group of the department. The political worker position was assigned to another classmate.

To have a good job in the department from which I had graduated was an excellent outcome for me. Although teaching botany was not my first choice, it was my second choice. My first choice was plant physiology. One graduate who was majoring in sugarcane research had been assigned to the position in the plant physiology group. However, I still felt satisfied and happy to be a botany teacher because botany was basic science. I preferred this to crop cultivation and crop breeding, both of which were more involved in fieldworks and research. It was not because I could not do farmwork, but I now knew that I did not want to be a farmer as my ancestors had been.

Class '77 graduated in January of 1982, and I started my new job in February. In the beginning, my focus was on familiarizing myself with the curriculum and learning more about botany. During my college years, I had taken only a couple of courses in botany, so my knowledge of the subject was limited. I had to spend time strengthening my background in this specialty area. I joined the teaching lecturers in the class as an assistant, helping prepare the laboratory section for the students. After I fulfilled the daily job requirements, I spent much of my time learning experimental techniques under the supervision of other professors and teachers. There were a couple professors in botany group who were well-known nationally for their research in plant anatomy, so my research and that of most other lecturers and assistant professors was concentrated in plant anatomy.

My tenure with the botany group was a short one, only about six months. By the fall of 1982, I had the opportunity to be a graduate student studying aboard. How lucky I was! I immediately set my plan to reach this goal.

Picture 9-1: Picture with leaders of Communist Central Committee and central governments (arrow pointing at me), during the Nineteenth National Student Congress of Federation in 1979

9-2: I was selected as pacesetter of New Long March of Guangxi in 1980.

10

MASTER JOURNEY

Four Big Pieces (1983–1985)

Under the guidance of Deng Xiaoping's Reform and Opening-Up Policy, opening the country gate and going out to the world was sweeping across the nation. In order to accelerate the intellectual development and to nurture a first class of scientists, the Ministry of Education of China began a significant program in 1978 to select young- to middle-aged scientists, researchers, scholars, and graduates from universities and research institutions to study and do research abroad.

The general procedure in this selection program included the recommendation of the candidates by their employment unit for those who had successfully passed the examination given by the central government and with the approval by the upper government of their city or state. These qualified students were sent to designated universities in specified countries by the state-funded programs.

In our college, a recent graduate student was sent to the UK for a PhD program around 1980. After he earned his PhD degree a few years later, he returned to our university. Because he was the only recent doctorate in our college, he immediately received attention and recognition by the university. He was respected by students and teachers as a young professor and was assigned to lead the science laboratory in the college. His academic achievement was well-known not only in our agricultural college but also in the country. He was the key scientist of the National 863 Project in biology. A few years later, he was promoted to the president of Guangxi Agricultural University and, subsequently, became minister of the Organization Department of Guangxi Zhuang Autonomous Region.

In order to accelerate the pace of reform and China opening up to world, another new national policy went into effect to promote and allow governments of the provinces and the cities to develop self-funded and self-sponsored programs to send students board.

Because Guangxi was behind the nation in economic development, especially in its education, science, and technology, it was quite challenging for Guangxi to compete at the national level for its quota of students to study abroad. In order to speed up technological and economic development in the region, Guangxi leaders decided on a self-financing program to send its own students aboard in 1982. This decision gave our classes '77 and '78 new hope and opportunity. When I heard the news, I could not calm my heart because I had never dreamed of studying aboard, but this might actually be a good opportunity for me.

The self-funded program of sending students aboard was first of this kind for the province, and it was different from later classes of self-funded programs. From the announcement of the plan to registration and final examination, there were only about two months for the process.

With such a short notice, coupled with the fact that most of the students had just reported to their new jobs after graduation, it was challenging for most recent graduates. This was especially true for those who had a job in the countryside. Consequently, most of the registrants for the examination were from universities and research institutes. Some graduates who were working in the city and government agencies also applied. There was a considerable advantage for those who were working as teachers at universities because these graduates had not only the time but also the study resources. Naturally, these graduates had stronger backgrounds and were more qualified intellectually than most other graduates of the same classes. I was lucky to be one of these people. I knew this was like a godsend, so I applied for this opportunity without hesitation. I received strong support from the Communist Party branches and offices of our department, including the teachers of the botany group.

All applicants were required to complete an application form, providing the major, the field of study, and the intention after completion of the study aboard. This application went through the political examination that was still widely used as a criterion in China. The test subjects were determined by the committees from designated universities selected by the Guangxi provincial government. The test questions relating to agricultural science were given by my alma mater. At least two tests were given by the teachers who had taught us during the past several years. This was a double advantage of both the '77 and '78 classes over other applicants who had graduated either much earlier or from other universities.

There were four tests given to the applicants of agricultural sciences. These were chemistry, plant physiology, and crop cultivation and breeding, and either English or Japanese language. It took a few weeks to announce the scores of the examination. The whole process—from application, taking tests, to scoring, and from political examination to final acceptance by students—was on a fast track. Everything went smoothly, and I soon received the acceptance letter as a member of the first Guangxi province self-funded overseas students.

This first class of students was from all over the Guangxi regions, with most from provincial universities and research institutions. A few came from various levels of government as technically specialized officials or key technical persons working in agriculture and manufacturing industries. The destination countries for these students were the United States, Japan, Canada, and Australia. About ten students in the agricultural sciences were scheduled to go to the US or Japan.

The timing of the decision meant that this class had only a few months of training in English because the government's plan was to send us abroad for enrollment in the fall of 1983. This required us to complete the application to graduate schools in March and April. A key requirement for completing the graduate application was passing the TOEFL. This language test was given only in a few major cities in China twice a year. Guangzhou City was the site for testing for the south of China.

Our training was carried out at the Department of Foreign Languages, Guangxi University (GXU), beginning in January and ending on June 13, 1983, a fast-track training.

There was a total of seventy students divided into three classes. The classes A and C were trained in English, while Class B studied Japanese.

I was assigned to class C, which consisted of thirty students. The same number of students was in class A. The reality of these two English classes was that most students were poor in English, with minimal oral and audio language capability. Our grammar and vocabulary were not good either. There were ten students in the Japanese class who were taught by teachers from the GXU.

The English courses were taught by invited faculty, one from the US and other from Australia. The teaching approach was to focus on building our verbal and reading foundation according to accepted methods of language training. The main topics included, but were not limited to, grammar, vocabulary, and reading comprehension. We all knew this would be an excellent approach, if we had enough time. Unfortunately, we did not. How could we learn enough in three months to build a sufficient vocabulary and significantly improve our spoken and understanding of English?

We had to add a greater workload to our daily schedule, with more hours for grammar, oral practice, and listening to spoken English on a cassette player. We spent a lot of time memorizing words and phrases and did as many practice tests of TOEFL as we could. According to most people, we needed eight thousand words of vocabulary and phrases, but the words and phrases learned in our classes would be considerably less than eight thousand. Many of us studied and memorized a small dictionary. All our efforts were directed toward getting a higher score on the TOEFL.

My English ability was not good in either reading and writing or in vocabulary and grammar. My comprehension in both understanding and spoken English was even worse. I needed to improve all aspects of my language skills.

We all know that the younger person is a better learner in a new language than an older one. Students from the north of China who speak the Mandarin dialect find it easier than those from the south who speak the Cantonese dialect. Some people had an affinity for learning foreign languages much easier than others. I was one of older students, speaking Cantonese and mostly a local dialect. None of this helped me to learn spoken English. I knew that I did not have a talent to learn the English language, but I had no choice. I had to speed up the process and learn as much as I could.

I recorded in my daily journal the steps I would take to learn English by spending an hour in each morning reading English and practicing my oral skill; attending all classes during the regular sessions; memorizing new words in my spare time during the lunch, evening, and at night; listening to the cassette player; holding conversations in English with other students and with teachers; and doing simulation tests of the TOEFL.

In order to better learn English, I asked my parents for some money, then using some of my own savings, I purchased a radio cassette player designed for listening to English tapes. When I entered the training, I estimated that I might have recognized and understood about two thousand words. Just as many other classmates, I forced myself to recite from a small dictionary. The words standing alone, taken out of the context of sentences and stories, had their meaning changed, making it more difficult to remember their usage and application. This made it more difficult to memorize. I might memorize a word today and forget it tomorrow, even if I repeated the word many times. By the end of the training period, I might have learned only about six thousand words. Although this approach to studying helped during the vocabulary portion of the exam, it was very little help in using these words in a given sentence. Once the exam was over, I gradually lost these words for good.

After training for only a few months, we had to go to Guangzhou City for the TOEFL test. My score was a little over five hundred points out of eight hundred points, a score that just barely passed the minimal requirement by many US universities. Most of students were in the five hundred-point range; however, several other classmates were able to score over six hundred points.

With the TOEFL score at hand, we shifted our attention to focus on the application to graduate school. Most of us hoped to get admitted and enter the program abroad as soon as possible. A few of students at my age had an even stronger desire to do so. There were multiple reasons for such rushing—one being that the Guangxi government hoped us to do so, and another was that we wanted to avoid the "long night leading to more dreams." This is an old Chinese saying that the more dreams one has in a long night, the more unrealistic a dream would be. People use this to remind themselves that unless your dream has become a reality, it would only remain a dream.

There were a number of challenges for me during my application process. I didn't have much information about the universities of the US. That was a time when computers and the internet were not available for us. I could only access limited materials provided by GXU and by our teachers. We shared information among our classmates, but there was even less information about the agricultural graduate schools. Making things more urgent was that when we received our TOEFL test scores, the deadlines for graduate school application had already passed at many schools. Fortunately, all of us majoring in agricultural science exchanged information and helped one another whenever possible. As a result, I quickly identified a number of agricultural colleges in a number of Midwest universities of the US that were appropriate for me to apply.

In order to have more certainty of admittance, I applied to Western Michigan University (WMU), a sister university with an intercollegiate relationship to GXU. WMU is a second-tier public university that did not have an agriculture college, and the closest department to my major was the department of biological science. This department offered only a master's degree and no doctoral program. If I wanted to pursue a PhD degree after my master's, I would need to apply to another university.

Since I knew all these drawbacks beforehand, why did I still apply to it? My reason for this decision was that the sister-university relationship between GXU and WMU permitted GXU to send a given number of students to WMU for graduate study. I expected my application to WMU to almost certainly be accepted. When I applied, I kept my options open so that after I arrived at the WMU, if it was not what I expected or wanted, I could still transfer to another university. Transferring between universities in the US was very common.

Because I wanted to study aboard as soon as possible, only the WMU admission would give me the best option. In addition, I applied to several other Midwest universities, including Iowa State, Kansas State, and Ohio State. But by July, with the exception of WMU, I had not received any letters of confirmation or rejection from the other universities. Because this was my only option and I did not want to delay my journey aboard, I decided to apply for my visa using the WMU admission IAP-66.

For me, studying abroad was equally important, if not more so than when I was admitted to Guangxi Agriculture College in 1977. This was a major turning point in my professional career as well. According to the situation and circumstances in China at that time, if I completed my PhD and returned to the college to teach, I would be recognized as a respected professional. This would not only help me attain the professorship, but it would give me the possibility of becoming a leader in the college. I had a world of reasons to celebrate this overseas study opportunity with friends and neighbors. However, I did not. Even my family members couldn't come up with a strong reason to host a large fanfare party. We treated this as an ordinary event, and only our own family got together for a dinner as a send-off for me to go aboard. With my government-subsidized suit, my luggage was really simple, easy to pack, and ready to go.

In October 1983, I said goodbye to my newly wedded wife and my family and embarked on a study abroad. I flew from Beijing to Chicago and then took an express flight to the Kalamazoo Municipal Airport in Michigan. I was picked up by a professor who taught economics at WMU. He took me to his home for an overnight stay, and then in the next morning, he drove me to the apartment that had been arranged for me.

WMU was founded in 1903 as a public university located in the southwest part of Michigan. It was about a two-hour drive from either Chicago or Detroit. Kalamazoo is a medium-size city with a population of about 750,000. The university was divided into the east campus and the west campus, with both sitting on hills with beautiful trees and flowers. The west campus was the main campus with the colleges of art and science, including the department of biological sciences, and several other colleges located there.

Few Chinese students had the opportunity to study aboard in 1983, and I was a lucky one. This feeling was even stronger whenever I recall my life of the past two decades. I had graduated from high school with excellent grades, but there were no college entrance examinations given and there was no opportunity for me to go to college; I had to return to my countryside as a farmer where I tried to become a young leader in our village, participating in various youth activities and leading a militia team participating in reservoir construction. I was selected for a trial cadre training, but I had no chance of becoming a cadre because I was asked to accept an arrangement by the Communist Party secretary of our people's commune to be a party secretary of our village. It was not until I entered college that my dream was gradually realized. As a graduate student now at WMU, my wish was that from now on, everything would be smooth for me and my family.

However, things were not always perfect, and there was always something happening that did not match the direction of my own plan. Less than two weeks after arriving at WMU, I began to experience an unplanned and unpredicted situation. I had chosen WMU only because of my desire to gain admission to an American university in order to get to the US as early as possible. After I had obtained my visa with the WMU IAP-66, I received an acceptance letter from Kansas State University. In comparison, there were a number of advantages for KSU over WMU, primarily because KSU has an excellent agriculture science program that would fit my major, and it offered a PhD program as well. Because my visa was issued based on my IAP-66 from WMU, I was required by law to reported to WMU. Now that I was in WMU, my application to transfer had to be approved by the campus administrator.

Because of the sister relationship between GXU and WMU, there was a total of eight Chinese students from Guangxi at WMU. There was a coordinator from both GXU and WMU in charge of this small group of students, so my transfer request had to be approved by these two coordinators, then it had to be approved by each of the two sister universities, and finally by the District Office of Education of Guangxi. If any one of these offices did not approve my request, my transfer would not happen. In my application of transfer, I gave three major reasons: first, WMU had no agriculture college, and therefore, it didn't have an appropriate program to meet my study goal; second, WMU required me to make up sixteen credits of undergraduate course work, and this requirement would lead to a tuition expense of six to seven thousand dollars, which would be a burden on the Guangxi budget; third, making up these courses would extend my time as a master's graduate student, which would not only increase my living expenses but was also not consistent with the policy of encouraging students to graduate and return home earlier in order to be of service to the country. My three-point argument appeared to be reasonable, but my transfer was denied.

When I was at WMU, I reported to the department of biological sciences, and the first thing I wanted to do was to select my adviser. Since my desire was to concentrate on plant physiology, I wanted a professor who was interested in doing research in plant physiology. I discussed this with the department chair, who suggested a professor with these interests. After I was introduced to this professor by the department chair, I had an opportunity to talk with him, and it did not take long for me to learn that he was not the professor for me. He had no active research program, had very few graduate students in his program, and had no research papers published in the recent years.

More than that, my first meeting with him made me uncomfortable because I got a feeling that he might not have directed the research of any foreign students, especially Chinese students. When I mentioned the possibility of completing my master's degree in two years, his answer was that it was absolutely impossible. His reason seemed to be that I was a foreign student with language barrier; therefore, I would need at least three years. Although his assessment of the time required to complete my master's under his advice might not be too far-fetched, the way he presented it to me made me feel unfriendly toward him. With that, coupled with the reasons I have described, I made up my mind that I should choose another professor as my adviser.

As school began in late August and I did not report to WMU until early October, I missed the class registration deadline. I could sit in classes without gaining credits only if the instructors permitted. Due to the fact that our class '77 major in agronomy at Guangxi Agriculture College did not include a curriculum with basic physics and calculus, both of which were considered required basic courses for biology undergraduates at WMU, I was required to make up twelve credits, with four credits each in calculus, basic physics I, and physics II. And I was required to take an English course as well. The normal requirement for an MS in the department was thirty credit hours, including twenty-four course credits and six master's thesis credits. After some discussion with the department chair, the requirement for English class was removed and changed to self-study and self-learning. These added undergraduate credit requirements significantly increased my challenge to complete the MS degree in two years.

The denial of my request for school transfer, the unsuitable professor to whom I was first assigned to, and the need to make up undergraduate credits frustrated and depressed me for nearly a month. This feeling of depression made me consider giving up studying aboard and returning home. Of course, this naive thought just flashed in my brain for only a moment because I had come so far, and the opportunity was too good to let it pass by. So I said to myself that I had to be courageously strong and deal with all the difficulties with my full focus and attention. I must raise my head high and make up my mind to overcome the challenges and difficulties I faced. I would adjust myself to the new environment and situations and complete my master's degree.

So I plucked up my courage and met with the chair of the department of biological sciences to request a new adviser be assigned to me. Perhaps it was due to my application for school transfer in the previous weeks that the chair apparently wanted to help me. He suggested three professors for me to consider. The first was an associate professor in crop nutrition, in his fifties, who taught soil science and crop nutrition. His interests were related to crop sciences and crop nutrition, which were related to my interest in crop physiology. However, he did not have an active research program for many years, and there were currently few graduate students, if any at all. Even though he was very friendly toward me, I could not pick him because I wanted to do research and needed an adviser who was actively involved in research. He was not.

The second professor, in his sixties, was interested in animal sciences and was the retired departmental chair. Although he had a research program going for years and was able to obtain funding for research during the past few years, I am not interested in animal science since this was not the plan of my study. He was not my choice as an adviser.

Now came with the third professor, who was forty to fifty years old and was a graduate of a prestigious school, the University of Illinois. He had been doing research in plant ecology and had published many articles in his field. He was recognized as an ecologist who had published many research papers, and his ecology textbooks were used in many universities and colleges in the United States. He also received regular funding from grant-providing agencies. Although his research interest was not completely aligned with my personal interests and my study plan, by comparison, he was a better choice for me because of his research activity, his reputation, and his graduate training program. This decision would mean that I would have to change the direction of my subject interest and research from the plant physiology to plant ecology.

After my academic adviser had been chosen, the next step was to sit down with my adviser to discuss my graduate program. My graduate adviser was responsible for developing a plan with me, including how and when to make up the courses, to complete MS courses, and to start the thesis research. He said that if I could follow his timetable and complete the requirements in every period, I could graduate in two years.

My god, this was exactly I wanted to hear! This really gave me a big relief. From that moment on, I would do anything that I could to make sure to follow his plan. In brief, my plan was this: in the regular two full semesters of 1984, I would take four courses each semester with a total of twenty-four credits; I would use the summer of 1984 to complete my makeup credits; and my thesis research would be conducted during the summer and the fall of 1984. I reserved the spring semester of 1985 without much workload except a few self-study credits so that I could focus on my thesis. My goal was not to try to get high grades or publish papers but to meet the requirements for my master's degree and graduate on time instead.

The arrangement and completion of course requirements might be relatively easy to achieve if enough time is available, but the master's thesis research, writing, and the defense of my thesis were more difficult to control. There were so many factors associated with thesis research, and any misstep during the process could delay the schedule by a big margin. As a result, I started paying attention to my study program from the start of my graduate school. I first set my thesis research topic as my priority. This was critical in order to complete my thesis on time. My hope was to select a topic that would be easy to handle. As long as I did my research, I would have data and results. With this in mind, I discussed it with my adviser and finally decided that the topic for my master's thesis would be entitled "Forest Relationship between Evolution and the Environment." This study included collecting information and understanding the current research by other researchers and the investigation of forest tree growth and evolution. Because I did not have a background in plant ecology and because I was just beginning this program, literature search and review in order to gain knowledge of plant ecology, especially the newest development in the area, proved to be a challenging task for me. Fortunately, I had my adviser on my side. He allowed me to access his files for all the publications related to the topic, and he had a study site selected for me.

I began my experiment in the summer of 1984. The main portion of the research was to collect data from a site of a forest owned by my adviser. Considerable background data had been collected in this study site of about a hundred acres by my adviser and his earlier students. Therefore, my research was a small part of his long-range study plan. Specifically, my research was to survey this forest for the species of shrubs on the forest floor and of tree species in the canopy and to measure at chest-height the circumference of each labeled tree. The data collection was straightforward and easy. However, because it was a hot summer with high humidity, I was soaked with sweat and fighting lots of mosquitoes every time I was out in the forest. Even with the use of mosquito repellants, which was only with limited effectiveness, I went back each day with knots of mosquito bites. Fortunately, it took only a few weeks for me to collect all data for my thesis.

With firsthand data taken back to the school, I felt so good about my position. My next step was to analyze the data. In the 1980s, there was no widely used computer platform available for me to use, and I could only use a calculator. Luckily, I did not have much data to analyze. I grouped and classified the data and did a limited statistically analysis. By comparing my data to that collected previously by my adviser, I was able to conclude that environmental factors influence the evolution of the forest and the speciation of the forest evolution requires destructive forces such as tornados and fires.

Around February 1985, I began writing my thesis, which was the most difficult part of my MS program. The main challenge for me was due to my relatively poor English, especially in writing. Fortunately, the writing process was set and carried out at my own pace. As long as I put enough time into the writing and made sure of the continuity of each chapter and section, the thesis should be acceptable.

During my writing, I got help from a female classmate who was friendly and helped me with class notebooks before, and now, she helped me with grammar and spelling in my thesis. I was so grateful to have such friends. Of course, I got much more help from my adviser, who read through the thesis and gave me suggestions chapter by chapter until the final version was completed. Because of the great support I received from my adviser and the assistance from my friends and classmates, I was able to finalize my thesis in April. After I passed my thesis defense and made the final correction to it, I delivered my thesis to the graduate school in May and applied for graduation in August 1985. I returned to WMU with my wife to attend the graduation and to pay a personal visit to my adviser with appreciation for his advising throughout my master of science.

Recalling this period of unusual experiences in my MS journey, I have a few important take-home messages. First, life is not always easy and straightforward. There are always twists and turns along the way that can make one grow up to be stronger. Although my life was filled with roadblocks and obstacles in the past, I could deal with them in my own country with many friends surrounding me. However, it was very different this time because I was in a new country with fewer friends around me. I had to solve problems almost exclusively by myself. I was glad that I had overcome the problems and had gotten my master's in two years.

Secondly, I had a new understanding of American society and of American people. Prior to my arrival at the US, or even a few weeks into the WMU, I did not think American students so friendly and professors so supportive and with flexibility in advising their students. I had realized that most people in the United States are friendly toward the Chinese.

Finally, my experience reinforced my original belief that no matter what, when, or where, as long as we stick to what we believe in and plan for it and work hard with a down-to-earth attitude, our chances of success to reach our goal will be high. These basic life lessons I learned undoubtedly became a cornerstone of my later career.

All our class '77 and '78 graduates from college had a job assigned to us with a salary of about fifty yuan per month. This money was to cover our monthly living expenses, including housing and utility costs. With some pocket money of our own and some with other expenses, generally we had very little money left. Basically, it was very hard to save any money with such a low salary. We were poor for all four years of college, but after we took the first job as assistant teachers, our lives still did not improve significantly. This was not unique to Guangxi region but across the Chinese nation because the salary for new college graduates were allocated by central government.

Now we were in the US, and we had an opportunity to change our living standard. For this reason, all my classmates at WMU had set a similar goal: by the graduation of our MS degree, we would save enough money for four big pieces (TV sets, refrigerators, washing machines, and radio cassette players) to take home. In the mid-1980s, people who owned these four items were looked at with green envy. Whoever had these four pieces was considered to have a symbol of the richest families. That was why most of us would do everything possible to save money in order to reach this goal.

Our Guangxi self-funded class of students was subsidized by the government at $380 per month to cover our living costs. This subsidy could be the lowest among the students from China, but recognizing the low income, poor province, and less-developed region of Guangxi, we fully understood the government situation and were satisfied with this subsidy. According to the then market price of four big pieces, we would need to save at least $2,500 in two years. The simple calculation for reaching our goal was that the total support for living that we received from the Guangxi government for two years would be $9,000. If we saved $100 a month, we could have saved $2,400 in two years, which could be enough to purchase these four big pieces. However, many of us wouldn't be happy if we just got four big pieces without taking home some American dollars. The exchange rate of the dollar against the yuan was about 1:2.5. Therefore, our goal was to take home at least $2,000–$2,500. To reach this goal, we needed to save at least $200 per month.

We set out to realize our goal by taking a very difficult and unusual approach that would never be understood by young Chinese students who are in the US today.

First of all, we played the housing card. It is well-known that in developed countries, most expenditures are related to housing, traveling, and food. The most expensive single item for us as foreign students is the housing expense, so it made a lot of sense for us to place this card on the top of our list.

In the first year, four of us lived in a two-bedroom apartment with a small kitchen area and a living room. Compared to the dormitory we lived in as students, or even an assistant teachers in China, this apartment was a lot bigger and more spacious. It was much better because it had its own bathroom. It was a relatively convenient apartment for us because it was close to WMU and only a few minutes away from my department by biking, or about fifteen to twenty minutes by walking.

The rental rate for this apartment was $240 per month, divided by the four of us at $60 each. A few months later, when we reevaluated our financial situation, we found that our housing expense was still a little too high. If we maintained this expense, it would be hard for us to save $4,400–$5,000 after two years. After a few discussions, we decided not to continue in this apartment for the coming school year, so we set out to find another apartment that would be less expensive. Through our effort, we found an old house located on the hill on the north side of the east campus, which was a little further away from the west campus. This single-family house, which was approximately eight hundred to one thousand square feet, had three bedrooms, a living area, and a kitchen. The rent was $160 per month, which was $80 less than the previous apartment. More importantly, this house could accommodate six persons, so we found two other visiting scholars also from China to corent this house. With $30 per month for each, this allowed us to save $30 per month, or $360 per year in rental expense.

Our second card was to save money on our food. Generally, most food was less expensive than now. A dozen eggs was twenty-five cents, while a gallon of milk was seventy to eighty cents. We bought the cheapest vegetables, fruits, chicken, and eggs available. There were discount prices on nearly outdated items on the special shelves in each supermarket. These shelves were always our destination when we did our shopping, and these items reduced our cost by at least 30–50 percent. In addition, we divided into three groups and cooked our food every day in order to save money. Our living habits and our choice in foods were different, so we could not cook and eat together as a group, which could have saved even more money. I paired with a visiting scholar Mr. Li, and because our goal was the same, we reduced our food expense to a minimum.

No traveling and leisure expense was our third card. During the two years at WMU, we never traveled or spent money watching sports and games. An automobile was the single most expensive item in a family, and none of us owned a car. Only one younger student who received his scholarship from WMU in his second year purchased a used car. I never thought about owning a car at all because my saved money was too precious to be used for leisure.

It was not until the summer of 1985, when I was sure that I would continue my PhD program, that I decided to buy my first old car. It was a $500 1976 Dodge Aspen. Due to the time limitation, I was not able to obtain my driver's license before moving to my next university. Although the gasoline was only seventy to eighty cents per gallon, if I had gotten a car, the expense would be a very significant portion of my savings.

Our fourth card was to use a bicycle and our two legs. Our bicycle was the main transportation for us in the spring, summer, and fall, when weather permitted. But during the winter, our two legs were our transportation. It was relatively easy to bike or walk in the first year because the apartment we lived in was on the west side of the campus, not only a short distance from the campus but also no hilly path or busy street. However, it was very different in the second year because we lived about two miles away from the west campus with an uphill and downhill street road. It was an hour of walking in snowy and chilly winter days. Sometimes, we did not see any other people walking on the hills except the few of us. We walked a few minutes to the bus stop to take a bus to the supermarkets, but when we missed a bus, we walked over an hour to get home with a full bag of food on our backs and another carried by our hands. We made our lives so very hard with one goal in mind, and that was to save enough money to take home the four big pieces along with some US dollars.

Two years passed by quickly because we played those four cards with considerable effort and made the tough decisions. Each of us was able to save more than $4,000 after two years. When I returned home to visit my parents during the Christmas holiday season in 1985, I brought with me two Hitachi color TVs, two Cannon cameras, one radio cassette player, and a washing machine. I gave one TV and a camera to my father-in-law. At that time, whoever had these luxury items was considered to be prestigious and was admired by many others. Although it was a challenge and with many difficulties for me the past two years, a glorious display of the four big pieces still made me happy and proud.

10-1: One of four big pieces: Hitachi TV brought home (1985)

11

FIVE PUBLICATIONS

PhD Program and Part-Time Waiter (1985–1989)

The spring of 1985 had finally arrived after a long winter. The weather had turned warmer, and the earth had begun its recovery. Everything that had made it through the long winter now began to thrive and embrace the nice weather.

My MS journey had shown a similar phenomenon because I had just experienced one of most challenging periods in my life. I was recovering from a depressing period of time when I was burdened by my study and challenging living environment.

Now it was about the end of spring semester, and I had passed my master's thesis defense and my thesis had been submitted to the graduate school for graduation in August. I was completely relieved with my master's at hand.

To appreciate what my adviser had done for me, I invited him to a dumpling banquet that I prepared, and I did the same to express my thanks to my friends, classmates, and my host family. In addition, several students and scholars from China held a party to thank a local medical chief scientist, Dr. Sun and his family. This Chinese family, well-known locally, often invited us to their parties, such as traditional Chinese Spring Festivals. At that time, there was a limited number of Chinese students and scholars at WMU, and their parties often included all the students from China.

Our goal was to earn a PhD degree. That was the reason that all of us from GXU had begun preparation to apply for PhD programs in other universities in the second year of our master's program. Compared to other students, I started my application a little late due to my much tighter schedule with all the coursework that I had to complete. It was not until the spring of 1985 that I had the time to submit my application.

I did not have a clear answer to the type of universities that might be appropriate for me to apply to for my PhD program because there were a number of issues I needed to consider. For example, I had to decide the major or concentration of my program. I had to choose either plant ecology or plant physiology. If I went for plant ecology, I would face the dilemma that it was not my original interest and might not be my future research and career goal. In addition, it would be more difficult to obtain a scholarship in plant ecology.

On the other hand, if I returned to plant physiology as I had originally set out to pursue, then my last two years of the MS program would not help in my application because the plant ecology program and the research that I did for my MS thesis had very little to do with plant physiology and plant biochemistry. Also, Guangxi government had made it clear that the government would not provide any more financial support for pursuing a PhD program. Unless we could obtain an assistantship or a scholarship from a university, we would return to China with only our MS degree. Because of this, our effort was focused not only on getting admitted to a PhD program but also in obtaining a scholarship from the school.

The funding for plant ecologists in the mid-1980s was limited, and the amount awarded for this field was less when compared to plant physiology and plant biochemistry. The most well-funded projects related to plant science appeared to be plant molecular biology and biochemistry. I thought I would have a much-better chance of receiving financial support from these areas. After carefully consideration of the pros and cons between plant ecology and plant physiology, I decided to apply for plant physiology with selected universities as my study concentration.

To increase my chances of success in admission and financial support, I decided to focus on second-tier universities that had good PhD programs in plant science. I tried to avoid top-tier universities and the hot areas, such as molecular biology. Through careful screening, I finally settled on a few universities that I considered appropriate. These universities were Michigan State University, Ohio State University, Kansas State University, and Miami University of Ohio. My goal was clear: I had to have financial support as my main consideration.

I began my application process at the end of 1984 but got serious in early 1985. I first communicated my plan to my MS adviser. He was very supportive of my plan, providing me not only with suggestions but also with a strong recommendation letter. With his help and a couple of other professors' reference letters, I submitted five to six applications. One of the universities, Miami University, quickly responded to my application by inviting me for a visit to its campus. This went well, and I was admitted to their PhD program in the botany department with a research assistantship.

In July 1985, I began another journey in my life, pursuing my doctoral degree. I hastily collected and packed my simple luggage into the old car that I just bought. Because I did not have my driver's license yet, I asked my friend for help. He drove my car with the luggage while his wife drove their car with their children to the Miami University. After a four-hour journey, we arrived at our destination: Oxford, Ohio, home of Miami University.

After arriving at the university, my first thought was that the campus is beautiful and that it should be a good place for my PhD program. The university is located near the Indiana state line, only thirty miles from the city of Cincinnati in the south and fifty miles from the city of Dayton in the north. Oxford is a small university town with a permanent population of about twenty thousand, in addition to the students.

Miami University was founded in 1809 with a campus that covers an area of about two thousand acres. There were about fifteen thousand students enrolled each year, both undergraduate and graduate.

For many years, the university has been named by the US *Fortune* magazine as one of most selective and valued top 50 universities. The basic criteria for its selection includes the national college admission scores (ACT and SAT), tuition, college graduation rates, degree of difficulty in finding a job after graduation, and the starting salaries, etc. The ratio of comprehensive scores to the cost of four years of undergraduate study provides an excellent value at Miami University. Additionally, Miami University has been named the no. 1 university for undergraduate teaching and the no. 1 best college town in America.

In the 1980s, due to the rapid development of new technologies, student enrollments in botany or plant science at the various universities decreased considerably. As a result, a great portion of universities had merged their botany or plant science with microbiology and zoology to form a department of biological sciences. After the merger, there were fewer universities with an independent department of botany or plant science. Miami University was one of these universities. This indicated that the botany department at Miami University was relatively strong with sufficient resources and academic faculty and staff.

The department had a dozen or so professors and associate professors, a few hundred undergraduate students, and a few dozen graduate students. There were a handful of foreign students, mostly from China and India in the department, and most faculty were very friendly toward the foreign students. The department chair was the former president of the Botanical Society of America, and after his retirement, he continued serving as a member of the American Botanical Council. The secretary of the department was a friendly and productive lady, capable of dealing with issues from students and faculty. In short, the botany department was a small, friendly, and accommodating department for foreign students like me. I fell in love with it in a few weeks of my arrival.

My academic adviser, Dr. Jerry W. McClure, was a world-recognized research scholar of plant secondary metabolite chemistry. He had a great influence on my life because he taught me not only the knowledge and research skills but also the growth of my personality. I was honored and delighted to have him as my adviser. I treasured the teacher-student relationship between us. I could easily claim that without Dr. McClure, I would not be the person I am today. Even after thirty years and after he passed away more than ten years ago, I still admire him very much and still feel his touches and effect on my family life.

Dr. McClure was born in 1933 and entered university undergraduate program at the age of sixteen. He graduated from Texas Technological University with a BS degree in agronomy in 1954. He joined the US Air Force for four years in 1955. Honorably discharged in 1959, he completed his master's degree at Texas Technological University in 1962. He obtained his PhD in 1964 from the University of Texas. After completing his PhD in 1964, he joined Miami University as an assistant professor, earning full professorship in 1973.

His research began early in his doctoral program. He made breakthrough discovery of flavonoids in *Flavonoid Chemistry and the Morphology of Lemnaceae in Axenic Culture*. As a result, his research paper was published in the journal *Nature*, which was highly praised by the scientific community. His accomplishment helped him gain the reputation as one of outstanding earlier American scientists in plant secondary metabolic substances.

Known as a class of chemicals in plants, the secondary substances, or secondary metabolites, were not found at an early date with any essential roles in plant life cycles. They are distinct from primary compounds such as proteins, amino acids, carbohydrates, and lipids that are closely related to every phase of plant growth. As the science advanced, we now know that these compounds are not secondary, but instead they are very important for plant life. One function is their defense against insects and diseases. Because the tradition has defined these thousands of compounds secondary metabolites or substances, its term continues to be used today.

It is generally agreed that research on plant secondary substances began relatively later in the United States compared to Europe. Generally, research and accomplishments in the US were also behind its peers in Europe. Dr. McClure was the one of a few well-known and respected US researchers in the area. He won the 1972 Sigma Xi Outstanding Researcher Award from Miami University. He received the West German Alexander Von Humboldt Senior Scientist Award in 1974 specifically designated for the most qualified scientists of the United States, as well as an Honorary Fulbright at the same time. When he accepted the award, the McClure family lived in Germany in 1974–75 as guests of the government, where he did research at Bochum University. He lectured in six countries in Europe, giving thirty lectures among the most famous universities.

In 1983, He was named Distinguished Visiting Scientist, Texas Technological University, in recognition of his outstanding contributions to the science. He received the Heinrich-Hertz Research Award the same year and was an invited chairman for the Conference on Chemical Aspects of Plant-Herbivore Interactions, 1983, for the prestigious Gordon Research Conferences for the furtherance of knowledge on the frontiers of science. His research had been recognized not only by the Botany Department of Miami University but also by the international scientific community. I was proud to have such adviser as my PhD mentor.

In addition, my adviser had other key areas that deserved my admiration. Dr. McClure was very approachable and an easygoing person. When I sat down with him, whether it was discussion of my courseworks, research topic, or even my family matter, I always felt very comfortable and had no hesitation. He often talked about his early days of college, air force life, his wife, and his daughters. He often spoke to us with humor and jokes, and his students felt particularly easy around him.

My adviser was a person willing to help others when needed. For example, my acceptance to his laboratory was not because I had good grade and research in my MS program but because of the potential of becoming a good student in his laboratory. It was only because of his help that I had the opportunity to go to Miami University. The students, especially graduate students in our department, liked to associate with and to surround themselves with him because he always responded whenever the students had problems. When I arrived at Miami University, unfamiliar with the environment, he drove me to buy food. When other students and I needed financial aid, he was there to help. When I wanted to save some money for future plans, he gave me a job trimming bushes and caring for his yard, paying me a normal fee.

Dr. McClure's approach to education was worth mentioning. He and his graduate students had always maintained a close relationship. From the first day I arrived at Miami University, he taught me not only scientific knowledge but also a life lesson, which was perhaps the most profound education I had in my life. This lesson was characterized with three words: *courage, persistence, fighting*, all of which were very important to me. These words became the guidance for my professional growth and became an essential part of success in my career.

He said that as a young person, courage was a key factor to get things started. Once it began, things might not always go smoothly; therefore, we needed a fighting spirit to overcome problems in a consistent and persistent manner. He believed that these three words were also applicable to scientific research and PhD thesis. He often reminded us that to judge the quality of a doctoral research, the number of papers published and the type of journals where those papers published provided a good measurement of a PhD program.

Jerry had a broad interest, and he was always optimistic about his life, his job, and his family. He and his wife liked music. There were a lot of classical music tapes and instruments in his home. He often played his music during his gatherings with students in his home. He also liked gardening, planting flowers and vegetables. He would grow his garden with lots of tomato, green beans, zucchini squash, and flowers.

My good impression of Miami University could also be extended to the International Student Office (ISO) and the International Student Exchange and Communication Office (ISECO). Director of ISO worked with high efficiency and was friendly toward international students. They helped me with my student visa and my wife's application for her J-2 visa. The director of ISECO was a generous woman. With the help of her office and ISO office, through the Community Program for Foreign Students (COSEP), all foreign students were assigned a host family.

We were glad to have as our host family someone whose husband was a professor teaching English at Miami University. This couple lived in a modest house built in the '50s or '60s, furnished with more cultural connotation. They loved flowers, plants, and pets—dogs and cats. They have repeatedly invited our family to their home for dinner on different holidays.

I had a memorable experience with international student housing at Miami University. Miami Manor was the school apartments for international students, located in the northwest corner of the university. There was a total of four two-story apartment buildings, each consisting of about twenty to thirty units. Most of the apartments were highly efficient apartment with one bedroom, a kitchen, and a bathroom. At the end of each building, there were four units of junior suites, each with two bedrooms. Between the buildings, there were playgrounds for kids not close to the busy streets and roads. The ground was covered with grass and trees, making it a beautiful place to play and live. In addition, it was only about fifteen-minute walking distance to my university department. Because of this convenience, we stayed there for four years until I completed my PhD. An excellent campus and good and affordable housing provided us with a relaxed environment that was good for study.

It took about eighteen months for me to complete my master's degree, which included a total of forty-two undergraduate and graduate credits. This was once considered impossible by some people, including the first professor who was appointed to me at the time of my arrival at WMU, but I did it. Now I took the same message with my PhD program because I wanted to complete my doctoral degree in four years. Generally speaking, a doctoral program requires four to six years. This, of course, would be influenced by many factors, such as curriculum requirement, especially the thesis or dissertation research and adviser's effectiveness. If the MS and the PhD are with the same program and the same adviser, five to six years to complete a PhD is possible. If the two programs are from two different schools and two different professors, it is very common for a student to complete a PhD program in four to six years. It was more of a challenge for me because I had changed not only my graduate school and my adviser but also my major, my interests, and my research direction.

For many students, it makes sense to take some time off from a difficult and intensive period of an MS program or at least to not put so much pressure on oneself with a new program. However, I was an exception to this because I felt that my age would not allow me to do so. I was now already thirty-two years old. If it took four years for me to complete my PhD program, I would be at the age of many young assistants, associates, or even full professors. Whenever I was in the lecture hall listening to a professor who was younger than me, I felt very uncomfortable and sometimes had a sour feeling about it.

The other driving force behind me was that I wanted to go home with my PhD as early as possible so that I could be in the leading position for good jobs. There were fewer students studying aboard in the 1980s, and PhD graduates returning to China were rare at that time. Therefore, recognizing my past experience as the president of student union and the branch party secretary of our production brigade, if I could earn my PhD and return to Guangxi Agriculture College earlier than other PhDs of Guangxi self-funded classes, I could be assigned to a key position in the college. I might have the potential to become the chair of the agronomy department or even the president of the college. Even with in a less optimistic case, I could easily become a full professor.

In speeding the completion of my PhD degree, I adopted a few key steps. For example, I placed all my required courses in the first and second academic years so that I would have less distraction in my research in the third and fourth year. I decided my doctoral thesis research topics as early as possible to avoid the bottleneck issues that could extend my thesis research. I worked hard and diligently on my research and, at the same time, summarized the data and published it as early as I could to facilitate and streamline my research in order to avoid an on-and-off research approach, which could disrupt the continuity and the productivity of my dissertation research. All these measures helped me speed up my PhD process.

Required courses for a PhD degree at the botany department varied among various concentrations. For plant physiology, the compulsory courses included biochemistry I and II, plant biochemistry, plant molecular biology, advanced plant physiology, tissue culture, ultra-anatomy of plants, and plant taxonomy. Among these courses, biochemistry was the most difficult for me. This course was taught by multiple faculty in two semesters. One of faculty responsible for the portion of plant secondary metabolite chemistry was also a member of my PhD program committee. This portion was closely related to my dissertation research. The knowledge I gained in the class greatly benefitted my later entrepreneurship.

Under the careful arrangement and scheduling by my adviser, I also took several self-study courses, which were mostly related to plant biochemistry and plant secondary metabolites. The purpose of this arrangement was not only to fulfill my total credit requirements but also to broaden my knowledge in the areas I concentrated on. I completed my coursework in the first two years as planned. Starting in the third year, my attention was completely shifted to my dissertation research.

To evaluate the quality of a PhD, my adviser had a unique prospective. For instance, for many people, a PhD graduate from a big-name school was considered the best. Some also considered higher grade point average (GPA) as a measurement of student's quality. However, Dr. McClure would add at least two more criteria to this evaluation. He felt that a good PhD student, under normal circumstances, should graduate in four to five years and have at least several publications in respected journals. Patentable technology and publication in top-tier journals were also an indication of quality of the dissertation research.

Because my research was on plant secondary metabolite chemistry and was not related to drug discovery, there was little chance that I could develop patented technology. Therefore, the goal of my dissertation research was to publish findings in peer-reviewed journals. I had this criterion in my mind since the beginning of my doctoral program. My adviser discussed with us that the earlier the publication of research, the better and faster to the completion of a dissertation. He promoted a practice in his doctoral training program to encourage his students to publish research results as early as possible and to include published papers in a dissertation. Early publications are not only good for early graduation of a PhD student but also helpful in job hunting even before graduation. This practice also increased productivity and reduced the possibility of dragging on unpublished research results because once a graduate has left the school, it is hard to find time to organize data and write papers for publication again.

To determine my research topic, I had several discussions with my adviser. My adviser took note of my intention for my research topic and getting an early start with my research program. I wanted my research to be part of his overall research program and a continuation of that of his previous graduate students, but with some innovation and to open up new research for the laboratory. For instance, the research in this lab had been on the accumulation and distribution of flavonoids and phenolics in barley and oat leaves for the past few years, as well as the effects of environmental factors on the accumulation of these second metabolites.

My research was focused on how these compounds were synthesized and accumulated as such. To understand this, I focused on the enzymes that might participate in the synthetic pathways leading to the accumulation of these compounds. In brief, my dissertation was to use the same barley and oat leaves as study materials to investigate the enzyme and their activities in various leaf tissues and compartments within the leaf. I was particularly interested in enzymes associated with the synthesis of cell wall phenolics. My research topic, established in the second year of my PhD program, was on "phenol-synthetic enzyme distribution, localization and the enzyme activity affected by environmental factors." Grass leaf cell walls contains a large amount of phenols, and these cross-linked phenols are synthesized by specific enzymes such as glucose dehydrogenase, peroxidase, polyamine oxidase, and lipolytic enzymes. Such catalytically chemical synthesis of cell wall polysaccharides with phenolics form a unique structure that affords the cell wall its rigidity and strong support of the plant tissues.

My thesis research went smoothly. I was able to publish five research papers from my dissertation. My first paper was published in 1989 in the journal *Plant Physiology*, which was the first chapter of my dissertation. There were two additional papers accepted for publication in the same year, which were placed as the second and third chapters of my dissertation. Chapter 4 and chapter 5 were from two other peer-reviewed paper published within a year of my graduation. The sixth paper was published after three years of my graduation with myself as the sole author in the journal *Phytochemistry*. Such high productivity in research was considered outstanding in the department because there was hardly anyone who could publish five or more peer-reviewed papers in a PhD dissertation in four years. As a result, I was awarded as an outstanding PhD graduate in the department, which made me proud of my accomplishment.

At the conclusion of my postgraduate studies and dissertation research, I had a few memorable experiences in my speedy completion of my PhD program. No matter what I did, I set my plan in advance and gave myself adequate time to prepare early, act early, and to start early. Once I started, I kept going until I finished, never letting other factors interfere with my plan. When things got going, I focused on whatever it took to get the experiment done. I was willing to work hard, and I never stopped in the middle of experiments or gave up halfway. These experiences were of great value that have provided me with an excellent foundation for my future business.

The accomplishment of my doctoral program brought me and my family a sense of sureness, so we decided to establish a family with kids before I had my real job. Having a real job was not easy for us at the time since I was still in school on one hand and held a J-1 exchange visa on the other. However, comparably speaking, having kids should be relatively easier because it was only a family issue to resolve. We were lucky because my wife was pregnant in January of 1986, and in October, our first son was born, which made me very happy to be a father at my age of thirty-two. Just as every other father who had experienced it, the arrival of my son changed my life, my family's life, and even our finances.

Speaking of our finance, my research assistantship was $500–600 per month, our rent was about $200, and our food about $50–60 per person per month. Total expenses on the apartment rental and foods was $350–$400 per month. Of course, baby expense was not included yet, which could be as much as $100 per month on average. We knew that it would be tight to make it if we just depended on only the assistantship income. However, barely making it was not in my DNA as a Chinese farmer. I had to save some money to cope with possible future difficulties. We also wanted to create a good environment for our children to grow up in; otherwise, I would consider it a failure as a father. Furthermore, I wanted to help my parents and my sisters and brothers as well because they were all poor in the countryside as farmers. Adding all these up, I came to the conclusion that I had to save as much as possible to improve our financial situation. If just by saving alone, we would not be able to reach our financial goal. I had to find another part-time job to earn additional income.

We carefully budgeted our expense on food, which we reduced to a minimum. We often purchased foods at the lowest prices, even if some of fresh produce was near its expiration date. We hardly bought any prepared foods or canned foods because these were usually more expensive. We clipped coupons and found special deals from every Sunday newspaper and drove to where less expensive food and produce were available. We ate more chicken and eggs because these were less expensive than beef and seafood. We never bought finger food and fast foods because of the high cost. In order to save additional money, we often organized a Chinese student group from Miami University in a carpool to buy fresh vegetables from an Asian supermarket in the Northgate Mall of Cincinnati, which was twenty-six miles away. We liked the variety, the selection, and the low cost of our preferred food in that store.

Starting from the first year of my PhD program, along with my adviser, we rented a garden plot from the Miami University to plant vegetables. Because of our farming experience, growing vegetables was our specialty. We produced sufficient amounts of fresh vegetables from June to September for us to consume. This helped us save a considerable expense on food.

According to the national classification on poverty, our income level was considered as poor, which qualified us for a program called Child Benefits for Women, Infants and Children (WIC) by the Department of Agriculture of the United States. With this program, my wife and my son received milks, eggs, and cheese monthly. This program helped our family considerably because this free food was sufficient for the mother and child.

The main part of our living expense was housing. Since we lived in the apartment of Miami Manor, the cost was fixed and there was little we could do about it. This was an ideal place for foreign students, which included twenty or so who were from China. All Chinese students got along well. We often organized parties, picnics, and hiking activities together. We were very happy to have such good group of friends around.

We also squeezed dollars out from our traveling and leisure expense. Our old and rusted Dodge Aspen stayed with us for three years until it was unusable. Our second car was 1978 Buick Regal costing two thousand dollars. When I purchased it, I did not realize the turbo engine was a problematic part of the car. It was about seven to eight years old with a good-looking body, but due to the frequently occurring problem with the engine, I sold it in less than two years.

During the four years of my PhD study, we rarely traveled or spent money on sports except for one trip we took. It was in the summer of 1987, my wife, my son, and I took a trip to Washington, DC, and New York. We drove our Dodge Aspen. Because there was no air conditioning with this car, we had to leave the window down. Our ten-month-old son was blown all the way on this trip, causing his whole face to become reddish. In order to save money, we would do anything possible, even if it was in an extremely hard situation.

We cut expense on our clothing and diaper. We brought some clothes from China not only for our son but also for my wife and myself. As our son grew, my wife used the sewing machine given to us as a gift by my adviser's wife, Mrs. McClure, to sew clothing for him. This machine was still in use more than thirty years later. It would not be an exaggeration if we called it an antique for us. We purchased minimal disposable diapers, but instead we used washable cloth diapers most of the time. Disposable diapers were used only when attending parties or for night sleeping.

After taking all these measures, we did save some money, but it was not anywhere near the financial goal that we set. Therefore, we had to come up with another meaningful way to increase our income. We decided to take part-time jobs as a waiter and waitress in Chinese restaurants.

The job opportunity for Chinese students was extremely limited. This was especially true for exchange students holding a J-1 visa, like me, and a spouse with a J-2 visa. The most jobs for the Chinese students were with Chinese restaurants. Only with the help of the international student office at Miami University did I obtain a work permit for jobs outside the school. The restaurant I worked for was called Jade Garden Chinese Restaurant, which was located in the Tri-County Mall of Cincinnati, thirty miles from Oxford. I usually worked twice a week, Friday and Saturday evenings, from 4:00 p.m. to 11:00–12:00 p.m. Occasionally, I might work on Sunday on an as-needed basis. A friend of ours also worked at the same restaurant and with the same schedule as mine, and he often rode in my car to work. My wife worked at another Chinese restaurant as a waitress. Her restaurant was located in Hamilton, about thirty minutes' driving distance from Miami University. Her schedule was two days on weekends and lunch on most workdays. Both of us worked until eleven to twelve o'clock at night on Friday and Saturday. When we got home, it was often past midnight. Our son was taken care of by a babysitter who also lived at Miami Manor. Every time we came back from work, our son was asleep. We brought him home and washed him before putting him back to bed. We then spent another half hour or so washing. By the time we got to bed, it was often past one o'clock in the morning. Such a challenging and difficult work schedule lasted for more than three years until I graduated with my doctoral degree.

Waiters and waitresses working at Chinese restaurants often received a minimal wage. Such a small wage was compensated by the tips received from the customers we served. Because tips were such important part of our income, we always looked forward to serving more customers. However, the restaurant owner often used a balanced approach to manage his restaurant business. In general, the workers preparing foods in the back of a restaurant were paid with a fixed salary per month, while in the front dining hall, service persons were paid with about $2 per hour, plus whatever tips we might receive individually. The dining room was divided into several sections, each with four to seven dining tables. To keep the workforce stable, the most and best sections with more tables was assigned to the full-time waiters and waitresses. For me, as a part-time and on an as-needed basis employee, the owner often assigned me three to five tables in the less visible section. Also, our boss often gave the best customers to the full-time waiters and waitress first, especially at times when the restaurant was not busy. This practice had led to some frustration for part-time waitresses and waiters. I realized that it was not easy to have a Chinese restaurant business in an oversaturated area. Unpredictability of business led to the uncertainty of our income. It was not uncommon for waiters and waitresses, just like the restaurant owner, who stood by the window, staring out at the parking lot and hoping for more customers to come in. Most of us felt very uncomfortable while waiting for work. Fortunately, our restaurant was a better one in the area, and we usually had a couple of busy hours on Friday and Saturday.

To maximize our tips and incomes, we often applied these strategies in our work. When we had customers at our tables, we provided speedy service. This was important because a faster service might give us one more rounds of customers to serve. Generally, slow service might mean two rounds of customers, but fast turnaround time service could get three. The more customers we served, the more tips we could receive. In addition, we tended to recommend more expensive foods to our customers if asked for recommendation. Similarly, we often recommended drinks, especially specialty drinks, to our customers when we thought it appropriate. We did what we could to please customers, including providing water and tea refills and other small items because happy customers often left more tips for us. All tips earned by each waiter/waitress belonged to them.

The jobs of the waiter and waitress were remarkably in alignment with the restaurant owners because the best interest of the owners was the best interest for us. When we sold more food in dollar value, the owner benefited from it, just as we had more tips. We always had some disturbing customers, such as certain customers who would be in no hurry to finish a meal and occupied the table a couple of hours, while other customers would not leave a tip no matter how good a job we had done. When we met such low-quality customers, we were frustrated, and our attitude toward them was often negative. We might try to push them to complete their meals as soon as possible. In contrast, when we had high-quality customers who tipped us 15–20 percent and, occasionally, 25 percent, our good mood would quickly rise; and we would say many thanks to them. In the restaurant service business, there was an unwritten practice in the US that if the service was bad or if guests were not satisfied, there could be less tip or no tip at all. On the other hand, if we provided a good service, a tip of 15 percent is the norm. My average tip was about 15 percent during my years as a waiter.

My four years with Miami University went by really fast. It was now May 1989. I not only finished my PhD dissertation but had passed my dissertation defense and was ready for the official graduation ceremony in August with a doctoral degree in botany. Recalling that experience, I can describe it in four words: *challenge, happiness, smooth,* and *satisfaction.* I had a lot of challenges during those four years, including difficult chemistry courses, a full load of study and research, a busy part-time job, and taking care of our son, etc. Fortunately, my wife and I had had a lot of difficult jobs in the past, so our mental state and our physicality no doubt enabled us to meet these challenges. Whenever we experienced difficulty, we would think about the money that we made as a waiter in one hour was equivalent to a half month of salary as a teacher in China. Our tiredness would disappear right away when the good mood was with us.

Happiness means that I had my wife with me all the time, a sharp difference from the two years of my MS degree, when we were separated in two continents. I was happy to have our son, who added a lot of pleasure to our family. And we had a bunch Chinese friends around, especially several Chinese families that we often played and socialized with. Two of these families were Zens and Dais. The former had a daughter, whom I had brought to the US when I returned from my visit to China in early 1986. The latter family had a son of about five to six years old. With my wife, these three ladies cooked delicious Chinese food for parties and gatherings that we all enjoyed.

My study and dissertation research as well as my thesis defense went smoothly with very few obstacles along the way. Although I encountered some difficulties from time to time, overall, my plan and my expectation were met. Even during our part-time waiter and waitress positions, where a lot of people often run into problems with their bosses, we had very few issues with our bosses. We were generally respected by others.

I was very satisfied not only with my PhD program, as I completed my PhD in four years, published five papers from my dissertation, and had a good financial position. By the time I graduated, we had a total saving of more than $20,000. With such an accomplishment, there was no reason that I wouldn't feel happy about it!

12

POSTDOCTORAL RESEARCH

Changing Immigration Status for My Family (1989–1992)

The spring of 1989 was a critical period of my dissertation preparation, defense, revision, and final submission for graduation. At the same time, there were a number of changes in the China. These changes had pushed me to the crossroad for a decision to either go home to serve my country or to remain in the US after my graduation. I was undetermined and hesitating, and sometimes I felt uncertain or even confused.

I had come to the US for graduate study with the financial support of the Guangxi government. According to the original plan, I should go back after graduation to participate in the reconstruction of the motherland. To return to my college to teach and do research was definitely the logical choice. In that same year, I attended the annual meeting of Plant Physiology Society in St. Louis, Missouri. During the meeting, I met a PhD graduate who was about ready to return to teach at Peking University. It was apparent that he had made a good decision by choosing to return because he was a key young scientist with support from the central government to set up and direct his own molecular institute at Peking University. He later went on to become president of China Agricultural University and vice-chairman of the Guangxi Zhuang Autonomous Region. If I decided, as he did, to return to China, I could have had a great opportunity to not only advanced my career academically but also possibly have an administrative position in my university. As the proverb says, "Past the village will not have the same shop again." This means that if you missed a great opportunity, then this opportunity would probably never return again for you.

However, the rapid development of the domestic politics had a great impact on my decision. As we know, the 1989 democracy movement in Tiananmen Square affected all students studying in the United States and around the world.

Some students in the US stood on one side of the national demonstrations, denouncing the undemocratic restriction of freedom and unwise authoritarian rule by the government. Other students did not agree, taking the opposite position and claiming that these students were naive with blind motives that did not help solve problems through democratic propaganda, considered by some as bullshit. The third group of students, me included, had the attitude that we didn't agree with either group. We were deeply concerned about the development and wished that each side could take a step back and find a solution through consultation. Unfortunately, the demonstration and the political development led to bloodshed in the Tiananmen Square. I was one of many who longed for democracy and hoped that our own country would be more democratic and for our living standard to improve faster. Especially after I had come to the US, I realized that our country was far behind in both democracy and economics.

On the one hand, our country needed us to go back to help improve our living standards, but on the other hand, the US had so much more to offer with opportunity and education, higher living standards, and democracy, all of which were good for our next generation and for future generations. In addition to these realities, we were also troubled with another issue: we were looking forward to the birth of our second son. If we went back, China's one-child policy could greatly affect my career and the happiness of my family. We knew we had to evaluate these risk factors that would certainly weigh on my later decision.

After some serious consideration and especially after consulting with my wife, I decided to stay in the United States on a temporary basis. I wanted to give myself more time to understand the consequences of the democratic movement in China, as well as what I wanted to do and what would be the best for my family. Meanwhile, in order to make better use of my time and my professional considerations for the future, I decided to take a postdoctoral position. This was the best possible option for me with a J-1 visa. The postdoctoral research experience, whether it was in China or in the United States, was necessary for my future career whether it was teaching and research at the university level or a research and development position in some pharmaceutical company.

In the US, whether a postdoctoral research position is a job or a "waiting for employment" work has always been somewhat controversial, depending on whom one asks. Some may say that the reason for a PhD graduate taking a postdoc position is because he cannot find a job or at least an appropriate job, making it a temporary work arrangement, which is better than being officially unemployed. This argument is stronger especially when a postdoc has been doing this for five years or more. On the other hand, many people feel the treatment of postdocs as unemployed is unfair, one-sided, and shortsighted. If we look at the faculty at the university level today, most professors have been through postdoc training. In other words, without postdoctoral experience, one is not competitive for positions at university and research institutions. A postdoc is a full-time, committed researcher. Because most research projects are closer to the technological frontier, the postdocs are able to learn the cutting-edge technologies. Two to three years of postdoc experience could allow a PhD to further mature to form independent thinking and establish research interests. This is critical for future scientists in the continuing advancement of our science and technology. I certainly put myself in the camp of the second group.

My application for postdoctoral position began in the spring of 1989. Based on the area on which I had focused during my PhD program, I chose a professor at Washington State University because he was considered one of the outstanding scientists in plant secondary metabolites. If I were accepted, it would be an ideal laboratory for me to further my research interest and skills. Unfortunately, even with the strong recommendation letter from my adviser and an excellent PhD research with publications, I did not have the opportunity to work in his laboratory. I then turned my attention to a second postdoctoral opportunity advertised in the journal *Plant Physiology* as a position with the USDA laboratory located at the University of Illinois at Urbana-Champaign (UIUC). This postdoctoral research position was on the biochemical mechanism of sugar and amino acid transport across the plant cell membrane. I applied for it, and to my surprise, I was invited for an interview a couple of weeks later. UIUC is about five hours' driving distance from Miami University. I visited UIUC in March, and after meeting my future adviser, I had a good impression of the university, the laboratory, and the adviser. He apparently also liked my application and immediately offered me the position, which I accepted without any hesitation.

A couple of weeks later, I received the official offer letter from UIUC. I looked at it, staring at the compensation, which was twice as much as my previous assistantship. I was happy, and so was my wife. We planned to move to Champaign in late May and report to work on June 1, 1989. It had been two very difficult years for my master's and then a challenging four years of hard work to complete my PhD. I had a lot of reasons to give myself a break, but I could not because we were expecting our second baby boy. We wanted to have full insurance with the new employer before he was born. And he came three weeks after we arrived at the University of Illinois.

It was emotional to leave the school, the program, my adviser's laboratory, and my friends at Miami University. To appreciate the help of the professors sitting on my PhD program committee, I invited them, plus the directors of the International Student Office and the International Student Exchange Program, to a Chinese dinner at a local Chinese restaurant. I then held a dumpling dinner for my adviser, Dr. Jerry McClure, at our apartment. Of course, we organized a party with most of the Chinese students who were at Miami University at that time. In return, our best Chinese friends and Chinese families organized parties for sending us off to new place. It took a couple of weeks to get all these arrangements completed, and we moved on UIUC to begin another page of our life.

UIUC is located in Eastern Illinois about thirty miles from the state line of Indiana. It is also located in a relatively small city with only about 120,000 permanent residences. Although being a college town, Urbana-Champaign, as twin cities, was only two or three hours by car from the major metropolitan cities of Chicago, Indianapolis, or St. Louis. The university sits on the west side of Urbana and the east side of Champaign. The school, established in 1867, has several national top 5 programs/departments, including computer engineering, civil engineering, and accounting, with agriculture, food and plant science, which are also very strong.

The campus is beautiful with its unique buildings of red brick walls and gray roofs. There are a number of well-known facilities such as Krannert Center for Performing Arts, where concerts by national and international are held for students and local residences. There is a large square of open space with dense grass surrounded by many buildings, including student union, the administration, chemistry, language, and life science buildings. This square is also an excellent place for student activities. We could see many students lying on the grass, taking a break from busy classes, chatting with friends, listening to music, or even playing light sports there. The campus is large because it was a substantial farmland on the south side of the campus of at least five square miles that was donated to the university.

USDA has many laboratories located in universities around the country. These laboratories are given a dual name and dual role as USDA labs and university labs. This arrangement is a win-win situation for both the university and the USDA. USDA provides an annual budget to these laboratories that are also under the management of the university. Students from the university may be supervised by USDA scientists who are also professors of the university. This dual role of faculty is especially useful in attracting young scientists because of the accessibility of graduate students to do the research that is important for USDA scientists.

There were three USDA laboratories within the department of plant biology that worked in the areas of photosynthesis. One was more focused on photosynthesis mechanism and the other on biophysical aspects of photosynthesis, while my adviser was interested in how the photosynthetic products (sugars) are transported across the cell membrane. These three researchers got along well. All students from these three labs often got together on a weekly basis. While sharing research progress, we often had a couple of beers with some snack food. We really enjoyed such informal gathering very much.

My adviser was in his late thirties with a family of four—his wife, a son and a daughter, both under the age of ten. His wife, a housewife, and he lived in an old house at Urbana, less than a mile from UIUC. To increase the living area, the adviser added a family room. He often biked or walked to UIUC when it was snowing. He was a warm and confident young scientist who was earnest and paid meticulous attention to his scientific research. He always wrote his papers for publication carefully and rigorously. He was also a very nice, gentle man who got along very well with other people. This had helped him later in his professional career as the president of the Plant Physiology Society and as the chairman of the Department of Plant Sciences at Oregon State University. I was proud to have such a capable young adviser for my first term of postdoc.

My research topic was to investigate how the sucrose, glucose, and amino acids (photosynthesis products) were transported through plant membranes. Key technology used include the isolation and purification of plant cell membrane from tissues. These cell membranes, once isolated from tissue and placed in an appropriate ionic strength of solution l, form a saclike body called vesicles. Because there were some technical difficulties to obtain uniformity of vesicles, I went through a lot of experiments with trial and error. We used various solutions with different acidic conditions under different temperature, along with high-speed centrifugation. Our goal was to obtain a homogeneous population of vesicles. With vesicles at hand, my next series of experiments were to perform sugar and amino acids transport experiments. In doing so, we placed radio-labeled substrate amino acids and sucrose in the solution and allowed them to enter the vesicle. Because the isolated biological membranes contained many biological characteristics of the membranes of plant tissues, the entrance into vesicles of the labeled amino acids or sucrose was either through carriers or diffusion. If by diffusion, the entrance might be limited due to the structural barrier of the membranes, which are composed of lipid bilayers. Therefore, by monitoring the amount and the speed of entrance into the vesicles, as well as the kinetics of the accumulation, this allowed us to make conclusion regarding to whether the substrates were carrier transported or simply by physical diffusion.

A two-year postdoctoral research, according to these technologies, resulted in three peer-reviewed papers. These publications described the basic technology in membrane isolation and purification and the transport kinetics of amino acids across the membranes by membrane protein carriers. The experimental methods and the biochemical properties of the transport served as the foundation for many research projects by this laboratory, which eventually led to the discovery of genes and cloning of the proteins responsible for the transporters.

I liked my job there at the USDA labs at UIUC, but by comparison, I was more pleased with the apartment we stayed in. We moved to the international student housing complex named Orchard Downs Apartment, located at the southeast corner of the campus. Many international students, including most Chinese graduate students with children, lived there. These apartments were best suited for family with kids because there were multiple playground facilities for children to play. In addition, a large group of Chinese students nearby was especially good for my wife socially. Young mothers often got together, chatting and sharing their motherhood experiences. Also, the front and backyards were covered with large trees and grass, forming a beautiful scene. Last but not least, the apartment was away from high-traffic streets, and there are many busses, making it a convenient, safe, and ideal place for young families with small children.

When we arrived in Urbana, we lived in a one-bedroom efficiency apartment. A few weeks later, we were told that a family with more than one child should not be in this apartment, so after our second son was born, we moved to apartment 1963A on the ground floor with some moisture that we did not like. The living room was big enough, and there were two bedrooms of adequate size, with the rent a little more than $200 per month, including utilities. This was not expensive because it was a little less than 10 percent of my compensation. This expense was considered normal housing for an average family.

There was a strong tradition in our family history with regard to how to raise a family. I inherited this and applied it to raising my family as well. The tradition was more focused on saving money while we still could for coping with any future economic hardship. In doing so, we ignored the importance of educating our children when we had all the resources available. We did not send our eldest son, John, to preschool when he was three years old. Instead he stayed with his mother at home because saving money was our primary purpose. We should have sent him to a preschool program since his mother was not able to speak English well, which was a real shortcoming for our son. That could be a possible reason why our son spoke English later than most other children. For this reason, we were quite worried about his intellectual development. Fortunately, Champaign County Family Services and a few other organizations had many educational programs for children, one of which gave free education to children with retarded and slow development. After we discussed our son's situation with the staff of Family Services, we had the permission to register him with Washington Elementary School, where there was preschool and elementary school education.

The Washington school was located on the north side of Urbana City with approximately a hundred pupils. This school provided free-of-charge education to families with an annual income level less than a preset level. The income level we had qualified us for this benefit. This was a half-day school for him. Our son really liked to go to school. He was excited boarding his school bus every morning, and he came back home happily on the same bus. He stayed at this school for two years, and it saved us at least five to six thousand dollars.

We took the same approach to raise our second son as we had his elder brother. We applied for the WIC program to receive nutritional supplemental food, and we used reusable cloth diaper as main staples. He wore his brother's clothes and those made by his mother. Above all, we made every effort to save money while raising our family.

To have fresh vegetables daily, we rented a small plot of land about ten by ten meters. The land was very fertile, and the water source located in the middle of field made it very convenient to water our vegetables by connecting a garden hose to the faucet. The rental cost for each lot was ten dollars, paid to the management office of Orchard Downs Apartment. We started planting in May and harvested over the next several months. We returned the plot to the office at the end of October. Because my wife and I had a lot of experience in crop cultivation, we were able to grow vegetables more than we could consume during the peak season. We liked this so much because with such a small effort, we could have sufficient fresh vegetables throughout the season, and it especially helped us save a considerable amount of money along the way.

Just as when I was a graduate student, I continued my part-time job as a waiter at a local Chinese restaurant. I worked on an as-needed basis, but often for two nights on Friday and Saturday evenings. My wife also worked as a part-time waitress at a restaurant and as a part-time technician with a professor at UIUC. Our son Michael was taken care of by a babysitter, a neighboring Chinese friend, when my wife was working. We saved this portion of our income in the bank for future use since my income from the postdoc was sufficient for our daily living expenses. We went through hard work and thrifty living for the two years of postdoc. Although the income from these part-time jobs was limited, it did add up. We had added more than $10,000 to our bank savings account.

As we headed into the second year of my postdoctoral research, our quiet life was soon broken as we faced a new challenge. My desire for temporarily staying in the US due to the democratic movement in China was slowly changing to a plan for staying longer. However, there was a two-year service requirement in our home country for all J-1 visa recipients based on the US national immigration policy. I would not be allowed to change my visa status. Even though the US government did not require Chinese students who came before the 1989 democratic movement to leave just yet, I was more or less concerned about how we could be able to stay in the US longer legally. According to my observation and analysis of the situation, I had a couple of possibilities. First, I could get a position at a university as an assistant professor or as a scientist. This would be considered as an outstanding scientist or someone with special skills the US needed, then I would be allowed to apply for H-1B visa, or even permanent residence status. Second, if the US government passed a law to allow Chinese students and scholars to change their immigration status, then I would not be required to do anything.

Regarding to the second possibility, the United States Congress had a motion under discussion of making it a law to grant Chinese students and scholars to change their status that was likely to be approved. However, this was a major political issue that would have to be adopted by congress and signed by the president. To play it safe, I thought that I should not put all my eggs into this one basket, but I should be more proactive in dealing with it. So I decided to apply for an assistant professor position at a university.

I started my plan for pursuing university tenure track positions. I consulted with my postdoc adviser and had his support in the spring semester of 1990. My approach was to review all advertisements related to plant science in various journals such as *Science, Nature, Plant Physiology*, and *The American Journal of Botany*. Since my undergraduate study was in agronomy, my master's in plant ecology, my PhD in plant physiology and biochemistry, and now a postdoc in biology and biochemistry, I had a broad spectrum of knowledge but with less specialization. This could work in my favor, but it could also work against me, depending on the specific position being recruited. Nevertheless, I set my eyes on those positions of plant physiology and plant biochemistry. After six months of my closely watching, positions opened. I found only about a dozen or so positions available that met my original broad objective. I selected five to six to apply for.

At that time, especially for an assistant professor position at a university, the competition was very fierce. There were between 100 and 300 applicants for every advertised position. For example, I applied to the Department of Biology at University of Maryland for a position with more than 150 applicants. The head of the recruiting committee was an immigrant Chinese professor. According to limited information from her about the application selection process, my application was selected in the elite list of the top 10. However, when deciding on three or five candidates for interview, my name was dropped. It was not because I didn't have enough research papers, because of the lack of research capacity, or because I did not meet position criteria in the area of the research. Instead, it was the school I graduated from, the modest journal my papers were published in, and the fact that I was a foreign candidate with English as not my mother tongue, as well as language barriers that were among the shortcomings for me. I also applied to Rutgers University for a position as a research assistant professor of turf grass research. I had an interview, but I did not get hired. Although I did not know why, I felt that the fact that the position might not have fit my background was the main reason.

My first attempt at applying for an assistant professor position did not yield what I had expected. I gradually realized that as a foreigner without an outstanding record, it would be very difficult to get these jobs. My application had to be very strong in my research program if I wanted to be competitive with other candidates who were US citizens. This led me to a decision to continue my second term of postdoctoral research. Of course, I also had a second reason for seeking this second term because I hoped the school would help me apply for the H-1B visa, a temporary work visa. I knew that the USDA lab where I was working could not make this change for me because no organization of the US government was allowed to recruit foreign nationals.

I started looking for a second postdoc in the middle of 1990. I met a professor from the Pennsylvania State University (PSU) at an annual meeting of Plant Physiology. After several discussions, the professor accepted my application to his postdoc position and, at the same time, agreed to help me apply for the H-1B visa. As a result, at the end of May 1991, I moved with my family to State College, Pennsylvania, where Pennsylvania State University is located.

I was amazed to see several of my previous classmates from our Guangxi alma mater at Penn State. One of them, with a family of three, was from the Department of Plant Protection at Guangxi Agriculture College, Guangxi University (GXU). His wife came as a visiting dependent. His son was very good at the computer and later graduated with a PhD degree in computer engineering and worked for Microsoft. Another, my classmate at the English training, graduated from the Department of Horticulture of GXU. His wife came as a dependent but later became a graduate student and graduated with a master's from PSU. A third student also came from the GXU. She and her daughter lived at State College, but her husband was one of earliest domestic businessmen, starting his business in the 1980s in China. She was influenced by her husband and became a businesswoman in the US. A fourth friend graduated with a MS in physics from Miami University and later earned a PhD from PSU. His family and my family had gotten along very well at Miami University. His wife was a housewife, and they had a son and a daughter. In addition to these four families, there were a few other Chinese friends or professionals at State College, and all of us formed a new social circle. We played, partied, and traveled together.

It was now at new place, a new university, and a new friends circle where I began my second postdoc. Everything was changing except one thing—our hardworking, thrifty-living, and saving behavior remained unchanged.

When we arrived at State College, we moved into an apartment at the Nittany Garden Apartments. This was for temporary accommodations introduced by our friend. It was a one-bedroom apartment located on a hillside, about two miles away from PSU, with a good environment. However, we stayed there for only few weeks because a family of four must live in at least a two-bedroom apartment. We knew this policy even before we arrived, but in order to save some money, we decided to accept this inconvenience. We then moved to the second apartment called Southgate Apartments, which was about a half mile from the Nittany Garden Apartments. This was a two-bedroom apartment for a summer short-term lease. Generally, a summer lease is about half of the cost of a regular school-year lease. We lived there for two months for a savings of about $250 per month. In August, we moved a third time in three months to Old Boalsburg Apartments. Although we had limited pieces of furniture, every move was a challenge for us and required a lot of time and energy. We accepted this hardship only in order to save a few hundred dollars.

This third apartment was in the basement, a two-bedroom apartment with less than half the windows above ground level. It was relatively dark and damp and not an ideal place to live. However, our main consideration was the price. It was $200 per month, one of the cheapest apartments in town. When compared to South Gate Apartments, the price was about half as much. This apartment was located in the west side of the PSU and University Park, about a mile from the university. From the apartment to the school, there was a hill with some slope, then across a few streets of the city of State College before arriving at the campus. It was about a twenty-minute walk and ten-minute bike ride to the school. Across from the apartment was an elementary school named Easterly Parkway Elementary School. This became the first school for our elder son to attend for the next a couple of years until 1993, when we moved into our own house.

We seldom traveled. It was not because we did not like traveling, but instead, we did not want to spend our hard-earned money on leisure activities. In 1993, our family finally decided to visit Disneyland in Florida. We took our newly bought used Subaru Legacy with our family of four and headed south. Because we needed two days of driving to reach the destination, we stayed midway in our camping tent. For many people, especially for kids, camping is fun, but not the way we did it. Our six-foot tent was too small for four of us to squeeze into. Making it worse, the tent could not prevent mosquitos from entering the tent. I hardly got any sleep that night. Fortunately, I was still young with energy, and the next day of driving was not affected. This was our second trip in five years after we took the first trip to DC and New York in 1990.

As my postdoctoral research was in progress, my personal situation was constantly changing. I was still in my J-1 visa, and without any change to my visa status, there was always a concern hanging over my head all the time. When I first arrived at PSU, I wanted to focus on my research program and hoped to get the program going before asking my adviser's help for applying for H-1B. I did just that. My research was on the right track with some significant progress. By the spring of 1992, I formally raised my issue to my adviser. He was in sympathy with my situation and accepted my request. After consulting with the department of biology, he agreed to help me with H-1B application processed through normal channels. This process required the postdoc position to be advertised and all applications to be screened and evaluated before I could be hired as the only qualified candidate in order to complete the application. Because the hiring procedures were complex, timing was a major concern.

There was only one opportunity each year to submit applications for H-1B. Because the number of applicants had always exceeded the quota set by the US government, a random selection of applicants often resulted in some applicants failing to be selected in the quota. If I failed in 1992, I had to wait until 1993. It was not that I could not wait another year, but rather, my two years of postdoc at PSU might end before I could submit my application again. In that case, I would be required to either extend my current postdoc for a third year or change to a third school for a third term as a postdoc. My family and I would be living in an unknown situation, which could create a lot of stress and pressure. In addition, I was near forty years old and did not have a lot of time to wait. Therefore, I asked my adviser to allow me to look for an assistant professor position while I applied for H-1B. I greatly appreciated his understanding and his support of my request.

Prior to my second attempt to apply for a university assistant professor position, I had an opportunity to speak to the retired chair of the Department of Biology at PSU. He explained to me how the process worked in selecting candidates for this type of position. Research universities like PSU would focus on three aspects: the doctoral adviser, the university PhD program, and where the research papers were published. If the university was lower ranked than PSU, the adviser was not well-known, and the papers were published in less prestigious publications, an applicant would normally not be selected. After listening to his words, I felt that I was in a very challenging position to compete with graduates from top-tier universities, so I dropped my target universities to second-tier schools. However, I kept my minimal standards, which was that the universities should at least have good research programs with sufficient graduate students enrolled. Otherwise, the university would become a teaching school with basically teaching as its main mission. If I were forced to go to even lower-ranked schools or even to two- or three-year colleges, it would not be my career endeavor and would make me less competitive since my mother language was not English. I did not want to have this kind of job.

After I established my criteria for target universities, I began searching for advertisements during the second half of 1992. I eventually submitted applications to a few universities. My application to East Tennessee University passed their screening selection as one of the top 5 candidates out of about 100 applicants. Then the chair of the search committee called me up for a phone interview. I thought I did all right with this interview, but my name was dropped from the short list of five candidates and I did not get an on-site interview like the other four candidates. I could not explain why, but I felt that the accent of my mother language could be a factor since this university had heavy teaching duties expected of its professors.

While I was worried about how to change my visa status and how to seek jobs in universities, the US Congress was discussing a law that would allow Chinese students and scholars to change their visa status. This debate was a result of the '89 Chinese democratic movement. As early as November 1989, Congress passed a resolution that allowed Chinese students to stay without the need for fulfillment of the two-year residency requirement for exchange students like J-1 visa holders. But the resolution was vetoed by President Bush although it was supported by the Senate in the spring of 1990. About the same time, Congress passed another bill, HR2712, for which President Bush used his executive order to insert into the bill the provision that protected Chinese, including all Chinese students and scholars who arrived at the US before June 4, 1989, and allowed them to stay in the United States until the situation in China could prove that there would be no longer any security concerns or discrimination.

Over the next a couple of years, Congress often brought up these heated issues for debate. Finally, Congress adopted a resolution called the Chinese Student Protection Act of 1992, the law that allow students to change their visa status to have permanent residency with a green card (officially known as a permanent residency card). This law made about forty thousand Chinese students and scholars eligible to apply for the change. This development profoundly changed everything for myself and my family. From now on, we were no longer temporarily staying in the US and no longer would be discriminated against in certain job positions. We could now make long-range plans for our career and our family finances.

Since 1989, I had been attempting to change my visa status, and now it had finally come to an end. It should be a good thing for me and my family. However, I was not totally happy about it because it was with a heavy heart and a somewhat bitter taste that I accepted my new status. First, in this new country and new society, I had to establish myself from scratch, which would be challenging. All my accomplishments and the trust I earned, whether it was from high school or branch secretary of Communist Party in the countryside, or as the student union president of Guangxi Agriculture University, had all disappeared. I had to start all over again from the same starting line or even way behind the line if it took into consideration my age, and without any advantage over the other graduates and the people surrounding me.

I was also a little worry that as a minority Chinese in the US, I would feel the discrimination that was still widespread in the nation. There were enough examples that we had experienced and felt in the past a few years. I had to adopt myself to the new environment and to the capitalistic system.

I really felt sorry for my home country, especially Guangxi Zhuang Autonomous Region, for sending me and supporting my study in the US with scarcity of resources there. Without its support, I wouldn't have had this kind of opportunity. Although there were many shortcomings in our country, I was in deep sympathy with her because I was born and raised by her. The reason why I stayed in the US could probably be due to my long yearning for freedom and for a free market economy and a higher living standard with a better education opportunity for my children.

Regardless of whatever the reason might be, I had chosen to stay in the United States. From this time on, I must set my goal. I wanted to have a good career and have financial independence. One day when I had reached my goal, I wanted to repay something back to my hometown and to my mother country.

With the legal status of permanent residency and a green card, I now had more job opportunities, with no more barriers to government jobs; and my selection range was wider. I had a lot more opportunities now than in the past because all US companies could have recruited Chinese graduates like me. As a matter of the fact, it was just about the same time that we changed our visa type and during the Christmas of 1992 that I got a job offer. The employer eagerly waited for my response!

13

FIRST JOB

Analytical Chemist (1993)

$\mathbf{M}$y first real job was as an analytical chemist at the Central Analytical Laboratories (CAL), State College, Pennsylvania. The laboratory was established as an environmental analytical laboratory around 1984 by a PhD graduate from Penn State University who came originally from Iran. Within eight years, the company has developed from a few employees to a staff of more than thirty. The services provided by the laboratory included the analysis of environmental samples and pesticide residues in various field trial samples.

Before I joined the company, a number of my friends and classmates from my alma mater were employed there. Because these Chinese valued their job opportunity, they worked hard and impressed the employer. Therefore, when there were positions open, the management asked his Chinese employees to help identify qualified candidates. My friend recommended me to the management team of the company, quickly resulting in my interview.

It took less than a month for me to complete the interview process, the job offers, and my acceptance of the offer. I formally began my employment with the laboratory in January of 1993. I was told that there were a few reasons for me to be quickly hired for this employment because the company's business was very good and they needed to hire more people for the workload. The company owners felt that I could be a good candidate who would be able to help the company's future growth. The owners had had good experience in hiring and managing Chinese employees who demanded only reasonable salaries, who worked hard, and who were able to finish their work independently and in a timely manner.

The laboratory services of this company were divided into three main parts: developing and validating pesticide residue methods; testing pesticide residues in crops, soil, and water samples; and testing environmental samples, including water, wastes products, and soil contamination by various chemicals.

Laboratory businesses were flourishing in the US because of a series of environmental laws and regulations passed in the 1970s. These laws included clean air, waste disposal, waste water discharge, and pesticide residue, etc. The enforcement of these laws reached its peak in 1980s. As a result, substantial tests were required for manufacturers, waste generators, landfill operators, gas station owners, and sewer water treatment plants. In order to provide uniform standards for monitoring and managing environmental industry, the Environmental Protection Agency (EPA) had published hundreds of analytical standard methods. Environmental testing laboratories must follow these standards to perform analysis of various samples. If the waste aftertreatment did not pass the minimal standards, it was not permitted to be discharged. As a result, tremendous works required environmental engineering and laboratory testing. These requirements provided the foundation for rapid growth of environmental laboratories.

The EPA also enforced a law called the Federal Insecticide, Fungicide, and Rodenticide Act (FIFRA) in the amended version passed in 1972. Under the provisions of FIFRA, all pesticides, whether they had been on the market, would be on the market, or were being experimentally tested for future market were required to go through field-trial experiments. These laws and regulations were mandatorily managed by EPA. If a pesticide was applied to any crop in different regions of the country or in different seasons, the field trials had to include all possible applications of the pesticide. The field samples were collected from different trials, different crops, different parts of the crops, or even different soils and water. These samples were brought back to the analytical testing laboratories and analyzed for pesticide residues according to the laws of FIFRA. Because the statistical analysis was required for documenting the data package, a substantial number of samples with duplicate or triplicate analyses were processed and analyzed for each pesticide. This led to many subcontracting opportunities for pesticide testing laboratories, including the CAL where I worked.

Before testing field samples to support a pesticide application for the market, specific analytical methods must be developed and validated. There could be multiple methods for testing for each pesticide because the method of analysis for one crop could be different from another. The testing method for leaves could be different from stems. By the same token, methods for grains or for soil and water samples could be different from each other. It was only after a pesticide method had been validated that we could apply it to testing samples. These methods could be developed by the pesticide manufacturers or by an independent testing laboratory. Under some circumstances, there could be a cooperation between the chemical companies and the independent testing laboratories. Regardless of the different ways to testing and meeting the FIFRA requirements, there were substantial business opportunities for laboratories like CAL.

Our company was a contract research organization (CRO) serving chemical companies for method development and validation. This kind of service was an important part of business at CAL. In order to achieve a validated method, it could take from a month to six months of research and testing. Because method development and validation were considered as research and development (R and D) work, the service fees for such service were more or less based on billable labor hours, which was a high-profit margin service. Outsourcing firms sometimes helped testing laboratories by paying a portion of the equipment costs. If a CRO were selected by a chemical company, the relationship often lasted for years, helping the CRO achieve a long-term business opportunity.

Our laboratory was equipped with the instruments like gas chromatography (GC), high-pressure liquid chromatography (HPLC), gas chromatography-mass spectrometer (GC-MS), liquid chromatography-mass spectrometer (LC-MS), atomic absorption spectrometer (AAS), and inductive couple plasma spectrometer (ICP). These instruments were installed on two floors of the CAL laboratory building, which was approximately fifteen thousand square feet.

The personnel of the company were approximately one-third administration, one-third the scientists or analysts, and one-third the laboratory technicians. The technicians prepared the test sample and the analysts analyzed the samples and reported the data daily. After data was entered into the computer, the quality control personnel reviewed the data for accuracy. Finally, the certificate of analysis was signed by the designated person before reports were sent to our clients.

There were two subgroups in our laboratory: the pesticide group and the environmental group. The pesticide group was directed by the laboratory director, fort-five to fifty years old, who was also the company founder. The environmental group was directed by a young man with a BS degree, who was in his twenties. As deputy director, he was very good in both maintaining testing instruments and in performing testing using various analytical methods. He was a hard worker and a responsible manager of the environmental laboratories.

The success of the company, according to my observation, was due to both the excellent market and good management team. For example, environmental market and pesticides residue market were both excellent. The management team was very responsible and committed. The marketing director had good communication skills and was able to bring in large pesticide projects. A GLP-stamped laboratory was also critical for this CRO. Without meeting the GLP standards, major chemical companies would not use our laboratory for EPA projects.

From the first day I was employed, I knew that my life had turned another page. I must quickly adapt myself to this new environment and align my energy to my new job and a new goal. I knew I should quickly master the analytical techniques and meet the job requirements. According to the management, I would receive technical training because my doctoral and postdoctoral training at the university level were not related to the work done in this laboratory. I had never used gas chromatography (GC) during my university years, but my first job assignment was to used GC to perform pesticide analysis. Therefore, I went through training by the company founder, and I was very happy with the rapid progress I made. After a few weeks of training, I was able to perform test projects independently.

In addition to technical training, GLP training was required in order to work on GLP-related projects. All chemists and technicians must fulfill this requirement. Analysts who performed pesticide project were also required to have adequate education with minimal bachelor degree or equivalent of training. Qualifications and training records must be filed for compliance. These records should be ready any time for EPA inspection. Without these strict quality standards, major chemical companies would not risk using a non-GLP laboratory for their projects.

Our laboratory performed tests for pesticides in drinking water, which was different from a CRO project. As a result, our laboratory was required to obtain certification from each state where we provided our service. Also, the US had many superfund sites that were polluted and required a long-term response teams to clean up hazardous material contaminations. Our laboratory had to pass proficiency tests for undefined intervals in order to provide analytical services for the superfund projects.

There were eight Chinese employees working in this laboratory, accounting for about 20 percent of the total employees in the company. Four of us held the position of analytical chemists. Among us, there were three couples of husband and wife. There were pros and cons about this kind of arrangement for employment because a husband and wife could lose their jobs together, making their lives much more challenging when that happens. On the other hand, when two employees left the company together, the two vacancies would be more difficult to fill with qualified experienced employees. Whether losing a couple because they moved to new jobs or terminating employment of a couple would not be good for either the employer or the employees.

My wife's first job was as a technician at CAL. This had been arranged when I accepted my job offer from the company. Before my interview, Chinese friends suggested her to the management and had recommended her for a position if I were hired. Her main duty was to help analysts prepare samples. It was a relatively easy task for her, and she was very comfortable with the job assignments. Compared to her previous jobs as a waitress in Chinese restaurants, she liked the lab technician job much better, although the salary was not as high as we expected.

There were two other couples working for the company, the Kus and the Xis. Mr. Ku, who was responsible for LC/MS/MS testing, had a PhD from Penn State and was a down-to-earth chemist. He was proficient in using this most expensive instrument in the laboratory and generated good quality data that allowed the company to charge higher fees. This is especially true when a project was challenging and often could not be done by other laboratories. His experience with CAL made him a good scientist and LC-MS chemist, which benefited his professional career with future employers.

Mr. Xi was a designated analyst responsible for the ion electrophoretic analyzer and was the only person using this instrument in the laboratory. This made him a go-to person for projects that required the use of this equipment. This analyzer was considered a new analytical instrument specifically used for analyzing charged pesticide compounds that were difficult to analyze using conventional HPLC. Several major chemical companies contracted their works to our laboratory for method development and validation using this new technology.

Mr. Xi was smart not only as an analytical chemist but also as a businessman as well. He and his wife, both graduates of Penn State University, started buying houses and renting them to students while they both were in the graduate school. They purchased older houses and fixed them up by themselves before leasing them. Twenty years later, these houses had quadrupled in value. Mr. Xi started his own analytical laboratory in 1995, providing contract research and testing service to the pharmaceutical industry. His laboratory has been very successful and has grown to more than sixty employees by 2017.

After I received adequate training in analytical techniques and GLP, I began to perform testing independently. The projects I worked on were from the large chemical companies. Usually, I had a lab technician prepare a set of samples (usually eight to twelve samples) for me each day. I prepared a set of standard solutions. The prepared samples and the set of calibration standards were set up for analysis in the late afternoon. The samples were set to run overnight to increase output as the instrument automatically analyzed samples and standards. By the next morning when we got to work, the data was ready for analysis. I analyzed the data and calculated the results. If there was any troubleshooting work required, it was often done in the late morning to the early afternoon. This became the routine for my part of work, except for the method development and validation process, which required flexibility and persistent effort to complete a task. My job was not hard to do, but it was a bit boring. After six months, I felt that I had analyzed many samples and had made a lot of money for the company.

The other business of the company was the general analysis of environmental samples. Analysis of environmental samples was done by using a variety of instruments using EPA-specified methods. I did not have any opportunity to learn how to use these instruments, even if I really wanted to learn. I had to make up this lesson later when I became an entrepreneur, running my own laboratory.

I was paid $40,000 per year, and because we were living in a low-cost area, the wage was adequate for a decent living for a family of four. Plus, with the salary my wife as a technician, we had near $60,000 per annum. This placed us in the middle class. Because our financial situation had substantially improved, we decided to make some changes to our living standards. First we bought a good used car, a Subaru Legacy, which was a few years old at 80 percent new. It costed more than $10,000. The two cars we had owned before were eight to twelve years old that costed $500–$2,000, so we felt that our standard had been lifted with this car.

Our second major change was to purchase our dream home. By 1993, we had been in the United States for ten years. During this time, we moved to different apartments a total of eight times. The shortest time we had lived in one was only a few weeks, and the longest was a few years. Although we had minimal furniture to move each time, it did take time and effort to move. Now that we had formal jobs, it was about time to have our house so that we could realize the American dream.

We started our house hunting in the spring of 1993, right after I reported to work. Because we did not like old houses, we concentrated on relatively newer houses. However, after a few weeks of showing by our realtor, we could not find anything that we like. Some houses were too old while others were outside our budget. Therefore, we decided to build our own. We purchased a lot in a new development community that was about a mile away from the company where we worked. We decided on a floor plan provided by the construction company and made minor changes and upgrades before signing the contact. It took about six months to complete the construction. The house is about 1,600 square feet. Looking from the front of the house, it appeared to be one-story house, but if we looked at from behind, it was like two-story because the basement was at ground level with a walk-out door to the backyard.

The construction of the house was completed by early fall. Our down payment was $15K, so we borrowed about $100K to complete the purchase. The total amount of principle and interest payments was about $500–600 per month, which was similar to the rental rate in the area for a two-bedroom apartment. With so much better living conditions and ample space for our kids to play in the new house, we were so happy that we took this step to own our home.

By early fall of 1993, we could proudly say that our American dream had been realized. We had our green cards, a good used car, a new house, and two sons. Our life had indeed changed tremendously. My wife and I took our kids to school on our way to work and picked them up when we returned from work every day. We finally had some time to watch TV and to enjoy outside activities. It was about this time that I found time for fishing. I thought to myself, *This has to be a real American dream.* However, this type of smooth and easy life was soon broken because I was not satisfied with this type of life. I had a new goal in my mind: becoming an entrepreneur and owning my own business.

13-1: First dream house with my wife and two sons sitting in front

14

ENTREPRENEURSHIP (1993–2010)

PREFACE

"ALong Road from China" was the front page article in the commercial section of a Urbana-Champaign newspaper, the *News Gazette,* in 2004. The article described my entrepreneur experience and our successful company, which generated a positive reaction in the twin cities of Champaign and Urbana as well as surrounding areas. Its effect was even greater in the local Chinese community where fewer entrepreneurships had been established. With the publication of the article, many local residents became aware of the existence of our company, which had played a role in the region's economy.

The article focuses on how I could become a successful entrepreneur through the long road from being a farmer to a college student, a graduate student in the US, and then taking my first step into the business world to establish my company with no business experience and little capital. The article included telling about the development of my company from just myself to fifteen full-time employees, making a profit every year since 1997. It described the testing service we provided for the nutrition supplement industry with more than a thousand different tests and explained the assistance of our friends and the bank loan officer who played a role in the establishment of our business. It explained the rapid growth of the nutrition supplement market, a crucial element for the success of our business that had led to the sustainable growth of the business, and our plans for future development.

In 2010, the same newspaper again published an article entitled "Supplemental Gains" about our company's continuing success from 2004 to 2009. From the time of its first article, our company continued its development and growth, including the company's management team, the increase of employees to twenty-six, the global expansion of our customer base with hundreds of customers, and the global recognition of the company as a reputable independent testing laboratory.

I was probably an entrepreneur earlier than most students from China. Frankly speaking, if we looked at my business and compared it to the other successful businesses over the last ten years, my success was only small feat. However, in the '90s, and especially as a new immigrant to the US, my entrepreneurial spirit was exceptional, especially under the circumstances of little capital, no patented and advanced technology, not knowing the market, and without any management experience. I was able to tenaciously pursue my dream of becoming an entrepreneur. My quest for financial independence under a very challenging environment and conditions was unique and courageous. I was proud of myself for having realized my dream. In order to undertake the description of how I was able to accomplish this, I divided this chapter into the subjects of preparation, establishment, development, maturation, and merger and integration.

SECTION ONE

Preparation (1993–1994)

$\mathbf{M}$y personal character and working style were that if I wanted to do something, I just did it and never hesitated. I am a doer instead of a procrastinator. This valuable trait had been with me since I arrived at the US. When I said that I wanted to have my master's degree in two years and my PhD in four years, I did it. When I wanted to shift my career goal from seeking a professorship at universities to working in a company, it took me only a couple of months to do so. And when I wanted to have our dream home, we built it and moved in six months later. All these accomplishments were associated with my doer attitude and as an action taker.

In the late summer of 1993, we had our highly anticipated dream home, with spacious rooms equipped with several pieces of furniture and a color TV. It was our first time to own a home, and we were proud of this achievement. My wife and I enjoyed watching TV, which we had never had a chance to do before. We had ample space in the lower level for kids to play with their small toy cars and trains. As an immigrant to the US, owning a home, having a good job, and having a happy family were considered symbols of the American dream that most of us would try to reach. A rational thinking and behavior after achieving this dream would be to settle down and enjoy the happy life going forward.

However, my dream was different from this. In my view, a house, a new car, and an easy life was not my American dream. I wouldn't settle down for this kind of ordinary life. From primary school to secondary school, from high school to college, from returning home to becoming branch Communist

Party secretary, all these experiences were somehow and somewhat related to management and leadership. I was now working as an employee without much freedom for someone else. I often felt uncomfortable if someone looked over my shoulder when I worked. Similarly, I did not like to be controlled and have my life arranged by others. I wanted financial independence, and if I settled down with my current job and my dream house, I would be just like an average person. I preferred a challenging life with greater purposes. I wanted to create my own business, which I hoped would lead to my accumulating wealth for my family so we had financial independence.

Yet to achieve the American dream, especially financial independence, is easier said than done. I had no idea of what I could do to achieve my dream. I was at a complete loss for a period of time. During my master's and PhD programs, my concentration was on basic research. What I learned in both graduate programs had little commercial application or commercial potential for my business venture. In addition, I did not have anyone with whom to consult for business ideas. I felt that my life was in the three-pronged fork. As the proverb says, "Men fear being in the wrong mountain, while women are afraid of marrying the wrong man." Although I had the determination to pursue my professional career and the economic independence, a series of problems that I was facing threw me into a spin. At the time, nobody knew me better than my wife, who had observed my depressed mood. She approached me with care and said, "Don't worry about it. If you were not ready to go into business right now, you could wait for a better time. Most people, as employees, are still happy, and we could be the same. If you're not liking working under someone, you might go back to school and continue the effort in seeking future career as professorship."

Since I left my postdoctoral fellowship from Penn State, I have had no regrets about this decision. I had already focused my attention on the industry and business world. I hoped to pick up what I didn't know as soon as I could so that I could use what I had learned as an employee of the laboratory for when I became a businessman in the future.

Although I had a good start in my first job, within a few months, I often carried an unhappy face, mainly because of the high risk involved in pursuing my business venture. I was also concerned about how to get my wife to go along with this pursuit. As a mother of two, all her attention was concentrated on how to raise our children in a good and stable economic environment. Because of this, she did not like the risk, especially the entrepreneurship risk. But at the same time, she also knew well that it was my nature that once decided, I was always determined to carry it through. Here, opposition was not the best option, but her full support was. She encouraged me by saying, "The United States is a free marketing economy. You have experience in leadership and social skills. If we work hard, it is possible for us to make a career out of it." These few words sounded simple and might not seem as having much real substance, but for me, it was the encouragement and support that I needed.

Now with my wife's support, I no longer needed to persuade her to accept my business venture. I knew that for a business novice like me, the support of my family, especially my wife, was particularly important. If my startup failed, it was not only my sacrifice but also that of my family. This sacrifice included not only time and energy and the loss of leisure but also all our savings. My wife was an especially loving mother. The money she saved over the past a few years was so precious to her, and she would do anything she could to tightly hold on to it. Getting her support for my business plan really improved my emotional mood considerably.

My personal career had always been to not be satisfied with the status quo of a current situation but to constantly search for another dream. In order to achieve my new goals, I was not afraid of the challenge and the hard work or even of making sacrifices. These characteristics had been nurtured since my childhood. I gradually matured with my determination, confidence, and persistence. After I joined in the Central Analytical Laboratories, I slowly realized that these characteristics were indeed in line with the qualifications of small business entrepreneurs. Especially since America is a free marketing economy that provides plenty of entrepreneurial opportunities. It encourages young people to start their businesses. The government has many different programs and funds to support entrepreneurship effort. With such favorable social and market environment, coupled with my arduous spirit, I felt strongly that it was worth a try!

The founder of our laboratory was an immigrant from Iran. I admired him very much when I knew he started up and now owned a rapidly growing company. His experience of success really encouraged and inspired me. By comparison, he and I had many in common since we both were immigrants, received our PhD degrees from US institutions, and we both had similar characteristics as doers. Since he could start his laboratory testing business and build a successful company, why not me? This analysis strengthened my determination to venturing into my own business.

Then the most concerns I had were not my determination, being afraid of challenges, or a persistent spirit, but instead, it was what business I should be in. Generally, most businesses started with at least one good, sometimes unique, technology, especially with patented technologies or products. With an innovative technology, one could obtain funding from Small Business Innovation Research (SBIR) or Small Business Technology Transfer (STTR) funds from the US government. It is also possible to attract investment from venture capitalist and angel investors.

Unfortunately, my six years of graduate school had not given me any unique technology that would be appropriate for a good business plan. My tenure with Central Analytical Laboratory (CAL) for only a few months did not provide me with sufficient knowledge and skills to formulate my business ideas. Although I had learned certain operation techniques in gas chromatography, I still lacked the experience in using high-pressure liquid chromatography. I was a novice to many other types of instruments, such as liquid chromatography-mass spectrometer, gas chromatography-mass spectrometer, and inductive couple plasma spectrometer. I had little experience in equipment repairs and maintenance. In brief, I had no patented technology and only limited experience in analytical chemistry and almost no laboratory instrumentation skills.

So what kind of business I could start under such circumstances had become a major concern for me. I analyzed and evaluated my ideas again and again for over a month and couldn't come to any conclusion, so I turned to my wife and hoped she could help me out. I knew that I shouldn't expect too much from her because she was just a housewife and knew very little about business. She took it lightly by saying, "You asking me about business is just like someone asking about playing piano to a cattle." However, she did say that we had been farmers for years and that our business shouldn't be on farming or agriculture-related businesses.

I agreed with her about that. Generations of farmers' life in my family history had prompted me to make a change. Since I was a child, I had realized that the farmers have always been a group of the population having the lowest income and hardest life in history around the world. More importantly, with the exception of a little gardening and crop planting, I knew little about the agriculture business. Many years later, I realized that agricultural businesses are indeed enormous both in the US and around the world. This made me feel that I was a little farmer who was naive and did not know the modern farming and agriculture products!

After a few more discussions with my wife, I finally focused my attention on laboratory services. The reason for this was that I was now employed as a laboratory analytical chemist, a position letting me learn more laboratory services business than any other businesses. Plus I understood that laboratory testing services required certain testing and instrumental technologies, making it a technology-related company. There were a couple of advantages for me to be in this type of business. The application of the technology did not require a high level of English skills or proficiency in English, which should have less impact on my ability to get my business off the ground. Chinese students, including myself, were known for our ability to do research using current technologies. This, of course, included analytical testing services.

Having decided the direction of my start-up business, I turned my attention to learning and mastering analytical techniques as soon as possible. I used every opportunity I had with my daily work to understand the laboratory testing business and technology. I paid attention to the market that our laboratory was serving, the laboratory information technology, and the instruments used. Even if there were some tests or technologies in which I was not involved, I still found ways to ask questions and to learn. My goal was to learn more skills through all possible channels and means that would be related to what I would be doing in my business in the near future.

I devoted considerable attention to the repair and maintenance of analytical equipment. Whenever I had opportunity, I disassembled and installed columns, changed filters, and repaired equipment. In addition to analysis, I performed sample preparation, which was done mostly by technicians and analytical methods development. Within about six months on my job, I was not only able to perform independent testing but also simple repair and maintenance of the gas chromatograph.

Meanwhile, I used my spare time to learn the basics of chromatographic techniques. I learned techniques from an analytical chemistry book. I found that application manuals and technical bulletins from the original equipment manufacturers contained a lot of excellent analytical methods, equipment usage, and repair techniques. By reading these books and product bulletins, I was able to accumulate analytical knowledge and chemistry techniques, which was particularly valuable when I applied it to my day-to-day operation. This, no doubt, gave me greater confidence in my business start-up.

As I made progress in learning business and testing technology, other issues emerged. How to find capital for the start-up was one of them. Analytical testing service requires an appropriate laboratory platform that includes many expensive analytical instrumentations. Without capital, how could I start up this laboratory?

My limited hard-earned cash of about $50,000 might seemed to be substantial. But this money was only about one-tenth of the cost of a decent start-up laboratory platform. Adding to this challenge was that we could not put all into my business venture because we had a family to raise. We worked so hard and saved this money with one primary mission in mind: to create a good environment for our children to succeed. It was obvious that we had to put away some of the money for this mission.

Purchasing our dream home in 1993 did not help with my finances. We had a down payment of about $12,000, which reduced our cash to barely $40,000. This amount of money would buy me one instrument. Yet one piece of equipment wouldn't form a laboratory platform for the business I proposed. Therefore, from the summer of 1993, I was deeply concerned about money day and night.

My wife took care of our money. Although I knew the approximate amount of savings we had, what I knew for sure was the $10,000 I invested in the stock market. One day, I asked my wife about our bank saving and checking accounts. She appeared to be expecting this day and answered that it was about $30–40K. She turned the question around by asking me how much I would want in my business. I told her that all that money wouldn't be enough. Not even waiting until I finished my answer, she immediately, with her eyes focused toward me, disagreed by saying no. She continued saying that "if we spent it all, how could we raise our two sons and support their schooling?"

"How much could we use for our business?" I asked.

"Probably about half, or about $20K," she said. Yes, I agreed with her because we had to save some money for our sons' education and major unexpected events. I clearly understood that my business start-up was a high-risk venture. If I was not successful, how could the family survive without any savings? Therefore, I must find a way to get capital from other sources.

There are a number of ways for a new entrepreneur to obtain start-up capitals. The most common ones are from the personal saving; borrowing from friends, parents, and relatives; and from venture capital investment and bank loans. The US government also provides funds to start-ups for innovation research and technology transfer known as Small Business Innovation Research (SBIR) and Small Business Technology Transfer (STTR), which I did not know about at the time. The grants from US government is free money, and there is no cost to the entrepreneur, if one can obtain it.

Cash investment from the entrepreneur is an integral part of total capital requirement. This is especially important for the first-time entrepreneur because all bank loan officers and venture capitalists are very serious about owner's investment. They evaluate the quality of a business start-up with emphasis on what commitment the business owners have made toward their business venture. When owners are willing to put their own money, sometimes all of it or most of it, into their business and when their personal assets are closely tied with their business, the loan officers or venture capitalists often see it as a strong commitment by owners, and they might be more inclined to provide funding. In contrast, if business owners do not want to take risk with their own money, banks and venture capital firms generally would not fund any business plan by new entrepreneurs. There is exception to this generalization wherein experienced and successful entrepreneur might be closely followed by a money manager, even if no owner's money is invested. Unfortunately, that was not for me because I was a poor college graduate with no business experience. Consequently, I had to show the financial institutions my strong commitment to my business venture. I did this by putting $20,000, 40 percent of my whole savings, into my business. This was a testament of my character and determination to take on the risk as a new entrepreneur.

Borrowing money from friends and relatives has been an effective approach commonly used by many entrepreneurs. In the business world, many friends, relatives, and parents are wealthy; and they frequently lend their money to new businesses, especially their relatives and family members, such as sons and daughters. Their capital is often later converted to company shares. However, this was not applicable to me because I knew few friends in the US, and the ones I knew were poor students with minimal saving. It was difficult for me to ask these friends for money because of the high risk of my business venture. In case of failure, it would be hard for me to return the money I borrowed, and I really did not want to lose my few friends. Besides, even if any of my friends were willing to lend me money, the few thousand dollars they had would not provide much help for setting up my laboratory. Therefore, borrowing money from my friends and relatives did not fit my circumstances at all.

Start-up funds of many small business come from the United States government. The United States, in 1982, passed the Small Business Innovation Development Act, which has played an important role in American business development. The Congress each year passes a legislation to provide funding to support innovative enterprises. For several decades, this small business support funding has helped build many successful high-tech enterprises. Because the technology innovation and technology transfer are the core of this government funding program, most recipients of the funds (SBIR and STTR) have been high-tech engineers and university professors, including graduate students and postdoctoral fellows. Unfortunately, I knew little about this funding program. Of course, even if I had known it, I might not have the technology that would qualify me for funding.

The opportunity for venture capital funding is enormous in the US. In this US capitalistic society, the more successful you are, the more likely you are to get venture capital (VC) funding. Sometimes, the capital follows you wherever you go if you are an extremely successful business person. In contrast, if you have no experience and it is the first time you are in the business start-up with no successful history to show or if you have failed in your past business, it is much harder to access venture capital. In addition to credibility and success of the entrepreneur, the technology in the business is also important. VC companies often want entrepreneurs to have patented technologies, excellent market prospects, and great market potential in order to achieve a successful investment. Because of the high risk involved for VC investment, they expect a return of several times, and even hundreds of times, the money invested. It was unfortunate that what I wanted to do in my business plan did not fit any of these criteria established by the VCs. I did not have any technology, especially patented technology. Our service market was limited with market potential, as well as return on capital, both relatively small and slow.

Since the channels for obtaining start-up capital from borrowing from friends, SBIR, or venture capital were unlikely for my business, the only option left for me was to borrow money from a bank. I kept my hopes up when I realized that the Small Business Administration (SBA), an agency of the US government, provides support to entrepreneurs and their small businesses. SBA loans are made through banks, credit unions, and other lenders who partner with the SBA. The SBA provides a government-backed guarantee on part of the loan. Because the risk to banks was lessened, I felt that SBA-guaranteed loan was my best option. However, in order to have success getting a loan, I needed to develop a convincing business plan.

Now my top priority was on my business plan, a job that I had never thought about. I did not have any basic business knowledge about writing business plan, so I had to learn quickly how to do it. To take on this, I borrowed two business books from the Penn State University library about how to start up a new business and how to write a business plan. Because I was still working at CAL, I read these books in the evenings and on weekends. These books gave me the basic understanding on the business start-up issues and procedures; however, several key issues in the business plan remained unsolved, such as what our service was, pesticide residue testing and/or environmental testing, who our management team and our marketing director were, what our marketing advantages and competitive strengths were, where our company should be located, and how much money should be borrowed, etc. All these issues had to be answered because they were indispensable to our business plan. I must find answers to all these questions before I could complete the plan.

My initial thought of owning my business started by the end of 1992, when I left the Penn State University for CAL. However, the final decision for setting up an independent testing laboratory was not made until the summer of 1993. Although I then set my eyes on laboratory services for environmental and pesticide residue testing, my decision was made not based on a detailed market analysis and the careful consideration of all related issues, but instead, it was solely based on the business situation and performance of the laboratory I was working for at the time. It was just because of this light and careless attitude that I misjudged the market badly that led to the difficulty of getting my company off the ground later.

As an immigrant without business experience, coupled with my less-than-fluent English, I did not have confidence in sales and marketing. I spoke to a colleague during lunch one day about the key person who was a contributor to the success of the company. He answered, without any hesitation, "The marketing director." I wondered and asked him, Why not the owner/founder? He said that in the establishment, the founder was more important, but now that the company was in its rapid growing stage, the person who could bring in business was more important than other employees. His argument appeared to be reasonable and convincing.

Indeed, this assessment had been described in all type of business books written about many successful businesses. As a result, I concluded that my start-up required an American native speaker to serve as the marketing director. Otherwise, it would be difficult to be successful. Discrimination in society, especially toward Chinese immigrants, would add to the challenge; and the lack of business experience with limited social connections in the US were my serious shortcomings as well.

To make up for these shortages, I started looking for a market director, but as we all know, a good marketing manager often demands a high wage and good benefits. This requirement would make it difficult for my start-up company to pay. Simply put, I wanted to save money in the early establishment and did not have a budget to pay for this position at all. Therefore, I had to consider either of two possible scenarios. First, I could employ a part-time marketing person who would be holding a regular job and would be willing to work one or two hours each day to market our services. I would pay this person a combination of basic salary, plus a higher commission rate and more incentives. If it worked out, I could convert this position to a marketing director and business partner later. The second option would be to partner with someone who could be the director of business development, hoping that this partner would, like me, accept minimal pay in order to ease the pressure on capital requirements in the start-up phase.

I first started searching for this marketing person or business partner among my colleagues and circle of my friends. It did not take long for me to realize that this kind of person did not exist, even if I extended my search to other regions. In June of 1993, I placed an advertisement in a newspaper named *News Gazette* in Champaign, Illinois, where I had chosen to build our laboratory. This advertisement described the criteria and qualification of the candidates and was published for a week. It did not yield any application for this position. Although the outcome was somewhat expected, I still did not feel good about it because now the two options to hire a marketing director did not work out. This led me to the third, the last option that was not really an option but rather a forced-on-me option.

This third option was actually somewhat expected. I knew from the beginning that our company did not have the resources or capital to attract a good candidate, especially one with the qualification I had expected. I had no choice but to accept the fact that I had to do it all myself. In order to meet this challenge as early as possible, I again began reading books written about marketing, and I made full use of free SBA consultants who were associated with the SCORE Association (counselors to America's small businesses). SCORE is a nonprofit association comprised of thirteen thousand-plus volunteer business counselors throughout the US and its territories who are trained to serve as counselors, advisers, and mentors to aspiring entrepreneurs and business owners.

In addition, I tried to learn directly from Mr. Hu, who had successfully established and developed his laboratory service in Baltimore, Maryland. I knew Mr. Hu by the introduction of one of my friends. Mr. Hu was also an immigrant from China whose laboratory provided contract study and testing to pharmaceutical industry for drug development. He was very successful in his business venture and by 1994, his laboratory occupied about twenty thousand square feet and had about sixty employees.

One day in the summer of 1993, I gave Mr. Hu a call, and he was somewhat surprised. After I introduced myself and told him that I planned to set up my laboratory soon, he expressed his willingness to help, but he said that "based on your current situation with only a few months on the current job, with no prior experience working in industry, you really haven't learned much about the business and the technology yet. It would be too abrupt to start up now."

I told him that "my employer company is performing so well and the testing technology is not difficult."

He responded, "What you have seen is only the surface and the like but understanding why and how small businesses succeed is far more than just being able to do a few experiments. Every new business faces full challenges, including finance, marketing, technical, and management aspects. To learn all this is many years of hard work and experience, therefore, to hurry up to start your business is very dangerous." At the end, he suggested that staying with the job for two or three years to acquire more business skills and testing techniques before setting up my own shop would be a wise idea.

Indeed, the more I listened to him, the more I felt that his suggestion was reasonable and made sense. Even so, I still did not want to follow it. It was obvious that I was a little naive, which was probably common novice behavior during the transition from student to employee of industry. Everybody knows that a few months were simply too short a time to learn a new industry and the techniques involved. However, the way I judged things was completely outside the ordinary. Of course, I was anxious or rushed to set up my company because of another reason: I was in my forty years of age. My best and most energetic age to start my company would soon pass me. I was in a race against my time and my age!

To set up a company, I needed a register agent and address to complete the registration process. This should be a simple question for most people, but it was not for me. I definitely wanted to consider two key factors: best for my business and my family. Good business and entrepreneurship environment is important for a start-up. Because business is not for all our life, a place good for living and education is equally important as well.

In considering the family life and education for our kids, I asked my wife for her advice. I knew that she had limited knowledge about US cities, so I did not expect any good suggestions in other geological locations other than the ones where we had been. Because I did not know much about other cities, all that I wanted was for her to give me her choice of a city among those where we lived during the past ten years.

There were only a handful of cities my wife knew. Her preference was Champaign-Urbana. The reason she picked this city was because she felt that the city was small enough, about twenty minutes driving from east to west and from south to the north, but big enough with a rich culture because of the University of Illinois and more than one hundred thousand population. It was one of the safest city with relatively low crime rate and with minimal race discrimination. In addition, the city was only two to three hours to the major metropolitan cities of Chicago, Indianapolis, and St. Louis.

The twin cities was the place for my first postdoctoral research. My impression was that most people at the city worked as professionals. There were many students from around the world and a good portion from China. My family had lived here for two years and had established good relationships with a number of friends, especially several university professors, including the chair of the department of plant biology. These relationships might give our business a helping hand, which indeed proved to be the case a few years later.

In addition to the easy life and the children's education, the city had a lot to offer as well. The low cost of living is one advantage for a start-up company because a new company usually has limited capital and lower payroll expense, which are important factors to consider. I knew this was critical for us since I would do anything I could to save pennies.

Another advantage was that in order to grow a company, a source of qualified employees is critical. The University of Illinois would provide a potential source for recruiting technical candidates. An analytical laboratory uses modern technology, and access to technical assistants is critically important. Testing service laboratories require methods and published peer-review papers that are available from the library of the university. The abundance of library materials and its accessibility was particularly useful in 1994 when internet was not as developed as it is today.

During the process of our site selection, I had considered the city of State College, Pennsylvania. We had lived in this city for more than two years and had established friend circles. More importantly, we just moved into our dream home, and we were happy with the city that offered us an easy life and safety.

To evaluate this option, I approached SCORE for help. After thoroughly discussing the pros and cons for this site, the SCORE counselor suggested to me that it was not an ideal city for my company. The counselor explained that generally it is not a good idea to establish a business at the same place that would directly compete with a previous employer. The rationale behind this suggestion was that as a start-up, my company would be in a weak competitive position. The existing laboratory might do what they could to compete with us. This fierce competition could lead to an extremely challenging environment for us. At the end, the existing company would come out as a winner while my start-up would have difficulty surviving. Although the expert's analysis was obvious and easy to understand, I still did not get it until I was a boss myself a few years later.

While considering the city of State College, I also looked at Washington, DC, and its beltway cities. One of best beneficial factors for being in the region was its proximity to many national government agencies. As we know, the government is a big buyer of services through its various agencies, especially since it has many projects that required setting aside a portion of the total project cost for small businesses. Relevant to our proposed business would be testing superfund contaminated samples from EPA projects. As a small and minority-owned business, our company was classified as an economically disadvantaged small business and was qualified to be a subcontractor for large corporations for national projects. In general, it is only with the small business set-aside that the small businesses have an opportunity to win a portion of major projects. This had to be the main reason for me to consider my business location near Washington, DC.

Another reason for me to consider the DC area was to recruit a business partner. I had a good friend working in Smithsonian Museum. He was an energetic person with personal characters similar to mine. I asked him to join my company as partner, which later proved to be unrealistic. I also realized that there were many small- to medium-size companies in the area, which could provide us with more business opportunities and partnerships. However, after driving through the area a couple of times to search for laboratories, I didn't like it. It was an expensive area to start a business because the cost of living was high.

When I visited Frederick, Bethesda, Gaithersburg, and Rockville, Maryland, areas, I experienced all kinds of traffic jam problems. Even if it took about thirty to forty minutes of driving from Frederick to DC, it took me more than an hour. Needless to say, my wife was afraid of traffic jams. Plus, I could spend at least an hour or more on the road daily, which I felt should be spent on my business.

The high cost of living would be a major burden on small business startups. This would be particular important for our laboratory because we had a severe lack of capital. All these pros and cons led me to conclude that the DC area was not a suitable place for locating our laboratory. Looking back at this decision, I felt that my judgments at the time did not apply objective evaluation. A proper selection of a company headquarter location is much more than traffic and the living cost index. The business environment, access to capital, and qualified employees, as well as convenience to customers are all very important to the success of a start-up company.

After about two months of consideration, I finally decided on the location of my business to be at Champaign, Illinois. In 1993, my family took a trip from State College to Champaign, pretending it to be a vacation trip to attend Qigong class, while in fact, the purpose was to do a marketing survey, to look for laboratory space, and to hire a marketing director.

Guided by a local real estate agent, we visited several buildings to determine if they were suitable for laboratory use. For a standard laboratory, we required bench tables, cabinets, fume hoods, adequate water, and electricity. Because there were fewer chemical and biotechnology laboratories at Champaign-Urbana and surrounding areas, it was rare for a construction company to build this kind of facility. To our surprise, we found a suitable laboratory building at Savoy Village, Champaign County.

That laboratory was built in the 1980s and hosted an agricultural biotechnology company until 1992. The building, in addition to offices, consisted of several quality laboratories totaling about four thousand square feet. The landlord agreed to rent only one laboratory of about seven hundred square feet for stage 1. We had the option to expand to another laboratory space as needed. This kind of flexibility was exactly what I looked for.

In addition to looking for lab space, I visited a few potential customers with whom I had set up appointments prior to the trip. I discussed with them our plans and hoped they would use our testing service. This was my first taste of marketing, and I was glad to receive two verbal commitments from the group of small companies I visited. This had indeed given me a little more confidence and more weight in my business plan, which would be finished later.

The third purpose of my trip was to put an advertisement in the newspaper about our search for a marketing director. I visited the Champaign *New Gazette* office. For this advertisement, I made a terrible mistake because I used the fax number of CAL where I was working to send my ad to *News Gazette* without any identifying information included. After the ad was posted, the *News Gazette* sent a fax of the ad using the fax number of my original fax. The ad information was exposed to the management of CAL.

It was quite a surprise for the company's owner to receive this fax. The owner called me into his office, with his face showing anger and disappointment. "Charlie, what's going on? You've got to be crazy! You are so naive and did not know how much money you would need to set up a lab. You have no idea how hard it is to do this laboratory! If you don't have $500,000 or more, don't even think that you could set up your laboratory."

I knew that I was wrong, plus my boss had hypertension. Therefore, I avoided answer his question directly but instead said, "Sorry, please forgive me for such an action without consulting with you."

I knew I could not forgive myself because this mistake led to a number of problems right away. I severely underestimate the challenging position I was in. I had no money, no technology, no market, and even no marketing person for my proposed business. Because I apologized to my boss, he still held hopes for me. He said, "If you give up doing your own laboratory, I would just let it go and take it as if nothing has happened."

After coming home from work, I talked to my wife. "What are we going to do now? If I want to do my own company, I must immediately leave the company, and you should, without exception, as well." My wife and I had had no intention of leaving the company this soon.

So she brought an unhappy face toward me and said, "Why were you careless? You exposed everything so early. There is not much we can do now unless you give up on setting up your laboratory."

Giving it up without a fight was not really in my DNA. I am a person who, once decided to do something, would continue until I reach the goal. My wife knows me well on this because, if we used an old saying in Chinese, "nine cattle can't pull it back." Therefore, she encouraged me by saying that "we should go ahead. 'A good horse will not eat grass left behind.' If you don't do it now, it would be even harder to make up your mind in the future."

That night, my mind was at a loss, my heart was beating faster, and I could not calm myself. The middle of autumn season was supposed to be good for life. But to me, I was hurt with a welted eye. I could not fall asleep the whole night.

As usual, I went to work the next morning. I told my boss that "since I have taken my first step, it is time for me to move on. If you want me to leave the company now, I have no objection."

My boss looked at me with a puzzled face and said, "Well, since you have chosen not to give it up, there would be no need to continue coming to work. You go to the accounting office to receive your wages, payable to the end of the month."

I returned to my office, put my belongings into a box, and then, under the eyes of my colleagues, walked out of the laboratory building. The more I thought of this, the deeper was the feeling I had for my boss. It was not easy for him to see an employee leave like this. He had done everything he could as a boss and as an owner. As expected, my wife was also let go a couple of months later.

By now, everything was a foregone conclusion. I recalled the challenges I had had up to this point in my life. None could be comparable to this one. I was so depressed that I felt like there was a mountain of pressure on me, making it hard for me to breathe. Now both my wife and I had lost our jobs, and there was no more income for us.

If it were just for me, it might be easier to deal with because a few pieces of bread might get me through the day, but now it was for a family of four. How could we survive without income? We needed food, the kids needed to go to school, we had a mortgage to pay, and many more things needed money each month.

In addition, our company was still a remote idea. We had not obtained any commitment of investment in our company, and we had no idea if we were qualified for a bank loan. If we could not get any investment or a loan, how could we start our company with just our own $20,000? Adding to this puzzle was the fact that I had no experience in business, and whether I could get my company started was still questionable. I felt completely blank and could not even taste my food for a while. In retrospect, this was really quite a scary period of time for me.

But "once the bow was released, there was no way for the arrow to turn back." Since I chose this road, I had to take it with the mind-set that there was no way of backing out. I asked myself a bunch of questions. For example, Is there still a chance if I don't do it now? If so, in the future, will I regret not taking action now? Why am I not capable of starting a business while others are?

I was constantly concerned about something, which was like the old Chinese saying, "Losing shoulders with loss of wife." Because of this decision, my wife and I had many sleepless nights. This hardship lasted for several weeks, and during this difficult time, we comforted each other until we were finally able to settle down. In the end, we decided that "without success is to fight to die," which was the strongest testament of our stand.

Along the way, during my attempt to make up the lack of capital, I tried to find an investment partner. If I were successful in this route, I could solve the most difficult problem, shortage of money. I contacted an environmental testing laboratory in Williamsburg, Pennsylvania, about fifty miles north of State College. The owner of the laboratory was Rod, and his laboratory had been in business since the mid-1980s. It provided environmental testing service with about ten to fifteen employees.

One day in November 1993, I met with Rod. After he introduced me to his lab, we sat down in his small conference room for a discussion. I thanked Rod for his interest, and I was given the opportunity to introduce myself and my business plan. I told him about my personal experience. I emphasized the market potential and told him why he and I should work together for my business plan. Rod appeared to be interested in what I presented. He was a straightforward person and immediately posed a question to me by asking, "Why would I be interested in your proposal?"

I knew his laboratory had no service offering a pesticide testing service, which was one of the brightest market segment for environmental testing laboratories. I replied, "Because I could bring in pesticide residue testing services to the laboratory, which is complementary to your current laboratory." I also told him that the business in our laboratory was now excellent because of the large projects outsourced to us from major chemical companies.

Of course, Rod knew this. Pesticide residue contracts from chemical companies were a high-profit business. However, he was doubtful about my ability to obtain these clients. He asked me how I could bring in the projects. This was a difficult question but a logical one for me because I did not know if I could and I could not make this promise by saying the experience I had or the connections with chemical companies I had established.

After Rod learned more about me and my experience in pesticide testing and method validation, he asked, "How are we going to cooperate?"

At this point, I thought to myself that he seemed interested in my project, so I answered him unequivocally, "I hope you would invest in my business plan, and I'll carry and execute it."

"How much does it cost?" he asked.

"About $150,000 or so." Obliviously, my number was a rough estimate. When I answered this question, I felt that the new venture would use his current laboratory facility and a lot of the start-up cost would be omitted or minimized. Under this assumption, we would just need one gas chromatograph and one gas chromatography-mass spectrometer, plus my salary.

I was excited because everything seemed going smoothly. Then, Rod got to the hard part of the discussion. He said, "Let me consider using my laboratory credit to help the new unit borrow $200,000 to establish the laboratory."

Not even waiting for the completion of his offer, I was almost jumping in joy by this prospect. However, next came the hard part. He wanted 80 percent of the ownership, and I would have 20 percent. He indicated that I could still receive the salary equivalent to what I was making before. He spoke about this to me with authority.

This proposal caught me by surprise because I had never thought about this distribution ratio. I wanted to do this business so badly. How could I accept only a 20 percent of the business, especially since the money provided to the laboratory would not be from Rod's own pocket but from a loan to the unit and we would need to pay the money back by proceeds from the new laboratory? I considered that Rod had gotten more of a share than it should be, so it resulted in the discussion ending without any verbal agreement.

After I returned home, I let my wife know of the outcome. Just like me, she felt very disappointed. This unsuccessful attempt did not help ease the pressure, but it added additional pressure on us because my plan to seek a partner was a failed attempt.

For this reason, I phoned Mr. Hu again for his help and his suggestions. I told him what had happened about meeting with Rod and my disagreement with the ownership ratio. I asked him what the appropriate ownership for my share should be when I brought the technology and the possible market.

He helped me analyze the situation and said, "For a technical share, 15–20 percent was the norm. If the technology was patented and unique, it could be more. Otherwise, 10 percent was still quite common in the marketplace. The technology you have is not unique because everyone can learn to use it. Therefore, 15 percent is plenty."

I still did not want to believe this and asked him, "If the company is successful, then Rod would take the 80 percent for nothing since the $200K would be repaid by the company and not by him."

Mr. Hu obviously knew this question beforehand because an entrepreneur without experience often had similar thoughts. He then emphasized to me, "Yes, you only see the successful side of the new business but ignore the fact that 95 percent of all new businesses are failures in the first three years. Rod uses his credit to borrow this money, and he will have to guarantee the loan with personal assets. If the business failed, he would be responsible for paying back the loan."

I remained calm without further expression. Mr. Hu was afraid I was misunderstanding his points. He explained, "If it were you taking such high risk for this venture and could not have a controlling interest and did not have the authority, what would you do, and would you continue the cooperation?"

His explanation enlightened me because I was convinced that it was a naive idea to ask for a controlling interest of the company based on what I could offered at this time.

I asked Mr. Hu what I should do. He replied, "You should be happy to own 15–20 percent, since you will receive your salary. If the company fails, you can take off without saying goodbye to him. On the other hand, if it is successful, your ownership would be enough to make you a rich person as well."

I went back to Rod the next day and told him that I accepted his proposal of 20 percent ownership with his borrowing of $200,000 for the company. Unfortunately, he was no longer interested in this venture. I don't know the reason behind this, but the most likely explanation would be that he would no longer considered me the right partner to work with.

The twists and turns in seeking a business partner without a good outcome struck me hard. The pressure on me continued to build. I was now left with only one option, and that was to apply for a bank loan. If I could not get this loan, I would be left with only my own $20,000 to start up a testing laboratory. Although I thought about using this small amount of money to start up, the monumental challenge to me was hard to imagine. At this point, I knew I must carefully prepare my business plan and hope to increase my chances of getting a business loan.

In order to write this business plan, I first decided the minimal amount of capital that was required. This capital would come from two parts: my own investment and the bank loan. However, the questions of how much funding would be needed and how much I could borrow, along with what would be terms of the loan and how the funds would be used were completely new to me. One thing that was clear was that I should ask a minimal amount of the loan because as a first-time entrepreneur, I did not have any credentials to help me obtain a large loan. I must use the lowest capital investment to get started. I did a thoroughly careful evaluation of the various costs such as lab equipment, glassware, chemicals, reference analytical standards. I needed two gas chromatographs, one equipped with electronic capture detector (ECD) for pesticide analysis and the other with photoionization detector (PID) and flame ionization detector (FID) detector for hydrocarbons and fatty acid analyses respectively. With these two instruments, I could analyze most organic contaminants of environmental samples and pesticide residues for pesticides projects.

In order to save money, I could only consider buying old, secondhand instruments, with a budget of about $50,000 to $60,000. There were plenty of other minor and routinely used instruments to be purchased, plus many chemicals and reference standards, with a total budget of about $15,000. The rent and utility would be less than $10,000. Principal and interest on loan would be about $20,000. I also planned for six-month working capital at $10,000. I felt that I needed a total investment of about $110,000. In addition to my own investment of $20,000, I still needed a loan of $90,000 from the bank.

In this simple estimate, I did not add my full salary compensation, but instead I added a small portion for family living purposes. It was clear to me that I could not pay myself a decent salary in the first year or two. This has been very common among the first-time entrepreneurs. Indeed, I had made up my mind that I was willing to work for two to three years free for this business. If it was not successful, it would be as if I were giving myself a few years of vacation. If it was successful, I would receive many times, or even hundreds of times, the amount I had invested. Such a high risk and high return ratio has been the norm of a lot of entrepreneurships.

With this basic amount of funding requirements, the next step was how to present it in the business plan in order to make sure that a bank official would see it as a reasonable and convincing business plan. The business plan included several major parts such as service scope, competitive advantages, the organization leadership, operational plan, and the financial plan. With the help and advice from a SCORE consultant, I applied my personal experience and knowledge, as well as the marketing information I had gathered for my plan. I did it step by step, section by section, chapter by chapter, really like a blind person moving through a river in slow, hesitant touching steps. I went back and forth many times.

After several months of my part-time effort, in December of 1993, I finally completed the draft of the business plan. This plan was forwarded to the consultant of SCORE for review and suggestions. The consultant gave an OK to my business draft with a number of suggestions. I was pleased with the positive assessment, and I revised the plan according to the suggestions provided in a couple of meetings with SCORE. By the end of February of 1994, the business plan was finally ready for submission.

My business plan started with an executive summary that summarized the main points from the business plan in a concise one to two pages. The aim of the summary was to achieve the attention of bank loan officers and, in three to five minutes, to answer the questions of market, technology, who, competitive advantage, and so on.

An important question addressed in the plan was the market we would serve. We had decided on environmental testing and pesticide residues analysis. Full analysis and market potential of these two market segments were discussed. This analysis included the competition and our competitive advantages. In fact, this portion of the plan was not easy for me because the reality was that we had fewer advantages compared to competitors, which led to the general description without hard evidence.

The operation plan was a relatively easy portion in the plan in terms of writing since I just needed to put down what I would do with my company. However, because it would be a one-man-show laboratory, I sometimes felt that anyone reading it might feel it boring. Nevertheless, in additional to myself, I included my wife in the plan plus a to-be-hired marketing director. The organization structure like this has to be typical for the first-time entrepreneurs without funding in place.

In my final part of my business plan was the financial operation. The projections of financial data are standard in every plan. I spent a lot of time on this part, and I could not even know how I was able to come up with several sets of data for projection of monthly income and balance sheet. When it was done, I was greatly relieved. The entire business plan was twenty-five pages long.

Our business plan was used for application for a small business loan. The US government had set up SBA loan programs specifically for small businesses in many banks across the nation. The SBA's primary lending program—the

7(a) Loan Program—guarantees as much as 85 percent of loans up to $150,000. By partnering with SBA, financial institutions accept, review, and approve independent loan applications from small business owners. Because of the SBA-guaranteed loan, the loss to the financial institution was limited to 15 percent of the total loan amount should a business fail. Because there is still some risk to the borrower, this interest provides the incentive for the financial institution to maintain the loan standards. On the other hand, the SBA-guaranteed loan reduces the risk to the lending company, which could ease the constraints and lending standards somewhat, making the loan possible to a small business. Otherwise, many small business owners wouldn't be able to obtain a conventional loan. The cooperation between private companies and the government has helped small business success possible.

Because I was still in Pennsylvania, there were some issues during my loan application. My company was to be established in Champaign, Illinois, applying to a bank at State College, Pennsylvania. This made it harder to be accepted by the banks at State College. If the loan were approved, then it would be very inconvenient to manage the loan in the future. Therefore, I tried to find a bank with a nationwide network and, especially, with locations at both State College and Champaign; but these banks were not in existence at the time. Mellon Bank was a regional bank but had no branch in Champaign. Nevertheless, I submitted my loan application to Mellon Bank, which denied the loan in just a week or so. This bank suggested that I borrow money from my relatives and friends to get started before applying to them again.

At the same time, I submitted applications to three banks in Champaign, Illinois, which included my personal financial statements. Among them, two banks seriously considered my business plan. They were First American Bank and Busey Bank.

In March of 1994, I drove more than ten hours nonstop from State College to Champaign for an interview with the two banks. On the way back to Pennsylvania, I ran into a very dense fog with rain and a visibility of only twenty-five to fifty-meter distance. I was frightened that evening while driving in the rain and fog that lasted for more than half hour.

The first interview was set for the morning with Busey Bank, a small local community bank with good reputation. I gave a brief introduction about myself and why I wanted to do this business. After a more detail discussion about my business plan, the loan officer asked, "Have you done marketing research?"

I replied, "Yes, I have."

He continued, "Do you know whether the environmental testing market is good or bad?"

"Yes, my understanding of the market is largely based on the Pennsylvania market, especially from our company's current business I have been seeing on a daily basis," I replied to the officer. By this point, I got a feeling that this officer might have known a lot about the environmental testing market.

This suspicion was indeed confirmed when he posed his next question, "Even though I don't doubt your ability, your proposed business is too challenging and too difficult due to the shrinking of the overall market." Apparently, his knowledge and information about the trend of environmental testing market was from a local environmental engineering company. His judgment on the market was indeed confirmed later by my company with the difficulty of business development.

The unapproved loan application by Busey Bank was a blow to my confidence. Because I had had no loan experience, this rejection made me wonder how bank officers evaluate each business plan. Since I knew that each loan officer might have different opinions about the market, I was hoping that the second bank, First American Bank, would reach a different conclusion than the Busey Bank.

My appointment was set for the afternoon on the same day as the Busey Bank. I met the bank loan officer named Kirdiz, who was probably about thirty to thirty-five years old. I sat down in his office with some nervousness. To my surprise, the officer asked me if I would like a drink. I did not know how to respond to his offer, so the best way was to decline. Our conversation was started just as that with Busey Bank, but to my surprise, after my presentation, the loan officer said that my business plan was well written, providing clear and convincing evidence to a certain extent, and that he liked it very much. One day many years later, Kirdiz asked me to allow him to use my business plan as a model for other entrepreneurs.

The assessment and conclusion from Kirdiz immediately made me excited. All I could say at the time was, "Thank you, thank you." Furthermore, I honorably said to him, "This is my first business plan. I had to learn it by trial and error. I am glad you like it."

I wondered whether this bank officer knew the environmental testing market or if he saw something different that the officer at Busey Bank didn't see. He said, "I like your personality and your willingness to risk your hard-earned savings in your business, which indicates you are prepared and ready to face the challenge."

"Yes, sir, I am ready and willing to work very hard to make my company successful," I replied with determination.

Even if the borrowing was an SBA loan, the lending standards for every bank remains high. If a business plan does not meet the criteria, no loan would be given. By the same token, every loan requires some kind of collateral or a guarantee with either cash or valuable personal assets. If the start-up business fails, the bank would try to recover as much as it can. The common collateral may include business assets such as equipment and account receivables or private property, such as cars, gold, bank accounts, stocks, and real estate. Kirdiz made no exception to my loan and said that "we need you to guarantee this loan personally, and I hope you would agree."

There was no choice for me but to agree to his request for the collateral. Kirdiz asked me the types of collateral I could provide. I agreed to include my 1994 Subaru Legacy and my stock market account with a current market value of altogether about $32,000–$35,000. Of course, my company assets, including laboratory equipment and account, would be a part of the collateral. A simple mathematic calculation indicated that if my business failed, I would lose at least $50,000 to $60,000. By comparison, the loss of the bank was limited to 15 percent, less than $14,000, since SBA guaranteed 85 percent of my $90,000 loan.

From the preparation to the approval of my business loan, it took about ten months. My hard work was finally yielding results. I received the $90,000 loan from the First American Bank, which was with my personal investment of $20,000, making a total of $110,000. This was my start-up capital, and I hoped that this money could help me realize my dream.

Although the loan interest may vary from bank to bank, in general, SBA loans are set at 2.5–3.0 percent higher than the prime rate as published in *Wall Street Journal*. My loan was an 8.75 percent eight-year loan, or 2.5 percent higher than the prime rate of 6.25 percent. There was a fee to the bank at about 1 percent and a 2 percent fee to SBA for the loan guarantee. For my $90K loan, about $2,700 was taken out at closing. Just like every other commercial loan, the total loan is divided into categories, each for a specific purpose. For example, our loan was divided into the purchase of fixed asset equipment, inventory of chemicals and standards, and working capital at a ratio of approximately $55,000, $25,000, and $10,000 respectively. The monthly payment of both principal and interest was $1,300. There was another restriction on how to obtain and use the fund. Every time I needed the money, I had to apply in advance with the reason of why, how much, and when needed. I signed the loan on May 16, 1994.

Obtaining this loan made me feel happy about my accomplishment for a moment. However, the next question was more than enough to make me dizzy. With this small amount of money, how could I establish a laboratory platform that normally would require half a million dollars in a standard business plan? It was obvious that I had to use an unconventional approach to equip our laboratory.

Although the loan application did not require a legal company name and address, the company must be incorporated and a federal employment identification number (FEIN) was necessary for closing a business loan. Along the way of my business plan preparation, I also paid attention to the incorporation process of my company. There were several different types of businesses under which I could incorporate: C-corporation, S-corporation, limited liability company, partnership, professional service, and sole proprietary. In deciding the type of the company for my business, I consulted with the SCORE and finally decided to adopt an S-corporation, which was determined to be most suited for my company. Most private and publicly traded companies are C-corp. The advantage of C-corp is that there is no personal liability involved. The major drawback is the double taxation, a tax is paid before distribution of dividends by the corporation and a tax paid by the individuals after receiving the dividends. Partnerships and proprietary companies have the best tax advantages but the greatest personal responsibility for the owners. However, an S-corp is in between these two types of companies, with minimal personal liability and taxed only once. No matter how much money an S-corp makes, the profit is passed to the owners who report to IRS in their annual filing of personal income tax.

Regarding the US taxation, I especially admire the tax laws for small businesses. For instance, if the company loses money in a given year, the entrepreneur does not pay any federal income tax in that year. In addition, the loss amount can be passed to the next year for tax filling. If the company is profitable in the succeeding year, the entrepreneur can subtract the loss from previous year before paying taxes. If the next year is still a loss, it can be carried forward to a third year and so on. This tax carried forward for the loss in reporting federal income tax is called tax loss carryforward. In contrast to this is the tax loss carryback. This method allows an entrepreneur to claim the taxes paid the previous year using the tax loss in the current year. It can be carried back for two years. Because most entrepreneurs often experience cash shortages during the start-up phase and are sometimes under tremendous pressure to make their start-up work, they are most likely to select the tax loss carryback method. However, one has to be aware that each person can have only one selection, either tax loss carryforward or tax loss ward. Once the selection is made, there is no way to change it. As most entrepreneur often do, we work very hard, day in and day out, on our businesses. We worked sixteen hours a day because we don't want to fail in our business. When we are successful in making a profit, we pay a higher tax rate (sometimes much higher) than those of the tax loss carryback. Such tax system is actually a very smart way to get an entrepreneur to work hard, but it also allows the government to receive more taxes from successful entrepreneurs.

To complete the company registration process, I had multiple options. I could hire a law firm to help incorporate my company for the cost of about $1,000–$5,000 for the incorporation service. I could hire a consulting company to complete the registration for me at a cost of about $1,000. This is especially true if I selected the state of Delaware to incorporate my business. The reason many companies, particularly large US corporations, are registered in the state of Delaware is because the business laws in that small state was extremely corporate friendly. Resolution of common issues about business practices have been remarkably predictable in most court cases. If I chose Delaware, since I would not run my business there, I had to depend on a service company with a fee of about $1,000 annually. A third option was for me to register my company myself. In order to save the money, I finally decided on the third option. I incorporated my company in March of 1994 in the state of Illinois. Because I was still in Pennsylvania, the registration address was my friend's apartment at Champaign County. I later filed an amendment to change the address to my own address after I moved to Champaign-Urbana.

The procedure for the registration of a company was simple, although there are considerable differences in regulations of enterprises in the different states. This simplicity was geared toward the small business start-ups. In order to attract businesses to its state, the state secretary offices across the nation often promote and provide incentives to entrepreneurs and businesses to attract new business to the state. The filing form of incorporation in the state of Illinois can be completed within a couple of hours. In this form, there is no specific requirement for capital. The business scope can be detailed, but it can also be brief and nonspecific, such as doing business as the law of Illinois allows. It requires the incorporator's address and a register agent within the state. The registration fee was a couple of hundred dollars for S-corp. The check and the application were sent to the secretary's office. Within a couple of weeks, my company was approved for its legal incorporation. We then took the document to the county recording office to be recorded as the final step of the incorporation process. During the past few years, such process has been shortened. The article of incorporation and application for FEIN from the IRS can be done online. The selection of an S-corp, not made during the registration in the article of incorporation, can be designated in the application of FEIN.

No matter how small it was, my company was required to fulfill all the necessary documentation process. For instance, we had owner's stock certificates, board of directors, board meeting minutes, etc. Because I am the sole owner of the company, everything was simple. I had meeting records for just myself, and I signed my own stock certificates. From the standpoint of records and documentation, my one-person company was just like a large corporation. I had done it all according to legal requirements.

Regarding the name of our company used for registration, I had a number of considerations. One of the names I considered was Li's Analytical Laboratories. The reason to consider this was due to the influence by the traditional culture of a family last name in China. After I realized that this was not a common practice in the West, plus the fact that it sounded awkward and not easy to say, this name was quickly dropped. Then I considered Advanced Testing Laboratories Inc. and American Analytical Chemistry Laboratories. However, the former was used by another company and was not available. Therefore, the latter was my logical consideration. As a matter of the fact, this name was not an ideal one because it was too long to say, making it hard to share and to exchange information with customers. A couple of factors were incorporated into this name. First, I wanted to include *laboratory* in it because this would made it apparent for anyone to know this was a laboratory. With the word *American* in it, this gave us, not only the letter *A* for alphabetical arrangement in front of various publications such as the yellow pages, providing us with visibility to readers, but it also was the country of USA, which might help in our future business expansion in China and in other countries. Because America is the greatest leading country in the world, if I had a chance to take this company globally, this name might help. Although this seemed somewhat ridiculous, it indicated that I had an ambitious plan.

Our laboratory was set up at W. 101 Tomaras Avenue, Savoy, Illinois. It was a few miles away from the UIUC and adjacent to Champaign City, making it very convenient to access both places. The laboratory was situated in a building that combined both the laboratories and the offices. We had rented a laboratory with about six hundred square feet and a small office of about a hundred square feet. The total rent was about $6,600 annually or about $550 per month. There were four laboratories in the building, totaling about four thousand square feet, out of more than ten thousand square feet of the building. I was particularly satisfied with the rent because I had the option to rent additional space on an as-needed basis. Because the laboratory required a unique setup with water sinks, fume hood, and specific electricity requirement, the rent was usually about 1/3 higher than normal office spaces. The rent I paid was probably about half the cost of those on the West and East Coasts.

After I had the laboratory, I turned my attention to purchasing and installing the laboratory equipment. In accordance with my business plan, I had only $50,000 for key analytical instruments. With this small amount of money, I had no choice but to buy old instruments. My first instrument was purchased in the early winter of 1993. I had learned from a friend that a lab in Maryland was closing down for good and that there was a sale for all the equipment. I drove for about six hours to the location and bought a gas chromatograph (GC), equipped with flame ionization detector (FID) and photoionization detector (PID). This equipment was specifically used for analyzing environmental samples. Especially because our plan called for testing gasoline contamination, a PID was required for low detection limits. To make this instrument automatic sampling and injection, I also purchased a purge and trap autosampler. The total cost for me was about $20,000, which was about 30 percent of the cost of a new instrument, which otherwise would cost about $80,000. To bring this equipment home, I bought an old Toyota van for a few hundred dollars. The equipment was stored in our garage until the spring of 1994, when I moved it to Champaign, using yet another car, a Chevrolet Celebrity. Due to the age and the conditions of these two automobiles, I quickly disposed of them after I got the instruments transported.

In addition to this set of equipment, I purchased another old GC equipped with an FID. This equipment was used for the analysis of nonpolar compounds such as fatty acids and cholesterols. In order to use this equipment for analyzing pesticide residues, I purchased and installed an electron capture detector (ECD) on it. Because this detector is highly selected toward halide ions such as choline, most pesticides can be analyzed with this detector at trace amount.

I used this instrument for fulfilling the pesticide analysis described in our business plan.

The third piece of main instruments was a high-pressure liquid chromatograph (HPLC). This equipment is mainly used for analyzing water-soluble compounds. There was no immediate usage of it because our business plan did not call for such equipment. However, I wanted to install this equipment to increase our reputation and, at the same time, to seek out other testing opportunities. This was indeed the case about a year later, this equipment was used for vitamin analysis.

These three major instruments, plus a few other minor equipment, comprised our initial laboratory platform. Our minor equipment was a water bath, an oven, balances, glassware, etc. The total cost for this lab was about $80,000. When all was said and done, the account in our bank was less than $30,000. Our fixed cost of rent and loan payment was about $2,000 per month. Even if I did not take out any salary, this amount of cash was not enough to cover our operation for one year. This meant that the company had to have income in the next few months; otherwise, the cash would run out soon and the survival of my company would be in jeopardy.

Because all these instruments were old and out of calibration, my first job was to bring them back to the original equipment specifications. This became a huge task for me since I had little experience in repairing and maintaining instruments. Making things worse was that I had no budget to hire an expert or consultant to help. Fortunately, we had the equipment manual describing the assembling and parts. This gave me a good start by reading it over and over again. Once I had a general understanding of the instrument as a whole and the function of each part, I dissected the instrument and ordered all necessary parts, including all consumable filters, seals, and wafers. I cleaned up each part, and with the new parts, I was able to assemble it back together and recalibrate the instrument. While I carried out my job, I got a lot of telephone support from the original equipment manufacturers (OEM). An example was that I installed a new ECD on the second GC according to the technical support of at least two experts from the equipment OEM who also helped me with the instrument installation qualification and performance qualification. By using this GC-ECD, I was able to pass the proficiency tests set by Illinois Environmental Protection Agency.

Our HPLC was made some fifteen to twenty years before by Waters. It was an old model, and Waters has already discontinued this model. I followed the manual with certain support from Waters. I took every component apart for cleaning and then put them all back together with the necessary new parts needed. With these installation and repair experiences, my confidence in maintaining and repairing GC and HPLC got a big boost. This had actually become an important asset to my company because I was no longer afraid of equipment break down over the next ten years. During this time period, I hardly hired outside experts to repair our instruments, thus saving company a lot of cost in equipment maintenance and repair.

At about the same time I performed equipment installation and calibration, I had many other jobs ongoing. For one, I completed our service brochure. This was indeed a difficult task because I needed to know what I could provide and how much I could charge for my service to our customers. Since my previous job was only on pesticide residue testing and I had no experience in environmental testing, setting prices for environmental sample analyses proved to be quite challenging. If I set the price too high, it would scare away the customers. If our fees were not competitive, it would make it more difficult to develop our service business. However, if our fees were set too low, it could give people an impression that this was not a sound laboratory and a reputable company, which might not help in attracting customers either. Therefore, a balanced approach was critical for our laboratory so that we could provide a competitive service at a reasonable service fee. Based on these principles, I finally decided on a fee structure at about middle range in the market price while stressing our faster turnaround time service.

The practice of setting up service fees in the range of the average of the market was based on three sources of marketing information. Our customers or potential customers had the firsthand information on pricing. When they came to us for a quotation, they often let us know approximate fees they were currently paying. To be able to attract customers, we would need a fee not exceeding those fees. Service brochures from competitive laboratories were extremely useful when writing my own brochure. Some of the competitors' brochures might be collected from industrial shows; others might be acquired through our customers. With this information at hand, I was able to complete our service brochure in a few weeks.

Marketing brochures with service fees were the main marketing materials most often sent to customers. The marketing brochure was frequently tailored to specific industry and customers. As an example, the brochure sent to chemical companies for pesticide residues projects was very different from those sent to environmental engineering firms. I ended up preparing at least two general brochures or templates in order to deal with these different customers.

The logo of the company was through a thoughtful process. I wanted to have two components included, the capital letters of AACL, which stands for American Analytical Chemistry Labs, and a circle with a green-blue color of four letters representing green chemistry. Once I had decided, I drew a sketch and had a service company complete the logo. I finally had it made as a seal stamp. All my marketing materials and my business staples included this logo. In the US, the stamp seal is used only occasionally because most of important documents are signed with a personal signature. The seal stamp might be used on stock certificates and some specific documents or on certain reports if requested by the customers.

The lesson in purchasing laboratory chemicals and reference standards was costly to me. For the first time, I purchased testing standards based on the chemical parameters listed in my service brochure, not taking into consideration the actual tests performed at any given time. Therefore, I spent $3,000 on standards, but only a fraction of it was actually used. Most of it was wasted because many tests listed in the service brochure were not even required, even before the standards had expired.

General liability insurance was required by state law. Our company purchased this insurance at a cost of about $1,000 annually. The second insurance was also important—professional liability insurance, which insures against errors and omissions due to mistakes made in the testing. However, the professional insurance was generally expensive but not required by the state law in Illinois. I did not have the budget for this insurance; therefore, I had to take on this risk without insurance. A few years later, when our company made a profit, I began paying for this professional insurance.

After several months of preparation and hard work, I finally opened the laboratory for business on June 1, 1994. This day had not come easy at all. From the time I left the university and joined the employer, decided to be an entrepreneur, learned technology, acquired business knowledge, wrote the business plan, applied for the SBA loan, to the preparation of the laboratories and equipment installation, I experienced and overcame all kinds of challenges and difficulties. Therefore, to some extent, getting my laboratory up was a small feat and made me feel satisfied and accomplished. This was a small cornerstone for me therefore. I should have every reason to celebrate this achievement.

However, in the grand opening of our laboratory for business, we had no ceremony, no gathering of our friends, and even no other employees present this event. Only my wife and I congratulated each other. I spent my day in the laboratory while my wife was at home. We both felt that there was nothing to be displayed and deserved celebration. We felt that this small achievement set us up for more challenges ahead. Therefore, my head now was filled with all kinds of concerns, especially on how to get our business off the ground.

It is almost universally true that to start a new project always takes more time than expected. Getting our first customer was our priority. Even if I had done some marketing and had a few early verbal commitments, I had no idea whether these commitments would translate into sales. Therefore, only after we received an order from them did the commitments mean something to our business. Making things more challenging to our laboratory was the fact that Champaign, Illinois, is in a region with fewer businesses, especially manufacturing businesses. This geographic location and farming business greatly limited our business opportunity in environmental testing. Let alone the fact that if I were able to convert the commitments into customers, it would still be hard for me to get the second, the third, and even more customers. In brief, I did not have much confidence in my ability to sell our testing service.

Equally challenging to me was whether I could deliver our testing results on time. That I had no experience in doing environmental testing wouldn't help. Whether my experience in pesticide residue testing would be helpful or not was unclear. Although I had done a few trial tests during the last couple of months, when it came to the real-world samples, my confidence in getting accurate results was not high. In additional to quality results, our customers required on-time delivery. Although the environmental samples could be contaminated at different levels on different days, or changed all the time, long-term monitoring for several years could had produced the base line level of testing data. If my testing result was far off from what was in the database, then the customer would notice right away. Therefore, producing reasonably accurate results was prerequisite for our laboratory.

A critically important issue was to finish tests and report the results in five business days. This was a standard of delivery many customers were expecting. Some customers might accept a two-week turnaround time on certain projects, but only two to three days for rush projects. This was particularly challenging to me without experience. I had to make sure that I was capable of dealing with both the quality and the fast turnaround requirements.

Even if I had many concerns and worries, I had opened my door for business. I had no way to back out. I had to move ahead, fighting to succeed. If I failed, I not only would lose our $20,000 but also would be responsible for returning the bank loan money. More importantly, my credibility would be blown, and this would be detrimental to my future career. It would also be disastrous to my family and my children. Therefore, all that I had to do now was to do whatever it took to give my business the best chance to success. I would not stop until I reached my dream.

14-1: Moving back to a small old house at 601
E. Colorado Ave, Urbana, Illinois

14

ENTREPRENEURSHIP

SECTION TWO

Start-Up (June 1994–December 1995)

Creating my own business brought me and my family into a long and difficult journey. In the entrepreneur world, there was a famous saying, "Once an entrepreneur starts his/her own business, it was just like marriage. It would be hard to divorce later." It is not only the investment of money and time but also a scary time for the spouse and children's lives. Although my company was not running normally yet, I already had a deep feeling about this experience.

When we were at Pennsylvania, we fought to have our dream home. Finally, we had it. However, in order to pursue my dream, my family had to leave that home and move back to Champaign, Illinois. The move this time was harder than any other time of the past because we had just moved into our dream home and our kids loved it so much.

Every time we moved in the past, we knew exactly what we would be doing; but this time, we didn't. We had no idea of what we might end up with in short term or even in the long term. In addition, we were apparently returning ourselves to the life of a graduate student in a small rental apartment without knowing when this kind of life would end. Whenever I thought of this, I felt depressed and guilty toward my family.

In order for our children to complete their spring semester, my wife and I decided the moving should be in two steps. I would move first, and then she and the children would move later. I left State College, Pennsylvania, on March 1994 and moved into a small apartment with about six hundred square footage in Champaign. The rent was a little over $500 per month. My wife continued taking care of children and selling our house in Pennsylvania. We were lucky to get the home sold in the summer with a few thousand dollars' profits. The sale was closed in July, and I returned to Champaign with my family.

Champaign, Illinois, was a place my wife and I liked a lot during my postdoctoral research. None of us thought at the time that we would be back after only three years. On the one hand, we were glad to be back because we had a number of friends and professors with whom we had good relationships, but on the other hand, we were a little afraid and nervous because I was worried about how to get our business going without failing. As usual, I visited my postdoc adviser and all professors I knew. I explained to them the purpose of my return and hoped they would give me a hand when needed as I pursued the business endeavor.

One day at dinner, after we had settled into the cozy apartment, I asked my wife whether we should try to buy a small house. She answered it without hesitation, "This apartment was not bad, except its smaller size. The school for kids is not that good either." Although we did not bring all our furniture with us, the few pieces filled the apartment quickly. I certainly did not feel good living in such a crowded condition.

Yes, I had to agree with my wife. We had just moved from a house that was three times as large as this apartment. "Should we go ahead and buy our own house since we still have enough money left from the sale of the house for down payment and a mortgage?"

"That would be good. It would make us feel better." She agreed.

A simple discussion between us was sufficient for me to make up my mind to buy our second home, even if it were smaller than our first one. We started house hunting right away and hoped we could have it in a couple of months so that our kids could go to better schools in the fall.

However, during our mortgage application, we met some difficulty. One day, I went to Busey Bank asking for $100,000 mortgage after we indicated to the bank officer who met with us that we would put down 15 percent of total house cost as down payment. To our surprise, this officer looked at us and said, "Charlie, do you know what you are doing? Who knows if you could make a living with your company? If not, how could your family get by living daily under such circumstances if you still want to own a house?" His attitude and the way in which he spoke to us made us feel extremely uncomfortable, and he nearly killed our hopes of owning our house.

I returned to our apartment with a heavy heart. After rethinking over it all, I did a simple math: If the house was $100K and we put down $15K, our borrowed money would be $85K. With a mortgage rate of about 7 percent and with a fifteen-year loan, our monthly payment would be about $700. I knew that Busey Bank did not have confidence in my business or in me as a person, but his had no effect on my decision to buy a home.

I thought to myself that if my business did not produce this $700 monthly to pay my mortgage, I could work in a restaurant as a waiter, and I was sure to make this amount of income. My wife knew me well and did not express her opinion because she knew that her husband did not like people who spoke of his inability.

I even went a step further on this, thinking that "if we could not get a conventional mortgage from a bank, we could find another institution that might loan us the money, even with a higher mortgage rate."

I had looked into this option already and found that this kind of lending agency often required 2–3 percent points higher than a conventional mortgage from a bank. Taking this approach would increase our monthly mortgage payment from $700 to $800, but I was not afraid of this $100 monthly increase, which I considered still bearable.

After the rejection of my mortgage application by Busey Bank, I made my next appointment with the First American Bank, which had loaned us the money for our business. I had not wanted to apply to this bank because I felt that it had done a lot for us with the SBA loan.

My appointment with the mortgage loan officer of the bank was set for two days later. To my surprise, this bank agreed to my application without asking any questions. This obviously had something to do with my SBA loan officer, Mr. Kirdiz, because the mortgage officer mentioned him a couple of times. Our mortgage rate was good, and the closing costs were standard.

My wife murmured to herself, "Mr. Kirdiz is so good to us." From that time on, we made up our minds that all our future banking would be with this bank. The bank kept its faith with us, and we would do the same in return. That has been exactly what has been happening ever since.

Once we were qualified for mortgage from the First American Bank, we purchased a house at 601 E. Colorado Avenue, Urbana. This was an old house built in the 1950s. Although it was not an ideal house, it was in a school zone for Yankee Ridge Elementary School, plus this house would be a transitional one for us, so we settled on it. We knew that if our business failed, we would be forced to move to a new place for job, but if we were successful in our business, we would have the financial capability to buy a bigger house.

As soon as my family was settled, I began putting my full energy into the company. My first task was to get our first customer. Although our environmental testing market was confined to Champaign-Urbana and the surrounding area, the pesticide testing service to chemical companies was outside the state of Illinois because the difference between two markets, the marketing approach, and strategy were different. Therefore, I had to divide my time into the two parts—that of the local area and those outside the state. In our business plan, we had grouped pesticide residues in water, or wastes, into the environmental industry category. I started with those people who a few months before had made a verbal commitment to use our laboratory service and hoped that at least some of them would keep their word and use our services.

In fact, I was lucky to get two small engineering firms committed to sending samples to my laboratory. I was glad to have them, but to get a third and a fourth company and more customers proved more challenging than expected.

The difficulties were in two aspects. First, there was no credibility established by our laboratory. Because the environmental industry is a regulated industry, every testing laboratory should have some accreditation in order to convince customers to use our services. We did not have any certifications and no operational history of our laboratory. Similarly, we had limited manpower and resources available. Our personnel structure was like a one-man show, which made customers feel uncomfortable. All these factors put us at a disadvantage to compete for customers. Second, the environmental industry was a mature industry and the laboratory testing services were overcapacity. There were more than a dozen environmental testing laboratories in the area of Champaign and the surrounding area where there was a very limited market. Every potential customer had had their contract laboratories lined up for years. Under these circumstances, it was hard to persuade potential customers to switch laboratories and come to us for service.

Despite all these shortcomings, I tried to find reasons to put us into a better position to compete, but I failed.

For instance, one day, I drove to Danville, a small city about thirty-five miles away to meet the manager of a municipal wastewater treatment plant. As usual, I introduced myself and then handed him my company's service brochure. I explained why we could service his plant better for his testing needs. He asked me, "How many people are in your lab?"

"There are three. We just started."

Right after I answered, I was worried about my answer of being a mom-and-pop business, so I immediately added that "we are hiring and expanding the scope of our services."

The manager then asked, "Do you have EPA certification?"

"Not yet, but we are preparing our application to the State of Illinois and hope to be certified in the near future," I replied.

"Well, why don't you come back about this time next year?" I knew this was a polite way of refusing my service offering. He apparently wanted to send me out of his facility in a way that I really had not expected.

Although I was disappointed with the outcome, I understood it because I knew my laboratory had little to offer. My lab was new, and no one knew its existence, plus the fact that it was small, with just myself and my wife. And our lab equipment was old and outdated. More importantly, we had not been accredited yet. With all these issues, it was a no-brainer for a thoughtful manager to trust this laboratory until I proved otherwise.

The failure of persuading the water treatment plant to use my testing service did not make me lose heart in pursuing my marketing. I continued visiting other potential clients in the area. Unfortunately, the outcome was similar, and I had only two engineering firms who had previously committed to using our service.

The first company was called Midwest Environmental Engineering, which provided inspection and engineering service to the area gas station owners. As part of their work, they required monitoring buried gas tanks for oil leakage. Water and soil samples were collected and sent to laboratories for testing. This underground storage tank leaking monitoring business was a hot market segment in 1980s, and the fee for this test was about $250 per sample. But now it is about $50–$100.

The second company, Soderman and Associates, was also a local engineering firm doing a lot of area construction projects and waste landfill sites. They collected ground water samples in a couple of area landfills for us to analyze. The monitoring was tested every quarter using a set of parameters approved by Illinois EPA. These two companies were our first customers.

With more effort, I was able to get a few more customers over the next a few months. However, the number of customers was small, and each customer had limited samples for analysis. By then it was clear to me that these few customers and the sample volume would not be sufficient for us to survive, so I expanded my service area to over fifty miles away. I visited almost every waste treatment facilities and manufacturer with little success. Most of these companies gave me a similar answer: "We have contract labs already and don't need your service at this time. If things change, we will contact you."

At the same time, I also looked into EPA national projects in my attempt to identify projects where my laboratory could apply as a subcontractor of a large company that was usually a winner of the large projects. Most EPA or other national projects contain a requirement in the request for proposal (RFP) to set aside a portion of the project for small and disadvantaged businesses. I was a minority from China and qualified for the set-aside projects. However, my effort did not yield any results.

Now I realized that my company was facing a steep challenge in the environmental testing market. This agricultural state of Illinois, especially in the south and central part of the state where few manufacturers were located, made it worse for us because the environmental testing market was confined to local laboratories for convenience of sampling and delivery.

I was under pressure to turn my emphasis to the second part of my business plan—that of pesticide projects from major chemical markets. I thought to myself that since I had some contacts with a few chemical companies and certain experience in testing pesticide residues, this might help market our services. If I could get one pesticide project, my company could survive.

In my effort to pursue this market, I went through an incredibly difficult process. It was in the summer of 1994, when I got appointments with both Uniroyal Chemical and DuPont & Co. as a result of my persistent effort in marketing. Since they were the appointments I had been looking for, I had to make every effort to prepare marketing materials with the hope for the best results.

After my marketing brochure was completed, I decided on how to travel to these two companies. One night, I said to my wife, "In order to save money, I want to drive because flying for this trip is expensive."

"How far it is from Champaign to Connecticut?" My wife asked.

"There may be more than a thousand miles one way, which would take about fifteen hours of nonstop driving." I answered her with a guess.

"Isn't it too far to drive by yourself alone?" My wife sounded worried about it.

"Then we can go together and take turns driving so that one of us can take a nap when not driving." I was pleading for her to agree with this plan.

My wife, who knew me well, wanted to share the responsibility and be by my side, so she readily agreed. At that moment, I had only heartfelt gratitude for her. We discussed how to deal with the school absence of our older son, who was in his second grade and who could miss several days to a week of school since we did not have any relatives as a babysitter to help. Our younger son was at kindergarten, and it would be relatively easy to deal with. Consequently, I decided to make my appointments with the two companies on a Friday so we could leave Champaign right after school on Thursday. We had overnight driving and could get to Connecticut by the next morning. After the appointments, we would have the whole weekend to drive back, and our sons' school on Monday wouldn't be affected. This arrangement was more centered on our children's education than our convenience, and of course, it was beneficial to the laboratory operation as well.

We packed our small suitcase, loaded our car, and then waited for our son to be released from his school. We drove straight through to Connecticut, stopping only for gas and for restrooms. When we got to central Connecticut, it was about 6:00 a.m. I arranged my family in a motel, and after I washed myself and put on my suit, I drove to my first appointment at 8:00 a.m.

The representative at Uniroyal Chemical was a senior scientist who was responsible for outsourcing their pesticide residue projects. He was about fifty to sixty years old and a very friendly person. He politely invited me to a small office and let me introduce myself and my laboratory services. Despite driving overnight, I was excited to have this opportunity and did not feel tired at all. At the closing of my introduction, I once again thanked him for his arrangements and said I hoped that the company would consider our laboratory as one of their outsourcing service partners.

The representative asked me, "How many employees are in your labs?"

"There are four right now, but we are hiring," I replied.

He said, "You should understand that all of our projects are done in accordance with good laboratory practices (GLP) regulations, which are enforced by United States Environmental Protection Agency (USEPA). If not done properly, our experimental data may not be considered valid."

"I know it, and our operations will be in compliance with the GLP." I was afraid at this point that my answer was not convincing, so I further explained. "Our staff has had considerable experience. We have an analyst with a PhD degree and an employee for quality control. I perform the final check and provide compliance statement for GLP projects."

The meeting came to an end in about an hour, and the representative finally said, "I have confidence in your ability to do a good job because you did our projects previously at Central Analytical Laboratories in Pennsylvania. But now, we don't have any new projects to be outsourced. Most of our projects, after more than ten years of research and testing, have been basically completed or are near completion. Indeed, most of the studies have been reported to the USEPA. If EPA approves the reports of our projects, we have fewer projects that need to be subcontracted out. Until then, we wouldn't know. If more are required by EPA, then there might be opportunity for your lab."

I did not know whether a meeting ending this way was normal, but I felt that he was comforting me and leaving me with a gleam of hope. This was better than straight out turning me down. Regardless of what it meant, I was still grateful to him because, after all, he was willing to meet me and at least possibly consider my laboratory services in the future.

Right after the meeting, I hurried back to the motel to my family. There was no time to take a break or relax because I had another appointment with DuPont in the afternoon in Wilmington, Delaware. It is about 250 miles from Central Connecticut to Delaware, a four-hour driving journey. So we packed our kids into the car and got on the road immediately. The time frame did not allow us to eat lunch at any restaurant, so we got some fast food and ate it in the car. Again, we drove straight to the next destination without stopping. By the time we got to Wilmington, it was about 2:00 p.m. I left my family in a nearby small park for rest and drove on to DuPont for my appointment.

The head of outsourcing pesticide projects at DuPont was also a PhD scientist. He invited me to his office, and I followed a similar procedure as I had at Uniroyal Chemical. I introduced my laboratory and answered all questions that this representative asked. For any questions that I could not answer, I promised to get back later. At the closing, I pleaded the same way as I did with Uniroyal and hoped that DuPont would consider my laboratory as one of their outsourcing testing labs.

My second meeting of the day ended in a similar way as the first one; DuPont sent me out its doors politely. Viewing this in retrospect, this was normal because this was the first time they had heard about my laboratory and it was impossible for them give me any promise.

I returned to my wife and children somewhat in a depressed mood. The time was now about 4:00 p.m., and I did not have time to think about these two meetings. Instead, I had to decide right away whether we should drive directly back to Illinois or stay at a motel overnight. If we chose the latter, there was a motel expense. Being in the situation where I desperately wanted to save every penny, spending the night in a motel obviously would not make me happy. If I chose to drive straight home, we would be extremely tired since I had gone more than twenty-four hours without sleeping. My unhappiness with not getting projects from these two chemical companies did not help.

The distance from Delaware to Champaign, Illinois, is about seventy miles, requiring about twelve hours of driving. But if we started driving at 5:00 p.m., we would not get home until the next morning. In the end, saving money overtook the concerns of tiredness. We got in the car, took turns driving, and kept ourselves awake by talking and chatting along the way. After a night of agonizing, we finally got back home safely the next morning. Because I was so tired, I fell asleep immediately and slept for several hours. When I woke in the afternoon, I had partially recovered my energy.

This attempt of marketing our service to chemical companies did not yield any meaningful progress, and with the environmental market being so limited, I realized that the difficulty was much greater than I had ever anticipated. The idea I had described in my business plan to have a pesticide residue testing market from major chemical companies appeared to be childish and unrealistic. Without establishing my laboratory as a creditable GLP laboratory, it would be impossible to become a contract laboratory for GLP projects. Therefore, I had to start from square 1 and build our company to meet the GLP basic requirements. One obvious indication would be that we must pass the auditing by these chemical companies.

How to get a passing grade on the GLP audit was now my focus. During my marketing, I kept saying that there were four employees in our company. This was one of many issues I needed to address. The reason behind this was that I had a friend from the same undergraduate college who was a PhD student at the University of Illinois at Champaign, Urbana (UIUC). His wife was an as-needed lab technician at UIUC as well. Both were willing to help us as part-time employees on an as-needed basis. I had a verbal agreement with them that if we had a GLP project, we would need them to work for us. If we had more business that required additional employees, they would be the first and second to be hired. With these two persons, plus my wife and I, it was a four-employee structure. This structure would actually fulfill our organizational chart, making us be able to meet the GLP regulation.

The GLP standards clearly stated that the person who performs testing must be audited by a second person, such as a quality control manager, to ensure that the testing methods are followed through. The quality control personnel cannot participate in data generation, unless the data is to be audited by a third person. Both the data generator and the quality control person are not allowed to be the same person and to approve the final report of the study, which requires a third person, such as the president, CEO, or laboratory manager. In brief, different personnel among these three positions must be clearly separated functionally and operate independently during the process of data production, data review, and final report approval. Full compliance with GLP was strictly required by EPA. No chemical company would take any risk to delay or abandon their project if the laboratory failed to pass an EPA review. As a result, selecting a qualified contract laboratory is critically important to the reputation and economic interest of the laboratory. Therefore, from all these important considerations, it was not hard to understand why my first marketing effort to major chemical companies did not yield desirable result.

With the organization structure in place, I turned my attention to completing our standard operation procedure (SOP), which is a part of the total quality system documentation. It defines the policy and procedures in our operation in a recognizable set of standards. When chemical companies and EPA agency audit a laboratory, this is a must-see document. I spent a few months completing it, and it played an important role in our laboratory later.

As the progress of documentations such as SOP was made, I continued updating our progress to Uniroyal Chemicals, DuPont, and a number of other pesticide manufacturers. After nearly a year of effort, I received an indication that our laboratory might become a contractor of Ciba-Geigy, a major pesticide developer and manufacturer. The company invited our laboratory to send representatives to their GLP training class. For this reason, a newly hired PhD and I enrolled in this training. In order to reduce expenses, we decided to drive about thirteen hours from Illinois to North Carolina.

We participated in this training class for two main purposes. First, it is a two-day formal training, which I did not have before. Previously, when I worked at Central Analytical Labs, I had a simple training, organized internally. The training by Ciba-Geigy was different because this training was specifically designed for its contract laboratories on the one hand and meeting specific GLP requirements for its pesticides projects on the other. The goal of the training was to make sure all their contract laboratories were able to produce results in full compliance with the GLP regulations. The class size was about thirty people who were mostly quality control directors and compliance officers. I was pleased to be included in the class along with about a dozen or so contract laboratories. Once this training was completed, our laboratory was placed on the list of their outsourcing laboratories. This training also helped me establish communication channels with Ciba and some other contract laboratories.

This training had indeed brought us new marketing opportunities. Not long after the training, we received an audit request by Ciba-Geigy. The company sent a couple of their quality control staff to our laboratory for a preliminary review of our operation. I did not know if they came directly from the company headquarters in North Carolina or as a part of another trip to the Midwest contract laboratories. Regardless of where they were from, to have them in our facility said a lot about our progress. It indicated that they were serious about using our testing service. This was a preliminary audit. They spend a half day looking over our SOPs. Before leaving, they gave us a number of suggestions on the improvements necessary to meet their outsourcing project standards.

In the next few months, I made the change to our SOP and operations according to Ciba-Geigy's requirements. Once I made the improvement, I informed Ciba-Geigy and hoped they would send a second group for quality assurance and quality control (QA/QC) to formally audit our laboratory. Much to my surprise, they soon sent a four-member working group to review our laboratory, including SOPs, total quality system, and personnel records. Although this audit wasn't completely satisfactory, the audit reports were, in general, meeting their basic requirements with a few identified changes. One of the deficiencies was that our laboratory did not have a fireproof storage cabinet for GLP documents, so I purchased an old fireproof cabinet from a friend of an employee at Ciba-Geigy who brought it to our laboratory in his pickup truck when he was on a job in the Midwest.

After the audit, I held my head up high with the expectation of soon getting a project from Ciba. This, indeed, turned out to be true. In the summer of 1996, they sent my laboratory a project for method validation. The work order indicated it as a small project with limited analysis. It was only a few thousands of dollars, but I did not consider the size of the project as important as getting the opportunity of being their contract laboratory because with the first project, if we could deliver it well, we might have more projects on the way to us. It was for this reason that I had our part-time PhD work on the project under my supervision. Although it took a few weeks to complete it, I was happy with it because our study report was also accepted by Ciba-Geigy.

As we prepared to receive more projects from Ciba-Geigy, they informed us that their outsourcing practice was undergoing a change, resulting in less outsourcing. The immediate outcome was that many projects were taken back to the company for its own employees to complete internally in order to reduce the layoff of its employees. This development was very significant to us because it indicated that if only a limited number of projects were outsourced, the projects would first go to large and established contract laboratories. We might not see another project from them any time soon, which was the case in the coming months.

By now, I was further convinced again that the outsourcing market for pesticide residue testing had headed downhill, a trend that actually started a couple of years earlier. I recognized this signal when I had visited Uniroyal and DuPont some months before, even if I had not been prepared to accept it because I needed this market so much for our survival. It was unfortunate that this development at Ciba-Geigy forced me to accept this fact.

My company had been in operation for about six months. Although I was able to recruit more than a handful of environmental customers, the business volume was small. By the end of 1994, we had generated only a little more than $10,000 in revenue. This was not enough to pay the interest and principal of our SBA loan, not to mention our rent of the laboratory and daily consumable expense of our operation. Under such terrible financial conditions, my plan of taking $1,500 per month from the business to cover our family expense was suspended in order to save cash.

The pressure was on for me. At times, I did not know what to do to improve our situation. One day at our dinner, I talked to my wife about it and hoped she realized what we were facing. "According to our current business income, it was impossible to receive a payout from the company."

"I noticed this already, so what can we do to make it better?" she asked.

"We should find ways to generate some income to cover our family expenses."

My wife had already understood what I meant. She said, "I can find a job working in a Chinese restaurant to earn some cash for our living and other expenses."

I was thankful and said, "Thank you. It is really hard for you. My decision to do this business has brought you back to the waitressing position in a restaurant."

I knew it was a little unfair to her, but what other options did we have? She took action immediately and worked at the Yanjin Chinese Restaurant. She could still hold accounting and technician positions in our company, but because there wasn't much for her to do in the company, she worked about twenty hours a week, mostly lunch every day and weekend evenings. Her base salary and the tips together totaled about $1,500 a month, which was more than enough to cover our living and mortgage expenses. This greatly reduced my concern.

The difficulty in our business was also reflected in cash flow, which was noted by our bank loan officer, Mr. Kirdiz. As a normal part of the loan reporting process, I was required to provide the bank loan officer information about our business progress in addition to the request for fund release and usage. As a result, Mr. Kirdiz was well aware of our situation.

One day in November 1994, I went to see Mr. Kirdiz to report our recent business development. To my surprise, as soon as I sat down with him, he said to me, "In view of the small amount of cash flow your company has generated the last a few months, I propose to help you by deferring the principal payment of your business loan. Specifically, by the end of November 1995, you are only required to pay the interest but not the principal of the loan in order to improve the liquidity of your company."

"Thank you very much, Mr. Kirdiz." I did not know what else to say for this such good news. We then signed a supplementary contract with the bank. In doing so, our monthly expense on the loan was about $800 per month versus $1,300 per month otherwise.

Due to these two initiatives, the pressure on me was eased substantially. It allowed me to focus all my energy on the development of our business. In order for my business to survive, I must make adjustments or even make a change in the direction of my business. I wished for a miracle that would give me an opportunity to revive my company. At the time, I indeed saw a niche market that I was not aware of previously.

An old saying that goes well here is, "One successful man needs three helpers." In retrospect, my business got help from a number of people. When we experienced major challenges and difficulty, we got the help from the loan officer of the bank. We indeed got even greater help from a local businessman named Mr. Draze. Draze had established his trading and marketing company in the late '80s. It was located about a few miles from Champaign. The main business was to import raw nutrition materials from other countries, such as China, and then repackage and sell them to manufacturers of dietary supplement industry. He had noticed a description of our laboratory from a local newspaper article that described our grand opening for business. One day, I received a call from him saying that he wanted to meet me at our laboratory. He said that he would be bringing a few samples to see if we can help him test the products. His company needed a laboratory to do quality control testing, and the resulting report would be provided to his customers as a certificate of analysis to help with his marketing and sale of products.

I was waiting anxiously that afternoon for his arrival. I thought to myself, *Is it too good to be true?* I had never heard anything like a customer who brought business to us without any marketing being done. He arrived at our lab at about 1:00 p.m. that day. After we introduced ourselves and shook hands, he stated his question right away. "I knew your laboratory from the newspaper as an environmental testing lab. However, my samples are nutrition samples that I want to have tested. Specifically, these few samples are fish oil, primrose oil, and borage oils. I hope your lab can help us out."

As I listened to his request and offering, I was totally shocked with how little I knew about nutrition supplements and about the nutrition supplement industry. I told him, "I did not know the terminologies and the products, so I don't know if we can help in testing."

Mr. Draze recognized my concern about the testing methodology and further explained to me, "There is little you need to be worried about it because I can provide you with the testing method and the report format of the analysis, or the certificate of analysis, for you to follow."

His willingness was greatly beyond my imagination. As a customer who went this far to help us, I had no reason not to be serious about it. In general, service providers only try to find customers, and it is rarely the other way around unless the demand from customers exceeds the offerings of service providers. If that was the case, it should be an excellent indication of a prosperous market in the industry. Through some more discussion, I slowly came to understand that any business practice was a two-way street. In this case, Mr. Draze was looking for something his current testing laboratories could not provide him, which was that he wanted a fast turnaround service at a reasonable price. This was hard for him to get from an outside laboratory. If we could help him solve the problem, it would make both parties happy and should be a win-win relationship moving forward.

Actually, his methods were not relatively simple in that they required only a gas chromatograph with FID director. This instrument was already available in our laboratory, so I accepted his order request with thanks for his kindness in sharing the testing methods and report format. Not only with that, he also provided me with the cost that he currently paid to the other lab. It took only a few trials to qualify these methods before I used them for testing.

The short conversation with Mr. Draze gave me a lot of information about his company and the industry. We developed a very good relationship in the coming years. He used our laboratory almost exclusively for his testing needs. As a matter of fact, our 30–40 percent of revenue in the first one to two years came from him. More importantly than the business he gave to us, he introduced me to the nutrition supplement industry that was in its initial growing stage. In a sense, Mr. Draze's introduction of our laboratory to this new market played a decisive role in our survival and success in the coming years.

Because Mr. Draze was such an important partner of our business, I praised his contribution to our laboratory wherever and whenever I had an opportunity. For instance, in the article on our business in the local newspaper, I included him for helping our business. At his seventieth birthday party, to which I was invited but could not attend, I wrote a nice letter to him and wished him a happy birthday and a healthy senior life.

In addition to the bank loan officer Mr. Kirdiz and Mr. Draze, I received help from my friends and professors. A professor from the Department of Plant Biology at UIUC helped me whenever I had urgent needs for certain rare chemicals or, occasionally, laboratory equipment for certain tests. The professor let me use his laboratory and made me feel as if I were at my laboratory whenever I needed his help. To appreciate his help and support, I invited him and his wife to our company Christmas party every year.

It was due to the service we provided to Mr. Draze that I made the decision to redirect our services from the environmental industry to the nutrition supplement industry. To understand more of this industry, I began to gather information through various channels. One of the most important step I took was to attend an annual meeting of the National Nutrition and Foods Association (NNFA) held in Nashville, Tennessee, in the summer of 1995. This annual conference brought together many leaders, CEOs, vice presidents, R and D directors, and quality control directors of leading nutrition companies around the country all together under one roof. The attendants also included United States Food and Drug Administration (FDA) officials and heads of nonprofit organizations. Apart from the academic seminars and lectures, a major focus was on the larger exhibition hall where hundreds of companies were exhibiting their products and services. The exhibition venue was huge with thousands of attendees walking around the floor. It was an eye-popping event for me. To participate in this grand gathering of health and nutrition people broadened my horizons about this industry. I never thought of nutritional supplements and health food market as being this big.

This show was a platform for buyers and sellers to exchange business ideas, to sell and buy products, and to understand the latest development of technologies and new products. Exhibitors included raw material suppliers, raw material importers and exporters, brokers, marketers, and distributors, as well as manufacturers and chain store buyers. Most attendees from exhibitor companies are primarily company leaders and marketing staff. There were also some consulting and laboratories service companies like me at the show. These companies intended to look for customers and sell their services to the industry.

Prior to the meeting, I compiled a service brochure according to the information I got from Mr. Draze and other sources. The experience in testing products from Mr. Draze helped me considerably in the preparation of my brochure. In the exhibition hall, I stopped by every exhibitor and talked to the exhibitor personnel. If the company's quality control personnel was present, it was my number 1 target, then in turn, it was the quality assurance personnel, scientific officer or R and D directors, and finally the chemists. If the president and vice president were present, they were also my targets because these people were the decision makers. I handed over my service brochure and my business card, and when I was given an opportunity by the customer, I introduced my laboratory service. Otherwise, because exhibitors did not like us to interfere with their focus on selling their product, I just introduced myself and got a business card from the exhibitor. It was an intensive and tireless effort for a couple of days on the show floor because I wanted to talk to as many people as I could and collect as many business cards as possible.

In addition to this NNFA show, there were a number of other shows held annually or semiannually over the years. The Natural Products Expo West and Natural Products Expo East are large industrial shows for our industry. These shows were attended by a few thousand in the 1990s to sixty thousand attendees and thousands of exhibitors worldwide in 2010s. In addition, there are a number of other related shows such as functional foods show, raw material supplier shows, and contract manufacturing and packaging shows. Although there are many different conference and exhibitions in this industry, each focuses on more specialized areas. Some are replicated and overlapped. Over the years, I often attended three to four shows annually. My practice, adopted at NNFA in 1995, had been in use until 2010. We had only a couple of exhibitions over the years. Mostly, my goal was to get as many connections and as much contact information of potential customers as possible. My approach of walking through the exhibition hall and talking to every booth person about our service was really a hard job, with several hours of walking and standing, until the closing of exhibition hall at 6:00 p.m. My marketing approach like this was more targeted and more effective.

From the first national show, I learned a few things about the food and nutrition industry. First, the industry, especially the nutrition supplement industry, was rapidly growing. The government had recognized this by passing a law called the Dietary Supplement Health and Education Act of 1994. This act provided foundation and direction guidance for the industry that was actually started in the 1980s. Second, because this industry was in its infancy stage then, there were a lot of business opportunities for different companies, including our laboratory testing service. Third, in order to catch a share of the laboratory testing service market, I must establish a contact profile for the industrial members and a set of testing methods in order to meet the demands of the customers. From that time on, this industry gradually became the focus of our service.

In order to seize the opportunity, I took a few important steps over the next a few months. For example, I revised our service brochure according the marketing information collected during the shows, making it more closely reflect the requirements of the industry, such as adding testing parameters of vitamins and herbal products. I adjusted the service price to match the average pricing structure of the industry in order to be competitive. I communicated with potential customers in a timely and consistent manner. My strategy was to include more testing parameters as long as we had the equipment platform and the technology to do so. We adopted an average market service fee structure. Recognizing that we were a new laboratory to the industry, our price should not be too high, but it should not be too low either because I did not want to give an impression in the marketplace that our laboratory was inferior as compared to other laboratories.

Another major action I took was to shift my energy from environmental testing to nutrition supplement testing. This strategic change was very important to my company, especially with the possibility of failure in our current service to the environmental and chemical companies. However, I knew I must make it a smooth transition because I could not just simply stop the service to environmental customers. Therefore, in a short period of time, I continued providing service to existing customers, and I stopped marketing to new customers of that industry. On the other hand, I spent the bulk of my time on marketing, developing analytical methods, and testing to nutrition supplement customers. This transition was basically completed in 1997. With a set of testing methods at hand, I was confident in our ability to serve our customers.

In addition to methods development and routinely performing testing, as part of my job, I actively marketed our services by submitting our updated brochure to the list of potential customers that I had collected during the show. The electronic email at the time wasn't well-developed, so my main approach was to mail our service brochure, followed by phone calls. Within a few months, we received very good response from these customers. The momentum continued toward the end of the 1995 and beyond. As a result, our revenue was increased from a little over $10,000 in 1994 to more than $70,000 by the end of 1995. This was very good news for us, and from there on, our service kept growing. Starting in 1997, our company made a good profit every year.

Recalling the first two-year process of building my company, it was a memorable and difficult experience. During this period of time, my wife and my whole family paid a lot for my business venture. It was not just the loss of money but also the physical and spiritual burden. In the most difficult times, my wife was the breadwinner and shouldered the burden of our family life.

Her actions removed my worries from my daily work and, at the same time, lifted my morale.

Additionally, I got help from our bank loan officer and a local businessman who literally got us a new business direction. Through this, I had a deeper feeling on the old Chinese saying, "A fence is stabled with three piles, a man's strength needed the help of three men." In order to build a successful business, one person's effort is limited. It requires a good business environment, and it needs help from friends and colleagues or even customers. If we use the more fashionable term, it must be teamwork and a collected spirit. This is a good lesson I have learned.

The Christmas of 1996 and New Year of 1997 were a period of our happiest days since the previous five years. My wife and I were greatly relieved. My family finally had a happy holiday. Since 1993, we had been constantly under pressure and stress because of my entrepreneur venture. Although I still had a sour feeling during the holiday, my feelings had shifted from being worried about the survival to seeing the growth of our company. I was still under pressure as a business owner. It was different kind of pressure now for growth. I wanted to build a growing business from here on.

14

ENTREPRENEURSHIP

SECTION THREE

Business Development: First Five-Year Plan (1996–2000)

The Dietary Supplement Health and Education Act (DSHEA) was passed in the United States Congress in 1994. This law was cosponsored by senators Tom Harkin and Orrin Hatch and signed into law by President Bill Clinton. This law is significant in American history regarding to nutrition supplementation in our diets. It provides legal foundation and the framework for the development and growth of the nutrition supplement industry.

There are ten major sections in this DSHEA. First of all, it describes the current status of the medical and health care industry. The thorough investigation and survey, as well as research and assessments of the health care industry, have led to the conclusion that despite about 10 percent of total GDP spent on the health care industry in the US, there are still various problems in achieving a healthy society. Nutrition supplements are the right solution to some of these problems. This basic assessment is a significant event because in a sense and from the national prospective, this regulation has elevated nutrition supplement as a national strategy and its importance as an indispensable part of national economic system. The federal government has set up agencies and offices around the country to manage and execute this regulation and the dietary supplement market.

DSHEA has provided the definitions of nutrition supplement and nutrition labeling provisions. Among them, two components are important: nutrition labeling and safety of products. It states that parameters shown on the label should be tested by a laboratory to confirm the ingredients on the label. The safety analysis includes pesticides, heavy metals, pathogens, and toxins. To complete many of these tests requires an in-house laboratory or an independent testing laboratory. This testing requirement had created an excellent marketing opportunity for our laboratory testing service.

In the first national industrial conference and exhibition show I attended at Nashville, Tennessee, in 1995, I noted that a strong emphasis of the conference was on the DSHEA legislation. It was a well-attended forum on dietary supplements industry perspectives and challenges. Many attendees were interested in the new regulations and wanted to understand what this law meant to their business. This law marked the beginning of a healthy industry. It was not perfect because it lacked some of the key components. For example, the law did not include any causes to define the structure/function of a product, which led to the confusion in the marketplace. Some individuals and some companies made claims without real scientific evidence, which seriously confused consumers on how to select the right products for their health. When products claim an exaggerated function or claims to be disease healing, a claim equivalent to medicines, it violates the FDA regulations for medicines. The worst claim was found to advocate that their products were capable of curing all diseases. These types of claims were clearly misleading and an illegal business practice. To overcome this kind of problem and all related issues, Congress passed another regulation in 2000 named structure and function claims (see 21 CFR 101, 2000). The legislation is important and beneficial to the nutrition supplement industry. With this regulation, false claims, whether on the label, on the product sheet, or posted on the website, were to be investigated and monitored by the FDA and attorneys from private industry. Significant fines and enforcement action would be applied to those who violated the regulation.

These two regulations have helped our industry achieve rapid and healthy growth. However, we did not stop there. The nutrition supplement industry was challenged by the pharmaceutical industry as well as by certain consumers who did not agree with the direction of the industry. The reason for the former was that nutrition supplement manufacturers did not have current good manufacturing practice (cGMP), a regulation that was established and enforced in pharmaceutical industry to ensure the quality of the medical products. Without these regulations in nutrition supplement industry, the nutrition products produced could not be guaranteed, and therefore, the quality was questionable. For this reason, many industrial members of dietary supplements got together and pushed through a regulation called United States Drug Manufacturing and Packaging in 2003. With the same group working together in a consistent effort, our own version of cGMP regulation was passed and signed into laws by President Obama in 2007. This regulation also set up the action for an enforcement timeline in three phases according to the size of the companies. A company with five hundred or more employees was required to be in compliance by the end of 2008; companies with fifty to five hundred employees by the end of 2009; and companies of any size by the end of 2010. Any company that did not meet compliance standards with cGMP would be punished by the FDA. It was because of this cGMP regulation that the market of laboratory testing service was given a real boost. The law requires all raw materials of nutrition supplements be tested for their identity and safety, all the final products be tested for accuracy as described in the label, and each product tested for their solubility, stability, and safety.

These three regulations have guided the US, and to some extent the world, step-by-step in the right direction for the development and expansion of the health food market. In each of these laws, an important component was the testing of products. Federal regulations have always been the important boost to the markets subject to the regulations.

I was new in my foray into the healthy food and dietary supplement industry, so these regulations were new to me as well. Therefore, I was determined to master the regulations, especially those related to laboratory testing service, as fast as I could. I wanted to be in the forefront of this new market and take every opportunity to develop our business. This rare opportunity occasioned by these regulations would become the best medicine for our company to succeed in the coming years.

The transition of our company from a difficult stage to a profitable survival stage was completed by the end of 1996. This achievement was important for our company because from that time on, we were not fighting for survival but instead for growth and expansion. We had the basic foundation to develop our laboratory into a reputable third-party testing company. To do this, according to the analysis of market and the situation of my laboratory, I developed our first five-year plan focusing on the following aspects.

Improving my laboratory equipment platform took the center stage. Due to our business growth, I decided to increase the installations of lab equipment and the update of older instrumentation to newer ones. In addition, I spent considerable time developing our standard operating procedures (SOPs) and standard analytical methods (SAM). All the newly hired were trained according to GLP standards. These areas of investment were enormous, including money and time. It was a consistent effort on my part because I wanted to make sure that we had the right system in place for both the operation platform and the management of personnel.

To cope with market demand, I developed and expended our service scope. By the end of the five years, my goal was to reach at least a hundred customers. Our services would cover all aspects of the nutrition testing markets and most parameters labeled on nutrition products. At the same time, I decided to phase out the environmental testing and contract research organization for pesticide residue market from chemical companies. Our focus would be on nutrition supplement and functional foods.

Along with the expansion of our service, I wanted to grow our revenue and profit, hopefully every year. Our goal was to increase our service revenue by at least 50 percent annually, with a positive cash flow and profitability. With this performance, I hoped to pay off the SBA loan and accumulate capital to build a stronger foundation for the second five-year plan of the company.

My five-year plan provided only a few general goals. It was not specific enough for many reasons. This was a small company with only three to four employees in the beginning of the plan. I was busy with daily testing work. Therefore, the plan was gradually adjusted and improved as the plan moved forward. I was satisfied with these goals because if I could achieve them, my company would be moved to another stage. Now I came to work with a happy face, which was a sharp contrast from the previous years when I carried a depressed mood most of the time as I worked because I was constantly struggling for survival. I was confident that I could achieve my goals by the end of the first five years.

To specifically execute my plan, I first expanded our laboratory space from 600 square feet to 1,300 square feet, including two laboratories and an office. With that, I could install more equipment and accommodate six to ten employees working at the same time, which should be good enough for us to use as we worked toward the end of the plan.

In order to deal with the increasing numbers of samples and the numbers of tests per sample, I finally hired our first full-time employee at the beginning of 1996. My wife also quit her job at the Chinese restaurant. I then hired a second full-time employee by the end of the year. Before that time, I did everything myself from sample preparation, running tests, equipment calibration, and maintenance to marketing and customer support. With two newly hired employees who were adequately trained on SOPs and analytical techniques, I gradually transferred most of the tests to them. As a result, I had a more time to develop our SOPs and testing methods as well as our marketing and sales. In addition, I used more time for quality control of the testing results.

My wife worked as both a technician and an accounting clerk. She was able to adapt to the job quickly, even if she had had no knowledge or experience in accounting. To further improve her knowledge in accounting, she took a few courses in accountancy at a local community college. The software platform we used was QuickBooks, which made our accounting simple and easy. My wife was able to easily do billing accounts payable and accounts receivable as well as financial statements. It saved us a lot of time in accounting, and we were fortunate to have this software.

As our company continued to grow, I hired more PhD and master's graduates as analytical chemists. The reason for me not to hire more undergraduates was that the tests we performed were quite challenging, and I wanted to have the best-qualified employees for the jobs. However, regardless of different level of graduates, all employees in our laboratory had to go through systemic training, including SOP, safety, and technical training before they were allowed to carry out our laboratory tasks. The chemists had to pass the method qualification evaluation before they were allowed to analyze samples independently.

There were considerable technologies and analytical methods used in our laboratory. As a nonchemistry major, I had to learn and master all analytical techniques that were routinely used in our testing. I often learned and accumulated information along the way. I realized that it was only after I had established a set of training standards and analytical methods that could make it easier for training new employees and for completing tests in a fast turnaround manner.

Adding employees brought the need for adding instruments to our laboratory. We had installed two older GCs and one even older HPLC to start our service in 1994. These instruments now were not sufficient to handle our sample volume. Adding to the problem was that they had gradually gotten close to the end of their life cycle. Therefore, starting from 1996, with our positive cash flow and having paid off our bank loan, with the gradual accumulation of cash on our balance sheet, we decided to purchase better used equipment or brand-new ones. For instance, we purchased a new Shimadzu HPLC and an excellent refurbished Agilent GC. At the same time, we also purchased a humidity and temperature-controlled environmental chamber and a biosafety fume hood. With these additions, we were able to accommodate our customers' demands for more service, and we expanded to product stability tests and microbial analyses.

A highlight of our first five-year plan was to establish our SOPs and hundreds of SAMs. This was particularly important to our company. As a result, I spent considerable amount of my time and energy on these efforts. By the end of the five years, I had written three large volumes of SOPs. In addition, these SOPs were revised on a regular basis, usually once every year in order keep them current.

In the beginning, I grouped the analytical testing methods with the SOPs, but later I found that the frequent revisions and amendments of the methods made them difficult to go along with the SOPs. This led to the separation of the SAM from the SOPs. Because a significant portion of the SOPs had been prepared and audited by chemical companies, this part of the work was indeed fast to complete. One emphasis in our SOPs was to include only those that were repetitive and easy-to-follow procedures. If a given procedure was difficult for an average chemist to follow, it should not be included in the SOPs. Once procedures were written as SOPs, we were expected to follow them without deviations; otherwise, the FDA and the EPA would consider it a violation. To our business, it was critical for us to have a set of standard analytical methods (SAM). According to our customers' test requirements, I made every effort to develop an analytical method for each test. To speed up the method development process, I adopted a few fast and effective approaches.

When a customer requested a specific test, my first step was to review the chemical structure of the organic compound in question. It is well-known that a relationship exists between a chemical structure and a testing method used for best possible results. Over the years, I paid attention to summarize this relationship and was able to recognize it at my first glance. With this information at hand, I could easily pick a separation column, select a mobile phase, and set an optimal temperature to achieve the best separation of a mixture of compounds for accurate quantification. An example of this is that when a compound contains a nitrogen atom in its structure, the HPLC mobile phase often contains ion-pairing ions or phosphate buffer to give the best peaks shape and resolution. Some of these techniques could be learned by reading the technical reports from manufacturers, while others could be learned from product bulletins from suppliers. Because these techniques were derived through many rounds of experiments, they often provided me with a starting point in my method development process. These invaluable techniques became an indispensable part of my effort to complete hundreds of methods.

Once a method had been determined, I wrote up the first draft of the method. This method was then used in the laboratory to determine if it worked as the method described. Frequently the method might require some adjustments before it was finalized. In the first few years, I often carried out the whole method development process by myself. It was toward the end of this five-year plan when the other chemists took part in the method development. Consequently, I was the one who knew the most methods and naturally became the company's most versatile person, mastering all technologies in analyzing nutrition supplements. I became a go-to person for all kinds of questions of analysis in this laboratory. This greatly benefited my marketing and customer support service later as well.

Through the development of the SOPs and SAMs, I learned a lot about how one could grow into a career, even if it was not one's major in college. A number of the people originally thought my college major was in chemistry; otherwise, I would not have gotten into the laboratory testing service. They were somewhat surprised to know that my study was in agronomy and botany. Therefore, it is not what you learn in school but what you want to do and accomplish. As long as we have certain basic knowledge and skills, we can develop various other skills and become experts in a specific area. There are numerous examples of this that in the traditional practice of "what you learned is what you should do" is no longer applicable in today's society. The most valuable asset accumulated in our laboratory is our several volumes of SOPs and several hundred SAMs. These documents enable us to build a reputation of producing fast and high-quality testing results. Without them, it would be hard to imagine how I could manage our daily laboratory operation.

Although establishing SOPs and SAMs took a major portion of my time, I constantly made my best effort on marketing, which I felt was equally important in growing our company. A strong marketing program was the lifeblood to enable any company to grow. I started from no experience to now understanding how to do marketing effectively. In fact, my approach to marketing was focused on relationship marketing. This marketing method is often used to describe a marketing focused on customer loyalty and long-term relationships. It also emphasizes a close relationship to be established as a priority before selling services to customers. This relationship marketing is a simple form of the well-known customer relationship management (CRM), which refers to practices, strategies, and technologies that companies use to manage and analyze customer interactions and data throughout the customer life cycle with the goal of improving business relationships with customers, assisting in customer retention, and driving sales growth. The CRM is sharply different from a short-term marketing approach where one emphasizes the short-term sale but not the long term relationship. It is a new method of marketing and is widely used in recent years. Specifically, I adopted this marketing method in our business by using resources to establish and maintain a good relationship with our customers and by promoting mutual benefits and a win-win relationship between our laboratory and the customers. There is basically no place in today's market for the older approach of marketing that depended on gifts and favors given. Rather, fair competition and mutual respect are the basic business ethics in today's world.

I started the relationship marketing method in the third year of business for our company. I did it step-by-step by first getting customers to try our service, then developing a relationship with the customers, and finally investing resources to maintain a good and long-term close relationship. Specifically, my practice can be summarized into several aspects.

Through various industrial shows and other channels, I identified the key persons in selected companies in our industry who were in charge of contracting tests to independent laboratories. These key persons include the quality control manager, the R and D director, and the designated chemist or staff. I collected their names, addresses, and phone numbers in my database for future contacts.

I then dealt with them on equal and mutual footing. When I faced a customer, I tried to make eye contact and listen to what the customers wanted and what their concern were. My goal was to make customers feel that I would be a trusted, honest, and good partner for them.

Once I had a customer using our service, I did what I could to keep the customer happy, which is prerequisite for a long-lasting relationship. I did this with multiple critical approaches. I kept contact with our customers and tried to understand what they needed on a regular basis. I paid attention to whether they got from us what they were expecting and what we could do better serve them. I stayed in contact with them through phone calls, emails, and our company's newsletters, etc. For major customers, I arranged to visit to them at least once every other year.

Customers were like my gods. I did everything I could to make them happy. Whenever a customer asked for special attention or a favor to test their products, I often accommodated these requests as long as the request was reasonable. I recognized that many good customers would not demand something unless there was an urgency or a serious problem that needed a solution for them as soon as possible. One such examples was that a customer needed to ship a product with a truck that was waiting in the loading dock, but the testing report was required before loading the product. In this case, as a service laboratory, I often set aside other work and completed the tests for this customer.

In addition to meeting the requirement of a turnaround time schedule, the quality of the testing results and the customer service after-test reports were submitted. These were all equally important. Our goal was to make sure that our customers were satisfied with these three aspects of services: quality results, fast turnaround time, and timely customer support, which were the building blocks of the CRM.

Another important factor to be considered when building a long-lasting relationship with customers is reasonable pricing. Although most customers followed the testing fees provided by us, they usually expected a reasonable pricing structure. As long as our prices and services were competitive, they accepted it. A significant portion of our customers took the quality of test results and the timely professional customer support over pricing because the former two were more related to their daily responsibilities and workload while the pricing was paid by the company and not by the employee involved. In other words, if time were money, receiving their test reports and helping them solve problems would outweigh the slightly higher fees. That was why we emphasized our fast turnaround time and our quality testing results.

Our customers were quite diverse, including manufacturers, distributors, brokers, and retail stores. Some were small companies, while others were large corporations. Over the years, I had developed an approach to differentiate them in my attempt to make then all happy. For example, when a customer placed more stress on quality and turnaround time, I made sure we did just that. Indeed, most long-term and large customers belonged to this group. For some price-sensitive customers, I paid more attention to service fees in order to please them. The smaller companies were included in this group. There were always some customers who demanded not only fast turnaround but also a deep discount. It was often that these customers frequently shopped around for pricing in order to save a few dollars. Because the test volume for these customers was small, I dealt with them by patiently explaining everything, but by the end of day, I often let it go in order to preserve our pricing strategy and the integrity of our company. For large and long-term customers, I often provided discounts as a way of preserving our long-term relationship.

The first five-year plan passed quickly. From reviving the company in 1996 to the completion of this plan by 2000, we doubled our laboratory spaces from 600 square feet to 1,300 square feet with an annual revenue growth of more than 50 percent, from $70,000 in 1995 to more than more than $1 million in 2000. Our employee head count rose from two to ten. In addition, we had added instruments to the laboratory and completed our SOPs and written many SAMs. We also passed the Illinois EPA pesticide performance evaluation and received the EPA certification. All these accomplishments had laid the foundation for our company's rapid growth and expansion in the coming years.

14-2: Z. Charlie Li performed analysis.

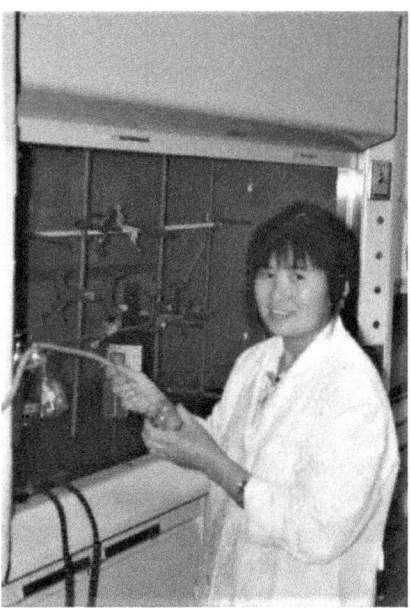

14-3: Lisong Zhang prepared samples.

14

ENTREPRENEURSHIP

SECTION FOUR

Business Maturity: Second Five-Year Plan (2001–2005)

Since we had successfully achieved our goals in the first five-year plan, I now had more confidence than ever with my second five-year plan from 2001 to 2005. I had a number of goals in this plan, including expanding our laboratory by at least three times to about four thousand square feet, adding employees by 100 percent to more than 20 full-time and part-time positions, installing additional instruments to meet the service requirement, completing our laboratory information management systems (LIMS), enhancing our capability to serve the demanding and more complex needs of our customers, and further raising the status of our laboratory nationally and internationally.

The expansion of our laboratory was officially called into action in 2002. At the time, we rented about 1,300 square feet of laboratories and office space, which was only sufficient to accommodate eight to ten part-time and full-time employees. Based on our plan, we would need at least 3,000–4,000 square feet of laboratory and office space by the end of this second five-year plan. In the current laboratory building, there was no more space for our expansion. Therefore, I had two possible options: either leasing another facility or buying a building for our laboratory.

At first, we set out to find another laboratory facility. After a few weeks of looking, I could not find any facility that would be suitable. Most vacancies were either not the right size, not in the right location, or simply not fit for laboratory usage. At about that time, the developer of the University of Illinois Research Park, Fox Development Corporation, learned that we were looking for space. President Fox wanted to recruit our company to the Research Park. I agreed that locating our business in the Research Park was a good option because we could make use of the university resources and networks, particularly being able to access the university library, student interns, and graduates, which would be beneficial for recruiting new employees. It could also help us improve the company's image and visibility. However, after twice discussing this with the developer, I concluded that leasing their space was not the best choice for us. The reason was that all facilities were built in a big-box structure. If I wanted a laboratory built or space remodeled, I must pay for upgrading it to fit our laboratory purposes. With three thousand square feet of laboratory and office space, I needed about $300,000 to remodel. In addition, if I signed a five-year lease term, my rental payment per month would be $4,000–$4,500, or an annual rent of about $50,000. Not only was this cost too high but also this space might not be enough for us in a few years. This would require the need for more space, and it could result in a substantial waste of the money that would have been used for the remodeling.

Precisely because of the lack of adequate leasing space in the Research Park, I decided on option 2. I would purchase and renovate a laboratory office building from an existing facility. I wanted the building to be at least 7,000–8,000 square feet, which should be sufficient for our laboratory needs over the next ten years. My wife and I set out with a realtor to find a suitable building, but after a couple of months, we could find nothing available for remodeling as our laboratory. After much discussion and comparison between buying and remodeling, remodeling a leased building, or building a new facility, we finally decided to purchase land and build our own laboratory facility. It turned out that this option was a smart one and became a key driver of our second five-year plan. It provided the foundation for our business expansion and the accumulation of our wealth in the coming decades.

We purchased a lot of about an acre in the Mattis Business Commercial Park, Champaign, in 1993, where the city had a tax incentive for owners to build in this park. The tax incentive included a five-year real estate tax exemption and tax exemption for purchasing building materials. Before the sale contract was signed, we hired an environmental engineering company to provide an investigative report on the site for an environmental and geological assessment. This was to ensure that there were no potential environmental issues and that the geological topography would be applicable to our laboratory facility. Completing these two engineering research reports took a few weeks with a total cost of about $6,000.

Once the land was purchased, I immediately hired an architect to help design the building and facility. Initially, I took the floor plan of the laboratory building we were renting as our basic design. I listed all the requirements for a functional laboratory and office spaces for the architect. These basic requirements included but were not limited to power supplies, number of electric outlets, fume hoods with ventilation, lab benches, wall cabinets, and sinks, etc. The architect started his design after he had my information and the assessment reports from the engineer. It took about two months at a cost of about $25,000 to complete the building design and for the blueprints.

The next step was to take the blueprints to prospective bidders. I selected five area construction companies and asked them to bid on my project. In addition to the blueprints, I included the requirements for specific components about a laboratory facility. In order to be able to read the bid reports from the bidders, I hired the original architect as our consultant. It took about two months for three bids to come back with prices ranging from $1.1 to $1.4 million. The consultant and I discussed the bids point by point to assess the quality of bids. Finally, we decided to hire Tatman Construction Company for the project. This company had made the lowest bid at about $1.1 million, but the quality of the bid was equally impressive. Of course, this price did not include laboratory equipment and furniture such as ventilation fume hoods, blowers, laboratory benches, and wall cabinets. The delivery schedule was about one year.

It took almost one year from buying the lot, the engineering study, the laboratory design, the bidding process, selecting the builder, and signing the contract. It was now the fall of 2003. The Tatman Construction Company could not immediately begin construction because the entire design blueprint for the building had to be approved by the City of Champaign. The approval process typically took two to three months. The municipal engineering meeting was held once every two months, and if the design was not approved at the first meeting, we would need to redesign the building accordingly then wait for the next scheduled meeting in another two months. With all these unknown, we had no idea how long we might have to wait.

I was lucky with the selection of Tatman as our construction company because this company had a good relationship with the city municipal authority. Our building was well-designed to meet the city code requirements, and our plan was approved at the first meeting in about two months. By that time, it was November, and it was a time of the year in Midwest that the ground was likely to be frozen with snow. If temperature was below zero, concrete could not be poured, underground drainage pipes could not be laid, and the foundation of the building could not be done. Therefore, it was critical to get the foundation done as soon as possible before the ground was frozen. If we could erect the structure by the end of the year, then we could complete installation of laboratory equipment and benches during the winter months, even if it were cold outside. The installation of laboratory furniture, electricity, and HVAC was a time-consuming process that could require several months. The bottleneck of our project was to get the concrete foundation poured and the building structure in before severe winter weather came. We had already set our moving date to May 2004, when our lease was up for renewal. For this reason, we prayed to God to give us good weather!

I was lucky again with the weather. The snow came much later than usual in that year. Tatman completed the installation of underground pipes and concrete floor in the middle of December. They also poured the parking lot having thirty-five parking places. The steel frame and the concrete block structure of the building along with the flat roof was completed in January of 2004. The weather had turned cold and snowing, but by this time, our contractor had already begun the installation of furniture and had completed all kinds of other work inside the building. To assist the construction process, I made sure that I did what I was supposed to do in a timely manner. If there was any problem in our design that we missed or if there was an added job, I did my best to speed up the process, making sure that I did not delay any step of the construction on my part. Because of the united effort between the contractor and our company, the building construction and the installation of furniture were completed at the end of April and delivered to us at the beginning of May of 2004, when we officially moved our laboratory into the building. This nearly two-year construction project was finally completed.

We named our laboratory building JMT Technology Center. JMT are the initials of our three sons' names (John, Michael, and Tony). The building had a total area of 11,000 square feet, about half laboratory space and half offices and other purpose rooms—a conference room, break room, storage and utility rooms. The laboratory was fitted with 180 linear feet of high-quality and acid-resistant laboratory benches or tables, with cabinets and more than 100 feet length of wall cabinets. If this furniture were new, it would have cost at least $100,000. There were also five fume hoods, which were acid- and base-resistant. If they had been new, they would have cost another $40,000. There were ten laboratory acid-resistant sinks as well. All said and done, the laboratory furniture and accessories would have cost $200,000–$300,000 if new. But they cost us only about $50,000.

I had my laboratory built with such large space, equipped with excellent-quality benches and wall cabinets at a low cost due to my careful planning and budgeting. From the time that I decided to have my own laboratory built, I had looked for quality secondhand furniture. I was fortunate to find a laboratory that was closing for most of my lab benches and cabinets, a full-loaded semitruck of it!

The total cost for our laboratory building was about $1.3 million. We borrowed from a local bank for approximately 80 percent of the cost, with a down payment of 20 percent from our cash savings and free cash flow. Our payment was about the same as if we had agreed to be a tenant in the University Research Park. Our monthly mortgage payment would have been similar to that of the monthly rent. Therefore, I was very proud of this accomplishment and felt it was one of the best decisions I had made. I had spent a similar amount of money as I would have on the leasing option in the Research Park, but I now owned this quality building that would accommodate our business for the next ten years. It had to be one of the major cornerstones of our company.

In addition to the laboratory building, our plan included the upgrade of our laboratory instrumentation. To accommodate our growth, I purchased several new HPLCs and GCs to retire several older HPLC and GC. Through a few years of experience in using HPLC from the Japanese manufacturer Shimadzu, we really liked it for two reasons: ease of use and low cost. Their HPLC was good quality and cost about 20 percent less than its immediate competitors. If we had any problems with the instruments, their technical support team could help us solve problems at a minimal cost. For GC, we selected Agilent's because this company produces the best GC in the world. Even if the GC from Agilent was more expensive than other suppliers due to its technology and longevity, it was our best choice. From 1998 to 2005, we added ten new HPLCs and two new GCs. We also added other high-end instruments such as inductive couple plasma (ICP) spectrometer, gas chromatograph-mass spectrometer (GC-MS) and liquid chromatography-mass spectrometer (LC-MS). Our practice of buying instruments had changed from older with minimal cost to newer and easier use as our main purpose.

Our company required a laboratory information management system (LIMS). This software platform was critical for our long-term growth. Using this LIMS, we could track and manage our samples from receiving, testing, reporting, storing, and retrieving, all in digital and automatic format. These traceable operations were absolutely necessary for the satisfaction of our customers and to be in compliance with the FDA regulations.

The importance of LIMS called this investment to the forefront task for the company in 2004. That year was a year of our major investment. We not only completed the construction of the laboratory building and the installation of approximately half a million dollars in new equipment but now we also planned to invest $100,000 in LIMS. The LIMS was purchased from Thermo Fisher. After we installed the software platform, our information technology (IT) director took part in a technical training workshop, then he spent a lot of time customizing the LIMS based on our tests and day-to-day operation. The platform included a centralized computer system server, a database, and an internal network system. We had more than twenty of the company's instruments and dozens of computers networked to the server. The analytical data and the notebooks of laboratory tests were input into the server. The data stored in the server were retrievable for easy access to meet the requirements of customers and regulatory audits. The system required a full-time staff to manage it. As part of the IT expenses, we had several software companies with whom we signed contracts, costing us an annual total of about $30,000. These contracts included software usage right, technical support, and royalty fees. After several months of familiarization and training of our employees, the LIMS was finally put into use in October of the same year. The installation and customization of the LIMS was another major milestone for our company.

More major investment for us in 2004 was related to hiring more chemists and technicians. It was obvious to me that our completion of building facility, installation of new instruments, and the LIMS would give our business a boost. Therefore, I had to hire additional staff to accommodate this anticipated growth and expansion for the next several years. My strategy was to set up a short-term and an immediate-term approach. For the short term, I hired employees according to the amount of business we had had the prior three to six months, with a projection of the next three to six months. For the immediate term, I projected our business based on the industrial trend and the competitive position we were in. Since our main expenses were on personnel, I used a baseline revenue of about $140,000 per employee to consider our short-term hiring. Because of this disciplinary practice, I rarely under- or overhired employees in our laboratory. I had no records of firing employees during my tenure until the end of 2005.

Our newly hired candidates were primarily graduates from the University of Illinois (UIUC), although a small number of graduates from other universities was also hired. Résumés from candidates were obtained by job replacement offices at UIUC and Parkland Colleges of Champaign, Illinois, by a twice-a-year job fair organized by the UIUC, and by referral of current employees. I established an account with UIUC and with Parkland College so that I could make a regular search for qualified candidates. Once a candidate was identified, I brought him/her to our laboratory for interview.

When I reviewed the qualification of a candidate, I often looked at a couple of key items. First was the applicant's past achievements and the potential for future success. To evaluate the accomplishments, I paid special attention to the productivity and efficiency of student's college program and the years needed to finish the undergraduate or graduate degree. Since the average time to complete an undergraduate degree was four years, if the candidate needed five years, unless there was a special situation that had disrupted or interfered with their schedule, then I considered the candidate in the low tier in regard to productivity and efficiency. This would not fit our laboratory's fast-paced operation. When speaking to a potential employee, I mainly looked at the work habits and productivity of graduate study. If no paper was published in a master's program or fewer than two papers for a PhD dissertation research, unless there was a good reason, I would not consider the candidate productive. Secondly, I looked for candidates who were more bench-type chemists and technicians. Except for our marketing and customer support staff, we did not require a candidate to have strong English skills, but I looked for good skills in chemistry. Given similar qualification, I preferred candidates with the work ethic of a down-to-earth person who usually worked more hours daily and stayed longer with our company.

The labor laws in the United States were well established, and every company must comply with these laws when hiring. There is no discrimination by color, religion, gender, or age. Employers are required to follow these labor laws and must treat all applicants equally. In order to prevent lawsuits and litigation by employees and job applicants, as an employer, I often recorded and archived candidate qualification and answers in the interviews. This was especially important for our company to hire candidates who were foreign graduates.

Our laboratory was often asked why we employed foreign graduates. In general, many companies do not want to hire foreign graduates because of the strict requirements to comply with labor laws. US labor regulations specifically state that no employers can hire foreign graduates unless the graduate has a legal status and is allowed to work in the United States. Otherwise, the employers will be fined and disciplined. Most foreign graduates may apply for a twelve-to-eighteen-month internship program, and if approved, the company can hire the student for the purpose of practical training and as a temporary worker. However, when the practical training is over, the employee must be let go unless the company can help the intern obtain a working visa called H-1B.

The number of H-1B visa issued annually in the United States are limited and authorized by the United States Congress each year, which may vary in number. Because the number of applicants applying for H-1B greatly exceeds the work visa quota, it is difficult for all applicants to obtain this visa. To determine who gets H-1B depends on the time of application before the 1990s. Usually, the earlier an application is submitted, the better the chance of getting it. However, during the 2010s, it was based on a random selection process taking into consideration the qualification of the applicants. Once approved for H-1B, a student's visa will change from student to temporary worker, which is good for five years of employment. During this employment period, most H-1B holders usually go ahead and apply for a labor certificate authorization (LCA) and then an application for green card or permanent residency. This has been the main pathway for international students to permanently stay in the United States and to become US citizens. This application process typically takes two to five years. Another way to apply for a green card is as a prominent contributor, such as outstanding scientists or experts. The United States government has set special category for these foreign nationals to apply for EB-1B, which is a fast track, usually about one year, to receive the green cards.

In our small laboratory, however, we were not qualified for EB-1B application for our employees and our H-1B temporary employees had to go through the normal process, which included advertising for our openings, selection of job candidates from US citizens, followed by foreign candidates. In order to offer a job to the foreign candidate, an employer had to prove that none of the US citizens and permanent residences were qualified for the job as described in the advertisement before they were allowed to hire foreign applicants. All these procedures must be in compliance with the labor laws. Once an employee had the H-1B, it could be taken to a new employer. For every foreign candidate hired, employers spent not only time but also money since the advertising and application fees, as well as attorney fees, could add up to $10,000 or more. All these restrictions make a lot of employers not want to hire foreign candidates.

Our laboratory employed a number of foreign student graduates of American universities. I had several considerations when employing them.

They usually had an excellent educational background and possessed basic laboratory skills, plus they were more eager to have jobs and were willing to work harder to complete their job assignments. When they were offered a job, they tended to be more stable workers, which could be very important for a small business, especially one requiring highly skilled workers. Generally, training would take about six months to a year for a chemist to be able to perform tests independently in our laboratory. It was in our best interest to have a stable workforce with minimal turnover rate. As an immigrant myself, I knew how hard it was to find a decent job. Therefore, within the law, I was happy to hire foreign chemists and help them apply for the H-1B visa and a green card. Several excellent chemists working in our laboratory changed their visa status from student to H-1B and eventually to permanent residency.

Champaign County is a low-cost living area. Salaries of most employees were relatively low compared to those of the West Coast or the East Coast. Recognizing this, I tried to provide benefits to the employees, including medical health insurance, retirement contributions, and a year-end bonus. By adding all these benefits and salary together, our overall compensation was reasonably good compared to other testing laboratories in the area. My goal was to minimize the employee turnover rate and to make sure employees were happy with our workplace environment. I felt strongly that a stable workforce was undoubtedly a good, intangible asset for our company.

An important indication of the maturity for the nutrition supplement industry in the US was the comprehensive implementation of the regulation current good manufacturing practices (cGMP). This regulation has been considered as another milestone for the industry. The law clearly stipulates that good laboratory practice (GLP) is an important part of this legal requirement. Laboratories include manufacturers' own laboratories and independent third-party testing laboratories. The main part of the cGMP includes manufacturing operation, staff training, equipment performance, production program design and control, raw material quality, safety of product formulation, packaging specifications, trademarks and labels, comprehensive quality control and records, product distribution, product sales, product recovery, customer satisfaction and feedback, etc. Because it involves a wide range of areas, our company focused only on those that were related to our laboratory operation, which mainly included standard operating procedures, standards testing methods, equipment calibration and qualification, quality assurance, staff training, documentation, and record archiving.

Although our laboratory had built a strong reputation in the industry, we continued to experience challenges in the standard analytical methods. This had been the case with many other competitive laboratories as well. One major reason for it was that there were tens of thousands of nutrition supplement products in the marketplace, many of which were with complex formulations. The complexity of products made it impossible for a standard method suitable for testing such diversified products. For example, a simple method is good for a vitamin C supplement product with one single ingredient of ascorbic acid, but if this vitamin C was formulated with a dozen other vitamins, especially with a number of herbal ingredients, the method wouldn't work anymore. It is not uncommon to have a product with over thirty ingredients, and some may even contain a dozen or more of traditional Chinese medicines (TCM). We were constantly challenged with interferences among the organic compounds present in herbs. As a result, an established method for one customer's product might not be applicable to a similar product from another customer. As a third-party independent laboratory, our samples were from diversified customers, including manufacturers, importers, distributors, and retailers. We performed hundreds of test methods for several thousands of nutrition parameters in our laboratory. In addition, some of the samples contained low concentration of ingredients, while others had high concentration. Because of all these complexities, it was impossible for us to have one method for all parameters in one product or for the same parameter from different types of samples. Making things even more challenging was the fact that the formulations were constantly changing; testing methods had to be updated accordingly. Because of all these problems, our standard methods had actually become nonstandard. We allowed our chemists to adapt and make small changes to our methods to fit a specific type of the samples. Due to the complexity of the analytical methods involved, the new cGMP allows each testing laboratory to select the best method that is suitable for a given test.

The United States Pharmacopeia (USP) is the gold standard for pharmaceutical industry. In this USP, one method per parameter is required for drug analysis. Because the formulation was simple with one to a few active ingredients involved, the method development process is somewhat easier. Every laboratory testing the same drug usually follows the same monograph, and therefore, the testing results are more accurate and comparable across different laboratories. In contrast, there were no standard testing methods for dietary supplement published by USP until a few years ago. Even now, the methods described in the USP and National Formulary were not widely used because those methods might be good for only a limited group of products but not suitable for many others. Therefore, each independent testing laboratory continued using its own methods, which had led to the confusion of interpreting testing results from different laboratories. Regulatory agency and industrial leaders noted this in 1990s but had no real solution to it. This is one of the major concern of consumers that nutrition supplements are not manufactured to the same quality of standards as medicines.

The regulation on pharmaceuticals requires that each method for analyzing drugs must be validated before use. In general, the time required to validate a method takes several days to a few weeks depending on the methods under validation. If we wanted to validate all our three hundred methods by the USP criteria, it would take a chemist ten years to complete. In addition, we added methods on a weekly basis, and an older method may need revision as the formulation of products changed. This monumental work in validation makes it impossible and unrealistic for a laboratory to have every method validated. Fortunately, the cGMP regulations do not require independent testing laboratory to validate every method used but instead to use a scientifically sound and valid method. Because our methods were mostly from either other standards methods or from peer publications and technical application notes, they are therefore considered scientifically valid methods.

In order to enhance our credibility and to build our reputation among our customers, we decided to systemically validate our methods. Our approach was to set the priority in our scheduling with the most frequently used methods being validated first and the least-used method the last. For every validated method, we summarized all data in a validation report. After going through the validation process, our chemists had more understanding of the method performance, and it also served as a training tool for our current and future chemists. More importantly, these validation studies were used in benefiting our marketing and customer support. Many of our customers, when auditing our laboratory, usually praised us for using validated methods for testing their samples. Our ability for method development and validation provided us the reputation, not only as a testing laboratory but also as a service provider for method development and validation.

Another requirement of the cGMP is a training program for employees, designed to ensure that the laboratory has qualified staff to complete tests. Our company had two options to train a new employee: self-training and class-training. The former was based on an arranged study section for employees on specific SOPs and SAMs as well as safety and ISO manuals. The latter was set up to train employees in a classroom setting that could be conducted by internal experts or outside experts. In order to save money and to have a timely training schedule, I often acted as a trainer for most of internal training. FDA does not set specific requirements for staff training. As long as our employees were trained and documented, we were considered in compliance with cGMP.

The cGMP law is comprehensive and set specific criteria for all companies. However, the law does not tell us a specific way of how to meet the law requirements. This leaves companies with options for choosing effective ways to meet the compliance standards. For example, the law requires all that laboratory equipment be qualified and calibrated on a regularly basis, but how to do the qualification and calibration or how many times calibrations are needed to be considered adequate was not defined. Another example is that it requires all employees be trained, but how to train them is not mandated. One important point that FDA looks for is the records of the equipment calibrations and qualifications and the employees' training records, which should be as detailed as possible and retraceable. If an SOP has prescribed a specific standard procedure, it must be carried out. Otherwise, we will be found in noncompliance and the FDA regulatory audit would not be passed.

Full compliance with cGMP has been required for every company since 2010. However, prior to that time, we obeyed the regulations of DSHEA and the structure-function claims. I learned a good lesson related to compliance during the early 2000s. In my first five-year plan, our business was focused on nutrition supplement testing. By about 2000, we took another step to expand our testing service to the pharmaceutical industry by including testing for over-the-counter medicines. For drug analysis, we were required to follow the USP monograph without variation. If there is any significant change, the method must be validated again before it can be used. After some effort, we were able to attract a few customers of the industry, although our volume of testing was low.

It was because the service we provided to a company that manufactured both the nutrition supplements and medicines that triggered a FDA audit. On one day in 2002, an FDA official came by unexpectedly. After showing us her identification, she wanted to audit our testing results for a particular test we performed for this customer. When we received a product from this particular manufacturer, we did not know it was a medical drug because the request for a sample submission did not provide that information. Our chemist tested this parameter, not following the USP monograph method.

I had never had any experience with a FDA audit and had not even had any meeting with the regulatory agency in the past. Her arrival at our laboratory made me feel very uneasy. The FDA audit was for a product for which our customer had applied to FDA for New Drug Application (NDA). During the FDA review of the drug, the test report from our laboratory were used. The FDA officer asked for all related records of the sample analysis, including the chain of custody, sample storage, names of the chemist and technicians performing the test, the method used, the results deduced, quality control and assurance, the approval process, and the notebooks and data storage files. She started with our SOPs and then the test methods. She found that our chemist did not follow the method exactly as described and had even made a mistake in calculation. Because of this finding, she extended her review to a larger scale audit that included all other aspects of our laboratory operation. This was completely out of my original expectation because I thought it would be a simple audit on this one project for which we had charged only about $1,000. She spent five days in our laboratory. At the end of audit, she handed over to me a Form 483 that described her findings of noncompliance with pharmaceutical cGMP regulations. The Form 483 was actually a warning letter to our laboratory. She read each violation to me during an exit interview and had me agree to the findings with my signature before she left our laboratory.

In the beginning, I thought this warning was a really big deal for our company. It was not until later, when I searched the FDA website, did I find many similar warnings like ours published there. Some of the warnings were issued to major pharmaceutical companies, while others to small laboratories. Although there were numerous 483s on that site, it did not make me feel better about the situation I was in. I was very concerned that this kind of posted warning would greatly affect our business. I did not have time to think about what this could mean to our business, but instead I focused on my response on each item listed on the 483. FDA had set a deadline for my response, which was within two months. Accordingly, I made necessary changes to our SOPs and proposed new policies and procedures to clarify and overcome the problems related to our noncompliance. I set up SOPs on method amendments and deviation. I submitted the responses and the time table for implementing the changes to the FDA. The FDA would follow my response by conducting a second audit.

That was indeed the case. Another FDA officer came to our laboratory two years later. He first reviewed the listed items in our last Form 483 compared to my response. The officer audited our other operations against our standard corporate documents. We were confirmed to have made a great improvement but were still not fully in compliance with FDA standards for the cGMP of the pharmaceutical industry. The auditor questioned why we did not use a paper notebook instead of the electronic notebook we used. We explained to him that the digital records are easier to maintain. We also emphasized that our laboratory was a nutrition supplement testing laboratory and not a pharmaceutical testing laboratory, since our revenue serving the pharmaceutical industry was only about 5 percent of our total business. FDA wouldn't consider our points and our warning continued being posted on FDA website. It was not until a third audit another two years later that our laboratory passed the FDA audit and the warning letter was taken off the FDA website.

Through these FDA audits, I learned a great deal about regulatory requirements and how to prepare for audits. We must have well-trained chemists and technicians. All our work must be conducted in accordance with government regulations. We must have standard procedures in conducting testing, and these procedures must be followed without deviation. If there is any deviation to our SOPs and the testing methods, we must carefully document the deviation in as much detail as possible. The documentation should be archived and retrievable. Finally, we must have a strong quality control and quality assurance program to ensure the quality of testing results.

The second five-year plan passed by quickly. By the end of 2005, our company had grown significantly. Our customer base had expanded to three hundred to four hundred, and our revenue and income tripled. We had built our laboratory facility and installed many new instruments along with our LIMS. We increased the number of our employees to twenty-two. In brief, our laboratory had become a stronger and more reputable third-party independent testing laboratory.

14

ENTREPRENEURSHIP

SECTION FIVE

China Entrepreneurship Experience (1998–2010)

By 1998, our company was established as a recognized independent third-party testing laboratory in the nutrition supplement industry. At about the same time, China was opening up, and its economic reform was undergoing rapid development.

Guangzhou Municipal Government, supported by the central Ministry of Education and the Ministry of Science and Technology, organized the first forum and conference for scientific exchange of overseas Chinese scholars at the Garden Hotel in Guangzhou at the end of that year. I took my own entrepreneurial experience and testing technology to join the elite group of the Chinese from around the world attending this conference and forum.

I was one of hundreds of scholars who had an ambitious plan to help our motherland achieve a great leap forward in advanced technology, commercialization of new technologies, and to shorten the distance between China and developed countries. The delegates attending the conference included governmental officers and provincial leaders, leaders of major cities and economic development regions and zones, as well as key executives for domestic companies. Some of the delegates came to the conference hunting for technologies, while others came for recruiting technical experts. Still others wanted to lure the scholars to establish companies in their cities and regions. The meeting agenda included seminars on technology innovation, business planning and proposals, and matchmakers between government agencies and scholars.

The Guangzhou Municipal Government has introduced a plan to build a biotechnology island in the Pearl River Delta. Although I had prepared a plan to establish a testing laboratory in China, I did not have the opportunity to present it during the meeting. After some discussion with limited attendees, I found that my project did not attract much interest. It could have been that my technology was not innovative enough and might not have had the commercial potential. Therefore, it was not the subject of the forum. Nevertheless, I used this conference as my preliminary attempt to understand economic and business opportunities in China.

After I returned from the conference, while I continued focusing on my laboratory in the US, I kept my eyes open for business opportunities in China. One of my ideas was to find a partner in China with whom I could build a China laboratory. Toward this goal, I sought help from my friends. In 2001, through one of my friends, I was introduced to a possible business partnership with the Physical and Chemical Testing Center of Jiangsu Province. This center was located in Nanjing City, Jiangsu, China, where I met with the deputy director of Jiangsu government overseeing the center and the laboratory directors and managers of the center.

Our discussion was focused on how to form a cooperation and make changes to the center so it could become a private laboratory. At the time, the China was undergoing many changes, including privatizing nationally owned companies and enterprises, including laboratories. A good example of this change was that Beijing City-owned Beijing Physics and Chemistry Testing Center was under serious discussion for privatization, which was actually completed in 2002. I liked this business model and also proposed to privatize the Jiangsu Center. If I were successful in this transformation, I could then achieve two key objectives of having a laboratory platform and a government-lent credibility, or provincial seal, possibly with a budget that we could support. The laboratory platform was absolutely necessary for my China laboratory. To set up a testing platform, a significant investment would be required. This was not in my business plan, especially because there were so many unknown factors that could affect our business. In this case, our investment would be risky. To minimize the risk, forming a partnership with an existing laboratory was the best option for me.

The other factor would be to have the governmental credibility, an important factor because in a socialist country that had just opened to the world, most people believed in government's not-private laboratories. People would take the government stamps or seals over personal signatures, which are most commonly used in Western countries. Therefore, a partnership or joint undertaking with a government-owned laboratory would provide the credibility for our China laboratory.

Through serious discussions, we reached a preliminary consensus that we would reorganize the center according to the model adopted by Beijing Physics and Chemistry Testing Center. I, through my US company, would invest 1 to

2 million Chinese yuan into the laboratory for the purpose of updating the laboratory instruments and remodeling the laboratory. My other contributions would be the laboratory management experience and testing technologies, as well as helping with marketing to international trade companies, both in China and in the US. And I would make a verbal commitment to keep all current staff in the center employed. The center would provide the current laboratory platform, the current customer roster, the certifications from government agencies, and the day-to-day operation and management. Under this format, my company and the government of Jiangsu Province would each own 50 percent of the new company. I was very happy that this verbal agreement had been reached. As a side trip, I visited several main scenic spots of Nanjing.

After I got back to the United States, although I still had some concern about the verbal commitment of such a substantial investment, which I felt was a high risk because of my lack of business experience in China. I looked forward to the commencement of the project as soon as possible. According to the schedule agreed upon by both sides, I should have received the contract information from the center within a couple of months. However, several months later, I had received no information about the matter. It was only until after my friend in Beijing contacted the center did we learn that the center had withdrawn the plan due to a change of directors at the Jiangsu Province Productivity Promotion Center. As a result, this partnership venture was put on hold indefinitely.

I was not let down by the unsuccessful attempt to partner with the center in Jiangsu Province and continued to pursue my China business plan. Over the next couple of years, I returned to China a few times, seeking business partners mostly in three big cities, Beijing, Shanghai, and Guangzhou. I visited the Guangzhou branch of China National Test Center (CNTC) and discussed the possibility of cooperation with director of the center. He and a few smart deputy directors of the branch had already realized there would be an inevitable transformation of national and provincial laboratories to private firms, just like the model of the Beijing Physics and Chemistry Testing Center. They had established their own laboratory at an economic development zone in Guangzhou. Their private laboratory did not perform tests, but instead sent all samples to the branch labs of CNTC where they had arranged for tests. This practice would not have been allowed in the US and other countries because of the conflict of interest, but at that time in China, it was a common practice for people with power and authority. Perhaps because of the complex arrangement, they did not see a fit between my laboratory and their laboratory. Therefore, they recommended that I seek a partnership opportunity with their subsidiary laboratory in Shenzhen City, about a hundred kilometers south of Guangzhou City. Accordingly, I visited that laboratory and had several hours of discussion with the laboratory director. We both agreed there was an opportunity for collaboration, but we did not agree on specifics. To follow up, we emailed each other and spoke by phone over the next several months. For various reasons, we were not able to move the partnership proposal forward. Therefore, my second attempt to build a China business was not successful.

In addition to the Guangzhou Branch of CNTC, I tried to develop a partnership in Shanghai through one of my employees who had friends in the city. A visit to Shanghai and several discussions with a couple of people did not yield any progress. By this time, I felt that it was somewhat unrealistic to find a partnership laboratory in China. Therefore, I was forced to consider my last option to set up my own laboratory in China.

To begin this pursuit, I first decided on a location for my laboratory. Based on the analysis of the situation in China, I felt that my laboratory should be in one of three major cities: Beijing, Shanghai, or Guangzhou. Guangzhou and Shanghai were more business friendly because they had opened to the world earlier and the government policies were more liberal and more geared toward rapid development of the economy. There was an efficiency of the governmental operations, such as a fast business registration and approval process. On the other hand, Beijing was more bureaucratic, but with good order and safety, as well as better social behavior and activity. With many universities and central government offices located there, Beijing City had a lot to offer. For instance, there were opportunities for government funding, which would be good for a technology start-up. Therefore, there were strengths and advantages for each of the three cities being considered. Now the key factor influencing my decision was whether I could find a good partner. Because I had no friends in these cities on whom I could rely, the progress was slow.

I considered the options on a company location for a few months. Finally, through an introduction of my friend, I met Mr. Ling in Beijing. At the first meeting, we both appeared to like each other, and we decided to create a joint undertaking of a laboratory together. The partnership agreement included my investment of 1.5 million yuan in the company for 80 percent of the venture. Mr. Ling would invest his time and management into the company for 20 percent. I was responsible for the full set of analytical methods, laboratory management, and market development experience. In addition, I would help to develop the business of targeting companies in both the US and China that wanted quality control testing prior to their international trade. Chinese manufacturers and the US importers were our potential customers.

After several trips to China with a number of potential partnership negotiations, finally in the spring of 2006, I established my laboratory name as Beijing Zhenyuan Chemistry Technology Inc. in China. The company was registered in the Haidian District, Beijing, with a registered capital of 1.4 million yuan. The company headquarters and laboratory were located in Zhongguancun Bio-Medical Park, which was the property of the Beijing Municipal Government as an entrepreneurial incubator. The main anchor building was a large six-story commercial facility that hosted a couple dozen companies. Some of these companies were engaged in the development of medicines, some served the biotechnology and health care industries, while others provided a research and analytical testing platform. All tenants would be able to share and use the analytical platform after signing a contract with the park management committee.

I knew from the start that my investment in the China laboratory would be only enough to hire a few staff and for marketing and operation expenses for only one to two years. It did not include setting up the testing laboratory platform, which would require as least five times the amount of the registered capital. Therefore, we chose to sign a contract with the park director to use their analytical platform for two years.

Our contract consisted of three parts: the use of the analytical platform as we wanted, at the same time, allowing us to install necessary specialized equipment at our own expense, and the availability of analysts from the incubator for us to help in performing tests. The analyst on loan to us was on the payroll of the incubator but compensated by our laboratory. We agreed to pay a portion of the base salary, plus the hourly cost of the analyst when performing tests for our laboratory. In order to obtain quality testing results that were comparable to those of my US laboratory, I was responsible for training the analysts. In addition, I provided all standard operating procedures and standard analytical methods to the venture laboratory. Although, this was not the best option because the whole set of my methods and SOPs was exposed. However, in order to reduce the risk of more cash investment for this unpredictable business, it was our best choice at the time.

As agreed on between Mr. Ling and me, I was the chairman of the company. Mr. Ling would serve as president and lead the company to develop business and to serve our customers, as well as coordinate with the incubator. He would be responsible for hiring employees and managing the operation. I invited my niece from Guangxi to hold the position of accounting and treasurer for the joint undertaking.

After the company was established and the key positions filled, I thought everything would be on the track. However, a few months passed and not much business was conducted. I realized that my partner's time and energy were not really spent on this laboratory.

I knew that he had his own company selling used equipment in China in addition to this joint undertaking. At about that time, he had just gotten a contract to be a distributor of a US equipment company. That opportunity made him reevaluate the joint undertaking. After I spoke to Mr. Ling a couple of times and through a few emails, he unexpectedly quit the partnership in less than six months. I had no choice but reorganized the company in the Haidian District to become the 100 percent owner.

The failure of the partnership with Mr. Ling was a serious setback for my business venture in China. I hated to be in that situation. From the outset of my venture, I anticipated having a partner there to run the laboratory for me, with my focus to continue to be my US company. This decision was based entirely on the fact that our US business was in a rapidly growing phase and still had considerable potential for years to come, while the venture business in China was risky. I was willing to put some money into the venture, but I was not willing to spend my time and energy on something that was unknown.

I decided to hire a manager for our China laboratory, and through some recruiting effort, I hired a woman as our marketing manager. I knew that she was not the most qualified person for the job, but given the situation, she was my best choice at the time. She had a year or two of work experience after graduating from college. She began by learning the industry we served and the technology behind our service. It was unfortunate that her chemistry background was not good, and she did not have enough experience in marketing. With her lack of knowledge in the nutrition supplement industry, she could not stay with the job, and she resigned after only half a year in the company. This was another setback for my China laboratory.

When the woman resigned, she introduced her friend and classmate Mr. Chin to me. After interviewing him, I felt that the young man was a good candidate, and I hired him for our company. At the beginning, I proposed that I could pay him a salary plus stock ownership. To my surprise, he was not interested in company stock shares but demanded a higher wage instead. He said that he wanted to go back to school for an MBA in a few years. I knew this was a little unusual because most people would like a stock option. Anyone who did not like this option indicated that he would not want to work hard for the company long term.

After my repeated proposal met without success, I accepted his wishes in order to make him feel that I was serious about the success of the company; and to show that the future financial success of the company would reward him, I included the right of stock option for him in his contract. His responsibility included both the marketing and the customer relations, as well as coordination with the incubator and managing the company.

The young man showed his ability in the first a couple of months on the job. Under his leadership, our laboratory got off the ground and started getting customers. He had indeed pushed our laboratory forward slowly. In order to improve the visibility of the laboratory, in the fall of 2006, I applied for the Capital Award Program for Overseas Students and Scholars who wanted to establish new business in China. This award program was under the management of the Beijing Municipal Government. I made a special trip to China to give a talk on our laboratory service, and I was selected by the committee to be a winner of a 100,000 yuan award. Everything seemed to be going well for the first six to twelve months led by Mr. Chin. However, over the next two years, the growth of the China laboratory slowed. We could attract certain customers of manufacturers and exporters in China, as well certain importers in the US, but the volume of business stayed relatively small. The income and expenses were generally in line with revenue, resulting in a balanced cash flow, but the laboratory was barely surviving with no significant growth or expansion. By 2010, as dictated in the sales contract of my US laboratory, the China laboratories had to be transferred to my relatives.

From the establishment of China laboratories, the exit of the partner, the hiring of two different business managers, to the barely survival of our business and to the final exit from China when I transferred the laboratories to relatives, it was about six years of effort. This unsuccessfully entrepreneurial attempt was a good lesson to learn. Although there were many reasons that I did not achieve my original expectation, there were a few important and outstanding ones that are summarized here.

China's testing market did not open up as I had originally expected. My thesis on the market development in China was based on China joining in the World Trade Organization (WTO), which would open its private testing service market. My prediction at the time was that since China joined WTO in 2000, its testing market should be open in about five years. Under that assumption, if our labs could be established earlier, the business opportunity would be there for us to succeed. Unfortunately, this was not the case. The testing market did not keep pace with the economic policies in the manufacturing industry. The closed-door policy in testing led to the continuation of analytical services market that were served by the governmental and provincial laboratories.

My expectation was overly optimistic that the service market of China would be similar to the ones in the US and the EU, where most commercial testing is carried out by private laboratories, while the government laboratories mainly focused on law enforcement and public safety testing. China had only a few private laboratories, far less than the number of laboratories owned by the government. Several foreign laboratories, such as SGS, entered the China market only by collaborating with domestic governmental laboratories for obvious reasons because the credibility provided by the governments was so critical for success. There was no business like ours that had no affiliation with the government and that was 100 percent owned by a foreign entity. It was not until 2015 that the testing market gradually opened up for private laboratories. This was, undoubtedly, a serious challenge for the survival and growth of our China laboratory.

Most Chinese still did not believe in small laboratories and private laboratories but in national or provincial laboratories. This was due to the influence of Chinese traditional and social factors. People believe only in the government and in the Red Seal provided by government, not personal signatures. Even the law enforcement agencies had the same bias. This was why one of the world's authoritative multinational laboratories like SGS chose to partner with a China governmental organization. Our China laboratory was a start-up with no collaboration with a government entity, which made it harder for us to compete in the China market.

The business of dealing in China was very different from that of the US and EU. Chinese are more reliant on personal relationship. In the US, we also use relationships in our business, such as relationships in marketing and customer support. However, this is very different from the relationship practiced in China. The relationship there means special treatment, such as invitations to nightclubs, travel and dinners, gifting, red envelopes, bribery, and even kickbacks, etc. Our approach was obviously different from all these. I knew that I could not adapt to this Chinese relationship. I was unwilling to do it on the one hand, and on the other hand, I did not have the money to do so. In fact, from the very beginning, I just wanted to adapt the business model of my laboratory in the United States and apply it to the China laboratory venture. This was clearly not in line with business dealings in the national conditions in China. That might have been one of many reasons that we were not able to obtain projects from national and provincial governments but instead were getting small projects from manufacturers and exporters.

The Chinese people appear to be more superficial. This is why some small businesses, even with shortage of funds, spent money to show off or display its richness, such as driving a luxury BMW or Audi.

If we looked at the laboratory testing service, a small laboratory would have a fancy website to display nice equipment, even if the instruments might not belong to the company. In the quality of testing, it was not uncommon to hear that some testing results were falsified or the test results might have been unreasonably changed. It was unfortunate that some people just liked the reports with a big name seal but ignored the accuracy of the test results. Our small laboratory, with no big seal to offer, was certainly at a disadvantage competing in the marketplace.

The labor laws in China are not business friendly for small businesses. There are five types of employee insurance, or subsidies, a fund we needed to pay. They were retirement, unemployment, health, accident, and childbirth, plus a housing fund. As for business tax, it was based on the business revenue regardless of whether a business made profit or lost money. As a foreign-owned company, we were carefully dealing with government agencies and always obeyed the laws. These costs were a very substantial part of our capital expense.

In brief, my final conclusion about doing business in China is that it requires two key factors: money or personal commitment. If one wants to and is willing to do business by investing enough money, he may be able to do what he wants because money can be dealt to solve problems. Money can be used to hire competent business people who can lead the company and form all kinds of relationships with national or provincial laboratories and government agencies. Otherwise, one must commit himself to the business and do what it takes to be a successful entrepreneur. We did not have either of these key factors because I did not have not enough money, and even if I had, I did not want to spend the money because of the great risk. Furthermore, I did not want to make a total commitment to the China laboratory, especially my time commitment, since I wanted to continue my effort on American laboratory. Therefore, it was understandable and conceivable that our China business did not meet our original goal.

14

ENTREPRENEURSHIP

SECTION SIX

Positioning Company: Third Five-Year Plan (2005–2010)

The American Independence Day on July 4, 2004, had a special meaning for me and my family. We celebrated this important holiday along with the people around the Champaign area. We watched the parade during the day and the fireworks at night, then I invited our friends to our house to celebrate the tenth anniversary of our company, American Analytical Chemistry Laboratories Corp. It was exactly on this day that our company was written about by local newspaper, *News Gazette*, on the front page of the business section in an article entitled "Long Road from China." The article described my entrepreneurship experience and the success of our laboratory over the past ten years. And it briefly summarized our future business plan.

The paper introduced me as an immigrant from China, first as a graduate student with MS and PhD degrees working as a postdoctoral associate at universities and as an analytical chemist at a private laboratory. It then described why I wanted to become an entrepreneur, the challenges I had been through, and my determination and my capability to overcome difficulties and finally to successfully develop and grow our business.

Although my achievement may be minor compared to other major businesses, such as internet and social media start-ups, I was still notable in the 1990s in the Champaign area where fewer start-ups were formed in a less favorable business environment. It described the help I had gotten from the community and the university, especially noting a couple of people from the bank and a successful entrepreneur. The report summarized the testing service and the business scope of the company. As an independent third-party testing laboratory helping companies with their quality assurance and quality control on nutrition and food products, our company had provided a positive impact to human health. The article also reported our company staff, especially our management team, who had made it possible for our company to be successful.

It was a coincidence to celebrate Independence Day and the tenth anniversary of our company, as well as to have the special report in the local newspaper. It was a special day for us to remember, especially considering how many ups and downs we had been through over the past ten years. I really had a lot to be proud of myself, and I was very grateful for the achievements.

There is a popular saying that goes, "As a businessman who once started his business, it wouldn't be easy for him to stop," and so I didn't. I was now eager to continue growing my company. This strong desire led to our third five-year plan. Our goal in this plan was to expand our business globally and, by the end of the five-year plan, to have the company double its size and its business. We planned that the company would become one of the best nutrition testing laboratories in the US and that the company would have financial resources for merger with, and get acquisition of, other laboratories. Alternative to this was that our business performance and success would set us up as an attractive acquisition target by large companies. In other words, the company could develop to a stage that I could consider a merger and acquisition (M and A) opportunity or outright sell of the company at an appropriate time to reap the fruits of my entrepreneurship effort.

Then what would be the position and the condition that my company needed to be in order to appeal to a larger corporation as a target for M and A? To answer this question, I started an analysis of the marketing condition and the examples of laboratory M and A. The reality of the analytical testing industry at the time was that except for several large chain laboratories, most of the food testing or nutrition supplement testing laboratories consisted of only a few to a dozen or so employees. In addition, the growth of most laboratories was slow, and the profit was generally dismal. A great portion of the laboratories had no growth and no profit at all. Therefore, to have the ability to purchase other laboratories, my laboratory needed to reach the size of about twenty-five to forty employees with a revenue of about $4–$6 million, with a substantial profit, preferably in the range of $0.5 to $1.5 million annually. If I went this M and A route, I should hire a key person with a business management experience and capability, preferably with an MBA degree to lead the M and A effort. My analysis further indicated that purchasing other laboratories was a relatively risky proposition because the laboratories purchased would not necessarily bring profits into the company. In addition, the final goal of acquiring other laboratories would be to go public. In order to achieve this goal, we obviously would need to expand our business at least twenty fold. It would take at least ten years of effort in order to realize the possibility of achieving this plan.

Another way to develop an exit strategy would be to grow our company to a given stage and then to position the laboratory with excellent financial results to attract strategic buyers. There would always be M and A activity in the marketplace. As a matter of the fact, many companies are more or less dependent on M and A to fuel their growth and expansion. To reach this position, it was better to increase our laboratory staff to twenty-five to forty and to generate considerable profit annually. In addition, forming a partnership or cooperation with larger laboratories would increase the chance of being acquired. Because of more opportunities and flexibility compared to M and A and going public, I chose the second option as my main strategy for exiting our business. Therefore, positioning our company for sale was an important goal of this third five-year plan.

There was no conflict between going public or selling the company. Either route required us to continue growing and expanding our business. Our laboratory testing platform would need to be upgraded. Our laboratory operation and management needed to be streamlined. One way was to add more advanced instruments to the platform, and we needed to build a good management team. In addition, we needed to devote an effort into packaging our company. More specifically, we decided to accomplish two key objectives: the completion of installation and customization of our LIMS and ISO 17025 accreditation of our laboratory by International Standards Organization (ISO). With these two objectives reached, we would be able to further expand our business globally.

Our LIMS was installed in the last five-year plan, but the platform needed further improvement and customization. Our LIMS was appropriate for monitoring the sample flow and reporting but lacked the functional integration of the operations such as marketing and customer support. We also need to increase the security of the system network and the accessibility of users to chromatographic data in the server. The level of authority and approval process needed further refinement and enhancement. Each test and testing method that covered more than two thousand parameters must be input into this platform with the calculation formula built into the software system so that the testing results could be calculated automatically and reported. Our IT manager was primarily responsible for this upgrade and customization. It took us a couple of years to complete the project.

With a versatile LIMS in place, we now turned our attention to ISO 17025 certification. ISO creates documents that provide requirements, specifications, guidelines, or characteristics that can be used consistently to ensure that materials, products, processes, and services are appropriate for their purpose. ISO 17025 is specific for laboratory management system that sets the standards for global laboratories with the same standard yardstick. These international standards allow people to compare and market transactions at the same standard level with respect to the quality of products and the services provided by each company. Therefore, the ability to obtain an ISO 17025 certification is an excellent indication that the company has achieved the level of global qualification, which is important for a laboratory to move toward the global business opportunity.

During the early phase of our company development, we did not consider ISO certification because I felt that our company was too small and our financial resources would not allow us to do so. There are some considerable costs to be an ISO-certified company. In general, there should be a full-time employee responsible for the program, the ISO standard manual must be developed by a consultant, and the cost of this service would be in the range of $10,000 to $20,000. In addition, the cost to hire a certification organization would cost another $10,000 to $20,000. Furthermore, to have the certification maintained annually would cost a few thousand dollars, without considering employee's cost. That was why when my laboratory had fewer than ten employees, I did not think it was worth the effort. Now the company had grown to another stage, and in order to further improve the credibility and visibility, I came to the conclusion that the ISO 17025 certification was critical for our business expansion to move forward. As a result, we made the decision in the spring of 2005 to pursue this certification by starting the preparation of ISO standard manual. Our goal was to achieve the certification within the next two to three years.

Prior to the start of this certification process, I did careful analysis and evaluation on the best option or approach for us to take. The first option was to hire a consulting company for help in preparing the standard manual, monitoring the compliance of our laboratory operation with the ISO 17025 standards, and arranging for audits and response to the certification company. This would be the easiest route for me and our management team since all work would be carried out and managed by the consulting company. The cost of this full-range service would be in the range of $30,000–$40,000. The second option was to do it ourselves to save the money. Saving money had always been our consistent practice. Whenever we could handle it, we had never paid to hire a service provider before. After I read through the ISO standards, I found that the standards were not complicated, and it would be relatively easy to complete them by any experienced chemist. Therefore, I finally decided to do it myself.

To begin, I first selected a certification company. In the United States, there were only a few companies providing ISO 17025 accreditation service to analytical testing laboratories because there were not many testing laboratories wanting this kind of certification. The procedures for meeting the standards for certification and the cost of it differ considerably between certification companies. Since the purpose of our certification was to enhance our reputation and visibility and to smooth our operations, it was not necessary to have a big-name company to do our certification. Because all certification firms follow the same ISO standards, it was in our best interest to hire an accreditation company that could provide clear and simple procedures at a relatively low cost. As long as we had the certification, our customers would recognize our company as one of the elite laboratories that had achieved the international quality standards.

The certification would make our customers more comfortable in using our testing services.

The ISO 17025 certification standards include several aspects. The quality policy portion requires each laboratory to establish standards for the company management and the responsibilities of each management team member, quality assurance policies and guidelines, and quality assurance programs. More specifically, there are requirements for corporate executives such as the president/laboratory director to be fully responsible for the certification program and the quality assurance/quality control (QA/QC) manager's responsibility to execute the ISO qualification standards. In addition, the standards include the documentation management, staff training, operation, and other aspects of the provisions. The technical portion of the ISO standards includes testing platform, instrument calibration, technical training, standard testing methods, testing data review, reporting, etc. Because there are thousands of test parameters performed in our laboratory, we were required to define the tests we wanted to have the certification on, which should also include the testing methods. Because the vast majority of the testing methods we used in our laboratory were very different from ISO standard methods, to deal with this problem, I decided to select a small portion of frequent testing parameter with relatively well-defined standard analytical methods such as several vitamins and fish oil for our certification program.

After having evaluated a few certification companies, I settled with ACLASS. Before preparing the quality standard manual, I requested information about specific certification requirements from ACLASS. I studied the ISO 17025 standards carefully, noting questions for which I asked ACLASS for answers. I began drafting the ISO standard manual for our laboratory, taking into consideration our current operation. It took me about six months to complete our quality manual (QM). Some laboratories divided their ISO standards into six to eight chapters, while our QM standard consisted of two chapters: management standards and analytical standards. The management standards include policy and guidelines and the responsibility of each company executive and QA/QC manager. Analytical standards were primarily focused on technical aspects, including the establishment of testing methods, method validation and usage of the methods, sample reception, preservation and management, sample analysis, analytical instrumentation, calibration and usage, test results calculation, statistical analysis, and reporting, etc.

Although the certification process required all company management and employees on board doing this together, I and my QA/QC manager were the two key persons responsible for this program. After completing the QM, we followed the ISO standards starting with the employee training program. We had to ensure that each laboratory staff member understood the ISO requirements and carried out their work accordingly. Our QA/QC manager was responsible for specific duties in the laboratory auditing instruments, method performance, and documentation records, as well as making sure that the operation was consistent with the QM. This part of the work took us several months to reach compliance.

When we felt we were ready, we requested the certification company to initiate the process, which included the document review and on-site laboratory audit. The designated inspector(s) would visit a laboratory twice, first to review the corporate documents, especially the ISO QM, to make sure that the QM and other documents such as SOPs and testing methods that were established conformed to ISO standards. If there were any discrepancies, we were required to make corrections accordingly. The second audit was focused on experiments or tests of the samples with specific analytical methods. The chemists who performed the tests were required to follow the method as described. If there was any modification to the method, it must be documented. The inspector followed the experiment throughout to observe each step of the test. Major deviation from the method would result in a warning, and a correction would be required in a timely manner.

After two rounds of review and audit by ACLASS, the auditing officer finally provided us with an auditing report that identified the major and minor deficiencies of our nonconformance. This was a normal report for us with only a few major and a few minor nonconformances. With this report, there was no need for a third audit. We made corrections and improvements to each deficiency as described according to the timetable given. All responses from us were through emails. Once all correspondences were received by ACLASS, they reviewed them and made a final decision in which they approved our laboratory as an ISO 17025i–compliant company.

It took our laboratory about two years from the preparation of standards to the approval of our application for certification. We received the ISO 17025 accreditation in 2006. This certification not only enhanced our laboratory reputation in the global nutrition industry but it also benefited our business development globally and provided us with a program on the improvement of our internal management, process control, employee management, and overall quality control. This achievement was another milestone for our company after completing the laboratory building and the LIMS installation accomplished in the last five-year plan.

We upgraded our instrumentation platform in the previous five-year plan. However, the main equipment pieces added were high-pressure liquid chromatograph (HPLC) and gas chromatograph (GC), which was not enough because all these instruments were common among the average testing laboratories. In this third five-year plan, my goal was to build our laboratories into the industry's first-class. To achieve this goal, we would need to add a number of high-end instruments and a set of standard operating procedures and analytical methods and to train a number of high-level analytical experts.

For a few years, I was well aware that if we were to be more competitive in the marketplace, we must have our laboratories equipped with liquid chromatograph-mass spectrometer (LC-MS) and gas chromatograph-mass spectrometer (GC-MS). This strategic decision led me make a major investment by installing three LC-MS and two GC-MS and an inductively coupled plasma-mass spectrometer (ICP-MS). These instruments were expensive as new, but I purchased refurbished equipment to save between 25 to 80 percent. For example, the cost for a new LC-MS was about $300,000, and we got it at $50,000. As usual, all of used equipment were calibrated to the original specifications before use. These advanced instruments allowed us to test nutrition supplement samples at low concentrations, which was a competitive position for our laboratory. The other advantages of using LC-MS or GC-MS over the HPLC or GC were their sensitivity and minimal interference and faster analysis. Because of these precise instruments, our labs were able to provide more accurate and more comprehensive testing services than our competitors. This was especially true for certain difficult and unconventional analyses such as toxins. Furthermore, because of our capability, some large chain laboratories used us as their subcontract laboratory for difficult projects. We got not only the business from these laboratories but also certain customers' information that could help us sell our other services to those customers as well. Occasionally, we might be introduced directly by these laboratories to their customers for convenience of technical communication. This was an excellent word-of-mouth promotion of our laboratory. For those customers who had never used our service, once we got their first job, we would do what we could to keep the customer happy. In doing so, we could convert some of these customers to our long-term clients.

An important goal of our service was to provide a full range of services. Whether it was a common test, a special test, or a difficult test, we rarely turned down any testing request from our customers. I felt that if we did, our customers would be disappointed with us, which could result in losing customers because the customers would seek services from our competitor laboratories. Since we had the advanced instruments and experienced chemists to meet every testing need, my strategy was to retain every customer with us as long as possible.

We also had a number of other differential strategies in the works. If a new customer sent us an extremely challenging job, we were willing to accept it and carry out method development within a certain scope without charging the customer. This was different from many other laboratories that usually either did not accept the job or, if accepted, would charge for method development. By doing this, we might lose money with the first job, but it was worth it if we could retain this customer for other service opportunities that we could make money from. For our existing customers, our goal was to persuade them to use our laboratory either as their exclusive service provider or at least to use our laboratory for the majority of their testing needs.

Another effective strategy to develop and expand our business was to promote our name and our testing services through customer advocacy. As the saying goes, "Word of mouth is the best way to market products and services." I felt strongly that this word-of-mouth marketing approach was a key factor for our business development. This, of course, required substantial achievement and recognition of our laboratory by our customers. Our relationship marketing approach had played an important role in helping us to establish a core group of happy customers. These customers often introduced our service to their vendors and their customers. A significant portion of customer base came from this route. Because these customers trusted the word of mouth of their friends, colleagues, or their contractors, once they used our service, they tended to stay with us long term.

Because of the diversified customers with different objectives in their quality control program, the customers often had different requirements. Some customers placed more emphasis on quality results and fast turnaround time, while others looked for the best price. My observations were that there were a few characteristics for former customers. If their priority was quality and fast turnaround service, they were willing to pay the regular service fee and rarely negotiated price with us. They tended to trust us and were, therefore, most likely be our long-term customers. For the price-sensitive customers who came to use the laboratory testing service because the laws say so or their customer wanted them do so, these customers may take price over quality and fast turnaround time. They often shopped around for their tests and would negotiate persistently, even for a few dollars of savings. They tended to be short-term customers and frequently shifted service laboratories if they could save some money. Among our several hundred customers, most belonged to the first group that wanted the best quality of the testing results and customer service.

To deal with these diversified needs from our customers, I adopted a flexibly tailored to the customer. For the majority of customers, we focused on relationship building and faster and timely customer support. We ensured the best possible testing results for their samples. For the large-volume customers, we honored them as our preferred customers who received a discount. For the price-sensitive customers, we tried our best to explain to them that our prices were competitive if they took into consideration both the quality of testing results, the fast turnaround time, and our customer support. If all my effort failed, I would give the customer up. Over the years, I realized that there were always a few customers who would bargain with us on pricing every time. They were rarely satisfied and would negotiate again for their next job, which made me waste time repeating the procedures over and over. My experience had taught me that this small group of customers were not worth my time and effort because it was difficult to please them or to meet their expectations. Even if we got their first order, most likely we could not keep them for a second job.

Most of my effort in marketing was to focus on major and long-term customers. Although these customers used our service based not just on the pricing, we still wanted to provide a competitive price to them. For large and long-term customers, I grouped them according to their testing volume and the year they began using our service as gold, silver, and bronze customers by offering a discount of 15 percent, 10 percent, and 5 percent respectively. For the difficult tests that required advanced instruments, especially those tests that not many laboratories could provide, we often set a high service fee for this service. For top-tiered customers, we were willing to provide an added service, free of charge, to keep them happy. As a result of these efforts, our top 10 customers were fairly stable, and most of them had been using our labs for more than more than ten years. The top 10 customers generally accounted for more than 40 percent of the total business volume, which undoubtedly played a decisive role in the stability of our business.

By 2010, the end of our third five-year plan, our laboratory had made gratifying achievements. These accomplishments were also noted by a local journalist who came to me for an interview. He then published second report on our labs in a Sunday commercial edition of *The News-Gazette*, Champaign, Illinois. As the first article about our business was published in this paper five years before, the follow-up article reaffirmed the success of our business and its impact on the local economy.

14

ENTREPRENEURSHIP

SECTION SEVEN

Acquisition and Integration (2008–2015)

$\mathbf{B}$y 2008, our company had not only passed the FDA audits but also the ISO 17025 certification. These accomplishments had set our laboratory on the same level as the elite and well-known laboratories around the country.

Because of the steady and sustainable development of our third five-year plan, our company had caught the eye of some big companies and venture capitalists. As early as 2007, a New York–based investment firm came to us for a discussion of the possibility of merger and acquisition. This investment firm specialized in applying capital to purchase or reorganize small companies into a large corporation that would be directed to the market as a public trading company in the future. Their representative had a business plan in which they wanted to merge multiple small testing laboratories into an anchor laboratory. The purpose of this visit was, apparently, to understand what we did and the level of interest from us to join in his plan. I was very interested in his proposal, and I felt that this could be one of a few routes for me to successfully exit my business. If successfully integrated, I would be a stockholder of a larger corporation and could eventually cash out to conclude my venture. The shortcoming of this proposal was that it could take several years to accomplish. After a good three-hour discussion, both of us agreed to continue the dialogue. Unfortunately, the stock market took a downturn from the end of 2007 to 2008 and began getting worse in 2009. This worst stock market downturn since 2001 greatly affected the capital market, resulting in the suspension of their merger plan.

In addition to this venture capital company, almost at the same time, there was a London-based company that came to us as well. I had no idea what this company did and why they were interested in us. Nevertheless, I had a meeting with several delegates from the company in our conference room. They first introduced themselves and told me who they were and why they had come. Of course, they expressed their interest in knowing more about our laboratory and possibly acquiring our laboratory. From their introduction and presentation, I began understanding a little more about them. This company was a global company with offices around the globe. It was a London Stock Exchange/ The Financial Times Stock Exchange 100 index company doing business in more than a hundred countries and regions. It had about thirty thousand employees worldwide. Their service covered inspection, auditing and certification, and testing all kinds of materials, medical products, and foods. In the US, this company had employed several thousand people in various business divisions and subsidiaries except one area that was lacking—that of a food laboratory testing service. Therefore, their business hunters had identified our laboratory as a target for their acquisition with the expectation to complement their weakness in food testing. They definitely felt that our company would fit in well into their business plan.

After a few hours of discussion, both sides came to a common understanding that this was a first dialogue about each other's interest. From their standpoint, they raised two major concerns about our laboratories. First, the size of the company was too small, with fewer than twenty employees; and our business volume was relatively small. In general, the smaller the company, the less stability of the business because a small company management team tends to be less robust, with usually the entrepreneur doing the major management. Once the entrepreneur leaves after the company is acquired, it could lead to disruption of the operation since the transition to a new management would take time. This could lead to financial loss for the acquirer. Therefore, buyers often place more value on a company with a relatively stable business model and a strong management team. Second, the company had not been ISO 17025 certified. This did not meet the standards of a buyer that was a global and multinational company. They expected that our laboratory should achieve this certification before their further interest in acquisition. In the end, we agreed to continue the dialogue.

Since 2004, I had provided our financial statements to Dun & Bradstreet (D&B), a financial service company for their publication, which includes current financial information of most public and private companies. Our data could be viewed by any company authorized by D&B. The two companies who visited our laboratories were attracted to our company as a result of viewing our financial information. I was later told that almost all parties interested in acquisitions used the D&B database as a tool to identify acquisition targets. Some large companies may have a team specifically focused on acquisition. Although these earlier visits did not lead to acquisition of our laboratory, I felt good about the progress and expected to see more interest in the future.

One major yardstick used to measure the success of an entrepreneur was an acquisition or becoming a publicly traded company. Almost all entrepreneurs at some points of the business cycle consider exiting their business by selling it or issuing an initial public offering (IPO).

This had been on my mind since the first day I started my business venture. Through more than ten years of continuous development and growth, our company had basically reached this stage. Apart from the common practice of most entrepreneurs, there are several other reasons for me to sell my company. My business experience was limited to small private laboratory and might not be qualified to lead a large company, especially a public trading company. At the age of nearly sixty years, the energy I could devote to the company would certainly continue to decline. In addition, the market we served was relatively small, which would make it more difficult to grow unless we would expand to other markets. This could certainly be challenging for me without experience in those markets. Furthermore, I had originally hoped that my elder son would be interested in our business and possibly take it over one day in the future. However, having spent a couple of months in the laboratories, my son had no interest in it. As I grew older, I had become more conservative in my business venture. This was sharply different from a decade ago when I was a high-risk taker. The risk of acquiring other companies was high that was not consistent with my current conservative mood. Because of all these factors, I finally decided that our first choice was to sell the company.

Since I had made the decision to sell my company, I began with preparation and improvement of our financial data, an important component of our business package in 2007. There were a number of nice things going for us. For example, we had a qualified laboratory platform with a number of advanced instruments, we had a quality management team in place, our laboratory had installed and customized LIMS, our customers now numbered several hundred worldwide, and our business had continued growing. All of these were helpful in positioning our company for sale. However, we still had a few key items to prepare, including the company statements of profit and balance, as well as an estimated valuation of our company.

To evaluate the value of a company, the first step is to understand the company's financial position, including profit and loss, free cash flow, and the balance sheet. Every company needs an accounting system that is easy to access, review, and analyze. The QuickBooks we used in our bookkeeping helped achieve this goal. Because of this software platform, our book records and financial statements were standardized. We had entered each sale into the system daily, and a sales invoice was generated for each job. There was no cash transaction in our business, making it easy to manage. For the few customers who did not pay for service, these were logged as bad debt. We reconciled QuickBooks entries and bank statements monthly. These accounting procedures made our financial statements straightforward.

Because of the standard practice of our accounting system, there were only a few minor things that would improve our financial picture. These were the recognition of revenue and the control of timing of certain expenses. For example, while the year-end service could be billed the same year as the service rendered or the next year, we could bill a job that was partially completed in the same fiscal year instead of waiting until the completion of the job the next year. The same could be done for the expenses, especially on major capital expenses. The decision to bill or not to bill and to expense or not to expense which could have an effect on the financial statement. This practice had its limits, and I could do it only within the normal accounting practice. It is common for a publicly traded company to make certain financial decision on recognitions of revenue and expense at the end of each quarter or at the end of each year in order to meet the financial goal expected by investors. This consideration was certainly a part of our financial operation prior to acquisition.

In addition to getting our financial records in order, I prepared a preliminary analysis in order to assess the value of my company. To properly evaluate the value of a company, especially a small company like ours, was challenging, so I collaborated with a professor at the UIUC Business School to propose "the current status and market potential of food testing laboratories" as an internship topic for students. A group of intelligent students took on this research topic. They researched market, data collection, and statistical analysis on a variety of laboratories that had completed merger and acquisition three years prior to 2008. They concluded their internship project with a report on the topic. Although this report was not closely related to the industry of nutrition supplements and human health, it provided valuable information to aid in the valuation of our company if we were a food testing laboratory. On the other hand, our laboratory could not be valued according to the pharmaceutical testing laboratories because our market, or potential market, was so much smaller and our profit power was so much less than pharmaceutical laboratories. The research information led me to conclude that the valuation of our laboratory should be set between these two types of laboratories.

Time passed quickly. It was just like a blink of the eye that my business venture had reached its sixteenth year in 2009. I had completed the preparation of our financial records, our business development, and ISO 17025 certification. At the end of the year, I took the initiative and sent a letter to the British company that had been interest in us, indicating that we had made the improvements that were earlier suggested by its team and that we were still interested in becoming a member of the company family. To my surprise, this company had been watching us progress and had never stop searching for a food testing laboratory in the US. Once they received my letter, they quickly responded, indicating that they were interested in more discussion with us.

This company (here for convenience named the Company) sent several representatives to our laboratory for discussion just after the New Year of 2010. In the first stage, it seemed that we were not particularly serious. It was a general discussion exploring interest from both sides and attempting to understand our business and my expectation. I, of course, also wanted to know more about the Company and their plan. At the conclusion of the discussion, we agreed to continue further dialogue.

It did not take long for the Company to send me a preliminary contract describing the obligations and duties of further examination of our company. After I signed it, I gave them permission to look at our accounting records and our customer list as well as our management team and our operation. They needed this information to make an offer, which was apparently the first step to move forward. Selling a company is a lot like selling a house, but with more complex procedures and requirements. There would be several rounds of offering and counteroffering until both sides reached a finally accepted agreement.

We received an offer from the Company in early 2010, after which my job included the continuation of running my business as normal and preparation for and negotiation with the Company to sell my business.

There were three key questions for me with the offer. First, was the offer reasonable, and if not, how could I get a reasonable one? Second, how would the buyer and the seller reach an agreement on terms of the sale? Third, what were the buyer's plans to manage the company, and what were the requirements for my employment contract? The key to these three questions was a reasonable valuation of my company. It was only when the two sides came to an agreement on pricing that it was possible to proceed to the next negotiation phase.

So was the company's offer reasonable? What was the difference between their price and my original expectation? In other words, at what price could I accept? I started with a realistic analysis of our current business, especially the annual growth rate and earnings. With this information, I then compared my company with other publicly traded companies.

The valuation of a publicly traded company is largely based on the annual growth rate, profit, and free cash flow. The higher the growth rate and the higher the profit and net cash flow, the more valuable the company. There are important factor affecting pricing. A company holding patented technologies that can protect its intellectual property and defend its market is more valuable than the one without proprietary technologies. By the same token, if there is a high barrier to a competitor's entering the market, then the business is more valuable. Otherwise, the valuation of the company would be lower because competitors can enter the market, causing competitive pressure on products and services. If the cost of the business start-up is high, which would be, undoubtedly, a serious challenge to entrepreneurs to copy the business, the value of the company would be preserved.

After having analyzed the various factors of the market, I had a better understanding of my own laboratory. Our company was a technological company using a variety of analytical equipment such as HPLC and GC to perform services. However, these were not patented technology. Likewise, the equipment and analytical platform were expensive and required a large sum of capital to start up, which might limit a new player entering the market, but the capital needed was not a barrier to many well-funded start-up companies. In addition, our company had grown only about 10 percent in revenue and earnings annually in the past three years, which was not a fast-growing company per se. Furthermore, the industry we served had limited potential with a total addressable market about $500–$600 million, in which hundreds of laboratories were competing. All these factors made my company incomparable with most publicly traded companies.

According to the Company, their price offering was based on a combination of the P/E (price to earning), revenue, and earnings. I had originally asked for a P/E = 10 to determine the price, but they did not agree with me for a couple reasons. First, our company was a small company with only twenty-five employees, and our management was mostly centered around myself doing most of the managing. This kind of set-up could lead to instability if I decided to leave the company. Second, as a small company, we had a relatively smaller customer base, reputation, and credibility, not as good as larger companies, which might lead to volatility and an unstable business. Business stability was indeed an important consideration, sometimes even more important than growth rate for an acquisition because most buyers want to buy a company with a stable business. Otherwise, the value of the purchasing company would be greatly reduced.

It was for these reasons that the Company offered us a price that was lower than the common P/E = 10, using a P/E 5–8. This meant that the buyer would like to recover its investment in five to eight years. Through careful analysis and consideration, I felt the price range was in an acceptable range, so I decided to focus my attention on how to maximize the price in this price range.

My goal now shifted to reaching a price that both the Company and I could accept. As a small entrepreneur, we often make mistakes in two areas. First, we overestimate the value of our own company. There are reasons for this overvaluation because almost all small business owners have worked very hard to get their businesses established and to grow it to its current stage. They devoted not only themselves, but also their families. It is a human nature that they want more money for their businesses. Second, we often look at our own business with bias. We tend to see the positives, the accomplishments, and all the good stuff while ignoring the shortcomings and disadvantages. This is especially true when we compare our businesses with others.

There were fewer known M and A cases in the nutrition supplement industry. All the references obtained were for food and pharmaceutical testing laboratories. The food business is a stable and matured market with growth of about 2 percent annually over the last decades. This slow growth in food market had resulted in food testing laboratories having a growth rate of less than 10 percent, with stagnation in profit margin and cash flow. The laboratory capacity was saturated, and competition was fierce. In contrast, the pharmaceutical industry had been growing more than 10 percent a year, with the laboratory testing business greater than that, with the long-term growth rate still intact. The nutrition supplement industry was in between those two industries with a growth rate of 5–7 percent annually. This analysis supported the notion that an unbiased position on valuation should be between these groups of laboratories.

As an entrepreneur, we often carry the mind-set of "by luck" and "give it trial." We often come the conclusion that the buyer's price is too low and that we could counter with a higher price. If not accepted by the buyer, we could then drop our price. There was nothing wrong with this approach because it is, indeed, the backbone of negotiation for any M and A deal. But one thing we should be aware of is that if we want a ridiculously high price to start, we might scare the buyer away, resulting in the loss of the selling opportunity. Therefore, a smarter way to deal with an offering is to fully maximize the value but to not let the buyer feel that you are severely overexaggerating it; therefore, you have no interest in selling.

According to my basic understanding of these problems, I started my negotiation with the Company by raising the question about the basis for their price offering. They responded by saying that it was based on the operating income of P/E at 6–8. They answered my question on the P/S (price/sale) multiple, based on the range of one to four times annual revenue. The P/S of their recently acquired laboratories ranged between two to three times annual revenue. Clearly, all the answers provided uncertain elements, depending on many the factors underlining the business and the market we were in.

As far as I knew, the price to sale ratio was not a decisive factor in evaluating a company, but it was, nevertheless, an important factor that is frequently used as part of the valuation process. For most mature and stable large companies, market capitalization was within the range of 1.5 to 3.0 times annual revenue. I knew that this P/S approach was not the one I wanted, so I intentionally let the buyer know that I wanted to evaluate my company based on profit.

The buyer agreed with my point and explained that our laboratory was different from other laboratories because of our high profit margin and net profit. Their price was based more on our earnings than on our sales. They did not agree with my using ten times our profit as a base for the price. They explained the risk involved in acquiring a small company like ours.

I attempted to persuade the buyers that their offer was too low by reemphasizing the strength of our laboratory and its continuing growth within the growing market that we served. They agreed with me on this but said that "it was because we saw this market opportunity that we wanted to acquire your company, or else we wouldn't be interested in your company." I certainly agreed with their analysis, and the reason that we had a higher profit margin than other laboratories was partly due to the fact that I was doing more than one person's job daily. They felt that if I were an employee, not the owner, I would have more than one person doing the same jobs, and therefore, our expenses would be considerably higher and the profit margin would be lower.

During the course of negotiations, there were two key elements that I was not aware of at the beginning. First, the buyer's price did not include bank deposits or debts. Our company had a considerable amount of bank deposit with no debt. This would allow me to withdraw all the cash from our account before sale. Second, I could put all expenses to be considered as a onetime expense and a nonrecurring cost, which could then be added back as profit. Because the buyer's estimate was mostly based on earnings, adding a one-time expense would increase our total profit. This addition of the one-time expense as income helped our valuation considerably.

After several meetings, we finally reached an agreement. Prior to this agreement, all data provided by me was in the form of a printout of financial statements and a list of customers and sale information, which served for the buyer's quotation. The buyer obviously wanted to know the entire financial results, our customers, and operations in order to justify the agreed-upon price. With this agreement, the buyer was allowed to access our books to examine all data related to the offering. However, this was not the sales contract but a simple precontract document. It simply stipulated the requirement for secrecy.

Auditing our books was the most important review for the buyer. In order to understand our business, our sales, and our expenses, the Company wanted to confirm the authenticity of the data I had provided. The financial review was the buyer's most important work. If they found any inconsistent data or customer information, they could back out of the contract or renegotiate the contract at their discretion.

For my part, I had done my homework and had gotten our financial records in order, and I was confident that our books could pass their audit. In the end, I was really thankful to have QuickBooks as our financial platform because all the financial data could be accessed through this record. I was also lucky to have LIMS in place for our operation, which was also easily examined by the Company. The minor questions raised were a few expenses that looked unreasonable for large corporations but were not uncommon for small companies like us. A good example of this was the gasoline expense, in which small companies might not be able to separate expenses between the company usage and personal usage. To prepare for the possibility of these questions, I had listed the expenses, especially those likely to be one-time expense, in case the questions were raised.

In addition to the financial records, the buyer focused on our operation, including our management team, our customer base, seasonality of sales, and the top 10 and top 20 customers. Included was the trend of sale to these top-tier customers over the past a few years. From this information, the buyer might be able to assess the stability and trend of future business. At this point, the buyer did not find any information that materially deviated from what I provided earlier for their offering. Therefore, the two sides moved ahead to the stage of negotiation on the sale contract.

The contract of sale was prepared by the buyer's law firm, and after I got the contract, I hired our lawyer. The contract was divided into a dozen sections, each with a number of subsections. From the term definition, purchase price, purchase content, requirements for prior to the transaction of the business, and the afterward operation of the company to the buyer's and seller's responsibility, employment, and confidentiality, etc. The contract was about forty pages long, but the main aspects included corporate ownership, corporate finance, corporate clients, company property, mutual responsibility, and my employment contract.

Immediately following the definitions in the contract was the corporate legality and ownership of the company. I provided the corporate registration documents and stock certificates in support of the company solely owned by me. This was critical for the buyer because once the sale was completed, the buyer would not anticipate any claim from anybody or entity to the ownership of the company.

My sole ownership of our company made it easier for the buyer to clarify the corporate legality issue. Because of the limited potential of the market that my business was in, I did not hire anyone who might want corporate stock as part of their compensation. I had not pursued any venture capital or angel investor because I could not have any use for this kind of capital for our business.

The management team was promoted internally. In addition to raising the salaries and an annual bonus for our key management and employees, I offered stock options to them. When the stock options were offered to them, I used the earnings of our company multiplied by half the growth rate of our earnings, which I felt was similar to the valuation of the publicly traded laboratories. The goal of my stock option offering was to motivate our employees, especially management, to work hard and long term for the company. When the company was successful, the employee would be benefited. However, all the stock options we had offered for several years were let go without execution. The reasons were unknown, but perhaps it was because I did not give the employees a clear statement of their rights to ownership and the method to purchase the options that they had little confidence in the company. Or perhaps, it was because they believed they could make a better investment in the stock markets than in our company stocks. Since no employees had purchased their options, I continued to be the only shareholder of the company.

Regarding the financial data, the Company sent their accountants to review our QuickBooks. They found no problem with it. The most time that was spent was on the one-time expense items. In the end, they came to an agreement with me on the items listed.

When auditing our business and operation, the Company was more concerned about the stability of the company business. Because this requirement is common in every M and A, most contracts contain a provision of guaranteeing the business performance. For example, the buyer requires the seller to maintain the revenue and earnings for one to three years. If a seller does not meet the goal, there would be a penalty or a reduction of price to the seller. In contrast to this penalty clause, there was a reward clause as well. In this case, if the company's performance exceeds the expected goals, then the seller would receive an additional price or fees for managing the business successfully. Because I knew my company and my industry well, I was confident that I could meet the goal in the short term but did not want to bear too much responsibility in the longer term. Therefore, I did not want to make a promise on the performance. As a result, I guided the discussion with purpose of no promises and no guarantees. Later, the Company's business performed much better than expected, which made some people feel that I was not getting the value I deserved. This also made me pity myself a little.

At first glance, I thought there was nothing further to be discussed about what the sale was or what they had purchased. But an important portion of the contract was that the buyer was very serious to know what they had really paid for. Therefore, a list of what I was selling had to be clearly listed in the contract. It was everything, except the laboratory building and the furniture. The sale included the business, the laboratory equipment, the technologies used, the list of customers and the corporate documents, as well as knowing everything about our business. The Company asked for a specific list and a checkoff on it to be completed.

At the outset, I wanted the Company to purchase our laboratory building, but I learned that they were not interested in owning a lab building. The Company had bought a lot of small companies, most of which did not include any real estate. They, like many other big companies, did not want to own real estate because it was not easy to depose of a property if the company wanted to relocate the business. As a result, I had to concentrate on negotiating a contract to lease the laboratory building to the buyer. Our laboratory building was owned by my other company, JMT Group LLC, established in 2004. My laboratory, American Analytical Chemistry Laboratory, signed a fifteen-year lease contract with JMT Group, which would not expire until 2019. Unless it were a part of the contract, the buyer would have to fulfill the contract requirements. The rental income of this laboratory building became a source of an important income for us after the sale of our company. I feel that this long-term lease of my own company building to my own other company was the wisest decision I had ever made.

Another provision in the contract was our responsibility and liability. The purpose of this provision was to make sure that I, as seller, guaranteed that the company was not in any litigation, or under investigation for any potential liability. The Company was very clear that they did not want any product testing liability or environmental responsibility prior to acquisition. The main point here was to assure that we were not being sued for errors and omissions as a result of testing products from our customers, nor did we have any pending case of product liability. Potential environmental liability is a major concern of any acquirer because of the exceedingly high cost of fines and litigations.

For a laboratory, the focus is on environmental pollution, improper disposal of chemicals, or biosafety. There was no choice to avoid this provision but to accept the responsibility. All that I tried to do was to reach a time limit that was as shortest as possible.

I was selling not only the company but myself as well. What I mean by "selling myself" is that I had to sign an employment contract with the buyer. This contract was an important part of the whole purchase contract because the Company needed that provision to ensure that the business they purchased would be stable with me on duty. As a normal acquisition of a small company, the employment contract for the seller (owner) would usually be one to four years, depending on the nature of the business. Therefore, I spent a considerable amount of the time negotiating my employment contract and finally reached an agreement to work for thirty months. In addition, they also wanted the current management team to continue serving. This was understandable since the buyer would not like to have a management team turnover before they could get their team in place.

From the discussion, I gradually realized that the buyer had no intention to send a manager to take my position. Therefore, I was named in the contract as the site manager of the laboratory and the director of food testing of the Company USA, Inc. I reported directly to the vice president of this division in the US. In other words, I would run the laboratory just as what I had been doing. During this two and a half years of the contract, I must dedicate myself wholeheartedly to my job and to the Company. The buyer had the right to sue me and to claim my financial responsibility if they found me not seriously fulfilling my duty. One example was that because I had other businesses, I was not allowed to spend more than 5 percent of my working time at these companies, and if I went beyond that, it was likely to be considered that I had not devoted my whole effort to the Company.

The labor contract also provided my salary, vacation, year-end bonuses, and insurance benefits. In the beginning, I did not expect a high salary because I used a couple of old-fashion criteria to evaluate my salary range. First, I used a manager of a small laboratory with fewer than thirty employees, a job that should not be too difficult to do. Second, I used the low cost of living at Champaign, Illinois. Consequently, I was not prepared to ask for a higher salary than I had given myself in 2010. However, my wife did not agree and strongly suggested that I start with higher salary request, which I did. To my surprise, I was able to negotiate a salary and benefits that were almost 50 percent better that I originally expected. Obviously, the Company considered my compensation along with other managers in the Midwest in the US. My performance and contribution to the company in the next several years indicated that I was worth every penny of it since this laboratory under my management was the best performer financially among the Company laboratories.

The contract included a provision for setting specific requirements and restrictions after the completion of my service contract, covering confidentiality and noncompetition. I was restricted from setting up laboratories or any other companies that would directly compete with the Company for one year. This also applied to working in a competitive laboratory. When the contract expired, I would be an ordinary employee just as any other employee who could seek employment at will. The Company could fire me for any reason at any time, and of course, by the same token, I could resign and leave the Company at any time as well.

There was one other precondition set up by the buyer that required me to completely divest my Beijing laboratories. In the beginning, I had intended to sell both my US and my China laboratories together to the buyer. Unfortunately, the buyer had no interest in acquiring my China laboratory.

There were a few reasons for this. Our Beijing laboratory was small in size with only a few employees, our revenue and customer base were limited, and we had not made any profit yet. The buyer already owned many laboratories in China and Hong Kong, including one in Beijing. They did not want another laboratory in the same city. Perhaps more important was the fact that there could be a substantial cost for auditing our laboratory due to the difference in accounting standards between our China laboratory and the buyer. An anticipated cost would be far greater than the value of the laboratory. Another provision in the clause of the contract was that I was not allowed to give advice or help the new owner of the China laboratory. Otherwise, I would be financially responsible for the consequences.

I gave in to this provision and transferred the company to my relatives in China. Because of the strict stipulation that I was prohibited from helping the new owners, the laboratory survived for a couple of years from the foundation I built previously, but due to the lack of a competent person to manage it and without my technical support, it slowly lost its customers and finally ceased to exist.

We used the small conference room in my attorney's firm for the contract negotiations. My attorney and I were sitting on one side of the table while the buyer's attorneys and their negotiator were on the other side. We went through the contract sentence by sentence. The lawyers on both sides were particularly responsible, and my lawyer explained each clause to me and answered every question I had. No matter how hard we tried, there were always some questions that remained to be resolved. We returned to the questions we had not agreed upon again and again on the same day or in following days. It took us one week to reach a unanimous agreement on the purchase contract. We signed the contract on December 31, 2010. By then, my American Analytical Chemistry Laboratories Corp, founded in 1994, was successfully sold.

Another driving force for the completion of this sale on December 31, 2010, was that because there was an economic downturn in 2008–2009, the US Congress passed the Economic Stimulus Act, signed into law by President Obama, that lowered the longer-term capital gains tax from 20 percent to 15 percent; and the state tax was lowered from 5.0 percent to 3.75 percent in

Illinois. These temporary tax reliefs were set to expire by 2010 and to revert to the original tax rate. With a 5 percent difference in the federal tax rate, I could pay a considerable more amount in long-term capital gains if I could not get the deal done in that year. Therefore, I told the buyer there would be a deal or no deal by the end of 2010, which motivated both sides to complete the contract on the deadline.

On January 1, 2011, my company became a subsidiary of the Company. For me there was no change in my work or in my routine. The only change was that I was not the owner but an employee of the laboratory. Just like other employees, I earned my wages from my service to the company. However, I had more responsibility than any other employee because of my position as the director of the laboratory. I continued to manage the laboratory and develop the business for the laboratory and for the Company. One basic measure set for me was that I had to make money for the company. Because of most of the responsibilities I had retained, I was still busy as usual. As I promised all employees, it was my responsibility to make sure the performance of the laboratory was good so that everyone in the laboratory would have a job. Therefore, I could not relax, and I had to do my best on this job.

In addition to my daily job, a considerable part of my time was spent on the integration of the company. The Company, from the day 1, required us to quickly complete the integration process. Because the Company had grown from various acquisitions, it had considerable experience in integration, and our integration was expected to be on a fast track as well.

The first task of integration was our accounting. It was most important for the Company because revenue and income must be seen and should easily be accessible by the company executives and as a requirement of public security rules. Before the acquisition, we used QuickBooks for our accounting, but the Company used a different system, which meant the systems were incompatible. Additionally, our service included thousands of tests, and the platform from the parent company had not been set up for this. Therefore, we started with a new customized platform that was based on the financial platform of the parent company. Fortunately, the corporate had a strong IT team, and setup of the platform was taken over by the team. All what we were required to do was to provide the testing parameters and the prices to the IT department. Within a few months, we had completed the financial integration by May of 2010.

At the same time, the integration of all staff training, professional ethics requirements, and staff responsibilities into the corporate structure was carried out. Before acquisition, our company required each employee to sign a confidentiality agreement. We had professional ethics agreement with employees, but the one from the Company was more detailed and broader. There were specific rules regarding bribes and gifts listing the consequences of violation of the agreement. There was strict requirement concerning fraudulent behavior before acquisition, but the Company did not allow this kind of behavior with a strictest term and penalty. Independent and unbiased testing results to ensure the integrity and professionalism of our service were strictly enforced.

The corporate office particularly stressed the safety of our employees because any accident might significantly cost the company. A major accident especially could cost money, employee days off, and compensation. Therefore, all employees were required to undergo safety training. Once trained, each employee electronically signed the training records, which were required, along with all other important documents.

I was aware in the beginning of the acquisition that the parent company would give the power to managers of the laboratories at the local level. Therefore, I felt that I had authority in our operation and management. Unless there were any major issues, I was not required to report to upper management on my daily work. The upper management usually left us alone. I was satisfied with this because literally there was no one watching over my shoulders telling me how to do my job. I was basically free to exercise my authority.

Marketing was a key element with which there was difficulty in integration. The corporate office required us to first align our marketing plan and practice with the strategic plan of the Company. For individual markets served by each subsidiary, the corporate let us continue the marketing approach that was already in place. The specific service market was still the responsibility of each subsidiary. All subsidiaries might share resources and information for the mutual benefit of other units. The corporate had a couple of critical requirements for marketing. All marketing information directed to customers could not be exaggerated. For instance, we could not claim that our laboratories were the best among the competitor laboratories. It was all right if our customers praised us, but we could not promote our message like that. In addition, each subsidiary unit was to continue to maintain the established customer base and projects and to develop our business relatively independently.

In terms of operation, there was not much that needed to be integrated because I was given the authority to run this laboratory as I had in the past. However, due to the annual financial budget and a range of approval procedures, I felt challenged because my hands and feet were literally tied by all the rules and policies set by corporate office. For example, in every October of the year, I had to prepare a capital equipment budget for our laboratory for the coming year. I could not use an estimate approach since the Company wanted the reason of purchasing any equipment. I could develop a list for replacements and for new instruments that were needed. Whether it was for replacement or for new equipment, I showed an amount of revenue for justification for buying it. The rule of thumb was that if we wanted a good approval rate, it would be better to have a budget plan to recoup the cost of the investment in two to three years. The budget plan would be given to the division head, who then submitted it to the corporate financial department. There were several authority levels in our division. For example, as a laboratory manager and director of food testing, I had an approval limit of about $5,000. The head of agriculture service division that our laboratory was grouped under had a $50,000 limit. Anything that cost more than that amount required the country vice president's approval. My power of approval limit meant that I could not purchase any equipment that cost more than $5,000 without application and approval from the upper management. In general, the dollar limit to me was only available for buying chemicals and lab supplies.

There were quite a few restrictions on hiring and offering benefits to employees. The company had an equal employment opportunity policy in place. For every vacancy in our laboratory, I reported to the upper management, then to the corporate human resources (HR) department. From there the position was published on the Company website. All applicants applied from the website. The screening was carried out by the corporate human relations department (HR), according to the job description and the applicant's background. Once the applicant passed the screening, the information on the qualified candidates was forwarded to me for further consideration.

Our laboratory set up a three- or four-person recruitment committee, chaired by me, to do the interviews and to make final decisions for selecting candidates for hiring. We forwarded the name of the candidate to HR for final approval and for communication with the candidate. This was quite different from what I had been used to doing because when I owned the laboratory, I decided everything by myself. In addition, the wages and benefits of the new employees were described in the job description advertisement. If the final offer was found to be materially different from the posting, the hiring would not be valid and the process had to be started over again. With this the Company policy, I was not given the authority to offer salary and benefits to new hires. Even for the annual raise, whether it was the inflation-based salary increase or a special promotion raise, I did not have much say in it. I could only work with the annual rate of pay increase set by corporate.

When I was in charge of my own company, it was easy to set an employee's salary and benefits. Because I took the relatively low cost of living at Champaign area, I set employees' salaries slightly lower than those of equivalent chemists in other areas. As a result, the average wage in our laboratory started at a relatively lower level. To make up for this, I often offered bonuses and company-paid health insurance. After joining the Company, I found that the average wages in our group was lower than other employees among the Company laboratories. In addition, there was no bonus offered to the average employee and only partial payment on health insurance. Because of all of these, I felt strongly that our employees deserved some upward adjustment on their salaries. Therefore, I worked diligently on the behalf of the employees for several months by proposing to HR the importance of setting the salary level of this group equivalent to that of other laboratories within the Company. By lobbying my upper manager and the HR director, we finally got an average increase of 7 percent on our salaries.

The business performance, measured by both revenue growth and total profits under my management, was much better than many other laboratories in the Company. We generated substantial profits and increased employee numbers by 50 percent in a few years. However, I could not fully participate in the company's bonus program because the financial performance was accessed at the division level, not at the laboratory level. Since a number of other laboratories did not perform well, which affected the total bonus pools, this resulted in a payout not matching the level I had expected. Fortunately, I received company stock equivalent to 10 percent of my salary in March of each year based on the market price of the Company stock, which made me feel better. Unfortunately for the average employees, there was no opportunity for profit sharing. I was disappointed in this outcome but could not do anything to help. Our employees could only expect a 2–3 percent increase annually in their salaries set by the corporate office.

Toward the end of each year, I had a difficult job to do, which was to work with every employee on the annual raise. Prior to the discussion of the salary increase, we performed an annual evaluation of each employee, using a scale of 0–6 on a couple of dozen appraisal items. If an employee achieved an average of 3, they received an average raise equivalent to the rate set by corporate at 3 percent, providing this was the corporate rate of increase. If an employee got a score of greater than 3 or less than 3, then the employee would receive a raise of more than 3 percent or less than 3 percent. For those who received a score of 0–1, it was unlikely that they would receive a salary increase. In the end, the total increase for all employees in our group must be within the limit set by the corporate. As the frontline leader of this laboratory, I felt disgusted every time because I would always have some employees dissatisfied or even in a bad mood and depressed.

It was even more difficult to promote an employee, especially if the promotion was associated with a raise in compensation. Just like hiring an employee, most of the promotions were advertised on the company website. The procedure for selection and interview was similar to that of hiring employees. There were fewer chances for a pay rate increase aside from the annual rate increase. It was hard for me to get approval for my employees who were recommended for raises in the midyear. Because of corporate policies, my hands were tied, and I could not really do much to increase benefits for our employees.

Another HR-related practice was that as a member of the Company family, we needed to increase the diversity of our employee base. Before acquisition, our laboratory was more weighted in a greater proportion toward foreign immigrants. Now corporate required us to increase diversity. Because of this, some strong candidates who were foreign nationals could not be selected and hired in this laboratory.

It took us about a year to basically complete the integration. During my tenure with the Company from 2011 to 2015, it was a relatively smooth sailing for me. I did not encounter any major difficulties or problems. My relationship with upper management was also good. More importantly, my relationship with laboratory employees was normal. Briefly, my major accomplishments were reflected in four aspects: building the laboratory as a fully capable and fully equipped laboratory with several high-end liquid chromatography-mass spectrometers, expanding the customer base by 30 percent, increasing employees by 50 percent (from twenty-five to thirty-eight), and growing revenue by nearly 80 percent. Our lab had become the model laboratory acquisition example of success that the Company had taken over in its recent history.

The great acquisition by the Company of our laboratory had some of my friends wondering if I had sold my company too early and too cheaply. But I didn't think so. Although on the one hand, I somewhat underestimated the role of the cGMP regulation on the laboratory testing business in nutrition supplement industry, there were other contributing factors to our business as well. In addition to my leadership and the collective effort of our management, our association with other subsidiaries of the Company also played an important role because a good portion of our business was introduced and forwarded to us by members of other units within the Company. The name recognition of the Company might have also helped. Our advanced laboratory equipment platform and well-qualified chemists had positioned us as one of most qualified laboratories in the Company, USA. This made us a go-to laboratory for difficult analytical projects. Without all this and the collaboration from members of the Company family, we wouldn't have achieved such a glorious performance. On the other hand, after I sold my business, I made timely investments in the real estate market. It was the best time for investing because of the real estate downturn and the beginning of the stock bulk market, where I have had a significant appreciation. Therefore, I was quite happy with the decision I had made, and the timing of the sale of the company had been appropriate.

After serving the Company for about four and a half years, I resigned from my manager post in 2014 and then from employment in the spring of 2015. I was motivated to make this move because I wanted to take a break and finish this autobiography. By then we had financial resources sufficient for our retirement and for our family. Just as many other successful entrepreneurs who worked so hard for their business, we often choose to retire earlier and spend our time on other interests that might be more meaningful to our lives in the future. Of course, it was hard for me to leave the laboratory that we had been so passionate about, and it was hard to leave our employees whom I had hired and worked with for so long. Fortunately, through several years of integration and the improvement of the leadership team, I could rest assured that the business will continue and all employees will be stable and taken care of in the foreseeable future.

14

ENTREPRENEURSHIP

Epilogue

$\mathbf{B}$ecoming a successful entrepreneur was a dream come true for me. In this challenging and difficulty course I had taken, I learned a lot. It was not only the knowledge but also the business skills that I could have never learned from text books. I have a new understanding of how the American market economy works and why the government encourages and supports the development of small business enterprises. Through my own entrepreneurial experience, I have a further understanding that the opportunity will always be given to those people who have prepared for it. My experience has shown that for a successful entrepreneur, we must have a few important character traits and attributes, as I have summarized below.

First of all, anyone who wants to establish a company must have the necessary character traits of a business person. This must include both the innate factor and the nurtured results. Innate factor means that some people were born with a good business sense (gene) and are not afraid of challenge and hard work and are always willing to sacrifice the short-term pains for the long-term gains. Because of these demanding characteristics, most of us would not want to build companies or are not fit for doing business. However, this is not to say that a person born without the inherited entrepreneur traits cannot start a business because this person can indeed acquire such characteristics by longtime nurturing. In summary, all successful entrepreneurs share the same characteristics as a risk taker, never bending with challenges and difficulty, willing to make tough decisions, and having resilience and perseverance of the spirit. How I started my business and overcame the difficulties in my business are a good example of these characteristics. Without them, I would have given it all up easily.

Second, the success of entrepreneurs does not necessarily require a patented technology. It is, of course, important or beneficial to have a technology in order to reduce competition and attract venture capital or an angel investment, all of which would increase the likelihood of success. However, this is not a decisive factor that should stop entrepreneurs from starting their own businesses. There are many new enterprises that have not been built on advanced patented technology but on everyday "boring business." The most successful entrepreneurs started with what is happening in their daily life. They just come up with a better solution than the original businesses to make the same product or to complete the same service. My business may be regarded as such an example because my business used the common analytical technology, without any competitive advantage, but my service was better than other companies.

Third, successful entrepreneurs are always on the top of market. Whenever there is a change in the marketplace, they are able to adjust their business plan accordingly in a timely manner. Of course, this is not the same as those with a groundless and arbitrary change of direction of the enterprise. For instance, my original business plan was in environmental testing and pesticide outsourcing services. When I worked hard for a period of time, I observed that both markets were deteriorating rapidly. If I did not change the direction of our business plan to nutrition supplement market, we would not be here today. This made some people wonder if my success was due to my luck of getting on a bandwagon of a growing market. Honestly, some luck helps every entrepreneur, but every good luck is often given to people who have been well prepared for it. Since opportunity is available to every one of us, the difference is that some people are able to seize the opportunity, while others turn a blind eye to it and allow it to sneak past.

Fourth, most entrepreneurs can concentrate on doing one thing well. No matter whether that person is a first-time entrepreneur or an experienced entrepreneur, it is very clear that a person's energy and time are limited. We often talk about multitasking but not leading multiple business start-ups. As a matter of the fact, one start-up is more than most of us can handle. This is especially true for new entrepreneurs with unrelated business ventures. I actually have learned a lesson from this. When we just got our service business redirected from environmental testing to nutrition supplement testing and got a foothold established, I eagerly expanded to biotech services. The service was gene-sequencing services to researchers and universities. Because I did not have the time to do marketing research and learn the technology necessary for providing this kind of service, I hurriedly set up the business by hiring employees and purchasing equipment. This process took me eighteen months. By the time we were fully ready and started our service, the market had already undergone changes as a result of advanced and expensive gene sequencers available on the market. This generation of new sequencers greatly speeded up the sequencing work, which led to the steep decrease in the service price. This development put us at a disadvantaged position to compete with biotech centers located at various universities where the equipment was purchased using public funds and where they could afford to offer low testing fees. As a result, our gene sequencer became obsolete, and our service was no longer competitive. Another example was at about the same time that we tried gene sequencing service that I opened up a third business selling nutrition supplement raw materials. My reasoning was that since we served the industry with many raw material buyers as our customers, I could sell the products to those manufacturers as well. So I hired a friend to do this business. Because the sales of raw materials and testing services are two different businesses, the lack of my full-time commitment to it led to the failure of this plan.

Fifth, doing business in China is not easy and most likely not suitable for most entrepreneurs from the US. There have been many failed attempts from successful US entrepreneurs. Because the Chinese business rules and practices are different from those of the United States, many of us really have a lot to learn about that country. Our Beijing laboratory was not very successful because we lacked capital, and more importantly, we had no experience doing business in China.

Finally, as an entrepreneur, we should set goals for our business. When these goals have been achieved, we should then reevaluate our business for the next step to take. For many entrepreneurs, merger and acquisition is the goal. There is an old saying that goes, "No tree can grow to the sky." This is also something a lot of businessmen use to evaluate their business process or a publicly traded company. Every business has its rapidly growing phase before it reaches a plateau. If we can time and sell our business in the growing upper curve, it would be ideal. Unfortunately, just like buying and selling stocks on a stock market, this kind of timing is difficult. In addition, the market condition is constantly changing, which adds more unknown factors to our decision. Therefore, we should be happy if we can exit our business at the 80–90 percent of full value of the company.

15

MARRIAGE AND FAMILY

"First, bow to heaven and earth; second, bow to mutual parents; third, bow to each other." These rituals are part of all traditional wedding ceremonies in China, but this time, they were announced not by a priest but instead by a friend who presided over our thirtieth wedding anniversary celebration. It was indeed a bustling and very happy anniversary celebration with our friends for this wedding ceremony. This occasion was very special for me because I "married" my wife now in a ceremony that was very different from our first wedding and with a completely different purpose. We combined the celebration with the pleasure of being with our social group named HuanYan Nian Hua (beautiful flowers of aging) to make it a memorable event. Regardless of the name used for the occasion, its primary purpose was to have a good time with our group of more than fifty friends. As a group, we had been playing cards together for more than a dozen years. To have a happy life, we have always tried to find time to socialize and do things together. With our active participation, we wanted to set an example for the group. Therefore, we were excited to host everyone for this happy event.

This was a unique wedding commemorative party. In order to make it the best celebration possible, my wife and I worked with a number of enthusiastic friends, carefully developing a plan. We first planned for the banquet. Although it was a wedding ceremony, preparing a luxurious Chinese-style wedding feast with abundant food was not our objective. However, we still wanted to have plenty of food for everyone.

Our goal was to have fun, and we did not want to spend all, or most, of our time preparing food for a big meal. We decided to do a potluck-style party in which we each prepared a favorite dish to share. There was no pomp, no expensive banquet setting, no gifts, and above all, this was not only different from a traditional Chinese-style wedding but it was also different from a modern American wedding because it was not held in a church or any other special place and there was no presiding priest.

By early afternoon, several dozen friends had arrived at our home. We had a spacious house that could accommodate a gathering of more than one hundred people. Our event was scheduled to occur from noon to midnight; therefore, we needed to have plenty of activities planned in order to have maximum fun. Our friends had been divided into several groups to help with the planning. The first group was responsible for dinner arrangements. We, as the hosts, were to provide drinks and beverages while our friends brought in food for the potluck buffet. Therefore, only a few volunteers were needed to set up the tables and arrange the food. We used the ping-pong table for the food, and with so many different types of food, the table was barely large enough to accommodate everything.

The second group was the makeup group, which consisted of several lady friends whose main task was to help the bride with her makeup. It is not uncommon for an experienced professional makeup specialist to take a couple of hours to get a twenty-year-old bride made up. But to present a lady who was more than fifty years old as a twenty- to thirty-year-old, a young and charming lady, would be quite challenging. And of course, we had only amateur makeup artists who, nevertheless, took this job seriously. By working hard, they were able to turn my wife into a beautiful woman who appeared to be in her thirties. In addition, no wedding dress was prepared for my wife, so she wore a dress selected from her closet.

The third group was in charge of the ceremony. As our event was a reenactment of a wedding of thirty years before, combined with our thirtieth anniversary celebration, this group had the responsibilities for the wedding music that would be played, the greeting of the bride by the groom, a door ceremony, and choosing someone to take the role of priest to preside over the event.

The fourth group was responsible for the thirtieth anniversary program after the wedding ceremony, which consisted mainly of the bride and groom talking about their stories of love and romance while showing a series of PowerPoint slides. This was to be followed by singing love songs. Immediately after that, our friends joined in the singing and dancing.

Time passed by quickly. It was like the snap of a finger when it was already three o'clock in the afternoon. I dressed in a suit as the groom, waiting for my bride to appear. It had been thirty years since we had gotten married, and now my hair had turned gray. But at this moment, I felt that I was still in my thirties, eager for my "marriage."

This was so special for me. It was just like my first wedding, but there was no need to receive my wife and bring her home. All I had to do was wait on the couch in my living room. The bride finally came out of our master bedroom with several bridesmaids around her. I greeted her in a joyous voice, took the bride's hand, and brought her into the hall in harmony with the pleasant sound of the piano accompaniment playing "The Wedding March." As soon as the wedding music stopped, all our friends burst into loud laughter. We followed the program sequence of removing the scarf from the bride's head, taking a couple of drinks of the wedding wine, and kissing each other, all parts of any traditional marriage in many areas of China.

We had not arranged a Western-style wedding ceremony to be presided over by a religious dignitary or exchanging wedding rings; however, it was important to me to give my wife a ring. I gave her an excellent one with a value comparable to a new car. This was a gift that I would have given to her thirty years before if I had been able to afford it. Reality was that I did not have anything to give her then, but now I fulfilled my wish. And I felt quite happy about it.

The marriage ceremony lasted less than an hour, and as soon as it was over, the celebrations began with the wedding feast. There was plenty of food on the table with many different kinds of food, including various cuisines from the south to the north of China. Everyone took turns serving themselves the food and drinks. Adult men and women sat at two large tables, and kids sat at a separate long table. This made it convenient for each group to talk, drink, and joke with plenty of interaction among us, creating an extraordinarily happy and lively scene.

The banquet dinner took about an hour to complete, and by then, the next program had already begun in the family room. Everyone, except some of the children, were there, sitting on different couches and the carpeted floor. The audio and video systems were set up to run the program.

In that special era of thirty years ago, most love stories were quite different from today's stories of many young people. The uniqueness of our love story made it sound particularly interesting, and most of our audience was very curious about our story and were eager to hear it. In order to not disappoint our friends, I had compiled and organized a set of slides in PowerPoint presentation format. My presentation consisted of several dozen pictures beginning with my childhood and the beauty of my hometown, continuing on to my high school and college years, then to having my girlfriend and the undercover romantic process, ending with our marriage and our family. It took me an hour to finish my presentation. At the end of the slide show, the karaoke began with my wife, the bride, and I, the groom, then by the audience singing. I sang "The Moon Represents My Heart" as the first song. Although I am not a good singer, I did OK this time, probably because I was in such a happy environment. At the end of my song, I received hearty applause, accompanied by cheerful, loud laughter. The motivated and emotionally moved audience brought a liveliness to the room. Many of them sang happily and with such a joyful and happy setting, making the next two hours in our family room pass quickly.

Our friends had a wide range of interests, so our next program included several choices. Those who loved ballroom dancing or playing poker chose those activities, while others chose to chat and socialize. The nine-hundred-square-foot basement floor of our house was furnished with a ballroom dance floor big enough for five or six couples to dance on at any given time. Some friends enjoyed playing cards, our club's weekly event ever since the club was established about fifteen years before.

From afternoon till midnight, it was a long, unusual wedding and a memorable celebration. My wife and I were really happy that day. Who would have thought of such a late arrival of a happy marriage ceremony, especially as a "second wedding" with my wife? Compared to the first wedding in the scene and scale of that original wedding, this one was better and livelier, making my happy mood last much longer. The entire day brought me right back to my dreams of love, marriage, and family. I could not stop thinking about the many ups and downs of thirty-plus years ago when I was pursuing love. Many scenes from the past were brought back to my memory.

As I grew up, I was only aware of ignorant feudal thought regarding love and romance. As a young man, I silently pursued love. From middle school to high school, from the participation and activities of the Communist Youth League to becoming the Communist Party branch secretary, and from leading a militia team in the construction of a reservoir to the training of a cadre trial, for about five to seven years, I had many opportunities for love and marriage. However, I had never sought girlfriends or pursued marriage for a number of reason. Now, some of them appear to be quite unusual, if not ridiculous, looking at them from today's viewpoint.

I was greatly influenced by feudal thought and ideology. China was considered a closed-door nation in the 1960s and 1970s. In such a country, men and women were not allowed to express their feelings openly, to have romance, or to kiss each other. If they were not a husband and wife, men and women generally would not even hold hands in public or even shake hands with each other. In the countryside and remote villages, it was even worse. For instance, if there was something happening between a man and a woman, people would spit on them, and such shame could not be washed clean, even "by jumping into the Yellow River," as by the old saying. The gossip of the neighbors, especially that of the older women, could be like a knife sharpened enough to kill a person, especially for young girls.

I was impacted by the national policies of "later marriage, later childbearing, and family planning." This national policy, in its early stage of propagation, coincided with my high school graduation and returning home as a farmer. Then, my head was full of how to become a leader and a respected Communist Youth member. Because I was a member of a propaganda team, I had to set a moral example of later romance, later marriage, and later childbearing. Naturally, this led me to avoid developing any close relationships with girls, and I definitely had no ideas of romantic love.

My dream was to jump out of the countryside to become a national cadre or worker, an imperial food eater who could receive allocations of salary and food from the government. To live on these permanent allocations without worrying about the fluctuation of income was a dream of many young men and women. If I married too early, I would most likely never realize my dream.

The feudal ideology relating to girlfriends and marriage was widespread across many parts of the Guangxi Province, including our village. When I was in third or fourth grade in primary school, a female member of my class showed and expressed kindness to me. It would be considered a good thing for most kids today. But it was not good for me. My classmates laughed about it, making me feel very uncomfortable. One day, I met this female classmate on the stairway, and without giving any reason, I slapped her face hard, causing some pain and bruising. For this bad and naive act, I was asked to pay certain medical costs and to go to her home to apologize! That a pupil who had always been a good student and was only about ten years old to have shown such behavior fully indicated how much I was in bondage to feudal thought. It was also an indication of the failure of school and family education.

In the early 1970s, the whole country was hit hard by the Cultural Revolution, including our high school. The rules were particularly clear that no students were allowed to fall in love. Our class had more than 60 students. There were two classes in my high school year with a total of 120 students, equally divided between girls and boys. We all obeyed the school rules, and there were no boyfriends or girlfriends. At least I did not see any open relationships between boys and girls. Only a few classmates married each other later. I was a relatively skinny boy, and as a captain of our class, I had to take the lead to show compliance with the school rules. As a result, I never thought of having any girlfriend during my high school years.

After graduating from high school, for various reasons, I refrained from talking about girlfriends and romance. If I had wanted a girlfriend, there were many opportunities. However, because of my dreams to become a national cadre or a worker, I did not go any further than a comrade relationship, even though wanting a girlfriend and a romantic relationship is human nature, especially for a young man. During the second year, after I had graduated from high school, I heard that a female classmate had some difficulties with someone that she had dated. I was sympathetic to her and wrote a letter to comfort her. She wrote back quickly, which was followed by more letters from her expressing her love. If I had wanted to reach out, we might have soon headed down the road to love and romance.

My parents were generally not too keen on having a matchmaker find a match for me. They always considered that their son had the ability to deal with his personal life by himself. However, the neighbors and matchmakers tried to offer me words of advice and wanted to introduce girls to me, hoping to see results for their efforts. Some parents encouraged their daughters to get close to me as well. As I showed little enthusiasm toward all these attempts, the relationships usually ended quickly after only a short conversation.

So did I have favorite girls? Yes, I did. For instance, there was one whose surname was the same as mine. She was a year older than I, so she was like a big sister to me. We worked together in our Qiaobei Production Brigade and the Communist Youth League. We led the same militia team participating in the construction of the reservoir and even participated in cadre trial training in 1995. I liked her a lot and hoped to become closer than an ordinary friend, but for various reasons, I did not take the initiative. And she probably considered me as her little brother. However, we remained just friends for many years.

As far as having girlfriends, I had my own shortcomings too. I did not know how to sweet-talk girls or how to develop close relationships with them. I always seemed to be at the crossroads of trying to decide the kind of girlfriend I should have and what my future wife should be like. In the countryside, people hardly spoke about girlfriends. Instead, a young man often considered any girl the matchmaker could convince to marry him. There were few who gave a second thought to these decisions. In order to realize my dream of leaving farm life, I could not fall in love too early, and I should not get married before I was promoted to a cadre or recruited as a national worker. This idea had always prevailed in my mind and continued into my college years.

When I entered college in February of 1978, my dream of jumping out of the countryside and becoming an imperial food eater had been finally realized. Now, I was no longer concerned about being tied to the countryside as a farmer. It was time for me to think about my personal and family goals that I had never been able to do previously. From the first year of college, I started my pursuit of love, although my mind was still filled with feudal thoughts and attitudes.

How did I set my own criteria for choosing a future wife? My standards were relatively simple and could be easily summed up in three points. First, the woman must have a status similar to mine as an imperial food eater. This meant that she could not be a farmer. My ancestors were all farmers, and I wanted to change that symbolic status of my family. Second, she should be the type of woman who would be capable of taking care of our children and family in the future. Although this requirement was basic for ordinary people who wanted to marry each other, it seemed to be more important for me than for most other people because I placed a particular emphasis on family and, especially, on my children's education. Third, she must be able to sacrifice herself and support my professional pursuits. I had always thought that it was too hard when both the husband and wife each had a very successful career. If this were true of us, our home might not look like a home or at least not a warm home. Managing a home and a family requires full commitment and endeavor from one of the family members. It could be the husband or the wife, but for me, I wanted my wife to accept this responsibility and to support me as I pursued my career goals.

This criteria for choosing a mate was not necessarily accepted by many of my friends and certainly not by today's young people. I had been a farmer, so why did I not look for, or at least accept, girls from the countryside? Why could not both the husband and the wife be successful in achieving their own professional dreams? Why could not both husband and wife take care of the family but at the same time still be successful professionally? There were many examples of both spouses having successful careers. Making things more difficult to judge was the fact that when a young man and woman fall in love for the first time, it is hard to know if the criteria could really be applied. They do not thoroughly understand the inner workings of the other person and what that person's future behavior will be. Once I set the criteria, I would not change it. Today, I know that my criteria are not practiced at all.

As the result of setting such selection criteria for my future wife, I excluded girls who were residents of the countryside. As a common phenomenon, if you were promoted to a cadre, recruited to a state-run enterprise as a worker, or as in this case, entered in a university, you would attract many girls from the countryside who would like to be your girlfriend and future wife. More matchmakers would come to you and your family in an effort at matchmaking. My parents did not give positive answers to any of those matchmakers' visits.

However, I also had a pessimistic side. I came from a peasant's family and had five brothers and sisters. My family had always been a relatively poor family, and that put me in a disadvantaged position compared to the young men from cities. As the old saying goes, "The more children in a family, the smaller the piece of the pie each brother would get from his parents." In other words, a lot of girls, especially city girls, would not want to pursue someone from a family that had as many bothers like ours. It would be hard for them to accept my family history and the economic circumstances. Based on this understanding, I was afraid of making friends with city girls, so I narrowed my choice down substantially. This left me with only the college girls from the countryside.

My choice was terribly limited with these criteria. Making things even worse was the fact that there were only six female students in our class of thirty-two students. This was also the case in the other agronomy major classes, although there was a slightly higher percentage of female students in the majors of sugarcane and meteorology in our department. Among this small number of female students, only a few came from the countryside, which really created a limitation for me as I began to seek a girlfriend.

I did not see any opportunity in my class, so I turned my attention to those outside my college. Generally speaking, the proportion of girls to boys at medical schools is much higher than that of most other universities. Students in medical schools have a good professional and prestigious career after graduation. By contrast, I was an agricultural student, which was still attached with an "ag" label. This reality made me hesitant in approaching female students from other universities. Nevertheless, I made a couple of attempts to start a conversation with a girl who had graduated from the same high school as I had who was then a medical student. Unfortunately, I did not get any meaningful response from her.

In order to create more opportunities to meet female students, I used the summer break of 1979 to organize a summer camp called Climbing the South Mountain Camp. More than a dozen university and college students from our county joined in. Although there was a handful of female students, none were from medical colleges. I was somewhat disappointed in this regard, but we all had a good time at the camp.

Time flew by quickly. I had already entered my junior year of college when I gradually set my eyes on a girl named Lisong Zhang, who eventually became my wife. She entered the same college with the same major I was in, only six months later than I. Just as I did, she had to return to farming in her village during the Cultural Revolution. She would not have had the opportunity for college if it were not for the resumption of the national entrance examination in 1977. Furthermore, she came from a nearby village in the same people's commune as I had come from, a distance that could be covered in a sixty-minute slow bike ride. Although her father had been a respected bank clerk and her mother a good farmer, their status had been designated as rich class in the early days of the People's Republic of China. Because of such classification, she did not live the kind of life most of us got. As a result, she grew up in adverse conditions. It was exactly because she grew up in a difficult environment that she was self-trained and self-disciplined as a tough girl who was not afraid of challenges and hard work. Her character seemed to fit well with my selection criteria.

There were other considerations as well. Being from the countryside, she was more understanding in dealing with my family background. This was important to me because not having this kind of understanding could lead to a lot of confusion and uneasiness in the future. Also, Lisong was an introvert and a down-to-earth person. I thought that these characteristics would also be important in supporting my career endeavors in the future. After a period of time observing her, I felt that she was the one I would like to have as my girlfriend. I was told later that a number of other female classmates in my department also liked me, but perhaps because I had Lisong as my girlfriend already, I no longer paid much attention to others.

With my target set, I thought that I could have an open and romantic love story underway. However, this was only wishful thinking. It was only a few years after the Cultural Revolution, and many traditional ideologies and politics were still planted deep within our bones and bodies. All universities across the nation had policies that would not allow college students to have girlfriends or boyfriends or to get married. Since I was the president of the student union of the college, I should naturally set a good example for other students. However, I, along with some other students, did not comply with this policy, mainly because this was simply that most students were twenty-two to twenty-six years of age. I was twenty-six by 1980. This older college student population was a result of the Cultural Revolution that had disrupted normal college admission for ten years. To deal with this group of students, the school appeared to be using a strategy of talking tough but being lax in enforcement. Even if departmental officers knew some of the students were falling in love, they generally just "educated" the students but left them alone, or at least did not publicly denounce them. I chose to proceed in my love pursuit in "undercover."

Therefore, my love story progressed through a simple yet boring process. On the one hand, I could not invite my girlfriend to dinner or to watch a movie. We felt ashamed if we appeared together in a public place, and we could not let our friends and classmates know about our relationship. On the other hand, I had a low IQ in romance and making love because I did not know what words to use to please my girlfriend. Economically speaking, I was a poor young man, often with empty pockets and no money. So a loving relationship without romantic gifts or flowers was a good thing for me because I did not really have the money to afford anything else!

Our love story was secretly progressing. We still had opportunities to meet or could even take a short walk around the campus, including the campus pond. We saw each other several times a week because we went to the same education building, and we sometimes attended the same lectures. However, we rarely talked to each other about our lives or even about our studies. As my college time went by, each day my feeling got stronger, and I knew I should clearly express my love to her. I shied away from direct expressions or love words, so I decided to put my feelings in a love letter. I asked a female classmate to deliver it to Lisong at the end of my junior year. As expected, Lisong happily accepted my request to be my girlfriend. We formally established our relationship after we shook hands and had a little hug on the sidewalk by the big pond.

My love letter was another indication that I had a low IQ in this area. My letter was not really a loving and romantic letter because it had few words or sentences related to love and passion. It was a short letter, and when I read it to our friends at our thirtieth anniversary party, everyone laughed out loud. Some said that I had too often used the revolutionary words and the political slogans taken from the Cultural Revolution. Others said that they did not see from the letter that I loved Lisong. In the letter, I briefly introduced myself, who I was, why I wanted her to be my girlfriend, and finally said that I wished she would agree with me. Throughout this letter, loving, passionate, and romantic words were nowhere to be found. It was more like an information letter because the tone of it was such that "I want to let you know that . . ." It was also like a decision letter that implied, "You had better be my girlfriend." I felt so lucky because Lisong had not been expecting an elegant love letter from me. Instead, she knew who I was, and what I meant was more important than any gorgeous expression of love. Therefore, I got by her easily and was excused.

Our undercover relationship was successful. From the beginning until my graduation, few classmates really noticed us. My best friend, who was also the captain of our class, knew it because I asked him about Lisong's family being labeled with the status of rich class and wondered whether this would have any effect on our future career development and family life. Our captain came from the countryside with plenty of life experiences because he had three children who were being taken care of by his wife at home. I thought that if I could get his positive comments on my pursuit, it would give me more confidence. Of course, Lisong's best friend and roommate also knew about it. After Lisong and

I visited each other's parents during that summer and received their approval, we finally publically established our relationship.

My college life was quickly approaching the end. My love story and marriage issues had moved from the back burner to the front burner. The simple reason for this was that in China, all graduates were mandatorily assigned a job at various levels of government, institutions, or universities. It was a national policy that we could not select a job on our own. We must obey the assignment of the university. This kind of graduate assignment frequently led to the separation of husbands and wives when each of them was assigned to work and live in different remote cities or counties. These separations had created tremendous difficulties for families. Consequently, I wanted to do what I could to prevent this from happening to us. My first action was to let our departmental chair and the branch secretary of the Communist Party know that I had a fiancée who would be graduating six months after me. I requested that she be assigned to a job near me when she graduated. My request appeared to receive a great deal of positive attention from the department and graduate assignment committee.

I was the president of the student union at Guangxi Agriculture College, and my four-year college GPA was one of the best in my class. Therefore, the department had a plan for me to stay in the department as a member of a political cadre or as a student moral education instructor. However, that type of work was not what I had in mind. I did not want to be a political instructor anymore, but I wanted to be a professor. I knew that my rebuff to this kind of planned assignment might frustrate some members of the graduation assignment committee. Also, I had requested that there be consideration of a similar job for my fiancée. I believed that both the 1977 and 1978 classes, which graduated six months apart, would be assigned jobs at about the same time. My early application provided the flexibility for the department to accommodate my request. In order to be assigned together, I even expressed my interest in teaching at a two-year agricultural college in Yulin City, which offered only associate degrees. My strong leadership experience and my excellent academic records helped me convince the committee to reshuffle the job assignments to meet my expectations. Finally, I was fortunate to be assigned to the botany group of the same department from which I had graduated, and the department leaders promised a job for my fiancée. After graduation, she began her job as an assistant secretary in the same department.

Working in the same department was the best outcome we could have had. We were excited and eager to get married as soon as possible so that we could work together for our future. I was very pleased about the situation because my goal of becoming and marrying an imperial good eater had finally been realized. My dream of leaving the countryside, where my ancestors had worked for generations, had now been achieved. I felt that I had made history for my family. From now on, our family would no longer be a farmer generation after generation because we both held professional jobs. Unfortunately, this happy moment was soon replaced with worries as the new reality set in. How could we fulfill our desire to be married when I had no money and no apartment? Starting our family and planning for the future appeared to be quite remote for us.

Every graduate from college received a similar salary of about fifty yuan per month. Although our housing was given by the government with little cost, this salary was barely enough to meet daily living expenses. My bank account was empty, and my family continued to be relatively poor farmers. How could I save some money and get some furniture in order to get married? Borrowing from friends was not a good option because I did not know if I could return the borrowed money, considering the limited salaries we received. I was reluctant to ask my family for money because I knew their poor financial situation with my younger brothers and sisters still living at home. I felt that my parents had done more than their share for me during my four years of college. I would be embarrassed to ask for more money. After all these considerations, we finally decided to do what we could to arrange our marriage according to our financial situation.

The first college class after the Cultural Revolution graduated in February of 1982. There were millions of things to do and considerable problems to be solved by the government and by the university. One problem was the lack of dormitory rooms and apartments for new faculty. I was assigned to a student dorm, living with a couple of other new teachers. Without our own small apartment, it was impossible for us to get married, so I applied to the school for a single room in the summer of 1982. Although the university had a housing office, our application started from our own department. After my application was approved by the department, it moved to the college-level waiting list. There was a considerable number of new teachers coming to our college, and we all needed rooms. Under the severe housing shortage, the college was constructing a new building with one-bedroom apartments called the Bachelor Building. Because I was on the faculty and my fiancée was on the staff of the college, we were lucky to get one of these in 1983.

The apartment building was located at the southwest corner of our college campus. My wife and I visited it in 2017, just to recall our experience in this tiny apartment. The building had four stories and a total of forty units. Each unit consisted of one bedroom of about 120 square feet. It is only big enough for one queen-size bed, a small bed, a cabinet, and a desk. Three of these units shared a kitchen and a bathroom. Although it was small, it was allocated to us just in time for our wedding.

A relatively new style of wedding was called new way of new marriage. This was also called revolutionary marriage. The core concept of this style of marriage was to promote marriage without spending much money. I really loved this because it fit in well with my financial situation. Under this a concept and practice, I was not required to buy wedding clothes or a wedding ring and did not even need to prepare a banquet for guests. I could save all those expenses but could not save the cost of our bed, a set of drawers, and a dining table, all of which were absolutely necessary for our daily life. To solve this, I had to ask my parents for help.

At the back of the village where my family lived was Duqiao Mountain, where pine and fir trees could be harvested for lumber to make furniture. There was also a carpenter near my parents' home who had often helped other married couples make wedding furniture. My father asked him to make our furniture, and it took about two weeks for the carpenter to finish ours. Transporting it from my home to my college in Nanning City was another problem because the distance was more than two hundred miles away. There was no railroad nearby, with the closest one being about thirty miles away. No one had a car or truck in China, and there was no moving company either. Without a truck, there was no way to get the furniture to us. I had to ask all my relatives and friends for help. Finally, one relative was able to connect us with a truck driver who periodically came to Nanning with an empty truck to pick up cargo from the city and transport back to the countryside. This driver helped us get our furniture to Nanning. The whole process, from lumber preparation to receiving the furniture at our apartment, took us a few months.

Under normal circumstances, the gift and the wedding dress are not small expenses, but these costs were omitted from my wedding plans. It was not that I meant to marry my wife without spending money, but it was because I did not really have the cash for these expenses. Fortunately, Lisong was also very understanding and never asked for anything that I could not afford. In addition to the savings on the wedding ring, the wedding gown, and the wedding dress, her parents did not ask for dowry money and a gift, which were supposed to be a normal requirement in our tradition when a girl got married. I was very grateful to my wife and her family for their understanding and their generosity. I made up my mind that I would pay them back double the amount someday in the future when I got my finances in order.

There could have been more expenses if it were not for the new way of new marriage. One expense was the wedding banquet. The ten years of the Cultural Revolution had created a popular slogan, "Destroy the old fours for the new fours," which was deeply rooted in our younger generation. In that economic and political climate, many young couples took the lead in following this slogan and, opposed extravagance and waste. They held revolutionary wedding ceremonies. Weddings were mostly held in the form of symposiums and tea parties. To a poor single person like me, holding this kind of wedding was undoubtedly a very good thing! After I talked to Lisong and won the consent of both parents, I decided that we would adopt the new style of wedding ceremony for our marriage.

We registered with the government office where we obtained a marriage certificate in 1983 when I was nearly thirty years old. Looking back over the previous ten years, from a period of my attitude of indifference toward girls to the development of the undercover love process in recent years, I felt in my heart an unspeakable taste of joy. Many years of hard work and dream pursuing had finally bore fruit. This was a big deal for me, especially because without much expense, I was able to complete this major event in my life. I wished that I could have had the money to give my wife a more gorgeous wedding. I would owe it to her and to her family for a long time to come.

Our style of love and marriage was not influenced by our parents. In the past, the marriage of sons and daughters was arranged by parents. The young man and woman had no choice in their mates. This was a tradition of thousands of years in old China, but that kind of feudal thought and ideology was not with us anymore. Our wedding as revolutionary was both simple and completely different from today's modern weddings. For example, our son Michael's wedding took a year of preparation, including preparing and sending the invitations, choosing and reserving the wedding venue, planning for photo albums and video recordings, and choosing the best man, groomsmen, maid of honor, and the bridesmaids to participate in the wedding ceremony. They were married under the auspices of a priest, and then there was the reception, including the booze and dance. In contrast, when we got married, there was no wedding gown, no makeup, no flowers, and no bridesmaids or groomsmen. Our wedding invitations were sent by our friends through word of mouth. Neither parents nor siblings were invited to our college for the wedding.

The way we entertained our guests was to serve them with two plates of sweet candies, peanuts, and sunflower seeds, plus tea and cigarettes. The money to buy these "necessities" was about ten Chinese yuan, which came from my parents. There was little space for guests due to the furniture in our small apartment, so we borrowed the apartment of the teacher next door as our place for greeting guests, sitting, chatting, eating candies, and drinking tea. On the day of our wedding, Lisong and I were still at work in the morning. We came home in the afternoon, and by about 6:00 or 7:00 p.m., our guests started coming. They usually said a few words of congratulations and wished our marriage well. The guests sat for a few minutes, drank a cup of tea, smoked a cigarette or two if they were smokers, and ate a couple of candies. In order to make room for the next guests, each group usually spent only about five to ten minutes with us. We held this type of party for about three hours and greeted a total of some fifty guests.

After the marriage ceremony was completed, our wedding was officially considered finished, but we were actually only about half done. We still needed to go back to our parents' homes to have another wedding ceremony with each family, which was more complicated than the one at the school. Although our feeling was that our wedding ceremony had been completed, the ones at home were needed to satisfy the tradition of appreciation for our parents, relatives, and our friends in the village. There were two main reasons for doing this. First, my wife and I were both from the same people's commune where there had always been a tradition of young people inviting relatives and friends to the marriage celebration. If we did not entertain them, we could be considered mean, and our families would be subjected to sarcastic remarks and would be marginalized by the neighbors and the residents in the village. This could lead to the unfavorable treatment of them and unpleasant comments about our parents and relatives in the future. Second, I was once a cadre in the village, a member of the Communist Youth League, and the Communist Party branch secretary. I had a lot of friends and teachers in the village. It was better for me to express my appreciation to them through this marriage ceremony.

The tradition in my home area was that the groom's family would host a banquet party for relatives, neighbors, and friends, usually planned a few weeks in advance. Invitations were sent out, usually by word of mouth and occasionally by postcard. These banquet ceremonies included not only a big meal with plenty of wine for the guests but also the introduction of the bride to all the family members and VIP guests. It was usually a two-day event. On the first day, the family would host the distant relatives who had come a day before the ceremony. The groom's family also had helpers come on the first day to prepare certain foods that needed more time to cook so they could be served at the banquet the next day. Some of these dishes might include fried bamboo shoots and fried pork belly meat. Most relatives brought with them two baskets containing two pieces of pork, two packages of noodles, rice, and a red envelope called *hongbao*. The host family would return almost exactly one half of the gifts back to the relatives, meaning that they came with gifts and returned with gifts, and thus, symbols of luck stayed with both families. All other guests might bring only *hongbao* with money inside. And here again, the host would return to the guests a small portion of money, such as one to a few yuan. This complicated tradition has been in use for thousands of years and is still in use today.

The preparation of the banquet dishes was usually carried out by a group of neighbors led by a chef. There was an unwritten custom in our countryside that no matter who had a wedding or birthday banquet event, neighbors always voluntarily helped each other. In general, there were eight to twelve entrees, but ten per table was most common for an average banquet. Among the dishes, about one-third was meat and seafood, one-third was dried food such as rice, and one-third was fresh vegetables. It was not uncommon that a big pig was slaughtered for a wedding or birthday banquet party. The number of guests at an average ceremony was a few hundred. Meat for each guest was in the range of 0.3–0.8 pounds. With two hundred to four hundred guests, meat from a whole pig might be required. That is why many families often raised a large pig for these kinds of events. Otherwise, the host had to purchase meat from the free market. In addition to lots of meat, much wine was also purchased, which was a staple item on each table.

Depending on the number of guests sitting by each table, and assuming eight as standard, some tables required a lot of wine, especially when there were some heavy-wine-drinking male guests sitting at the same table. In that case, three to five liters of rice wine could be consumed. They might eat and drink for several hours. Each drinker would feel proud if he could be the one who got drunk first. Only when someone got drunk was the banquet, or the host, considered to have provided enough wine and dishes for the guests. Because there was so much food on the table, people could rarely finish it all, so what was leftover was divided and taken home by the guests at each table.

For our wedding ceremony, we purchased pork from the free market, but most vegetables were homegrown. There were about two hundred guests attending, half adults and half children. With eight people at each table, we had twenty-five tables of guests. The banquet was held at my family's home. However, due to space limitations, each round could accommodate only five tables at a time. With twenty-five tables to serve, we needed five rounds of dining. Each round included about one and one half hours of eating and a half hour of cleaning up and resetting the tables. Our banquet party ran from about eleven o'clock in the morning to around nine o'clock at night.

Another tradition in our countryside was that after the banquet, the wife and husband would be introduced to grandparents, parents, and relatives. It started from the oldest generations to the youngest (i.e., from grandparents to parents and brothers and sisters, and from uncles and aunts to nieces and nephews). My wife and I went around the prearranged circles where these guests were sitting. While my wife held the tea tray filled with candies and sunflower seeds, plus a pack of cigarettes, I was holding a teapot and teacup. When we walked up to the relatives, I introduced them one by one to my wife, and then we both invited them to have tea and candies. After they had drunk some tea and picked a couple of candies and/or some sunflower seeds and a cigarette for those who smoked, they left a *hongbao* on the tray. A *hongbao* was only a symbol of luck with a small amount of cash inside.

A similar banquet was also held for the bride's family. The way that guests were invited and food was prepared, as well as the way we introduced ourselves to the family members, was similar to the groom's family ceremony, except that my wife did the introductions. Traditionally, the families of the husband and wife held the ceremonies on the same day. But for us, we held it on two separate days. We completed my ceremony the first day and hers on a second day. There are only about twenty kilometers between my home and my wife's home. It was a two hours of bike riding on the hilly road. We were busy for two days, but we finally got through it.

When all was done, it should have been time for us to have a little honeymoon and enjoy ourselves. Unfortunately, that never happened because then most young couples never dreamed of having a honeymoon. Indeed, a lot of us did not even know the term *honeymoon* existed. This was completely different from modern marriages where young couples always make serious plans for their honeymoon and it becomes part of their life story. Unfortunately for our generation, the lack of money for a honeymoon was the standard for a married couple. Like us, most did not even have time for a vacation. As soon as our wedding was over, we went back to the college and started our work routine again.

At about the same time we got married, I had an opportunity for graduate education. I had already had an appointment for an interview with the consulate of the United States of America in Guangzhou concerning getting a visa to study in the USA. Therefore, our "honeymoon" was spent in our thirteen-square-meter apartment. I worked during the day and studied English at night. It was like a snap of the fingers when two months had passed by and I had to leave my wife and go to the US to pursue my graduate study. My heart was semibroken at the time because I really did not want to leave my newly wedded wife. However, for me and for every young person in China, nothing was more important than overseas study. I needed to sacrifice and bear the short-term pain for the dream and long-term gain. I felt sorry for my wife and myself because this goodbye seemed so rude and unreal when I realized that I did not know when I would be able to see my wife again.

In the next two years, both my wife and I experienced great difficulties. During the first year of graduate school, I had some unbelievable challenges in my life. I was not eligible for a normal school transfer, which forced me to accept a program that I was not prepared for. I was extremely depressed for a few weeks, and during this time, I wished my wife were with me, comforting me. For a brief moment, I even thought about giving up my studies and returning home to be with my wife. This naive thought, of course, only existed for a flash, but it still indicated that I really wanted to be with my wife.

At home, my wife was also not having an easy time. She worked every day. Without me, she worked during the day and took care of my mother and my cousin at night, both of whom lived with her after I left home. She had to make decisions by herself and learn how to live with my mother. Fortunately, she was an independent lady and she could deal with the general problems associated with her daily life. I could easily imagine that the greatest hardship for her would be our separation. This separated life lasted for two years until Christmas of 1985, when I visited home. I often told my children that we had a second "mini honeymoon" then.

Before my visit, I had already sent my wife a J-2 form that I had gotten from the Office of International Students of Miami University in Ohio. My wife's application for her J-2 visa was approved by the US Consulate, so we came back together to the US in January of 1986. From that time on, we no longer lived on two different continents, and we were happily starting a new chapter in our lives.

Our life was smooth for a while. Usually I went to school, taking classes, studying, and preparing for the dissertation research. My wife stayed at home as a housewife, trying to settle in and cope with the different environment. However, it did not take long for me to realize that there was a worrisome time ahead of us. There is an old saying that goes, "Established at thirty, for both family and professional career." This slogan says that a successful man should have a complete family, with children, and a good job to earn enough for the family by the time he is thirty years old. I had neither. Although I was worrying about both, I knew that I could not solve both problems at the same time because I was still a student. Therefore, we decided to have a family first. This should be easier for me because as long as my wife and I worked together, we would have a good chance of achieving it.

However, to have a complete family was not as easy as I originally thought. A simple reason for this was that once my wife arrived in the US, she also wanted to apply for graduate school. To ask her to give up the opportunity she had always wanted was hard. I was thankful to her that she finally agreed with me about not going to graduate school. As a result, she sacrificed her opportunity and devoted her whole attention to raising our children as her major responsibility.

To be able to take care of the family, Lisong needed to learn to drive, a skill that is very important for anyone in the United States. Therefore, the first thing I wanted her to achieve was to get her driver's license. My wife's English was not very good at the time, and no written examination was given in Chinese in the area where we resided. My wife required a translation from a Chinese friend of mine, and I did the same for my friend's wife who also needed a translation. Both ladies took the written driving tests on the same day through translation at a driver's license facility in Oxford, Ohio, and both passed the tests on their first try. They also passed their road driving tests a couple of months later. With the driver's license in hand, my wife was able to take care of all kinds of needs for our family, and this was critical when she decided later to become a waitress to help earn money.

Our reunion was strengthened daily by our desire to have a child. To my surprise, my wife was pregnant shortly afterward. This was our first child, and we went through all kinds of anxiety and concerns. We were thankful to have a very nice and qualified doctor from McCullough-Hyde Memorial Hospital in Oxford, Ohio, who took care of her starting in January of 1986. Our son was born in October of the same year. After labor, my PhD supervisor, Dr. McClure, and his wife came to the hospital to visit us. When Dr. McClure asked for my son's name, I told him that we had not decided what name to give him yet, and then I asked for his suggestion. He did not hesitate to suggest the name John. He explained to us that John was a name that anyone would like to be called, whether child, adult, or senior. We gladly accepted it and then also gave our son the Chinese name of Jie. Although my adviser has left us, he will be remembered by us and our family for a long time to come.

With a child in the family, we now felt that we were finally a complete family. I, just like all other new fathers, was obviously excited for our new family member. Part of my happiness stemmed from the tradition that all men should have sons to carry on the family torch to future generations. Although it was not common ideology in the Western world, in China, most families would want to have sons in order to be considered successful in the family tree. My father was particularly keen on this, and with John born, he was also very happy about it.

In no time, I became burdened with great responsibility and pressure. I was a PhD student who received an assistantship from the graduate program. The assistant stipend was barely enough for my family's minimal expenses, and it would not be sufficient to raise John in a way that most families raised their children. We felt that we could not create a decent environment for the child to grow up in, so after some discussion with my wife, we decided to find part-time jobs to supplement our incomes. There were no jobs for us to do other than work in Chinese restaurants. For several years, we worked part-time in Chinese restaurants—Lisong as a waitress and I as a waiter. Some of the money we earned was spent on raising John while the rest was saved for the future. Lisong not only took care of our son and me but also worked more than 50 percent of her time. One could only imagine that her job was perhaps more difficult than mine, but my wife always said that such tasks were not challenging to her at all. I knew that she had had plenty of hardship in her childhood and young adult life, including the hard work of plowing a paddy field and cutting firewood from the mountain. As a result of her experience in the countryside, it was relatively easy for her to adapt to the current situation.

Time flew by us, and before we knew it, our son was already two years old. During this period, my wife had learned how to become a warm mother and a good wife to her husband. She spent endless time at night with John because he cried frequently and ate many times during the night during the first few months. John was also a picky eater and required frequent feeding by his mom for the first three years. Even with breast feeding, part-time waitressing, and with little help from me, Lisong still did all the cooking for the family. After John was three years old, he began attending a half-day kindergarten, and Lisong finally got some relief from her motherhood duties.

Because I was from a traditional peasant family, I had long been influenced by the old feudal ideology of "More sons, more blessing and more happiness." There is a total of six brothers and sisters in my family. My father, although having little schooling in his life, often told us that "having people will make things available as long as we work together and are willing to work harder for them." My father and my mother were a hardworking couple. Together, they were able to raise six children. Growing up with such rich traditions, I was naturally deeply rooted in this ideology and wished to have many sons as well. When our first son was two years old, we already had begun thinking about having a second child.

However, the decision to have a second child was not as easy as one would think. First of all, I was an exchange student with a J-1 visa. The United States required that J-1 visa holders, after completing their studies in the US, must return to their home country to serve for at least two years before qualifying to work in the US. Because I was subject to this two-year rule, if I had two children, I would be in violation of the one-child policy in China. In this case, I could be punished or discriminated against when I returned home. If that happened to me, then it might be difficult to gain a good position, and my career could be jeopardized. The second concern I had was the financial stability needed to raise two children. In contrast to the challenges of returning home with two children, I would also face difficulties if we stayed in the US, especially since I majored in plant science, a field that had relatively few job opportunities after graduation. Without a good job, raising two children could be a real challenge for us. Even if I could find a job in this field, my salary might be too low to afford raising a large family.

Just as we were at the crossroads of the planning process, China's policy for students returning from abroad changed so that it was more friendly and accommodating. The central government of China had adopted a series of incentives and support policies to encourage overseas students to return home to serve. I analyzed the situation and came to the conclusion that the new policy would accommodate my two children if I returned. There was, of course, a certain risk associated with this assumption since, in the past, the country had been known for changing policies with each political movement. Therefore, I decided not to take the risk of returning to China and decided to stay in the US temporarily for the sake of our children. The financial stability needed to raise two children was, I felt, that whatever my job might be, as long as I worked hard, I should be able to afford them. This analysis of pros and cons helped us decide to have a second child.

When John was two years old, my wife became pregnant again. With the second baby on his way, I was also approaching the finish line for my PhD and beginning to seek a postdoctoral position. These three major events coincided well. I was so excited about these major cornerstones in my life, and luckily, everything went well for us.

But there was still one thing I was very concerned about. Our child was due in early June of 1989. I had only a partial student insurance policy, and the insurance for children was very limited. When our first child was born, we had most expenses paid for by the government's low-income welfare program. I did not feel good about this because it was subsidies and handouts. For this reason, I was determined to have a full insurance policy, and my new postdoctoral employer would help me with that. This motivated me to start my postdoc at the University of Illinois before our baby was born.

In the spring of 1989, China had a vigorous movement called the 89 Democratic Movement. The outcome of this movement had a huge impact on students studying in the United States. Just like many other students, I was concerned about the development of this situation in China in addition to the one-child policy. For the sake of our children, we decided to temporarily stay in the US. Within two weeks of our arrival in Champaign-Urbana, Illinois, our second child was born. His name was Michael Li with the Chinese name of Wen Li. There were two and a half years between our two sons, which was a good situation for us. Their mother could take care of them, and the older son would soon be able to play with his little brother.

With two kids, our family was now an average-size family. My wife and I felt the weight of our responsibility growing. We both wanted to create a good and warm home for our children's growth on the one hand, while our financial condition and resources were limited on the other. The wage I earned in my postdoc was barely enough for renting an apartment in international student housing at the University of Illinois and for covering our daily expenses. Our apartment had two bedrooms, a living room, a bathroom, and a kitchen area and was actually much better than those apartments we had lived in during my graduate study, although it was still a far cry from the housing of most middle-class American families. Also, our income from this sole source would not allow us to save for our children's future.

In order to become financially independent, I needed a well-paying professional job. Therefore, after three and a half years of postdoctoral research, I joined an environmental testing laboratory as an analyst in January 1993. My wife also had a technician's job in the same company, and as a result, our total income level put us into the middle-class society. However, as I was not satisfied with the status of being an employee, I started my own entrepreneurial venture in 1994, a move that created uncertainty and unpredictability in our finances. We were under great pressure for several years until 1998, when our company turned a profit that greatly improved our financial status. With a favorable financial situation, my wife and I had a new desire to have a third child, especially hoping for a girl. My wife was then forty years old, an age that was considered late for childbearing. Although we were somewhat worried about this, eventually our desire for this child outweighed the concerns.

Once this decision was made, my wife made some adjustments to her daily routine and embarked on preparing for our third child. God blessed us, and our third son, named Tony (Chinese name Cong), was born in 2000. Although not the girl my wife was hoping for, we all felt very happy with Tony. My wife now was busier than ever with all three boys while I, as usual, spent all my time and energy on our company.

As our company continued growing, our personal finances got stronger. As a result, we wanted to improve our living standard by increasing the size of our house and getting newer automobiles. When we started our business in 1994, we purchased a small fifty-year-old house with 1,300 square feet on Colorado Street in Urbana. Although the house was considerably roomier than those apartments we had lived in, our living conditions were still rather poor. For example, the kitchen cupboard was old, with a strong odor, and the basement wall leaked when it rained even moderately. In 1998, we bought a 2,600-square-foot house on Willow Bend Road in the city of Champaign that was built in 1994, consisting of two stories and included four bedrooms, a living room, and a family room. It was close to the new Barkstall Elementary School that was a walking distance of ten minutes from our home. Our children attended there and liked this school very much. We lived in the house for about six years. By 2004, we wanted to further improve our living condition by adding more space to accommodate the growth of our three sons. We also wanted to have a room where our parents could stay when they came to visit. This led to the construction of our own large villa at Summithill Place in Champaign with a total area of about 6,500 square feet in a three-story structure. The lower level is 2,600 square feet, with the base of the windows level with the backyard. It includes a bedroom, bathroom, ping-pong room, fitness room, bar, dance floor, and cinema room. There is good lighting and airflow, and it serves as a good venue for parties and gatherings. The middle level of the house, also 2,600 square feet, includes the master bedroom suite, living room, family room, study room, sunroom, lounge, and kitchen. The upper floor, about 1,300 square feet, includes four large bedrooms, two bathrooms, and a leisure room. The backyard of the house is large enough that we have been growing vegetables in our garden since we moved in. What we produce from May to November is more than sufficient for our family to consume. In most years, we have extra fresh produce to share with our friends. During the past few years, we have annually produced about three hundred to four hundred pounds of winter melon, and a portion of it has often been shared with more than a dozen other families. We have spent fourteen years of happiness in this house now. Our two older sons have graduated from college and have moved on to their respective new jobs, both out of state. Our third child, Tony, just left us for UCLA. The last few years, I could not imagine what our life would be like without Tony. One thing that is certain is that Tony's living with us reduced our anxiety and delayed our empty-nest syndrome considerably.

In addition to improving and expanding our living space, we made a decision to improve our experience with our automobiles. We drove a used and nonairconditioned Dodge Aspen in the 1980s; a Subaru, Toyota Camry, and Honda Odyssey in the 1990s; and we finally had the opportunity to experience a Lexus 430 and a BMW X-5. We have purchased more expensive automobiles in recent years, mainly because of our concerns about the safety and quality of our vehicles.

Having a large house and driving more expensive vehicles by no means indicates that we are living a luxurious life. Instead, we continue to have a living standard comparable to every other member of this community. Working hard, living thriftily on the basics, and never wasting food have been our philosophy and our practice since 1998. When we go on a trip, we never book luxury hotels, and we have never flown first class. When it comes to our daily living expenses, my wife always shops for discount food and daily items.

The one-child policy in China had led most of my college classmates to have only one child. As a result, at our college reunion most of them could not believe that I have three sons. They admired me and made me feel blessed and happy. Some of my friends regretted not having a second child. During the era when we were starting our families, few people dared to have multiple children because of the severe punishments that might be imposed in China, including fines and loss of jobs. One of my classmates once said to me that if he could start all over again, he would rather have had a second child and risked losing his job. This idea was representative of many people born in the 1950s and 1960s. It has become the history of an unfortunate generation in that country. Now these friends were even more disappointed because China has changed its one-child policy to multiple-child policy and even encourage more children with award and compensation to each child.

While I had a feeling of satisfaction when my classmates admired me for our three sons, we had full challenges ahead of us in raising them. One of the major issues was that I had little time for our kids because of the busy schedule I had with my company, especially in the critical time period when our older two sons were five to twelve years old. I had little time to play with them, communicate with them, or educate them. In this regard, I especially felt guilty that Mike did not receive much of my attention during this period. This could be one of the factors affecting his personal development and his introverted personality. His communication skills finally improved after several years of working at various jobs. If I could do it all over again, I would try to better balance my family life with my company work.

To raise a quality child, we need to spend resources on their education. This is a common emphasis in every Chinese family. We wanted our kids to be competitive after college and were willing to put our resources behind them. We had our children studying Chinese from four years of age. We sent them to Heritage Chinese School in Champaign-Urbana every Sunday and hired private teachers to teach them Chinese at home or in small groups with other kids, along with teachers to teach them piano. We wanted our children to participate in all these activities to make sure that they had a basic understanding of their roots, their parents' language, and of course, to develop their basic skills for a successful future career. We constantly reminded them that one-fourth of the world's population speaks Chinese. In a constantly changing and globalized economy, it was to their advantage to learn Chinese. In addition to education, we placed an emphasis on major disciplines by setting relatively high but achievable standards for our children, making daily routines simple and easy to follow, and limiting unreasonable demands on them. For instance, we required that our children eat what we cooked and put on the table, and we limited the purchase of fast food, canned foods, sugary drinks, etc. These emphases, plus our own moral actions, have helped our children establish similar habits by following our example. They shop for food values, do not waste resources, and have been saving money, following our family traditions.

Our eldest son, John, has a great interest in cars. His mind was somehow stamped with cars from his childhood, which was full of toy cars. This hobby carried over to his college days as well as his adult life now. It might have played a role in choosing his college major of mechanical engineering at the University of Illinois in 2004. After graduating from college, I thought I could persuade him to work in our company, but he did not like it after trying it for a couple of months. We, as parents, respected his decision. With motivation from himself and encouragement by us, he entered the Business School of the University of Illinois, graduating with an MBA in 2011. As soon as he earned his MBA, he began working for Ford Motor Company. He has been managing a software engineering program at the company for the past seven years, which he seems to like very much.

Mike likes computers better than cars. He entered the University of Illinois computer engineering program in 2007, majoring in computer hardware engineering. We have been very proud of him because he graduated from this top-tier program with an excellent GPA. This helped him land his first job in a communications company in Colorado Springs. To our surprise, he was successful with his employer. He was placed in an engineering position where he carried out independent research projects, and his leading role in his field resulted in his being recognized by the company as a valuable employee. He was promoted four times with salary increases and was given his company's stock options during the past five years. In addition to his regular job, he spent his spare time as a part-time student, completing his master's degree in computer science at the University of Colorado in 2016.

Our youngest son Tony's arrival has brought us both joy and annoyance. He was born more than eleven years after his next oldest brother, which often made him feel like he was the only child in this family. He picked up his oldest brother's interest in toy cars and usually played by himself. However, when his brothers were busy with their schoolwork or did not want to play with him, he came to us for our attention, and sometimes we played together. Our participation in his activities has actually prolonged our middle age and delayed the arrival of our empty nest. When we did not have time to spend with him, he went to the neighbors and played with children there. This helped him develop his outgoing character and fostered his communication skills. Like his brother John, after having passed the PSAT test, he entered the University of Illinois High School (Uni High). His cheerful character has earned him the reputation of getting along well with other students. He is one of a group of about a dozen classmates, all of whom have taken turns organizing parties and sleepovers. He was a happy high schooler and will enter college in the fall of 2018. He selected UCLA over the University of Illinois for his undergraduate, and we support his decision.

My father is now one hundred, and my mother is ninety-three according to their personal identification cards. In the old China, births did not occur in hospitals or clinics but instead occurred at home. No birth certificates were issued for newborn babies. Therefore, the record of a person's real age is often incorrect. My parents' ages are a couple of these examples. The records from our family tree show my father is ninety-five. My mother's birthday has to be based on the personal identification card, which could be different from her real birthday. As a result, she never had a birthday celebration given by us. Regardless of their real ages, they both are named the stars of the seniors in our village. Although my mother has some non-life-threatening conditions lately that cause her inconvenience, my father is still healthy. As their children, we have shown filial piety to the old. They have often been advised and persuaded to have a good rest and to live easily and comfortably as they are aging. However, the two never stopped working, especially my father. My mother grew a vegetable garden in a small plot, and for twenty years, until some five years ago, what she produced had been sufficient for the family to consume. In the past few years, we could see that the hardships of her young life have worn her down. Fortunately, she is still capable of most of her daily self-care.

In 2017, we organized a birthday celebration for our father's hundredth birthday based on his personal identification card. It has been the tradition in our countryside that most people celebrate their birthday one year ahead of a major birthday such as eighty, ninety, and a hundred years old. I invited a reporter from the Rong County TV station to come to report this event. The reporter was very surprised and impressed with the way my father spoke, thought, and acted. For example, the reporter asked my father, "Which floor do you sleep on at night?"

"Fifth floor," answered my father. Think about how hard it is walking up the stairway to the fifth and six floor several times daily without an elevator.

Then the reporter asked, "What do you do daily?"

"I harvest vegetables and bamboo shoots and sell them on the free market" was his reply. My father has been doing this for the past twenty to twenty-five years. Some of the produce they eat was grown by himself, some other vegetables were harvested wild from mountains and hilly areas, while certain items were provided by our family members. Recently, he even acted as the end seller of vegetables and fruit purchased from distributors or brokers. I like the transition from a self-grown business model to the purchase-and-sell retail model. His age gradually makes it more and more difficult to collect and harvest produce from mountain and the paddy fields. We were very concerned about his safety when he worked alone out in the paddy field and on the mountains. We tried to persuade him not to continue these activities and told him that if he needed money, we would give it to him. However, almost every time we asked him about this, he would say something like, "The money you have is yours—nobody would admit to having too much money! You have several children who also need money. You all should feel good when I can still work, so do not ask me to stop working." When I heard this, what could I say except to express my happy feelings for him? I had to accept the fact that for my father, making only one to two dollars a day by selling vegetables makes him feel happier than if I gave him a hundred dollars.

Another unique character my father has is that he usually does not take medicine for colds and the flu. He often told his children that taking medicine creates more problems than solutions. He also is disciplined with his food and eating habits. For instance, he drinks a small glass of rice wine daily, eats half a bowl of rice and half a bowl of soup for lunch, and half a bowl of rice and a cup of soup for dinner. He leaves everyone with the impression that he was born with a hardworking character and has not been afraid of challenges his whole life. We are so proud of him.

Although my father toils at this age, his mood is still good. Both parents are particularly proud of their children and grandchildren. In addition to their six children, there are fourteen grandchildren and six great-grandchildren. The grandchildren have great respect for them. Although we are such a large family, we all get along well with our parents. Some other families are filled with noisy individuals who have no respect for the older generation and who sometimes even hit their elders. I have come up with a recipe of three major ingredients for my parents' happy senior life: they live an active life style, they do not take medicine for even the most minor colds or cases of the flu, and they have a warm family relationship, living in a comfortable and relaxed atmosphere.

As our parents grow older, I want to see them more and more every day. Therefore, my wife and I established our schedule to visit them at least once a year. Every time I have gone back home, I have wanted to spend more time with them. My mother's hearing is completely gone, and she cannot hear us. So I just want to sit next to her for her to see me and talk to me as she wishes. When I am with my father, I often bring up topics about his past and his former neighbors. To everybody's surprise, my father's memory is still very good, and his simple math is better than many others at the age of fifty. All of us felt happy about our father's good memory.

We hope that our filial piety toward our parents will also serve as a role model for our children. The language barrier between our parents and our children has prevented them from effectively communicating, so their partial understanding of their grandparents has come through us as mediators. We want our children to respect them and share responsibility for them. That was the reason why we established an unwritten requirement for our children to provide certain gifts of money to their grandparents each year. In doing so, our children are reminded of their responsibility for taking care of their elders, which has been the tradition in China for a very long time. This should help cultivate our children's sense of responsibility and create a filial heart toward the old.

My parents never ask for money, but we give some to them every year. They usually deposit most of it in the bank. As long as there is money in their bank account or their pockets, their heart is steadfast. In addition to my parents, I have also dealt in the same way with my father-in-law and mother-in-law. My wife has spent more time with them than I have. Our goal was to provide the necessary resources, including money, caregiving, and medical care service. I am thankful to my sister-in-law, Zhang Liyan, and her husband, He Shenlin, for taking care of the in-laws so that we have less concern and more peace of mind to pursue our profession and our own happiness in the United States.

Because of being so far away from my parents, I have been unable to give them more care. As a result, I usually depend on my brothers and sisters. My brother, Zhenshen, and my elder sister-in-law, Chen Miqiong, lived in our home in the countryside. Their family and my father lived and farmed together until 2010. In 2008, in order to improve their living conditions and to expand their living space, we provided funds to remodel the old house and build a new addition. My mother has been with my younger brother, Zhenhai, and sister-in-law, Qin Xuemei, in Rongxian City since early 1990. A few years ago, my father joined my younger brother and my mother in the city. In addition, my eldest sister, Zhen Ming, and two younger sisters, Liming and Huiming, also live nearby. They all work together to provide care for our parents. Since my mother recently fell on the stairway, her health has deteriorated considerably. Fortunately, my younger sister Liming provides full-time care for her. We are very grateful to all of them. When they have financial needs, we always lend a helping hand. We hope to have a warm and harmonious family to allow our parents to live a happy and healthy life.

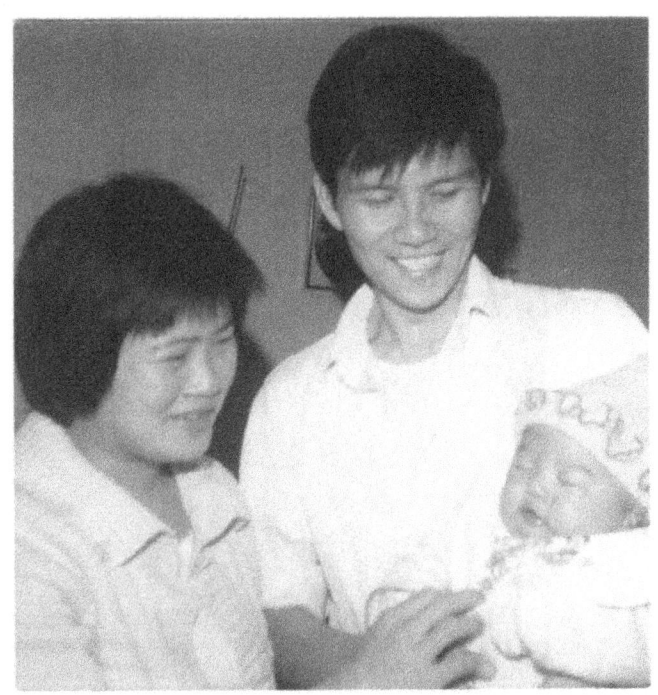

15-1: John was born (1986)

15-2: Expecting Michael (1989)

15-3: PhD Graduation with family and my adviser (1989)

15-4: Tony was born (2000)

15-5: Graduation from UIUC (2011) - John with MBA
and Michael with BS in Computer Engineering

15-6: My happy family (2015)

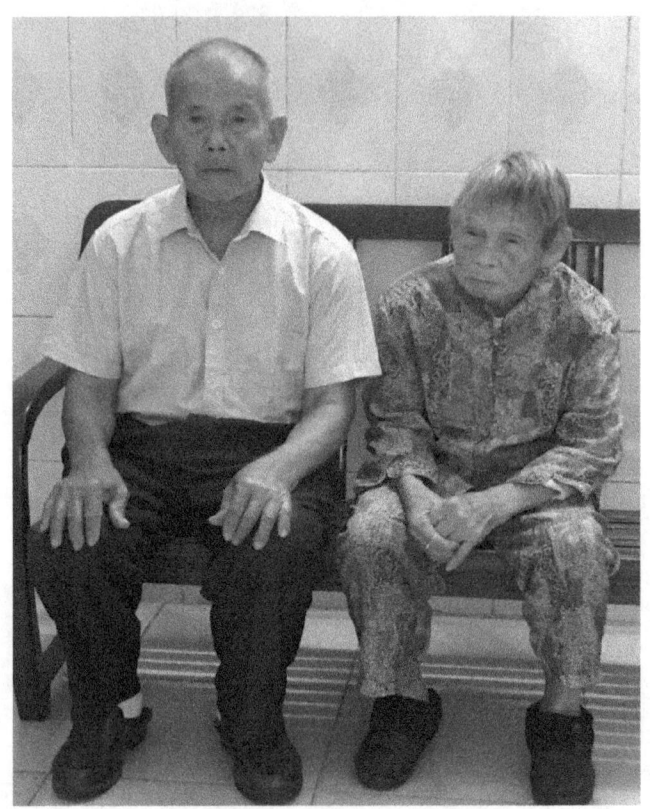

15-7: Father and mother (2015)

16

CHARITY AND VOLUNTEERING

I came to the United States to study advanced science and technology, but I feel that I have learned more about its marketing economy and competition mechanism, which are keys to America's ability to become an economic powerhouse. In addition, I have learned that a significant number of Americans participate as volunteers and donate selflessly to various nonprofit organizations and schools. One of the key forces behind this charitable spirit is America's tax policy, which has been very friendly to donors and contributors. This has become an important part of American culture.

There are usually two different types of charitable contributions: time and money. For the former, many ordinary people are willing to devote their time to help our society and the many groups and individuals who need help. Some volunteers help build public housing, some provide education and care for the elderly, and many more actively participate in various activities organized by charitable organizations. Their actions have brought love and warmth to the whole community. This kind of dedication is similar to those who, when we were young, advocated that we emulate the spirit of Lei Feng helping others in China regardless of remuneration. In regard to monetary donations, these are, as the name says, monetary gifts to society for the benefit of people through charitable and nonprofit organizations such as the Red Cross, universities, associations, foundations, churches, etc.

What I have been seeing and feeling deeply in my heart is the fact that church members donate a considerable portion of their income to their churches. Many rich people establish foundations and donate much of their wealth to these foundations to serve communities and society and even humanity around the world. Many people in the middle class make contributions to the schools from which they graduated, their alma maters, and their communities. The joint effort by millions of people in our society has led to the flourishing of this country's welfare services. Since my arrival in the United States, I have witnessed the important role of charity in this advanced country. My great respect for this led me to hope that one day I would be one of those volunteers and donors.

There is an old maxim that says, "While drinking water, don't forget the person who dug the well." I took this maxim to remind myself about thankfulness to those who had helped me in the past. After I exited my successful business in 2010, our financial status improved greatly. Therefore, we began to consider giving back to our communities and organizations where we grew up and were educated. This appeared to be a simple and sensible thing to do, but it was not easy for us to step into the ring of donors. We needed to convince not only ourselves but also my immediate family members and other relatives concerning any significant giving. I hoped that I could at least have their understanding that what we wanted to do would benefit other people and our society.

My wife and my three sons were very supportive of my dedication and plans for giving. Although my wife was discriminated against by others and suffered very unfair treatment during her childhood, when it comes to public welfare and monetary donations, she is charitable and generous. Our sons are even more so. They were born in the United States and were brought up to serve in the community and help the general public. They believe that as long as we are capable, we should contribute to society for the benefit of the poor and others needing help. However, when the issue of charitable giving was presented to my parents and my siblings, the situation was not the same. In fact, the reason for their concern was simple but reasonable. My family for generations, including most of my brothers and sisters, have been farmers. Their economic scale and income have been at the bottom half of their society, and they have needed money to improve their lives. Under these conditions, they expected us to provide them with more assistance. When they knew that we were going to contribute money for the benefit of the general public, they had a hard time understanding our rationale. Some of them said that we were a little stupid to give our money to others. Some felt that we did not care for them because we did not give to them and support them with more money. Most of them thought we were not paying enough attention to future generations and should be giving more money to our children and their cousins. Whenever I faced such questions, I always summoned the courage to patiently tell them the reasons and the benefits of our giving.

Our participation in charitable activities started around 1990. Our plan was to donate money each year to our alma mater, Guangxi Agricultural College, which was renamed Guangxi Agriculture University in 1992 and then was merged into Guangxi University in 1997. Our earliest donations were usually small, from about one hundred to a few hundred dollars. I sent a check of $200 to Guangxi Agriculture College around 1992, but for some unknown reasons, the university could not claim or cash the check, which was returned to me many months later. In addition to the problem in China, there was also a problem in the US associated with this check. As a result of sending this personal check to a university in China, the bank that held our account here investigated the matter on behalf of the government. To this end, I had to explain the facts concerning this transaction to the bank officer. As it turned out, my alma mater had no department that could accept a charitable donation from a foreign donor. By 2014, Guangxi University had yet to complete the process for accepting foreign donations. Therefore, I advised the Alumni Association to establish a bank account that could receive donations from overseas alumni. We have already donated to my alma maters of Miami University and Western Michigan University for about twenty years. We often receive promotional literature regarding charitable donations from these universities and their alumni offices. I also wanted to donate money to Guangxi University and hoped to have a similar relationship with them.

In addition to my commitment to small donations to my alma maters, I planned to make a relatively large donation to Guangxi University in 2011. This was right after the sale of my company. The plan I proposed was that we would donate $600,000 (equivalent in Renminbi, RMB, to 4 million yuan) to establish a Tropical Fruit and Functional Nutrition Research Institute. This institute would directly report to the vice president of research of the university. I also proposed to donate the total funds needed for the first two years of operation. This would require Guangxi University to provide space and certain equipment equivalent to 4 million RMB and the funding of 2 million RMB from either the Science and Technology Office of Guangxi Province or the State Science and Technology Department of China. The total amount of the funds needed would have been 10 million yuan. The main goals of the institute were to educate and train students, to carry out research and technical development of functional foods using the natural resources of Guangxi Province, and to build the institute into a prestigious tropical food research center. An important part of this plan was the sustainability of the institute by commercializing its technologies with start-up companies and technology transfers to established companies through partnerships. Unfortunately, this plan was not well received in a timely manner from the university.

After the nonresponse to our plan to build the research institute, we turned our attention to the road project in my hometown. My hometown is situated in a relatively undeveloped hilly area. Although China had achieved substantial development around the country, including many parts of the remote countryside by around 2010, the road to more than eight hundred people in our village had not yet been repaired. The road was only 4 feet wide with no asphalt or cement. Whenever it rained, the road was muddy and difficult to walk on. It was even harder to drive a small car on it. In order to improve and repair this road, the village committee convened a number of meetings for the villagers and hoped to mobilize people for raising money to repair it. Most of the villagers were not rich, and coupled with low enthusiasm for public charity projects, the plan to build this 1.5-kilometer road stood still for several years. It was not until 2012, when we donated 100,000 RMB to build this road, that a breakthrough for the project occurred. Under our impetus, other successful residents in the village also chipped in, and significant numbers of villagers agreed to donate according to the appropriate RMB per capita determined by the village. Our donation accounted for over 70 percent of the total cost of the project. As a result, after the road was built, the village commissioner erected a special showcase that contains a list of the donors where my name ranks at the top. Now every time I go home for a visit, the villagers always give me a thumbs-up. We feel a sense of hometown pride for what we have done on this charitable project.

Rongxian High School is my wife's and my alma mater. During the Cultural Revolution, all public high schools around the country were decentralized to various communes or towns, and the curriculum was reduced from four years to two years. This was the case for Rongxian High School, which was renamed Rongxian Chengxian High School. The Chengxian High School admitted students only from the Chengxian People's Commune. When the country resumed its entrance examinations in 1978, its original name was restored, and the source of its students was Rongxian County. That is why some of my classmates would not consider themselves to be alumni of Rongxian High School. My wife and I did not want to argue the history of this school but instead considered it as our high school alma mater. I have a deep feeling for this alma mater and continue my close relationship with it. During my college years, I kept in close contact with my teachers there and visited them during every summer break when I was in college. The school invited me back several times, asking me to give lectures to students on topics such as my experience of returning home as a farmer after graduation from high school, my college experience at Guangxi University, and my overseas experiences of studying for my graduate degrees. The occasion I remember the most was the New Year's holiday of 1986 when I visited home. I was invited to the high school to speak about my master's degree and PhD studies. Every time I went back to my alma mater, I received a warm welcome from the school leaders, teachers, and students.

In 2015, my wife and I were invited for a walk around the high school by the school principal and other leaders. When we realized that the chemistry building was the only original building left on the high school property, we proposed to the principal that we were willing to donate 2 million yuan RMB to remodel this building for use as an alumni center. The reason we liked this project was that we had spent two high school years in this building, learning chemistry and doing experiments. In addition, as a captain of my class, I also went to the same building every day to see my teacher and class instructor. Except for the primary designated classroom for our class, I spent more time in this chemistry building than in any other building while I was in high school. Therefore, it would be in my interest and the interest of other alumni to preserve the building. The building was classified as dangerous, and no one was permitted to enter it. Given that its foundation was still sound, it provided the possibility for remodeling. If the building were demolished and rebuilt on this site, we would not have any original structures remaining. Our passionate memories of this high school alma mater would be gradually lost. The more we thought about it, the more sympathetic we were. We made our commitment right in the front of the building to the school principal. Our proposal received great attention by the principal and vice principals, but unfortunately, it has not yet been approved by the Education Bureau of Rongxian County.

During the campus walk, we were also introduced to a couple of planned projects underway at the high school. The first project was to construct a canteen-sports complex building. This is a multipurpose four-story building, including a cafeteria and a dining hall on the first and second floors and basketball and ping-pong facilities on the third and fourth floors. The total cost of the construction was about 10 million yuan. This was obviously beyond our plan for charitable giving at that time. Even though they indicated to us that as long as we donated 2 million yuan, the building could still be named after us, I felt that it might not be appropriate for a donor to receive the naming rights when providing only 20 percent of the total project cost. In the West, this usually requires that a donor provide 50 percent, or more, of the total project cost. The principal then introduced us to another project. This was to build a high school south gate, which was budgeted at about 700,000 Yuan. We liked this project very much. Therefore, I immediately expressed our interest in making a cash donation to the high school for this charity project.

The main gate of Rongxian High School was rebuilt some twenty years ago. The door was facing the east and was located on a hill with a small slope. This was meant to give students the feeling that as soon as they entered the gate of the high school, they would be just like the sun rising from the horizon in the east, growing in personality, learning, and accumulating knowledge as they were climbing step-by-step to reach higher levels. Within this phenomenon, it is sometimes implied that as long as students enter this high school, they will increase their knowledge daily and will continue to improve and eventually pass the entrance examinations for colleges and universities. Personal development and maturity will accompany the accumulation of knowledge and skills. However, this school gate is slightly off the main street, and the traffic there is busy. As a result, it is not convenient for students entering the south campus. Recognizing the need for a second gate to the rapidly growing high school, which now has close to eight thousand students, the school board made a decision to build the south gate. With our commitment to fund the project, the school was excited. There had been very few charity projects in this high school, none of which had been considered as significant as our donation. The high school wanted to use this as a good example to promote and encourage its alumni to make more contributions in the future to Rongxian High School, their alma mater.

Initially, my wife and I wanted the gate to be the most gorgeous in the county and even in Guangxi Province. Therefore, we proposed to increase the gift to the project to 2 million yuan in order to make the gate as magnificent as it could be. However, after many discussions, the school board finally decided to build it according to their original plan, costing about one-third of what we intended to donate.

The United States government has a set of laws and regulations governing all charitable donations. One of the strict requirements is that only a qualified charitable organization is able to issue receipts for donations for the purpose of federal income tax deductions. This law greatly mobilizes the enthusiasm of the rich to donate. It is also an important reason why philanthropy in America flourishes.

In order to meet the requirements of American laws regulating charities, I set up a charitable donor-adviser's fund account with Fidelity Charitable Donor-Advised Funds. The funds I transfer into this account can be deducted from my personal income tax in installments according to the legal requirements of my annual tax return. Once the money has been put in this account, it can only be used for charity. I, as the donor, am not allowed to take the money out from this account for other purposes. Of course, this money can be invested in the stock market. In this case, we invested in several mutual funds with different investment objectives to balance the risk and annualized return. The return on these investments will stay with the charity account and grow year after year. Regardless of how much the value has increased or decreased, all money in the account must be used for charitable purposes.

The amount of money we placed in this charitable account was based on our current and future plan of donations. We used this account for our donations to my alma maters, Western Michigan University and Miami University. We also used the charitable account for each of the past five years to make a donation of about $5,000 to the University of Illinois at Urbana-Champaign (UIUC), where our youngest son was studying at the University High School. Our eldest son studied at the high school for five years, from 1999 to 2004, when we donated about $3,000 per year by personal check because our charitable account was not set up at that time. As a result of our donations to UIUC for eleven years, we often receive letters and sometimes invitations and holiday greeting cards from the president of the university or the University Alumni Association. Our name has been placed on their mailing list of donors.

However, this easy, direct, and convenient way to donate money is only applicable to American schools and is not available for any schools in China. In order to qualify for tax-deductible donations, a nonprofit organization in China must go through a qualification process. Only those that are certified by a licensed and qualified charitable institution in the US are allowed to accept donations from a US charitable organization. In the US, only certain charitable organizations are recognized by the Internal Revenue Service (IRS) as qualified. No individual, individual trust, or even most charitable 501(c)(3) organizations can donate money directly to a nonprofit organization in China.

To deal with this tax-deductible donation, I hired a consulting and charitable company named Give2Asia to help us with the application and qualification process. This company is a California enterprise dedicated to helping individual and groups of donors who are interested in Asian charities and nonprofit organizations. In order to donate money to our alma mater, Rongxian High School, Give2Asia used the contact person's name, address, and phone number that I provided to initiate the qualification process. After several weeks of auditing, Rongxian High School was found to be qualified for accepting charitable donations. The procedure of auditing and qualifying costed $1,000. Obtaining qualification status was the first step in the process. Since I wanted my donation to be in compliance with the tax-deductible regulations for donations, I worked with Give2Asia to accomplish this.

Fidelity Charitable Donor-Advised Funds is not qualified to transfer our donation to the high school because it is not a charitable organization. As a result, we had to hire Give2Asia for this purpose. We first asked Fidelity Charitable to donate the amount equivalent to 700,000 yuan to Give2Asia. After the 7 percent commission fee was taken out by Give2Asia, the balance of over 600,000 yuan was transferred to an account set up by Give2Asia. My high school alma mater then applied for the funds. With the greater benefit I received in my tax bracket, even though the commission fee was high, going through Give2Asia would still have been our choice. There was no other way around it. We had to pay the commission fee, which increased substantially beginning in 2018.

During the discussion with my high school alma mater on how to ensure the successful implementation of our sponsored project, I conducted a number of searches through the internet. I wanted to understand how the donor-sponsored project could be named and how the funds would be used. At first, I thought that there would be no guarantee on the project if we did not have a signed agreement between the high school and us. However, Give2Asia told me that if there was a signed contract, we then could not enjoy the tax deduction for our donation. They explained that none of the money donated to a nonprofit organization could be restricted by a signed contract, although the donor could offer advice or even request that the recipient of the donation carry out certain projects according to the donor's wishes. This was completely beyond our expectations as we did not know much about the matter. Since it was a tax-deductible donation, I had to contribute according to the law. Therefore, I changed my request for a contract to a verbal agreement that included our wishes. We moved the project forward with the donation for the construction of the south gate. In addition, I asked the school to allow a relative of ours to act as a communicator for the project since it was not convenient for us to monitor it from the United States.

The plan for the high school donation was formally signed in September 2016. When my wife, Lisong, returned home from visiting her mother, she was recommended by the high school board. Later she was invited by the Yulin City

Overseas Chinese Federation (YCOCF) to attend a meeting held in Rongxian for overseas Guangxi Chinese. She was warmly welcomed by the chairman of the YCOCF as one of the more than a hundred guests visiting Rongxian County's historical cultural sites and a number of natural sites during the two-day forum. On the second day, on behalf of our family, she attended a donation ceremony organized by our high school. This was attended by more than a hundred students, the leaders of Rongxian County and the YCOCF, and the deputy director of Rongxian County in charge of education. At the general assembly, my wife presented a symbolic check of 600,000 yuan RMB to the principal of the high school. The event was widely reported through Yulin briefings, Rongxian County television, the Guangxi Federation, and the Guangxi Foreign Affairs Network. My wife had always been a low-key lady, and this was her first public appearance, which made her feel proud of herself on this charitable occasion.

The construction of our high school south gate started on February 11, 2017. I was invited by the principal of the high school and was accompanied by the director of the County Foreign Affairs Office to participate in the groundbreaking ceremony. At the ceremony, I gave a short speech in which I wanted to convey a message:

"We donate our money to build the south gate of our alma mater. Although there are many reasons for our charitable action, the important ones are to thank and to show appreciation to our alma mater for educating us and to set a good example for other successful alumni to care about and to provide more support for our high school."

The project was completed on October 18 of the same year. At the completion ceremony, my wife, Lisong, was accompanied by a number of representatives from the high school and the county government, including several foreign affairs officers, the vice sheriff of the county, and many students of the high school. She gave a short speech in which she expressed our deep affection for our alma mater and how we always wanted to show love to our school and our desire to contribute and help our school become better.

Both my wife and I graduated from Guangxi University. Our relationship with our alma mater university has always been very strong. After our proposal to establish a food research institute failed to win approval, our plan for sponsoring some kind of project with the university continued.

In 2016, Guangxi University began preparations for the 2018 celebration of its ninetieth anniversary and proposed a number of projects that would need sponsorship. We looked at all the projects, especially those related to Guangxi Agriculture College. We decided to sponsor the renovation of the teaching building of the Agricultural College, which is the largest and the best-known building on the college campus. It was also one of a few key structures built around the time of the establishment of the Guangxi Zhuang Autonomous Region (Guangxi Province) in Nanning City. The construction of this five-story structure, including classrooms, laboratories, and the administrative offices for four departments was begun in 1956 and completed in 1958. The agronomy department was on the second floor. Our classroom and laboratory for plant physiology and botany were also on the same floor.

The reason for us to choose this project was because most of the advanced agronomy knowledge we learned was associated with this building. We spent most of our time in the building, attending lectures, engaging in self-study, and doing experiments. Our largest classes and departmental meetings were often held in the large classroom 124, and our first jobs were also in this building. In December 2016, when we presented our wish to renovate this building to our alumni association, the university changed the project investment amount from 2 million to 4 million yuan for the naming rights. As a result, we decided to look at other possible projects instead.

We continued to discuss our sponsorship possibility with the Guangxi University Alumni Association in 2017. This eventually led to a decision to establish a foundation with the university. On December 9, I attended the 365-day countdown to the Ninetieth Anniversary Conference at the university and signed an agreement with the Guangxi University Education Development Foundation to donate 1.5 million yuan to a foundation named Li Zhenchang Agricultural and Food Science Innovation Fund. Li Zhenchang is my Chinese name, which is different from my current English name of Z. Charlie Li. The signing also included the agreement of fund management and the price selection and award criteria. The 1.5 million yuan in the fund is the principal, and the annual return on its investment is to be used to provide financial awards to undergraduate students, graduate students, researchers, and professors who have made outstanding contributions to agriculture and food science in the areas of innovation and technology transfer. Our goal is to make one to four awards annually, totaling about 100,000 yuan. This assumes that a 7 percent annualized return on the investment of the principal is achievable. Our aim is to encourage more students and researchers to devote their efforts to innovation and commercialization of advanced agricultural technologies and products.

In order to meet the requirements for tax deductions under the US charitable laws, we again needed to have Guangxi University qualified as a nonprofit organization, just as we did for our high school project. For this, we hired the *Charities Aid Foundation of America* to help with the matter, including the application process and review of all relevant documents. The process is near completion. Our plan is to transfer the funds to the special account before October and to make our first award at the ninetieth anniversary celebration in December of 2018.

The two projects we did for our high school and our university alma maters are the reflection of our deep feelings and sincere appreciation for the schools from which we received our education. We were also proud of our accomplishment with these projects. Our contribution to the road project in our hometown had been praised by neighbors and friends. It is because of our efforts in these public welfare undertakings that we became the focus of the local media. Our families, including the older, contemporary, and younger generations, all expressed their appreciation for what we did for the hometown.

When I visited my parents during the New Year celebration of 2017, I was invited to a small symposium of the Li's Association of Rongxian County. It turned out that the association was planning to build an academy college. Academy college was the name used in the registration with the government, but it is actually for about ninety thousand clan members of the Li's ancestral temple in Rongxian County. The construction site includes about four acres of land. The main structures are the front, the middle, and the back halls, all of which are standalone temples. There are the side buildings and rooms in each side. All in all, the total floor area is about twenty-five thousand square feet with the cost of the project estimated to be about 15 million yuan (equivalent to about $2.5 million). The association liked for us to join the ranks and make a contribution to the project. After discussing the project with my wife, we finally decided to donate 140,000 yuan (about $25,000) to have a room crowned with our name as a gallery for our family's showroom. With this contribution, I also agreed to be the president of the American branch of the Li clan.

Worshiping and paying respect to ancestors in a clan hall is a tradition in our hometown. As a part of Chinese culture, this tradition has been in practiced for thousands of years. A clan commonly descended from a remote ancestor shares an ancestral temple, ancestral hall, or a small hall for large, medium, or small clans respectively. This is where every ancestor was placed in the last days of his or her life before passing away. It is believed that the soul of the deceased could ascend to heaven from this ancestral temple. Descendants worshiping their ancestors also do so in this ancestral temple. Our Li Hall is a small one because it extends to only nine generations, with descendants numbering about 120. Our hall was at least seventy years old and had not been well maintained. The structure fell apart recently because it was composed of mud bricks, which could not withstand any rain. As a result, our clan had no place to worship and pay respect to our ancestors.

At the beginning of 2017, I convened a meeting of the clansmen and proposed the reconstruction of our ancestral hall. My proposal was supported by most clan members. In my proposal, I called for a donation by each clan member of 150 yuan for the project. The remainder of the monetary requirement would be from our donations. The project was actually a lot more difficult than I originally thought because there was such a variety of opinions and behaviors from the clan members. Some did not want to donate money, and others did not want to build the two rooms attached to the hall that were not owned by the clan but had been inherited by two brothers who inherited it from earlier ancestors. Still others did not want to reconstruct it at all. With a project belonging to all clan members, the unification of these diversified opinions was my main job. The construction was stopped several times because of the arguments among a few members. I spent a lot of time and energy on it and finally was able to complete it on December 11 (Lunar New Year October 24), 2017. The total cost of the project was 160,000 yuan, and our donation of 120,000 (near $20,000) yuan accounted for about 75 to 80 percent of the total cost. In order to commemorate the success of this public project in the history of the Li clan, I organized and presided over a celebration ceremony. I praised and recognized the clan members who had made contributions to this project. On that day, just before the ceremony, we all worshiped our ancestors and payed respect to them.

The purpose of my public service has been to serve the community and our society. In my former cadres and various positions and capacities, I was always motivated by different purposes for different reasons. When I was a captain of the student class at the elementary and high schools, I used it as part of my personal growth and development. When I was a branch secretary of the Communist Party in our village, my goal was to become a national cadre as an imperial food eater. And when I was the president of the Student Union of the Guangxi Agriculture College, I wanted the experience to be part of my professional advancement and to help me get a better job after graduation. In another words, all my service had been based on certain personal goals rather than being oriented toward real public service with unpaid dedication. Since 2015, I have been involved in public and social service. This shift in my emphasis has led to my involvement with our Chinese association and the Chinese community.

The Chinese American Association of Central Illinois (CAACI) is a nonprofit organization, registered in the State of Illinois in 1999. The association's preparatory committee was initiated by several senior professors at the UIUC. They held the first of a couple of organizational meetings at the facility where my laboratory was originally located. With the exception of one other scholar from Mainland China and me, the rest of the organizational committee was from Taiwan and Hong Kong. The purpose of the association was to promote Chinese culture, to encourage Sino-American cultural exchanges, to help solve problems associated with the vital interests of Chinese immigrants in the United States, and to educate new Chinese immigrants to become integrated into the local community.

The board of directors is elected every year. In earlier years, most of the board members of the association had come from Taiwan and Hong Kong. I was the first-year board member from Mainland China. During the past ten years as more Chinese came from the People's Republic of China, the proportion of association members from Mainland China, Hong Kong and Taiwan has changed significantly. The association membership peaked in 2007 to include 159 families. Among these families, about 30 were from Mainland China. It was a medium-sized organization with a total of four hundred members. Most members participated enthusiastically in the various activities organized by the CAACI board. However, for various reasons, the association has not been further developed and expanded in recent years. It experienced a declining trend for several years until 2016. Then, under the leadership of the board of directors, our association was restored as a legitimate, nonprofit organization. The board successfully organized two major events, including the US National Independence Day Parade and the Hunger Food Packaging event, each attended by at least one hundred of our members and Chinese friends. These activities improved the status of Chinese Americans in the local community. The association also successfully cooperated with the Confucius Institute of UIUC, which helped the CAACI to reverse the continuous decline in association funds over the past few years.

Our 2017 board of directors was elected in November 2016, with nine members, and I was elected as the chairman of the association. There were two vice-chairs and six committee directors, including membership, culture, communication, social, education, and recreation/entertainment. As usual, all the board members served as volunteers. After a number of meetings of the Board of Directors, several goals were set to be achieved in 2017. We executed each program in the plan throughout the year.

We wanted to run this nonprofit organization as an enterprise. I emphasized the individual responsibility of each board member. For various reasons, this organization had been loosely organized and run for the previous few years, giving people the impression that the organization did not have a detailed work plan, and only a few regular activities were held each year. Now that I was in charge, I wanted to do more through each board member. I wanted them to have their own annual plans and then to execute and implement their programs.

One of our priorities was to increase the membership of the association. In order to reverse the decline in membership, we invited all past members to rejoin our organization. We made an effort to recruit new members by inviting Chinese and other friends to join our activities by talking with previous members. Through our efforts, we achieved a significant growth in membership, from 56 families and about 180 members in 2016, to 73 families and about 250 members in 2017.

Finance and accounting are the lifeblood of any organization. We needed to ensure that our books clearly recorded all income and expenses. This commitment resulted in the board adopting the QuickBooks Pro as our accounting system in 2017, and this helped us achieve standard financial reports, including profit and loss statements, balance sheets, etc. This was a big step forward for the organization because our past financial records were fragmented, making it difficult to report to the state agencies. More importantly, this accounting method was necessary to meet the expectations of our members in the CAACI.

An important and long-range project was to increase donations to our organization. The membership fee for each family and individual was thirty-five dollars and twenty-five dollars respectively. As a result, the total income from this source was minimal. If we depended on this as our sole source of income, we would not be able to organize many of the activities described in our 2017 plan. One of the solutions to this problem was to raise money from sponsorships, collaborations, donations, and volunteers. Our board of directors recognized this from the first day we were on duty. We used the Chinese New Year and other events, or holidays, to raise money. For instance, we visited a few dozen local companies, including a number of local banks and restaurants for their sponsorship opportunities. We strongly promoted and encouraged individuals to help the CAACI by donating money or volunteer time on various occasions. We were able to raise nearly $8,000 from individuals and companies as a result of the combined effort of our fund-raising committee and the board of directors. Along with this effort, my wife and I donated more than $1,200 in 2017. My family has been very supportive of the CAACI for the past ten to fifteen years by donating about two hundred to five hundred dollars each year. To conveniently and regularly donate to the CAACI, I have set up a charity account at Fidelity that has the name of the CAACI as a donation recipient. We plan to continue supporting our organization in the future.

To unite the Chinese of our community, the CAACI embarked on a plan to bring several small groups of our members and other Chinese friends under the umbrella of the CAACI for various recreational and other activities. Over the past decades, spontaneous groups and clubs have been organized by volunteers, including National Minority Dance, Folk Dance, Tai Chi, Ballroom Dance, Yoga, Mood for Love, and Field Activities Groups, etc. These groups have continued and maintained their regular weekly activities. Whenever there has been an opportunity with other event organizers, they represented the CAACI by participating through performance, such as our folk dance team that performed at a local retirement community and participated in Decatur at the Asia Culture Day. We resumed the CAACI Golf Tournament and organized the first CAACI Table Tennis Open, the first Tennis Open, and the normal outdoor barbecue activities, etc. These activities greatly benefited our members, promoted mutual understanding among Chinese, enriched our cultural life, and enhanced our physical and mental health.

Each year, organizing the China Spring Festival Gala has always been on the top of the CAACI agenda. This tradition has been with us as a community for many decades, and the CAACI has acted as an organizer for more than fifteen years. We, the 2017 board of directors, were determined to do our best to organize this event. The gala was open to Chinese members and nonmembers, as well as our American friends. We took a few steps to make some changes for the 2017 gala. First, we changed the food service from being served to self-serve, which helped reduce the cost by 40 percent from thirty-two dollars to eighteen dollars per adult, with a similar reduction for children. This substantial reduction in cost encouraged more Chinese to attend the gala. Second, we integrated into the pregala event a Chinese learning program for children. There were about fifty to eighty children who participated in the program. Third, all activity groups were invited to perform at the gala. This change overcame the exclusion of certain performing programs, which in the past had caused an uneasy tension between the board and the members. The programs included adult dance, crosstalk, singing, short story telling, etc.

Our Spring Festival Gala was very successful. We had a total of about three hundred guests attending the event. The mayors of both Champaign and Urbana were invited to the festival gala, and they gave us holiday greetings. In addition, with our invitation, the Chinese Consulate of the People's Republic of China in Chicago sent the office director and his staff to the Gala. The CAACI attorneys who had served without remuneration as our legal consultants since the organization was established in 1999 were also invited. Also, the dean and associate dean of the Confucius Institute were our VIP guests. The dean gave speeches on the education and mission of the institute, as well as about the HSK (Chinese proficiency test). On behalf of the board of directors of the CAACI, I welcomed all these distinguished guests, and I especially thanked the Confucius Institute for its support and cooperation. The gala included a semi self-served dinner, followed by fifteen programs and plays.

A major focus point at the gala was to recognize the donors to the CAACI. I praised them and issued each a certificate of donation. I especially recognized those prominent donors who gave $500 or more to the association. Our effort had mobilized the enthusiasm of the donors. As a result, this spring festival received one of the highest amount of donations in its history, reaching more than $4,000. In all previous spring festivals, I had been a participant, but this time I was an organizer. Through this event, I had a greater understanding of the importance of commitment of the many volunteers serving the CAACI.

The American Independence Day celebration of Fourth of July has been a grand holiday for all Americans, equivalent to the National Day of China on October 1. As an organization of the community, we wanted to participate in the Independence Day Parade, a decision well supported by the members of the CAACI and the local Chinese community. About two hundred Chinese attended the parade on July 4, 2017. Our drum dance and folk dance performances were highly applauded by the parade audience.

Another gratifying task of our association was to organize the 2017 lecture series. The content of the lectures covered a broad spectrum of topics, including starting up new businesses, investing and finance, and health and fitness. Our members and other Chinese actively participated in the lectures, and the feedback from the participants was excellent.

Midautumn Festival is another traditional Chinese holiday, also called Harvest Festival. In this festival, family and friends come together on the fifteenth day of August of the Lunar calendar to harvest crops and to celebrate. It's said that the moon is the brightest and roundest on this day, which symbolizes family reunion. This is the main reason why people think midautumn is important, and Chinese who are overseas use this festival to enjoy ourselves and to think of our relatives in China. CAACI organizes the festival each year, and there were more than 130 Chinese and American friends who participated in the 2017 year's Midautumn Festival. Each of us tasted a mooncake and enjoyed the hour-long program.

The HSK, an international standardized test of Chinese language proficiency, assesses the non-native Chinese speaker's ability to use the *Chinese* language in their daily, academic, and professional lives. It is said to be the equivalent of the English TOEFL (Test of English as a Foreign Language) for foreign students studying in the US. The HSK consists of six levels (levels I to VI). The students who pass level V or above are considered to be qualified for admission to Chinese universities. Our board of directors worked closely with the Confucius Institute and received support from the Institute for HSK programs. With funds available, we made a considerable investment in the Chinese Heritage Association, to which the Sunday Chinese School belongs. Our effort through a designated board director from the CAACI who worked with parents and teachers in the school yielded good results. In 2017, we turned around the declining enrollment of Chinese students. We had more than thirty children taking part in more than forty HSK tests. Most students achieved excellent test scores. In this regard, we are especially proud of our son Tony's nearly perfect scores for his HSK III and HSK IV tests. We did not realize how good our son's Chinese language was until he took the tests.

On June 9, 2017, a Chinese visiting scholar, Zhang Ying Ying, was kidnapped during the day on a UIUC campus street. The case has had a profound impact on the local community and even across the United States and China. As the chairman of the CAACI, along with other board members, I became actively involved in the case by organizing, leading, and participating in various activities, including helping Ying Ying's family. I was one of the organizers setting up a team to find the missing scholar, working with the UIUC Police Department to establish the case in the police network. Working closely with the Chinese Student Scholar Association (CSSA) at UIUC, we organized a series of activities, such as posting missing person announcements regarding Ying Ying in the community and the surrounding areas and looking for the car that was driven by the kidnapper. There were at least 200 local Chinese residents participating in this effort. Due to the high level of concern and media attention on the case, I was often invited by media outlets to speak about the concerns of local Chinese residents. This case has actually produced a positive effect on the popularity of the CAACI. Native and American Chinese, and many American friends, reacted strongly to the unfortunate incident and were sympathetic and enthusiastically helped Ying Ying's family. Many Chinese, especially those from the local Chinese church and from the CAACI, helped Ying Ying's family for several months by taking food to them and caring about their daily life while they were waiting for information on the developments in the kidnapping. In addition to spiritual comfort and support, many Chinese and community citizens across the nation donated about $160,000 to a GoFundMe account set up by UIUC for the expenses involved in Ying Ying's case, including the expenses of her family that was temporally staying in the US.

The case is now in federal court in Urbana, Illinois. Brendt Christensen was the suspect arrested for kidnapping the scholar. There is substantial unreleased evidence that points to the fact that Ying Ying was abducted by Christensen on Goodwin Avenue in Urbana. An FBI prosecution team has filed the case, approved by the US Attorney General, as a case qualifying for capital punishment. It is unfortunate that the case has been postponed several times and is still pending. The case most likely will not be tried until April of 2019.

At the beginning of December 2017, another incident occurred in Champaign-Urbana area that outraged the Chinese community. A local bus service company (Suburban Express) sent out an email promotion that stated, "You won't feel like you're in China when you're on our buses," which clearly discriminated against Chinese. It was debated and declared racist and in violation of human rights by the UIUC and by the *Daily Illini*. The CAACI and a local Chinese attorney also weighed in to condemn this racist and discriminatory behavior. The Board of Directors of the CAACI wrote a letter, signed by most of our members and Chinese friends in the community, to the Illinois Department of Human Rights and the Illinois Attorney General, requesting that state agencies investigate the incident and take whatever action needed to make sure this kind of discrimination does not occur again. At the same time, the CAACI also asked our members and other Chinese to boycott the buses as our immediate action against this unethical company.

The bylaws document of the CAACI is the most important document that governs our association. As a result of the constant changes in our world and technology, as well as in our short-term and long-term goals and objectives, it is in our best interest that our bylaws fully reflect these changes. For this reason, our board set out to revise and update the bylaws in 2017, forming a bylaws revision committee at the beginning of the year. Under our corporate attorney's guidance, and with the support of the majority of our members, the revised and updated bylaws were finally published and distributed to the members.

The two incidents of Zhang Ying Ying's kidnapping and the discrimination and racism by the bus service company have raised some serious questions for our Chinese community. All Chinese must unite to strengthen our reputation in this society. In order to achieve this, Chinese associations and organizations in the local community, such as the CAACI, must play a role in this effort. Until each of us gains credibility and becomes a valuable community citizen, we will not be respected or considered as equal to other races in the communities in which we live.

In order to achieve this long-term goal, the CAACI believed that a home where all Chinese could assemble and organize various activities was necessary. This home could be called a Chinese Culture Center, or any other name, with the main purpose of promoting Chinese culture, helping new immigrants integrate into US society, and developing good relationships with other community organizations and citizens. The concept of a Chinese Culture Center was proposed several years ago. Since then, it had been worked on by previous boards with slow progress. Therefore, it became a major task for our 2017 board of directors, and we established a Chinese Culture Center Committee to lead this effort.

I worked diligently on this project by investigating existing Chinese culture centers and similar centers in other areas of the country. I also had several meetings and discussions with the UIUC Illinois Research Park developer and the associate dean of the engineering college at the university and completed a preliminary business plan for the center. Ultimately, two plans emerged. My first plan was to build a ten-thousand-square-foot building at the UIUC Research Park with a first-floor plan that would accommodate basketball, volleyball, ping-pong, dancing, gongfu, taiji, and yoga, as well as classrooms, a library, an exhibition room, an art room, etc. The center of the building was to be two stories high, with peripheral areas on the second floor being about four thousand square feet that could be used for hosting businesses and as an incubator for new businesses. This plan called for $3 million to $5 million to be raised through donations. After some effort by the committee, we recognized the tremendous challenges we would face in trying to raise such a large amount of money; therefore, we downgraded the project in our second plan to build a steel building with the same first-floor facilities but without a second floor.

To discuss our plans, we held three town hall meetings. In two of those meetings that I organized, I provided specific details for discussion. At the same time, Lisong and I agreed to donate our commercial land lot worth about $80,000 to the CAACI as the building site. This second plan was estimated at a cost of about half a million dollars. We promoted this plan to all members of the CAACI and all Chinese in Champaign-Urbana. Our effort produced some encouraging progress with a total of seventy families signed up to be donors but who were not required to give specific dollar amounts in stage I. Among these families, five families committed to giving at least $20,000 each. I was so pleased to get this support from members and friends. However, after the analysis of my survey with about twenty questions on building the center, I estimated that the total verbal commitment was approximately $150,000. This was still far short from the $500,000 of the total project cost.

I went to several banks and spoke to a number of bankers about a loan of $350,000 for the Chinese Culture Center. Unfortunately, all the loan applications required a guarantee either by all the board of directors or any single person. In addition, we were required to provide a sound business plan with three years of past financial statements and the projection of profit and loss for the next three years. These requirements made it impossible and unrealistic for us because our financial statements from the past three years were not well-documented. Furthermore, our future projection was not encouraging either. We concluded that until we could raise all the money needed to build this center, the project could not proceed.

Beginning in 2017, I set out a plan to organize the Guangxi University Alumni Association of America (GUAAA). Although this plan progressed slowly, I was able to work with a couple of other alumni and finally achieved this goal. We registered the alumni association as a not-for-profit organization with the State of Illinois on February 8, 2018. I was one of three incorporators of the GUAAA, and I completed the bylaws for the GUAAA in the same month. In addition, I applied for a federal employment identification number and IRS tax exempt status as a 501(c)(3) organization. By February 28, 2018, the association was formally established, and I was named the president of the first board of directors of the organization.

The purpose of the GUAAA is to promote and foster appreciation of Chinese culture and Chinese Zhuang Minority culture, to promote fellowship among Guangxi Chinese and Chinese Americans in the United States of America, to reach out to other community organizations, to promote and foster good relationships with our alma mater's Guangxi University Alumni Association, to assist and promote academic and cultural exchange between Guangxi University and American universities, to provide forums for the discussion of issues of common interest, and to encourage excellent fellowship among alumni members. With two years' plan in place, we will work diligently to grow this organization and serve our members both in the short term and long term.

For the past eight months, we have organized a number of activities benefiting our alumni members. The board of directors was a strong advocate for keeping a legendary and historical agricultural building in our university, which otherwise could have been demolished for another project. The association has organized a Chinese New Year gathering, a spring picnic, a summer golf tournament, etc. In addition, we have established a WeChat platform for the association and a website for our members to share and exchange information.

GUAAA led a sixteen alumni delegation team to attend the ninetieth anniversary of Guangxi University in December 8, 2018. The board of directors has done tremendous jobs along with the University Alumni Association. One of the major accomplishments shall be seven alumni from the USA as main speakers of serval discussion forums in several colleges. The reputation and influence of GUAAA was excellent after the anniversary.

We have been very pleased to receive appreciation and recognition for our volunteer work and our charitable donations. In addition to the media exposure of our alma maters, Rongxian High School and Guangxi University, we were also honored by the Foreign Affairs Office, the Overseas Chinese Federation of Guangxi Province, the Overseas Chinese Federation of Yulin City, and Rongxian County. On January 23, 2017, I was invited by the Guangxi Overseas Chinese Federation to attend their sixtieth anniversary celebration.

On December 8, 2017, the Foreign Affairs Office and the Overseas Chinese Federation of Yulin City invited me to be their adviser for overseas Chinese. On December 9, I was invited to be a visiting professor of Guangxi University. Becoming a college professor has been one of my dreams for the past few decades. When I graduated from college, I taught at the same college from which I graduated. When I was a postdoctoral fellow, I attempted to get a faculty position in a US university, but then I went to work in industry and eventually started my own business. My dream of being a professor someday had never changed. When I return to visit my relatives at home, some people often call me Professor Li. They might feel it is appropriate to call me a professor because they do not know what my profession is. They might think that I am a professor in a US university because I have a PhD degree, or they might just want to make me feel better with this title. Whatever the reason, it does make me feel honored, but a little disappointed. This unpleasant feeling renewed my interest in a professorship. As a result, one day I expressed my desire and interest in doing some teaching and research for my alma mater, Guangxi University. My interest was given careful consideration, and the school board finally decided to hire me as a visiting professor at my alma mater. I was honored on December 9, 2017. I was very grateful for this honor and plan to devote part of my time giving some lectures to students and possibly collaborating with some researchers at the university in the future.

16-1: We are the key donors to the construction of our hometown road (2012).

16-2: South gate of our alma mater Rongxian High
School, built with our donation (2017)

16-3: Donation of 1.5 million RMB to establish a
foundation named after Zhenchang Li (2017)

16-4: Appointed as a visiting professor of Guangxi University (2017)

16-5: A main contributor to the construction of
Rongxian Li's Study College (2017)

功 德 榜

树有根，水有源，族人成家、立业、打拼或漂洋过海，也追溯到我们的祖宗。怀念祖辈，敬拜祖先，光宗耀祖是我们每位子孙义不容辞的责任。全体宗亲同心协力于二零一七年农历三月十九日巳时在原址上修缮了李氏厅屋，同年农历十月廿四日辰时进火大吉。宗亲们的捐资立榜如下，以励后人！希望子孙后代团结合作，努力开拓，再创辉煌。

修缮执委会：李振昌 李振安 李雄林 李 敏 李 强

赞助芳名 （金额单位：元）

李振昌 张丽松夫妻 12万

李振海1000	李惠明1000	李春原500	李 杰 500
李 文 500	李 聪 500	李振成250	李振东200
李振森200	李振奎200	李振明200	李刚海200
李春炎200	李汉清200	李桂清200	李漫漫200
李 鸿 200	李振杰150	李振模150	李振权150
李金海150	李振清100	李振连100	李定期100
李 永 100	李 敏 100	李 坚 100	李 强 100
李春英100	李连清100	李春良100	李春凤100
李春连100	李丽明100	雷桂兰100	浦静丽100
黄秀红100	李建宏100	李鸿榕100	李炷璋100
李裕民100	李 奔 100	李秀兰100	李 洋 100
李水清100	李思莹100	李海新100	李 潞 100

集资芳名 （金额单位：元）

姓名	人口	金额	姓名	人口	金额	姓名	人口	金额	姓名	人口	金额
李恒南	2	300	李彬南	5	750	李振新	2	300	李振才	2	300
李振成	5	750	李振昌	6	900	李振清	6	900	李振东	6	900
李振生	4	600	李振森	4	600	李振海	3	450	李振安	6	900
李振权	3	450	李振模	3	450	李振杰	3	450	植广清	1	150
李春原	1	150	李 永	4	600	李 敏	4	600	李定期	3	450
李 成	4	600	李汉林	5	750	李定富	4	600	李学林	7	1050
李文林	3	450	李 惠	5		李定有	1	150	李 坚	5	750
李定贵	5	750	李 志		900	李	4	600	李原生	2	300

16-5: Donated 80 percent of the cost to construct
Li's Clan Hall in my hometown (2017)

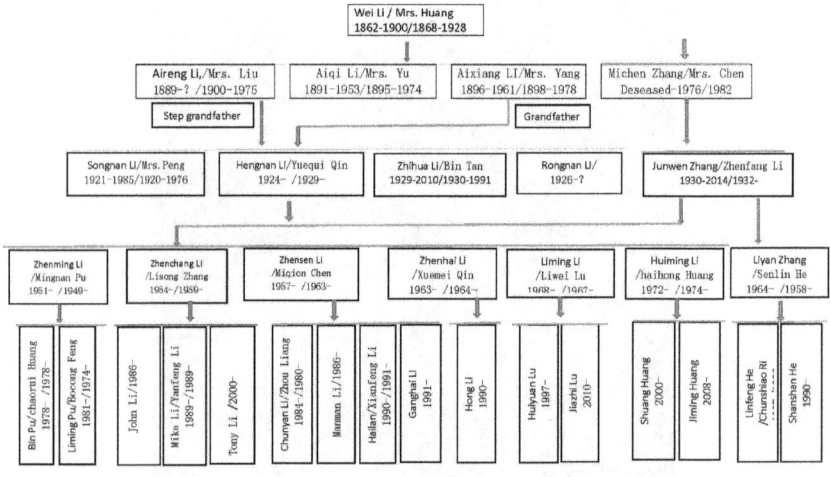

INDEX

production team, 7–9, 12, 18–19, 23–24, 30, 32, 41–44, 46–47, 60, 62–63, 67–68, 72, 74–75, 78–79, 85–86

Q

Qiaobei, 1, 20, 43, 50, 52, 63–64, 66, 70, 76–79, 255
Qiaobei Production Brigade, 43, 50, 63–64, 66, 70, 76–79, 255
Qingshou monastery, 1
Qin Xuemei, 275
QuickBooks, 195, 232, 237–38, 242, 291

R

Red Guards, 40, 44, 48–49
Red-Storm movement, 49–50
Rice Temple, 4, 10
Rong County, 1, 4, 41, 48, 52, 273
Rongnan, 5
Rongxian High School, 53, 283–84, 286, 297, 299
Rusticated Team, 59–61

S

7(a) Loan Program, 165
Shimadzu, 196, 205
sideline business, 32–33, 37, 39, 44
Siqing, 41
Small Business Administration (SBA), 153, 155, 164–67, 173, 178, 185, 194
Small Business Innovation Development Act, 153
Small Business Innovation Research (SBIR), 149, 152–53
Small Business Technology Transfer (STTR), 149, 152–53
Socialist Education Movement, 12, 40, 48

south gate, 134, 284, 286–87, 299
Southgate Apartments, 134
Soviet Union, 15
Spring Festival, 18, 39, 48, 71, 292–93
Spring Festival Gala, 292–93
standard analytical methods (SAM), 194, 196, 208, 217, 225
standard operating procedures (SOP), 184, 194–95, 208, 210, 217, 226
State College, 134, 138, 157, 161, 165, 176
steel movement, 13
Stone Foot Elementary School, 19
structure-function claims, 211
Suburban Express, 295

T

Tatman Construction Company, 203
tax loss carryback, 168
tax loss carryforward, 168
thatch, 37–38
thirtieth anniversary, 251, 258
Three Differences, 59
types of businesses
  C-corporation, 167–68
  limited liability company, 167
  partnership, 167, 214–17, 223
  professional service, 167
  S-corporation, 167–69
  sole proprietary, 167

U

Uniroyal Chemical, 180–82
United Camp, 49–50
United States Drug Manufacturing and Packaging, 193
United States Environmental Protection Agency (USEPA), 181–82

United States Food and Drug Administration (FDA), 188, 193, 196, 205, 210–12, 230

University of Illinois, 106, 128, 156–57, 183, 201, 206, 268–69, 271–72, 285

University of Illinois at Urbana-Champaign (UIUC), 128–30, 132, 170, 183, 188, 206, 233, 278, 285, 290–91, 294–96

V

vesicles, 130

W

Wang Hongwen, 57

Washington, DC, 122, 157

Wei (chairman of Guangxi Province), 49

Western Michigan University (WMU), 103–5, 108–10, 113, 118, 282, 285

work points, 24–26, 30–31, 33, 41, 45–47, 52, 67, 73–74, 84

World Trade Organization (WTO), 219

X

Xi (analyst), 142

Xiaodong Reservoir, 68, 70–72, 79, 86

Xiu River, 1

Y

Yang Shi, 5

Yao Wenyuan, 57

Yuekuei Qin, 7

Yulin City, 54, 259, 286, 297

Yulin City Overseas Chinese Federation (YCOCF), 286–87

Yunkai Mountain Range, 1

Z

Zhang, Lisong, ix, 200, 257–58, 261–62, 266–67, 286–87, 296

Zhang Chunqiao, 57

Zhang Liyan, 274

Zhang Tiesheng, 58

Zhang Ying Ying, 294–95

Zhen Ming, 275

Zhongguancun Bio-Medical Park, 216

Zou Shi, 5

CPSIA information can be obtained
at www.ICGtesting.com
Printed in the USA
BVHW030955180719
553829BV00003B/58/P